Purpose in Form

The Necessary Basis of All Ethics

By
Robert B. Davis II

Cover Image by: Peter Hermes Furian,
   Enhanced license through: Fotosearch

ISBN: 978-0-9978464-5-4 © 2020 All Rights Reserved

Dedicated to the best possible future;
Even if that is one where I am proved very wrong and must be greatly reformed.

"Many people have an aversion to infinity of various kinds. But there are some things that we do not have a choice about. There is only one way of thinking that is capable of making progress, or of surviving in the long run, and that is the way of seeking good explanations through creativity and criticism. What lies ahead of us in any case is infinity. All we choose is whether it is an infinity of ignorance or of knowledge, wrong or right, death or life." David Deutsch, *The Beginning of Infinity* (459)

Table of Contents

Introduction 1

Key Terms and Concepts 19

A Note on Citations 25

Part 1: Bad Mythologies 27

    Chapter 1: The Myth of the Finite 31

    Chapter 2: The Myth of Materialism 61

    Chapter 3: The Myth of Coming into Being 75

    Chapter 4: The Myth of Meaninglessness 93

    Chapter 5: The Myth of Secularism 107

Part 2: Return to Truth and a Solid Foundation for Life 127

    Chapter 6: Purpose in Form 131

    Chapter 7: Religious Reading and Interpretation 141

    Chapter 8: The Christian Ethic 175

    Chapter 9: Metaphysics of Mind 197

    Chapter 10: Christianity and Jung 209

    Chapter 11: Eastern Enlightenment 229

    Chapter 12: The Great Revealed Truth of Divine Intimacy 253

    Chapter 13: The Great Mystery that Divine Perception is Dependent on or Connected to Physicality 261

    Chapter 14: A Modern Religious Story 277

Part 3: Sticking to the Strait and Narrow 303

    Chapter 15: The Problems with Pantheism 307

Chapter 16: On What is Meant by "Certainty" and Other Epistemological Issues... 317

Chapter 17: Creator, No Creator? One Cause, No Cause?.............. 331

Chapter 18: The Christian Doctrine and the Gettier Problem of Knowledge.. 339

Chapter 19: On Tolerance... 351

Chapter 20: The Problem of Personified Evil 363

Conclusion.. 369

Epilogue: Atonement.. 377

Introduction

<u>The Need: The state of the world and our part in it</u>

The cultural state of the U.S. and the broader modernized world has been called a "crisis of meaning" (Pattakos, Psychology Today). In the U.S. more people died of drug overdose in 2016 than U.S. soldiers died in the entire Vietnam War (Welch, CBS News).

It would be too bold to say that if one or two more dissertations about meaning had been out in the air, this could have been avoided; but meaning and purpose in life are certainly large contributing factors to the continuation and exacerbation of drug abuse. In absence of a clear purpose, it's easier to just get high and escape all the apparently pointless toil. Rats addicted to cocaine will self-detox when allowed to play with healthy rats in a larger, less sterile environment. But people are not like rats. Rats don't wonder, "But what is the meaning of my relationships and enjoyment with these other rats? Is it worth anything at all?" But many humans do, especially when many others are braying about how this is all meaningless and (contradictingly) how we as humans are even evil. We need to be able to satisfactorily (and that means truthfully!) answer these questions for the modern audience that has abandoned the old mythologies that once served as either answers or dampeners to these kinds of questions.

There are still many traditions of valuing life that are alive and well, and there are many people who, whether they follow a particular tradition or not, value their lives and the lives of their friends and family at least. I am not claiming that nobody understands meaning, or that there aren't even a majority of people who get through life just fine without being greatly bothered by the

Purpose in Form

insane existential angst going around. But there is surely enough loss of meaning to cause concern and call for a recapitulation, at the least—and one in a language that can be understood by those disturbed by our muddled belief systems in the modern world.

Poignantly, how many people struggling with thoughts or attempts of suicide, fighting against or falling into drug addiction, or dealing with rage and resentment at being picked on or being an outcast have turned to someone they still trust and asked them whether they think life has any meaning? What would you say if your child or student asked you, "What's it all about? Why is it so hard? What is worth this?" Would you have an answer?

And, importantly, would you be able to back up that answer? Modern westerners have been raised to criticize and to question (to our credit, as author David Deutsch astutely demonstrates in his book *The Beginning of Infinity*). What good is it to offer a placating "yes" (i.e. to lie) if you will not be able to answer their inevitable next questions: "Why? How do you know?" Though people have still tried to get away with this subterfuge; Sam Harris has recommended this approach and "a whole generation of social psychologists recommended 'positive illusions' as the only reliable route to mental health. Their credo? Let a lie be your umbrella." (Peterson, 87)

But what can be truly said? If we say "Because God loves you" that answer is more than likely not going to reach the person in crisis. Traditional faiths face great challenges today, and the rise in popularity and discussion of atheism, and in many cases the intellectual caliber of its proponents[*] has put people in an apparent bind between mind and spirit. "We have been living through a period of more than a quarter of a century in which all our grand narratives have collapsed… The explanations for our existence that used to be provided by religion went first, falling away from the nineteenth century onwards. Then over the last century the secular hopes held out by all political ideologies began to follow in religion's wake." (Murray, 1)

In fact, it has been much longer than that. Already in 1949 Erich Neumann in his book *The Origins and History of Consciousness* talked about "the modern decay of values" and stated "The disintegration of the old system of values is in full swing. God, King, Fatherland, have become problematical

---

[*] Even though that should do nothing to strengthen or justify the arguments, see Deutsch on epistemology.

Introduction

quantities, and so have Liberty, Equality, Fraternity, love and fair play, human progress, and the meaning of existence." (390) The chaos we see today is something that has been brewing, growing, and festering for well over a century.

Because of this progressive decay, answers to the deep questions of life that once worked like "God loves you", "meaning is in your relations to others", "meaning is whatever you make of it", or "we all find our own meaning" have all been seen through to be the same—one pass of the buck and then turtles all the way down. And, given the extent of our crisis of meaning, I would not be surprised to learn that many modern, intellectually-minded people have taken to abandoning the pretext; I would not be surprised if an increasing number of distraught individuals have turned to a trusted friend, parent, or mentor and asked whether they think there is any meaning in life and have received the answer "no".

One flagrant example of this is the modern author and philosopher David Benatar, who writes about his beliefs in anti-natalism—the belief that human life is of such poor quality that it would be better not to exist, and the ethical conclusion this leads to that it is immoral to reproduce—but I think there are many who would give less direct, but equivalent answers of nihilism[*]. And I wonder how many people who are so horrified and outraged by the modern horrors of school shootings would yet blench at the question of meaning and wonder "Should I lie?", and how many would say "no" to the questions of meaning and not see the implications for the world they're creating (as well as the contradictory belief in the value of truth—of being honest—without a reality of meaning to support it, but we'll get to that later).

In his book *The Madness of Crowds*, Douglas Murray points to even more societal and political uproar and connects it to the collapse of our grand societal narratives (from which we derive meaning). Murray states, "Far beneath these day-to-day events are much greater and much bigger events. It is time we began to confront the true causes of what is going wrong." (1) However, Murray for the most part ascribes the "true cause" of all these

---

[*] Benatar goes to great lengths to distinguish himself from nihilism, and I do not ignore this. But I do take the time to show decisively that anti-natalism cannot be meaningfully distinguished from nihilism. So I say nihilism here, but I will give this distinction due consideration in due course.

symptoms to some surreptitious actions and motives occurring in modern individuals, finding their roots in Marxist academics. For example, he says that the current social push to turn "hardware into software" (i.e. biology into social construction) and vice versa "is at the foundation of the current madness." (106)

While there is some truth to this, and from a social and political lens it is appropriate to put responsibility and blame on those acting irresponsibly (especially when they should know better), and highlight the most proximal active causes of confusion in our social interactions, Murray is quite wrong to say this is anywhere near the foundation of the issue. The drive to disregard biology and human nature and the belief that one can rewrite all social norms and common sense in fast-sweeping reorientation movements is a symptom of a deeper confusion and erroneous assumptions.

It is only through beliefs in the meaninglessness of life (nihilism), the unreality of purpose, and doubt of the reality of truth itself that people feel inclined and even obliged to rewrite and make up scientific consensus around political claims and personal grievances. The loss of orientation to and foundation in our deepest beliefs in meaning, purpose, and truth is what has laid the ground work for the growth of these contradiction-impervious ideologies (see Murray, 58). As Murray himself concludes, "In an era without purpose, and in a universe without meaning, this call to politicize everything and then fight for it has an undoubted attraction." (255) Or, as Erich Neumann said almost a century earlier, "even [a] delusive frenzy of mass possession is zealously desired by an ego emptied of all meaning." (443)

Though in this instance Murray does recognize the deepest roots, and throughout the book does a good job at tracing the current political hysteria and conflict to its proximal roots, he does not go all the way to the foundational cause as he suggests. His book does not cover the questions of meaning and purpose, nor does it offer any answers to the anxiety surrounding them. This book aims at bringing up those exact issues in the fullest light and offering a sufficient address to them which can be used for personal reassurance and healing, as well as new, relevant and relatable, direct addresses which can be used in social intercourse when confronted with confusion and denial on the issues at hand.

Dr. Jordan B. Peterson wrote a widely successful and acclaimed book *12 Rules for Life* which aimed at orienting one's self properly and accepting the

Introduction

burdens of life voluntarily. This book seemed to become most popular with men, young and middle aged, and Dr. Peterson has observed that the social overemphasis on rights and entitlements and dearth of discussions of responsibilities created a vacuum for his work; people, especially men, are hungry for responsibility, and wanting of inspiration and direction to take up a purpose. *12 Rules for Life* does an excellent job at filling this void—at inspiring hope and encouraging action for those in whom the latent drive toward activity in the world is already simmering, waiting for permission or catalyst to get moving. But *12 Rules for Life* (in many ways to its credit) is a practical book; it works with this crowd who is for the most part ready to work, and it starts with many presuppositions and assumptions about life and how we do and should look at it.

Today, in addition to those merely momentarily disheartened, there are many who are much further lost and beaten down by the demons of our age to be merely awakened and moved by some practical wisdom. Many have heard all the traditional advice, but are so plagued by thoughts and narratives of meaninglessness, purposelessness, ultimate relativism, and the overwhelming apathy and shame these naturally breed without recourse that they cannot get to a place of willingness to act, to try out a new path and give it some time to sow and bear new fruits.

Dr. Peterson suggests that meaning found in individual conscious experience is the solution to nihilism (xxxiii). But nihilism, as we will fully elucidate later, can be characterized by a disregard and devaluation for one's own consciousness and experiences. How is one to override nihilism with that which it is actively destroying?

For those whose ship has already been mostly sunk by nihilism, such a proposal seems naïve and entirely inapplicable. *12 Rules for Life* is wise and inspiring, and fits perfectly in its niche. This book is for a different niche, one deeper in the pits of despair; this book is for those whose intellectual demons have already claimed victory, and for those who know and love people for whom this is the case. The project of this book is to take on the demons of nihilism in all their forms, on their own ground—without starting with any hopeful assumptions that they can target and subvert.

12 Rules for Life doesn't discuss what purpose is, where it comes from, and how we know it's real; it doesn't tell us foundationally why our consciousness is significant or our lives are worth living. This book does. Though in pursuing

Purpose in Form

this goal we sacrifice much of the readability and entry-level discourse for recursive depth and technicality, this is—I think—exactly what is needed and necessary.

Author Yuval Noah Harari says that humanity has to agree on a central story[*], and that we don't have forever to sort these things out. Carl Jung was of a similar opinion, and Edward Edinger called our current incoherency a "very dangerous state of affairs" ("Individuation"). Maybe they are right. But I am not writing this book because you need to agree with me (or rather, to agree with my reasons and explanations, á la Deutsch). I am writing it because you do agree. I believe in this book are some core undeniable truths that we all already accept. And I'm not talking about freedom; I'm not talking about the American Dream; I'm not trying to sell you on something that I think you should believe in by pandering to those of you who want to believe relative ideals are universal. I am talking about truly universal truths. I am talking about things that are unquestionable, not because they are my favorite dogmas or because I'll cry blasphemy if you say otherwise, but because you cannot question them without contradicting yourself. Now I know, that seems presumptuous to say the least, and human rebelliousness is forever undaunted, so many of you already have a host of objections up to bat and waiting on deck to bring me down a peg. But hear me out and then decide.

Why are things we all necessarily agree on important? To some extent, I hope the answer to that question is clear to you. I mean, it might be better for the world if I was merely crazy and the need I see for writing a book on inevitable truths was mistaken and the book proved uninteresting. But I don't think I'm *that* crazy. Odds are, you know exactly why we need this book. Many people today, and within the last 50 years especially, have declared (specifically or through action) that they do not believe in any truths; they believe the concept of truth is an arbitrary construction. Student protestors at Pomona and Claremont Colleges, protesting the appearance of Heather Mac Donald, a conservative political commentator, wrote "The idea that there is a single truth—'the Truth'—is a construct of the Euro-West that is deeply rooted in the enlightenment… the idea that the truth is an entity for which we must

---

[*] Curiously, he also says all stories are false, and he completely misdiagnoses nihilism, conflating it with Nationalism and what he perceives as selfishness and aversion toward globalism.

Introduction

search... is an attempt to silence oppressed peoples." (Murray, 136) In response to this idea, Murray states:

> 'The Truth is a construct of the Euro-West'. It is hard to think of a phrase which can at one and the same time be so wildly misguided and so dangerous in its implications. If 'The Truth' (in scare quotes) is a white thing, then what is everyone else meant to live in and strive towards? Truthfully, the worrying thing about such cases is not that young people would regurgitate such positions. The disturbing thing is that they have been taught them. (136)

Steven Pinker, Brett Weinstein, Dr. Jordan Peterson, Jonathan Haidt and many others in recent years have come out about the problem that has been growing in academics for decades. David Deutsch was the earliest that I have seen on the issue; when I read his book *The Beginning of Infinity* in 2017 I was impressed by the topical accuracy and pleased to see others speaking out in agreement with Dr. Jordan Peterson's assessment and concerns. Then I checked the publication date of the book and was astounded to see that it was published in 2011. What I had just been reading as quite topical was suddenly revealed as incredibly prescient and now all the more important and revealing given its proven accuracy. Peter Boghossian, James Lindsay, and Helen Pluckrose all deserve honorable mentions for their efforts to sound the alarm on the growing—and now quite established—problems in academia, to which they took a much more hilarious approach (though frightening in its implications) (al-Gharbi, "Academic Grievance Studies").

Within the last five or six years, society beyond college campuses and public schools have started to notice something new going on—whether they are acutely aware of it, what it's called, its origins, and whether or not they like it all aside. Perhaps a few who own their own businesses or work for themselves remain mostly unaware of these social disturbances (apart from exceedingly odd news stories every now and then, written off as marginal cases rather than growing social norms). And whether gripped or swayed by the notions of nihilism (in various forms), standpoint epistemology, neo-marxism, or antihumanism (under any of its chosen benevolent monikers) or not, so much of the world looks around in confusion and asks, with all seriousness, "What is it all about?"

Purpose in Form

If you're reading this I dare say you've asked that question or something like it. People feel disturbed all over the world, for an endless list of immediate reasons. But many can see the reduction of questions of nihilisms and meaning to echoes of a fundamental loss of orientation toward our deepest questions. And as I have just stated I believe the social and political hysteria of the present decade also traces its origins to these fundamental questions, which become problems when not satisfactorily answered: Who are we? What do we believe in? Do our beliefs matter? What even is it to believe? What is it even to be? Do I even exist in any real sense?

Without answers to the elemental questions, as we can see, the questions begin spiraling and we begin asking questions that may not even make sense. But we ask them, and we cannot dismiss them lightly. And without adequate answers we start looking for new grand narratives to orient us, and start charging down new paths with great vigor and zeal, desperate to escape the vacuum of disorientation and anxiety of agnosticism, often without regard for the potential and even emerging consequences and further implications of our new ideas and systems. Something seems better than nothing; and the new and magnanimously clothed seems far better than the tattered remnants of the dogmatic and (even worse) patriarchal past.

In search for the basic truths which answer the fundamental questions of meaning and purpose, which have the most rational explanations to support their answers, in Part 1 of this book we will look critically at questions and explanations about life such as: Is life finite or infinite? Is life meaningful? What is the significance and reality of consciousness in life? Is life purposeful? We will compare the explanations of the generally pessimistic answers to these questions to the more optimistic on both the levels of metaphysical and scientific analysis. In Part 2, we will extrapolate on the side of the truths that win out in these explanations and provide extensive supporting evidence and a concrete central metaphysical conception that we need to keep with us to stay in accord with truth.

When gripped by the questions of our modern age, at whatever stage of the spiral and despair, make no mistake, there is not a cookie of an answer you can be handed and have your problem solved. All such answers are in appearance only and the despair is only quieted until it is done chewing through the rinds of deception or word play. The questions are real problems, and real problems require real work. Without real work, there is no real resolution. So while I do

Introduction

believe I have outlined herein some very real and undeniable truths, it is not merely by reading the words and mentally "nodding" at the concepts and moving on that one benefits from these truths. The resolution comes from integrating them, becoming them, living them—which, in fact, means dying into them. "Every bit of learning is a little death. Every bit of new information challenges a previous conception, forcing it to dissolve into chaos before it can be reborn as something better. Sometimes such deaths virtually destroy us." (Peterson, 223) "Be ye transformed by the renewing of your mind." (Romans, 12:2)

It takes real sacrifice to reach the real truth. And you face genuine fear. These problems, these questions of our times, are our adventures—our demons to fight and dragons to slay—and we must undertake them wholeheartedly and see them through, so that "we also should walk in the newness of life" (Romans 6:4). There is no semblance of success nor second hand achievement for those who are genuinely touched by these problems. So while here is a record of an adventure completed and the results gained, each one who would have peace and share the fruits of this quest with others must first take it into themselves and make it real.

We must give our lives to universal truths. Not because the truths demand our lives, but because universal truth is, by definition and genesis, already superordinate to our lives and contains and fully suffuses our lives whether we pretend to give them or not. "To accept the truth means to sacrifice." (Peterson, 213) So in order to be in accord with truth, we must recognize that our lives ARE given, and we must act accordingly. We must live and act subservient to truth. "For we can do nothing against the truth, but for the truth." (2 Corinthians 13:8)

None of this is to claim that we are infallible. We are entirely fallible beings. There is much "knowledge"—all of it, actually—within the realms of relativity that is to be infinitely questioned, tested, and improved. Nothing in this book should be taken to encourage a dogma. My previous book on epistemology I stand by completely. We cannot know almost everything, and we should always remain skeptical. I do not ask you to put down your skeptical attitude here either. I merely believe that what I am going to relate to you here are universal truths that cannot be uprooted or avoided in any real sense—or at least until we are prepared to leave behind the most central concept of our own being. Eventually we may reach this point when we pass completely beyond what it means to be human, but not before. So for all intents and purposes, these are things we all agree on (even people who might claim not to be human would find these concepts at the core of their being[*]).

As I will show, there are truths. There are relative truths—things we are working on with our best running explanation—and, I think, there is one absolute truth (as I detailed in *Jnana Yoga*), as well as some tight corollaries or variations on that truth which leave us with some real knowledge. This one truth and its associated entailments are stated in human language, and are looked at from a limited perspective, and such formulations are fallible, but if we can pierce the meaning of the words, the truth they point to is something beyond such fallibility, which I hope to sufficiently show. (Again, this is not to say I believe we should end questioning or criticism in any arena.)

And yet there are some people who don't believe in truth at all (or so they say). There are others who claim truths but believe they are grim. Both of these points of view I believe are fundamentally flawed and I hope to show that that is so.

How we are to approach extreme ideas and claims through reason and the necessity for a metaphysical discussion in this case

Preliminarily, I must say that there are some seemingly extravagant claims made in this book. But the first part of this book is in large part a response to and refutation of David Benatar's works in antinatalism. In his works, Benatar says the following on outstanding claims "[on] whether it matters that my conclusions are so counter-intuitive… my answer… is an emphatic 'no'… a view's counter-intuitiveness cannot by itself constitute a decisive consideration against it. This is because intuitions are often profoundly unreliable—a product of mere prejudice." (Benatar, BNHB, 205). And, as Steven Pinker puts it, "cognitive queasiness is a poor guide to reality." (424) Here are some of Benatar's extraordinary claims: "coming into existence is a harm even when a life contains only an iota of suffering." (BNHB, 205); "There is nothing regrettable about some future state in which there are no more people." (BNHB, 183); "it would be better, all things considered, if there were no more people (and indeed no more conscious life)." (BNHB, 164)

---

[*] An odd aside, but one that I think may actually be necessary today and so I offer as a genuine address.

Introduction

I also draw on David Deutsch's book, *The Beginning of Infinity*, given his demonstration that explanations are the keys to scientific thought—that "there is no explanationless theory"—, and his expert testimony and illustration of the properties of infinity. Here are some wild claims from Deutsch: "The fundamental theories of modern physics explain the world in jarringly counter-intuitive ways... The existence of a force of gravity is, astonishingly, denied by Einstein's general theory of relativity, one of the two deepest theories of physics." (107); "the distinction between a 'natural' disaster and one brought about by ignorance is parochial." (207); "All knowledge originates from the same source as dreams." (238); "All fiction that does not violate the laws of physics is a fact. [And] some fiction in which the laws of physics *appear* to be violated is also fact, somewhere in the multiverse." (300).

In the realm of human thought in the pursuit of truth and reason outlandish claims are not to be dismissed out of hand, as Benatar points out. And as these quotations demonstrate the depths to which we will entertain what could potentially be immediately dismissed as nonsense by those unwilling to put in the mental efforts, such allowances must also be extended to the claims I will make as we go. We are here to dive into technicalities, context and pretext, assumptions, and fully delineated explanations to see what really makes sense as a cohesive view of and approach to the world.

History has shown us that, if we are interested in truth, we cannot merely dismiss a proposition because it seems far out or doesn't match with common sense (or our sense of what common sense should be). Neither should we reject a conclusion because it is far out and disagrees with our preconceptions, nor should we reject a conclusion because it is far out and is something that we would like to believe! There are people who believe blindly in wish fulfillment and have no cogent explanations. There are people who believe things that are completely insane as well as immoral and are beyond discussion. There are mathematicians who believe in God and ones who believe in "watches that came into existence spontaneously; asteroids that happen to be good likenesses of William Paley" (Deutsch, 452) and endless more of "the strange, ridiculous conclusions which some of the greatest geniuses have derived from the principles of mere reason" (Hume, 3-4).

The question is not, "is this idea really odd?" Nor is it, "could someone use this idea as wish fulfillment?" Nor, "could someone use this idea for immoral insanity?" The question is: "is the explanation good, and is there tested evidence in support of the idea?" Just as we cannot whisk Benatar away by saying he is too grim to be right (and how greatly his sympathizers and supporters would writhe at such a dogmatic rejection) the conclusions in this book should not be viewed as too religiously apologetic to be rejected out of hand (as many materialists and antinatalists would doubtlessly like to do—"ah you just believe that because it's what you want to believe, because it would be nice for you!").

"Optimism cannot be the right view merely because it is cheery, just as pessimism cannot be the right view merely because it is grim. Which view we adopt must depend on the evidence." (Benatar, BNHB, 210). But Benatar misses a key element in discerning truth, which Deutsch makes abundantly clear in his book: "There is no such thing as a[n]... explanationless theory" (Deutsch, 15). All data is "theory-laden", which means we never merely look at "the evidence," but rather we take in information through a filter of our expectations and underlying notions (Deutsch quoting Popper, 10). Dean Radin states the problem even more drastically: "Our deep beliefs determine what we view as logically reasonable and what we consider morally and ethically self-evident... and [this] hidden 'hypnosis' of belief actually determines to a greater degree than is commonly known what we can consciously perceive" (113).

Thus, if we look solely for "the evidence", we likely find merely what we expect to find, and to see a world which conforms to our basic beliefs (seek and you shall find). So the real question of pursuing truth is, primarily, what are the competing fundamental explanations which support our beliefs? Are they rational, are they consistent, and are they proven or disprovable? Examining the explanations of our basic beliefs is quite different than looking at the supposedly independent data of the world and trying to build a consensus or conclusion off of it (that is the empirical approach, which Deutsch dismantles in his book); looking at the explanations of our beliefs is a look at our metaphysical beliefs and assumptions, something we have turned away from and avoided for far too long.

Because it has become something of a taboo, I will say briefly, that metaphysics does not strictly mean religious, nor is it averse to science. Philosopher David Hume speaks lowly and dismissively about metaphysical theorizing and speculating:

Introduction

> The weakness of this metaphysical reasoning... seem[s] so obviously ill-grounded, and at the same time of so little consequence to the cause of true piety and religion... The argument 'a priori' has seldom been found very convincing, except to people of a metaphysical head who have accustomed themselves to abstract reasoning, and who, finding from mathematics that the understanding frequently leads to truth through obscurity, and contrary to first appearances, have transferred the same habit of thinking to subjects where it ought not to have place. Other people, even of good sense and the best inclined to religion, feel always some deficiency in such arguments, though they are not perhaps able to explain distinctly where it lies, a certain proof that men ever did and will derive their religion from other sources than from this species of reasoning. (55-57)

And, just as he declares, so many modern intellectuals dismiss metaphysical concerns out of hand. Sometime shortly after the enlightenment, most philosophy left metaphysics behind as though we could do without it, or at least that we had had enough of it. This is part of what has been called the "Death of God"—but that does not mean that metaphysics is God, nor that metaphysics is necessarily religious.

The enlightenment, it is no secret, is largely identified as a rebellion against and rejection of religion. "Nowadays, secular people often see the Enlightenment as a battle between two mortal enemies: on the one side was science, with its principle weapon, reason, and on the other was religion, with its ancient shield of superstition." (Haidt, 134) And as religion had handed us a metaphysical dogma for so long, which we were told not to question, through the enlightenment western society left behind the field of imaginative speculation[*] and "stuck to the facts".

But what really happened is that the first few adjustments to our worldview occurring during the enlightenment were accepted as our new metaphysics, were quickly erected, then left in the darkness of our unconscious and inattention; and even when we discovered that these models were scientifically insufficient, though we began teaching new theories and calculations, the area

---

[*] Or so they liked to think—though that creative process is actually a key element of science itself; see Deutsch's book for discussion.

of our underlying assumptions about the nature of the world remained unexamined and wasn't updated. These initial assumptions included the heliocentric model of the solar system and the rejection of the geocentric (and thus anthropocentric) model (which Deutsch chronicles as the genesis for the "principle of mediocrity"), the Newtonian paradigm of materialism and determinism (viewing the universe as a machine of isolated components and parts colliding), and the ideas of empiricism and positivism (that objective data is merely there to be observed and learned from, and that the only things really real and worthwhile are those which are to be measured).

Though the Newtonian system is long out of date, we still primarily believe in materialism and see the world as composed of physical Newtonian objects. Though we now know so much about how we process information and how our perceptions are mediated, we still cling to the idea of ourselves as objective beings merely taking in data and reaching conclusions about it. Thus, examining and updating our metaphysical conceptions is in fact crucial to science, in that it keeps our mental models of the world and its functions up to date with science itself. Metaphysics would only be amorphous and unrelated to reality if you were a relativist (or a religious dogmatist) committed to creating a dogma of your own imagination, unconcerned with the imperative to verify it to any degree.

But, as with self-fulfilling religious readings which we will discuss later, just because you create something that serves your purposes does not make it true. That is to say, the theory of ultimate relativism is wrong. There is an objective world which determines the reality of truth claims, and value is not an arbitrary social construction[*][†]. Thus approaching metaphysics from the perspective of ultimate relativism (or worrying that relativists will take advantage of it) is a straw man. Metaphysics is just our conjectures about and corresponding models of the fundamental nature of reality. In line with Deutsch's theories, metaphysics is the underlying EXPLANATIONS we have

---

[*] As we will see in this book, the proposition underlying relativism that values are arbitrary and meaningless comes from the underlying metaphysical assumption that our consciousness is insignificant.

[†] This is something that for the most part I got wrong in the final section of my previous book *Jnana Yoga*. The conclusions reached in this book, therefore, are to be seen as a revision of and superordinate to any of the conflicting ethical conjectures made in my previous book.

Introduction

for why and how what we see in the world (through science) is how it is.

One can certainly forward bad metaphysical explanations. But one can criticize these and forward better ones, ones more informed and in line with scientific evidence and theory. Thus metaphysics is not inherently relative and amorphous, and can and should be part of the scientific culture of conjecture and criticism, as this work will illustrate.

Since for centuries we have ignored the underlying assumptions about the nature of the world (metaphysics), we have neglected updating our structures and now, curiously, though we know the data of modern scientific theories, we still think of the world much as humanity did at the beginning of the enlightenment—materialistic, objective, external, mechanical, etc.

The problem of moving beyond empiricism David Deutsch deals with conclusively in his book, *The Beginning of Infinity*.

Materialism has curiously withstood so many attacks, including being entirely scientifically uprooted by the theory of relativity and the discovery of the subatomic worlds, but we have hung onto it in our minds inexplicably. It is my hope that here with the detailed look we will take back into our metaphysical theories and assumptions, and through the help of the colossal task of cataloguing evidence and meta-analysis of experimental data done by Dean Radin in his book *The Conscious Universe*, materialism will be finally uprooted as a fundamental metaphysics and cast out of our modern conceptions[*].

Also, in way of an introduction, this is ultimately a religious book as well as it is a scientific and philosophic one. Yuval Noah Harari, in his book *21 Lessons for the 21st Century*, asks if religion might play a role in healing the world, though he concludes that this is doubtful[†]. I, however, believe that religion, at its most basic, is exactly what we need.

While many modern western intellectuals have inherited aversions to religion in a multitude of ways, we are yet inundated with newly emerging

---

[*] We are talking about foundational metaphysics here. Quasi-Newtonian, materialistic conceptions are useful at a certain level of abstraction in physics, and this is perfectly acceptable. But this recognition of its usefulness as a model on one level should not be continually confused as its viability as a metaphysical conception.

[†] Though, again quite confusingly, at the end of the book he concludes that experiencing the mystery of the self—chiefly through meditation—is the route to salvation for the world...

terrible conceptions of reality that are incoherent and unreasonable. What religion, at its most basic, offers as an alternative I believe is coherent, reasonable, provable, and beneficial.

Though we should not and cannot take the bible entirely literally, for example, I hope to thoroughly show the underlying religious conception and explanation (explicit or otherwise) of the world and humanity is the correct one—that it is true. "It will always be the one, shape-shifting yet marvelously constant story that we find, together with a challenging persistent suggestion of more remaining to be experienced than will ever be known or told." (Campbell, 1)

In this light, I will be illustrating why the rationalist community should return to an ultimately religious foundation of metaphysics; not one that is merely dogma, but one that we are driven to through reason and science. The effects of this basic orientation toward the foundations of life will determine how we view, approach, and act in the world.

Aside from demonstrating the necessary truth and reality of a fundamental consensus on the nature of life, which uproots nihilism and materialism, I am not here going to take the additional task of defending religion as a whole or making the case that it does more good than harm in any or all cases. There are many objections to religion and faith, and many have merit. However, in the process of rejecting flawed ways of thinking and examining real ethical problems within religious dogmas, modern western intellectualism has made a critical mistake of basing itself on foundational theories of the meaninglessness and finitude of life. Religion, for all its faults, is on the side of truth in supporting a basic view of life as meaningful, purposeful, and human life and consciousness as significant.

I will show that these points are not merely faith based dogmas that we should accept because of their utility, as so many atheists and intellectuals suggest about religion, but rather that they are realities we can be entirely confident in based on a rational investigation into metaphysics; and further that we can see the irrationality of the alternative metaphysical conceptions and their resulting orientations towards life.

The discussion of the merits of religious philosophical systems and/or their moral problems is both fascinating and worthwhile, but is beyond the scope of this book and would only serve to distract from the fundamental issue of a revised metaphysical conception that I think is absolutely necessary in the west

Introduction

today. Thus, though in many ways this is only the beginning of a discussion, since anyone who speaks on the apologetic side for religion must inevitably face the many objections of disillusioned western minds, the basic conclusions reached in this first approach stand on their own and, regardless of however else one sees the extended moral nature of religious dogma, faith, and catechisms, the reorientation I will describe here can be accepted without necessarily further affirming any particular dogmas or abandoning the western epistemological approach to rationality of a culture of open conjecture and criticism.

Purpose in Form

Key Terms and Concepts:

Paul Bloom says "we reason best when we have help, and certain communities help reason flourish" (54), and Jonathan Haidt supports and emphasizes this conclusion, making it perhaps even more dire:

> We must be wary of any *individual's* ability to reason… But if you put individuals together in the right way, such that some individuals can use their reasoning powers to disconfirm the claims of others, and all individuals feel some common bond or shared fate that allows them to interact civilly, you can create a group that ends up producing good reasoning as an emergent property of the social system. This is why it's so important to have intellectual and ideological diversity within any group or institution whose goal is to find truth. (105)

It is only through social interaction, conducted in the proper ways, that we can hope to approach truth. As Jung says in his introduction to Neumann's book, "Ultimate truth, if there be such a thing, demands the concert of many voices." (xiv) Thus, though books of rational deliberation may appear to be monolithic achievements within themselves—and philosophy is a common culprit of carrying this veneer—all non-fiction books should properly be seen as forms of conversation. Authors are speaking with others, criticizing or praising concepts and ideas, forwarding their own conjectures, and awaiting further interaction—criticism or praise—with their inputs.

I have done my best to make this book as accessible and comprehensible in itself as possible. However, it is best and most fully understood as part of a conversation. In fact, a podcast conversation between Dr. Jordan Peterson and

Purpose in Form

David Benatar served as a central inspiration for the direction this book takes and the problems it attempts to resolve. But there are much bigger players in this conversation than these two. All the authors I reference are part of the conversation in some way—though they may not be otherwise directly connected to each other. There are two big voices of particular note whose work heavily influences the entire conversation herein, and you may well not have read them. These are *The Beginning of Infinity* by David Deutsch and *The Conscious Universe* by Dean Radin.

That being said, I have done as much as I can to make full readings of their work unnecessary. In the section where Radin's work bears extreme importance, I have taken the time to list in some detail his findings and quotes from other experts reviewing the same material that he presents. And here I will list several key concepts, mostly from Deutsch's work, which will help the reader enter with some understanding of the ideas being pulled from other sources. And one knows where to go to see the reasons for these assertions; the text will, therefore, be riddled with references to extended discussion as "See Deutsch".

<u>Fallibilism</u>— in his own words Deutsch defines fallibilism as "The recognition that there are no authoritative sources of knowledge, nor any reliable means of justifying knowledge as true or probable." (31) Deutsch emphasizes that it is "fallibilism," meaning the continual seeking for better explanations and the willingness to notice, admit, and adjust for errors, "not mere rejection of authority, that is essential for the initiation of unlimited knowledge growth—the beginning of infinity." (9) Deutsch holds fallibilism as the key element to successful reason, science, and indeed society as a whole.

<u>Culture of creative conjecture and criticism</u>—This phrase and variations of it comes from Deutsch's work, who defines this approach as the key element of all progress in modern western society (so long as it is based, as it must be, in an acceptance of fallibilism). This is, essentially, the golden foundation of science and western philosophy. It is a description of the creative process underlying the process of knowledge creation and discovery, and therefore of science itself. It also includes the acknowledgement that "we reason best when we have help, and certain communities help reason flourish" (Bloom, 54) Jonathan Haidt's work *The Righteous Mind* greatly supports this idea. "The

truth will emerge as a large number of flawed and limited minds battle it out." (Haidt, 107)

Conjecture—this term, included in the concept above, will be used in this book and is not to be looked down upon as a pejorative suggesting lack of concrete foundation. Rather, it is an honest assessment of the first step in discovery and the search for truth. It is a key to the creation of knowledge and progress. In all cases, conjecture is used in a positive or neutral light and is never meant to call into question some ideas for "merely" being conjectures. Conjecture, in Deutsch's use, is identical to Jonathan Haidt's use of the term "intuition" as the foundation of our rational thinking process.

"Theory-laden"- Deutsch borrows this term and concept from Karl Popper, and uses it in uprooting the idea of a sterile "empirical" approach of people "just looking at the facts". There are no sterile facts. All facts or data is "theory-laden". We see facts through a lens of underlying theory and explanation which we have accepted, regardless of whether it is was a conscious formulation gained through rational development or an unconsciously assumed bias inherited from some story or higher level theory.

Explanations- "There is no explanationless theory." Deutsch also attacks the idea that theories can be removed and abstract—commenting only about effects without conjecturing an underlying explanation of the causes, speculative though it may be. Explanations are the key element of rational thought. It is our explanations of data and theory which compete and are sorted through rational collective criticism. Theories that withhold discussion about their underlying explanations attempt to avoid criticism and rational discussion (whether this is conscious and intended or not). Once again, Jonathan Haidt's work supports this conception in that we reason to explain and justify, not merely to find and forward the truth. It is only through collective criticism of our conjured explanations that we move toward the truth.

Deutsch's Epistemology claims- Knowledge is not and will never be justified, and therefore we should not look for knowledge to be justified. All knowledge and ideas come from "the same source as dreams" (Deutsch, 238). This idea is a marvelous step forward in epistemology, but is something we do not hold well to in our pursuits of reason and truth. We believe knowledge can be justified simply by hearing it from "experts" or from some favored source. Deutsch's claim is that knowledge never gains its status from such justifications, but rather "fallibilists expect even their best and most fundamental explanations to contain misconceptions in addition to truth" and are interested in creating knowledge through the only truly effective means available—constant skepticism and open inquiry, improvement, and change (9). The radical element of this opens the true skeptic up to the possibility of gaining knowledge out of many uncommon and even unseemly sources (such as religious dogma, perhaps). "A true scholar is receptive to ideas regardless of their origin." (Pinker, 390)

Universal explainers/constructors- This idea comes from Deutsch's assertion of the universality of reason. Since reason has infinite reach, humans—who are capable of reason—are "universal explainers", and because there is a tight correlation between explaining, understanding, and controlling (or working with) humans are thus "universal constructors" as well. Now this sounds very idealistic and would seem to fall prey to Jonathan Haidt's criticism of the "Rationalist Delusion". But Deutsch does not claim that humans are perfect reasoners; in fact he reinforces fallibility as an absolute in our nature. And because Deutsch correctly, and in coherence with Haidt, conceives of our reasoning process as a social endeavor (requiring a culture of open inquiry and criticism), rather than as primarily accomplished by individuals, his conception is not undermined by Haidt's criticism. The claim is about human potential when we operate under the correct systems, and though this is an ideal, it is not an unreachable one, difficult though it may be. And further, the marginal effects of striving towards this ideal are significant in themselves.

Ignorance- Much like the term "conjecture", ignorance has a negative connotation for many people—perhaps especially intellectuals. However, in his work David Deutsch shows that ignorance is merely the necessary and inescapable reality of life. It is a logical corollary to the infinity of existence. If existence is infinite (which we will discuss), we will always be ignorant of infinite information. This is not a pessimistic conclusion, nor an insult to humanity. We are universal explainers and we have universal reach; but we are limited beings in an unlimited universe (or multiverse, as the case may be).

Key Terms

Thus, ignorance is merely a natural and logically necessary characteristic of our being. I will use it in this book in many instances, and it is never intended to be insulting or degrading. It is merely remarking on a fact of reality. We are all ignorant to many things, and our ignorance is neither surprising nor shameful (excluding cases of *willful* ignorance). This is how I always read the Buddha's comments on the ignorance of humanity—merely as a diagnosis of the reality, not as a disdainful judgement.

The Principle of Mediocrity- The principle of Mediocrity is an intellectual rule of thumb about humanity. It developed after the enlightenment as we learned more about our universe and displaced the geo- and anthropocentric models of thought about the universe. After taking a rational look at our location in the universe, accompanied by all the rest of the "Death of God" components, we concluded that we are insignificant beings in the universe. Deutsch takes this idea to task in his book from a secular lens, arguing that we have underestimated the universality of reason, and the enormous import the potential for reason in the human species has for the physical universe. He says that though this principle has become a mainstay of scientific thought, in terms of searching for truth, you would be much better served to use simply the inverse or negation of this idea (Deutsch, 45).

Form- as found in the title, and associated with the term "physicality" in the text, form is a reference to so-called material reality—apparently finite objects and bodies. It is, largely, a term used to avoid the word "creation" as found in religious texts, though the same domain is generally indicated. Form is the physical phenomena we perceive as the world and think of as Newtonian objects, but it is most often used with an emphasis on the body (one's physical form).

Anti-Natalism- (or "antinatalism," unhyphenated) the philosophic thesis, championed by David Benatar, that human life is of such poor quality (so full of suffering without redemption) that it is immoral to reproduce, and thus bring more beings into the suffering of existence.

Religion- When I say that this is a "religious" book, and when I talk about "religion" throughout, I am using Leo Tolstoy's definition of religion meaning,

Purpose in Form

specifically, "religion is the bond between man and God... if it does not bind man to the infinite being, it is not religion." (88-89) I believe this is the true meaning of religion at its core. I understand that many readers have a deep aversion to *organized* religion, at the very least, and they would perhaps like me to use a different term all together (like spirituality or reverence, etc.). However, I believe that the term religion is appropriate and I will use it in this positive and perhaps apologistic light throughout. Please note that whenever I use the term religion I am talking about a conscious connection to the infinite, and not about any organization(s) or sect(s), unless specified otherwise.

A few other key terms to remember will be listed throughout the book as we come to them.

A note on citations:

I have decided to use in-text citations, with an author's name and page number where applicable, throughout the book. In some ways this clutters the text and is inferior to endnotes in this sense, especially in what I have already been told is quite a dense book. However, I find the importance of the source paramount, in that I often use quotes from authors in contexts they would not likely be found supporting—like using Benatar to argue against himself, or Hume to argue for a traditional religious conception, etc. Therefore, the author's name next to the quote is an integral part of the effect and context of the argument.

When I was reading *The Hero with a Thousand Faces* by Joseph Campbell, I found all the sources being removed to the endnotes incredibly annoying, as I would read a religious quote and not know the source being brought into the discussion without constantly flipping to the notes section. It makes sense for more scholarly works that cite mostly scientific studies to list these at the end, where they can be checked if necessary, because the titles and authors in those cases are relatively unimportant compared to philosophical and religious sources used in an argument.

Additionally, there are a few authors whose citations will be unique. First, I quote from multiple books by David Benatar, thus the quotations must be distinguished further. Therefore, quotes appearing as simply (Benatar, #) will apply to the book *The Human Predicament*, which I quote from the most. Quotes cited in-text as (Benatar, BNHB, #) come from his book *Better Never to Have Been*.

Another common citation oddity will be concerning the book *Don't Be a Jerk* by Brad Warner, which is a translation and commentary on Dogen's work. Quotes cited as (Dogen, #) refer to Warner's direct translation of Dogen's words. Quotes cited as (Dogen/Warner, #) refer to some commentary from Warner on the essays by Dogen.

Quotes from Jung's prolific work will be given fairly standard abbreviations. And quotes from Joseph Campbell come almost exclusively from *The Hero with a Thousand Faces*, though one quote comes from *The*

Purpose in Form

Power of Myth and is thus marked 'Myth'.

It is also an interesting age when it comes to citations, with so many memes and YouTube videos spreading quotes and ideas, and people accurately or inaccurately keeping the correct sources connected to these as they spread. I had to remove a few quotes which I liked and which helped the progression of the book, but for which I could not find original sourcing. I also directly cite quite a few YouTube videos and even songs. It is truly a new era and it will be interesting to see how the future generations update the citation expectations and requirements for the new landscape. For now, the old ways apparently still apply, and must simply be adapted for the time being.

Part 1: Bad Mythologies

What We've Done Wrong and How We Can Clearly See It Is Wrong

"It is our responsibility to see what is before our eyes, courageously, and to learn from it, even if it seems horrible." – Dr. Jordan B. Peterson (223)

Chapter 1: The Myth of the Finite

How It Began and Where We Stand (A Formal Address to the Rational Community)

> "The special mark of the modern world is not that it is skeptical, but that it is dogmatic without knowing it." G. K. Chesterton (Murray, opening quote)

One thing that the philosophic, rationalist, and educated communities—i.e. anyone who ascribes to truth as their highest virtue and goal, and believes it is reached through rational inquiry—must address and make absolutely clear is the question of the infinite.

Since the enlightenment and subsequent progressive move from religious order, rationalists have achieved the so-called "death of God", which among many other things has made it a clear statute that, within the halls of reason, it is not required that you worship a god or the God—there is no requirement of belief or faith, and that if one in the discussion derides another for not conforming to any recognizable belief in God or even for out-rightly declaring their disbelief in God, the former is not a true member of the society of reasonable persons; that is, we have accepted the reasonability that one may doubt God, and one may even make arguments for his non-existence that do adhere to some level of reason.

However, in this concession, far too much ground was given, for it was not clear (obviously) what one meant by "God". And so, when it was acknowledged that the God of traditional dogmatic or metaphoric description was open to doubt and the criticism of reason, there was a large sweep through that allowed people to throw out all accepted metaphysics, since they were apparently entirely based in dogma and not pure reason, and thus, looking back now, we have allowed into the accepted circles of discussion the possibility of finite existence—that the basic and foundational nature of life or existence itself may be ultimately finite, as so many things in our conception are (or seem to be).

When it was conceded that we rationalists would not require members of the house of reason to believe in or structure their arguments in accordance with any "God", on this new grand opening in came many who do not properly belong in the houses of reason. They, like the former men who would not dispose with their religious dogma to follow entirely the virtue of reason across whatever frightening vistas it might explore, will not dispose with their unreasonable tenants of non-existence, ultimate finitude, and/or surety of annihilation.

It is not that these topics should be taboo to discuss, for there should be no bounds on the purview of reason. However, reasonable discussions must be held to a certain level of, well, reasonableness, and they should require of their members, especially those of clearly high intellectual capacities a full and coherent account of their views, unless a clear and reasonable explanation of why such explanations cannot be given, can be given. And it is a necessary fact that the doctrines of non-existence, annihilation, and/or the finitude of life are entirely unreasonable, inexplicable, and cannot be supported in the category of vague "faiths" to which a reasonable rationalist tolerates in particular members.

Not only is it the case that these views themselves are unreasonable and unsupportable, but it is also supremely evident that the reality of the infinite is a clear and necessary truth which is illustratable entirely through reason. Thus, those who dogmatically espouse not only the certainty (which many do) but also even the possibility of the finite (so long as they remain dogmatic and unreprovable) not only uphold a belief they cannot (and often refuse to) substantiate, they also deny clear and powerful reasonable accounts to the contrary. Thus all beliefs in and accounts of non-existence, annihilation, and/or the foundational finitude of life and all those theories which rest necessarily on these assumptions should be viewed in the same way, when presented under the auspices of reason, that rationalists would view a dogmatic orthodox

The Myth of the Finite

religious pundit (an American Christian fundamentalist, say) expounding their doctrines before the community.

Unless there can be a clear and reasonable account of these metaphysical assumptions given, which also sufficiently addresses the clear and strong (and in fact completely necessary) reasonable account of the infinite, which has not been given to date, we must abandon these fundamental suppositions within the community of reason and uproot the systems based upon them; not because they are taboo, nor because we should never look in that direction or never have our work checked, but because the case is so clear in this matter that, though we do not restrict its continual discussion and reiteration, and reformulation and repostulation, we cannot allow large sweeping theories which comment on the nature of life and urge us to action to pretend to reason if they rest on these necessarily unreasonable claims.

Though I would not, for the sake of reason and humility, ever urge the quieting of the discussion and debate on the subject, and would not force others to mouth the truth that I hold, though I believe it is one of the highest and most certain truths we can light upon, I do believe I can say that the truth of the infinite is necessary, and it is self-evident (though of course this does not count as my explanation and I would not use this in an argument where there appears doubt[*]). But in addition to the necessity driven by the respect for reason alone, which should be more than enough for the community, we also must recognize the immense pragmatic reasons[†] that such doctrines cannot be blindly supported or allowed to be mouthed in the name of reason any further.

The consequences which follow from dogmatic beliefs in non-existence, annihilation, and/or finitude are extremely vicious[‡]. And although the pundits of these views may claim they can escape the threats of nihilism or that their morality remains intact, or that these views themselves are in fact moral views, it can be made clear that such distinctions which the pundits go to extravagant

---

[*] "What is 'self-evident' isn't always self-evident." (Pinker, 413)

[†] If any philosopher does not consider these part and parcel of the reason in itself.

[‡] They would, even if we were unable to prove so clearly the unreasonable nature of their foundations, force us to reconsider reason itself as a virtue, for if these things were reasonable, then reason itself would have to be redefined as a vice for the clear nature of its products; or, again, given all the other virtues of reason, we might be inclined to think that these things were in fact not reasonable, though we were unable to see why; but fortunately there is no such ambiguity.

lengths to define, remain unevident in themselves and do not appear as necessary to the inspection of reason which does not already approach with the goal of preserving a predetermined level of morality in the given conceptual structure.

These are strong claims it seems relative to the current accepted berth given to the discussions of reason. But I intend to fully support them and prove them beyond the levels of doubt which would be required for us to give to the pundits of annihilation, non-existence, and/or finitude to survive. It was not my original intention to make this a book about metaphysics or to take to task the general metaphysical uncertainties of the age, but this has become evidently necessary not only in pursuit of the goals at hand, but also out of concern for the state of reason itself and the state of the world and their futures (which we would hope are bound together). So the scope of the book proceeds beyond the elucidating of metaphysical certainties and discrediting of metaphysical assumptions, but begins with this in depth and decisive argument of what we must accept in reason, what we must reject and why, and then on to what our far better option is and how it is reasonable and how it is virtuous.

Disclaimer

Now I am as human as the next person, and my ability to conduct an exploration in pure reason is in just as much question. It can be seen that humans are not primarily rational beings, and people are far less rational than they think, including and perhaps even especially intellectuals! The faculty of reason is built on top of our emotional, subjective, and unconscious dispositions and drives, and our preconceived notions. "Intuitions come first, strategic reasoning second." (Haidt, 61) In the way to pure reason stands our very nature. And so when we set out to reason we are always influenced by values, perceptions, and dispositions, many of which are unconscious.

Even when one professes in good faith to be dedicated to reason and makes clear the great intellectual rigor of which they are capable, that is no good reason for us to assume they are successful, either in the process of their reasoning as it goes (every step of the way) or in their beginning from supposed blank or neutral grounds. "Expertise, brainpower, and conscious reasoning do not, by themselves, guarantee that thinkers will approach the truth. On the contrary, they can be weapons for ever-more ingenious

The Myth of the Finite

rationalization." (Pinker, 359)

Of course this applies to me just as well. As Deutsch rightly asserts, fallibility is the human reality and it is the bedrock of all potential pursuits of knowledge. But contrary to the fashionable disapproval of the human attempts at reason, I wholly agree with Paul Bloom's take on the issue of reason and rationality in humans, found in his book *Against Empathy*:

> It is one of the ironies of modern intellectual life that many scholars insist that rationality is impotent, that our efforts at reasoning are at best a smoke screen to justify selfish motivations and irrational feelings. And to make this point, these scholars write books and articles complete with complex chains of logic, citations of data, and carefully reasoned argument. It's like someone insisting that there is no such thing as poetry—and making this case in the form of a poem. (52)

Jonathan Haidt, who himself details the subordinate nature of reason, still concludes that we can reason effectively as a group. He also offers an evolutionary point to the effects of reason: "Language-based reasoning… evolved because it did something useful." (Haidt, 54) Reason being difficult, and humans being ill-equipped for pure reason, is quite different than reason being "impotent". It is difficult for humans to bear and raise children, and yet we are still so effective at this that many are driven to a hysteria over overpopulation. Something may be difficult and only marginally effective as compared to its imagined ideal application, and yet it may still be tremendously effective and advantageous to use said wayward tool over the alternative of not using said tool. This is to say that, though reason is something we are fighting against great odds to approximate and move towards, it is still undoubtedly powerful and EFFECTIVE, and is something to which we should rightly devote our energies.

Hume said the following regarding the significant effects of even abstruse reasoning (reasoning about reason itself, in this case):

> If a man has accustomed himself to skeptical considerations on the uncertainty and narrow limits of reason, he will not entirely forget them when he turns his reflections on other subjects; but in all his

philosophical principles and reasoning, I dare not say, in his common conduct, he will be found different from those who either never formed any opinions in the case or have entertained sentiments more favorable to human reason. (6)

And I *would* dare say such speculations, when truth is perceived in them (and so long as one takes ideas seriously as impulses to action[*]), do reflect even in common conduct in significant ways. Significant does not mean all-encompassing. Significant can be small. As Hume points out, extreme skeptics still exit through the door, rather than the window—they are not wholly converted by their passing impulses to doubt everything.

Yet, those who question more thoroughly and deeply than others will be more likely to come to new or different ideas which may shape their attitude and conduct as different from others (for better or worse). Again, the question is not whether one forever embodies their skeptic attitude and cannot be sure of the difference between a door and a window, but rather, whether such an attitude is entirely purposeless and has no effect or whether it is even somewhat effective, for any effect on the basic attitudes and actions in one's life is a significant change.

The same idea applies to all levels of reason, not merely to the extreme skepticism that Hume lampooned. We may not be reasonable 100% of the time, and when we do reason, we may do so with far less than 100% purity. But those are not the only important facts. It is important to know that we are so fallible, indeed. But another incontrovertible fact is that reason has been shown to be exceedingly effective in changing the course of human life and history. The case for reason is quite settled, and falling short of an ideal is not equivalent to impotence. Imperfect achievement through fallible striving is enormously effective compared to lack of any such efforts. That is the fact to remember: not that we are imperfect, so why bother? But that we are fallible, yet we are effective, so we do progress and achieve[†].

---

[*] "Since modern man has a highly developed ability to disassociate, simple recognition may not be followed by appropriate action." (Jung, CW, vol 9) Further, Jonathan Haidt points out that neurologically reasoning is well separated from the structures of motivation (Haidt, 66).

[†] This dichotomy between intellectual pessimism driven by comparison of human actuality to an imagined perfect state should be kept in mind as we proceed through

The Myth of the Finite

<u>My Prejudice and How It Will Be Mitigated</u>

When I first came across David Benatar, I listened to his debate with Dr. Jordan B. Peterson on The Renegade Reports podcast of CliffCentral. I was already a fan of Dr. Peterson, already rudimentarily working on this book, and already had deeply oriented my beliefs on metaphysics, the nature of consciousness and reality, and my outlook on the world.

My values are stacked against Benatar's conclusions, so naturally I found fault with him at nearly every step of the way. As one who is severely influenced by reason, who believes in the righteousness of reason and the profound effect that reason (for better or worse) has on the world and people, and one who really wants to be right and show off how right they are, I would love to take you through a blow by blow account of how much I feel Benatar is mistaken about and how I feel his argument fails at every step of the way in a detailed analysis of the debate and the arguments he presents in his books[*].

This, however, is not what is actually right to do, nor what is reasonable, for it is not what will actually be *EFFECTIVE*. What is important here is not to enumerate the inadequacies I perceive in someone who is of strong intellect but who has overlooked their basic assumptions and been slain by their own most powerful capacity—their own sword, as it were. Though it might be instructive to see the assumptions and missteps as they played out in the debate and in the presentation of the argument, and it might give us a clear understanding of the limitations of the intellect to catch its own pomposities and adhere to reason itself[†], this in the end would not produce the effect that I

---

our discussion; it is endemic in the world today, is epitomized in Benatar, and is a core tendency we aim here to eradicate. Hopefully, when one is finished reading and comprehending this book, they will be free from the despair at their own inherent and necessary ignorance and failings compared to an ideal, and regain the ability to view human imperfection and fallible striving as an inherently significant and worthwhile endeavor.

[*] Though, to be fair, after reading his books and thinking back on the debate, I saw how fundamentally the two men were not even talking about the same things and, I believe, Dr. Peterson was most at fault for not speaking to Benatar's understanding and claims, but rather arguing against his own approximation of those claims. Benatar, for example, kept trying to bring up and reassert his claim on the asymmetrical analysis of suffering in life, which Dr. Peterson did not seem to even address or ever really present a comment which showed he understood the claims being made.

[†] Rather than come up with a much more irrationally determined mindset and then to extravagantly "reason" a path around it with more investment, unconscious as it may

consider my highest goal. This might win me great esteem with those who would already naturally be inclined to agree with me. But it would not actually reasonably affect anyone who is partial to Benatar's point of view.

In taking the effort to deride the exterior edifices of his beliefs and arguments at each superficial point, even though I would be arguing reason, I would in fact be arguing *ad hominem*; I would be saying, with such effort, "look how many failures this man of intellect has overlooked, look how blind he is", which would just be a guise for me to say "look how smart and righteous I am." A natural revulsion in those who are not already leaning away from Benatar, and perhaps even in some that are would follow and undermine my arguments. I say this because I know how frustrating it can be to attempt to reason with one another, how much our emotions drive us to actions that may dawn the guise of reason, but are in fact irrational and unconsciously emotion-based and thwart our attempts to pure reason. I can fall at fault to this very easily.

So, instead of trying to uplift myself and win some favor or glory in a sweeping dissolution of what I believe to be Benatar's sophistry, the appropriate approach is to elucidate and examine the most foundational and essential assumptions and underpinning mistakes on which his entire argument and world view stands. That is to say, in line with the principles Deutsch describes, to examine the explanations underlying his claims, not to argue interpretation of evidences from different theory-laden perspectives. In doing this there is actually hope that those who are already biased against me will not enter into the crucial point of discussion with built up resentment toward my haughty naysaying, and that those who are on the fence or believe in the world view that Benatar claims to reason toward and support, can approach, begrudgingly or not, the basic foundations of their beliefs and be struck as clearly and unbiasedly as possible by what I believe to be the substantive evidence against their positions.

For these reasons I will concentrate on the suppositions in Benatar's work of annihilation, non-existence (or "coming into existence"), and the underlying

---

be, in keeping the grounds that have already been staked out than actually seeing if reason naturally supports the ground; this is actually how we all reason all the time and how all intellects work, see Jonathan Haidt's book *The Righteous Mind* for full discussion and illustration of this human tendency.

The Myth of the Finite

supposition of finitude, or the disregarding or evading of any consideration of the existence of infinity and the implications thereof. These underlying metaphysical claims and assumptions are not unique to Benatar, but are common throughout the intellectual world in varying degrees of transparency and lucidity. Benatar, to his credit, confronts them directly (for the most part) and puts them upfront for examination.

So, strong claims have been made. If I do have the attention of anyone who preliminarily opposes my world views, judging from who I oppose and who I support, even this introduction likely has them already more resistant than might be hoped in a pursuit of pure reason. And of course, though I collected this over time and tried as much as possible to eliminate bias from the actual concourse of reason herein, I am biased in my own ways too.

But let us take a breath—that is no platitude; seriously, take a conscious breath or two—and turn now to the crucial issue which I said was both self-evident and necessary, and completely supportable to reason beyond any measure of doubt that would allow the opposition room to adhere to their claims as determinants for action or as anything more than the not-entirely-written off fantasies of the infinite possibilities of imagination.

Let us turn to the question of the infinite, as reasonably as we can and let us not suppose—for the moment—that the conclusion of the infinite leads necessarily to any virtuous or vicious action, nor that the conclusion of the finite, or the negation of or agnosticism toward the infinite necessarily leads to virtuous or vicious action. This we can discuss later. But in order to affect the purest examination of reason, let us try to conceive, as far as we can, that neither option would for the moment be so life shattering that we cannot bear to suppose in its direction. Let us merely see what is reasonable within the bounds of the question: is life infinite or finite?[*]

---

[*] Note: one might argue on epistemological grounds that one cannot ask this question because it would be impossible to argue that one could know the infinite or prove it. This would appear reasonable on the surface but it actually has the underlying conception of finitude built into it. It asserts the nature and capacity of the one who conceives or reasons as finite. If we are to walk the epistemological path we must also go to the very foundations and ask the hardest questions. This I have done in *Jnana Yoga: A Skeptic's Journey to Knowledge*, and the conclusion there is entirely compatible with what we find here—namely, that the infinite is self-evident and is in fact an epistemological certainty. The questions of the conception of the self and how one could make this claim are dealt with therein.

Purpose in Form

The Preliminary Case for the Infinite

We will start the questioning off in favor of Benatar, and any such finitist or so called skeptic[*], for the question of the infinite seems a very hard one to put to anyone, so let's see if we can say anything reasonable at all, let alone conclusive.

We must answer three questions at least: 1) What does "infinite" mean? Or what would a claim of infinite existence consist of? 2) Where would we look for proof of the existence of an infinite? Or what can we expect as evidence in this case? And 3) Is the infinite a reasonable or even evident account based on the evidence we can see or our capacity to gather such evidence as defined? These three questions must not only be answered in totality in a reasonable manner, but the individual answers to each must be reasonable and coherent.

As to the first question, what does "infinite" mean? There are several ways to conceptualize this. The immediate problem is the problem of a definition for something that is indefinite by definition. This is one of the reasons that the question would seem so hard and that those who oppose such considerations might seem to be rational as well. So one of our first definitions—though it comes with a conundrum—is that the infinite is not defined or delineated. But the flaw here is in translating the reality into an all-encompassing word, not that the existence of the infinite would contradict itself. Merely we must concede that any word that we take as a token for the infinite will not correspond "correctly" to the thing-in-itself.

When we say "tree" we suppose that this word covers all the necessary elements that we know to belong to a tree (or the archetypal tree, maybe). Though there are odd trees that would not fit to the image we might have in our minds or even the definitions we would give, we not being botanists, assume well enough that this word corresponds to that reality and covers it. Though I might argue that assumption is unfounded and also assumes finitude, and that each and every tree (or any "thing") is infinitely complex, that is

---

[*] See *Jnana Yoga* for my full take on skepticism, but in short, skepticism is not rightly claimed or attributed merely to those who support a generally modern western intellectual secularized point of view—those who question traditions and "outlandish" claims. True skeptics must be skeptical of their own skepticism (i.e. possible bias) and thus there should be no such thing as an intuitively obvious ridiculous or outlandish claim, regardless of the splendor or horror it stands for.

putting the cart before the horse in the same way that it would be for someone to say that because the words we use most clearly do not cover the entirety of the supposed infinite existence, our claim to reason about this existence must be flawed—that is the pre-convinced finitude-ists trying to have their way.

Actually, though conceptually difficult, the definition of the infinite as non-definite is quite helpful, and it can be seen better when compared to the other formulations of this conceptualization; another way to conceptualize the infinite, which is perhaps the most iconic, though I think least clear (the previous obscurities notwithstanding) is that the infinite is endless; it has no end. This, however, is not like in mathematics where we suppose an infinite line—a sequence that continues "forever" in either direction but that is bounded to a narrow domain. It is actually more appropriate to say that the infinite is *unbounded*. There are and cannot be borders or bounds to its domain—its domain is simply all.

Thus we see that the "definition" of non-definite is actually entirely reasonable given the subject at hand. A definition requires the making-finite, the defining of boundaries, so these can be drawn to light in the description. So the infinite cannot be defined because to border it would be to miss it, to not indicate it. Thus our definition is apophatic, but it need not be an endless stream of denials until the end of time, for we can within our minds apprehend the concept of this necessity for aphophasis. We can know that when we talk about the infinite, we are talking about that which exists beyond all boundaries and is without end. This conception does not, and cannot by definition, give us an accurate picture to hold in our minds about the infinite, but it does give us an understanding of the nature of the infinite; the necessary qualifications it would need to uphold in order to be evidenced. There is still one more element of the infinite's nature that is important but we will return to that after addressing an immediate objection which arises.

The idea that we cannot adequately conceptualize the infinite, that we cannot capture it in boundaries less we destroy it and hold not what we seek, leads us perfectly to our next question in that it would seem we must here fail. The second question is "what can we expect as evidence of the infinite?" If we cannot, by definition, ever hope to present the infinite in its totality to the mind or much less to the eyes, then what real, persuasive evidence could we hope for at all? If the thing itself cannot be brought forth and pointed out, how can it be self-evident or even a mental whim beyond any hope of confirmation?

Purpose in Form

Now the real answer to this question is problematic because it does not on the surface seem to be reasonable. We must consider, however, that we are not beings who know perfect reason, and that many things that are reasonable do not appear to us immediately as such though they are clearly before us. Take the example of the existence of a positron. We know these particles exist. We knew that for some time. But when we went to characterize them we struggled until, after 17 years of puzzling over the problem, Richard Feynman gave the clearest description which agreed most consistently with our best mathematics that a positron is an electron moving backwards in time (Muller, 231).

Now if, upon first discovery, the positron was seen and one of the observers said, "Well, that's clearly an electron moving backward in time!" he would have been at least and at best ignored. It was only after the struggle to comprehend the nature of the reality presented, that the seemingly absurd explanation, which agreed with the best mathematical formulas, could be presented and taken seriously. In that same light, seeing the real truth and reasonability of this answer lies in struggling to understand the world without it. In that sense it would have been more amenable to me to illustrate the arguments (or lack thereof) for finite existence first. But I wanted to put the hard task to myself and see if I could do better facing more difficulty. The inherent lack of a definition of the infinite is seen by those who propose finitude as a fatal flaw—that those in support of infinity have no answer to give and must only believe in this mere speculation on faith. But I believe there is an answer to be given and it is more coherent than anything supporting the finite (which is really nothing).

That being said I will answer the question posed directly and then I will explain and substantiate this answer. So the question is what evidence could we hope for given that we cannot capture, overview, or elucidate the infinite? The answer is that we cannot hope to gain or attain any evidence, but that the evidence is given immediately at hand. We cannot capture or possess the infinite, but it can be present—that is to say, if the infinite does exist, then it is necessarily everywhere. We cannot conceptualize, grasp, rise above and examine the infinite to establish its veracity as an objective and separate observer, but every moment we witness the undeniable reality of the infinite.

Pretty wishy-washy, eh? Perhaps. But maybe we can do better than leaving it here. As I said, I believe we are given *evidence* and I do not mean that this evidence cannot be examined.

The Myth of the Finite

Here we must return to the first question where we left our definition unfinished (necessarily, it seems). There is an additional, conceptually rational description of the nature of the infinite which bears immediately on the hunt for and the examination of the evidence at hand. The additional definition or description of the nature of the infinite is that it is self-saturating, necessarily. Infinity by definition is everywhere—for it is unbounded and unending—and thus, if infinity is the fundamental reality, we must find infinity everywhere we look. What that means is that the infinite would not be infinite if any substance anywhere were not infinitely divisible. For, if we were to find some instance of finiteness, it would contradict the reality of infinity.

In the mathematical description of Deutsch (though he was talking about number sets, the concept is well illustrated), he says any set of an infinite's constituents is equal to the whole. "The defining property of an infinite set is that some part of it has as many elements as the whole thing." (Deutsch, 167) That is to say, the infinite must be infinite (clearly), and the supposition of finite objects cannot be the ultimate reality[*].

This, again, bumps up against both our capacities for understanding and our preconceptions (which may be the same thing…). For, as we saw with the definition of the tree, with any definition we assume finitude. And since we are beings who function by nature largely on speech and definition and conceptualization, we seem to in our very nature assume finitude. However, that is very different from saying that our nature is necessarily finite which proves finitude. It is that we by nature or at least evolutionary custom assume finitude and that is our preconception. There is nothing reasonable about assuming this presumption, though it seems to underlie our very nature, is necessarily reflective of reality[†].

---

[*] "The universe is something infinite and incomprehensible. Man's life is an inscrutable part of this inscrutable 'whole'." (Tolstoy, 44)

[†] There is a good objection to be made that our assumption of finitude is proven by its clear efficacy, especially in light of our discussion that will follow. But this is actually not undermining, because the reality that life responds to action directed by conceptualization of finite objects does not prove that the infinite is necessarily impossible, nor that the finite is necessarily true. It is true experientially, certainly, and that is often what we have meant by "true" throughout the ages. But it does not prove beyond any doubt that our experience of reality must be in complete accord with the fundamental nature of reality. We cannot merely presume that we have comprehended nature to the core because we find our conceptualizations moderately (or even

Purpose in Form

Thus we must conceive that, despite our evolved and inherited biases, it is possible that we are fundamentally mistaken about the certainty or necessity of finitude, and that we may have inherited this mistake as a consequence of it being a very effective tool for certain kinds of life and pursuits within a greater reality that contradicts it (see previous note).

So, as we were saying in way of definition, the infinite must fully pervade itself. Though we do not exclude the possibility of finite apparition within the infinite (see notes), of which it must be allowed, this manifestation would be apparent only.[*] Thus, this quality of self-saturation makes it plain that the infinite would be immediately and imminently present. That being said, it becomes a bit more reasonable to say that we are given the evidence of the infinite before our eyes; we cannot grasp it, we cannot stand apart from it and judge it "objectively"[†], by definition, but we can nonetheless behold it. The

---

miraculously) effective. Thus, this is an inverse case to the discussion of reason presented earlier—reason is not impotent or unreal merely because we are not perfect at it; it is real and it has some significant effect, though not total. In this case, the hypothesis of finitude is undeniably effective for us, but somethings effectivity does not mean that it is fundamentally true. It can be true and significantly effective on a certain level of abstraction (like the Newtonian assumptions in physics), while not being fundamentally true.

[*] Now, one might say that wouldn't it be possible, strictly speaking, for the infinite to actually manifest "real" finite existence? This is a concession that must be made since the infinite must be infinite (and therefore infinitely powerful and infinitely impervious to the contradiction that in its infinite power it creates something that is fundamentally apart from it and different to it, which then destroys its own nature of infiniteness by making some boundary where it does not pervade...) But we will not take this as part of our argument for the existence of the infinite because it relies not on reason so much as "I have created a conception which can do anything, therefore it is incontrovertible"; therefore were rationalists able to prove finitude in some way, we would, if we held reason has our highest value and wished to remain true, then hold that the infinite is a necessarily unreasonable conclusion. However, this conception of an infinite divorced from its creation will remain very important throughout the book and is, though often not clearly formulated or even conscious, pervasive in the world; we will prove that this is, fortunately, (regardless of its possibility/impossibility) not the case.

[†] This likely brings up trepidation in the minds of rational, scientific-minded readers. We have been lead to believe that objectivity is the sole measure of truth and true inquiry. But that is not the case. Objectivity, or attempting to approach objectivity as much as is humanly possible, is appropriate and effective in the realm of finite observation and the search for finite truth. But this question is addressed in depth in

The Myth of the Finite

truth is revealed to us without and prior to our search and conquest for it.

Here we cannot insert an entire book on the discoveries of modern physics or the varying theories across the discipline. But we can cite some of what is necessary.

First and foremost, in all due candor, it is appropriate to say that the scientific community considers the debate between a finite or infinite universe a reasonable one. They too do not currently exclude the possibility of finitude from the realms of rational conception. But the distinction between a scientific conception of a/the universe and the philosophic question of existence itself or underlying, foundational metaphysical reality must be seen as paramount. Science may explore the bounds of a universe, given that they do not take the necessary definition of a universe to be "all that exists", and then science may wonder: if it is bounded, what lays beyond it and if there might be an end. This is all well and good for science as it functions almost exclusively within the preconceived notion of finitude which is inherent to the human race (though the infinite capacity of the imagination is perhaps overlooked as a cornerstone to that endeavor—though not by Deutsch).

In science, like in mathematics where there is the conception of bounded infinites which are accepted realities but do not answer or approach our question, the theories about the finitude of the universe and the possible multiverses, etc. do not address the same question that we address when we talk about the basic question of the finitude of existence or the existence of infinity or not.

But this is not to say that science cannot help us, nor is it to say that science can help us but never contradict us. As we said, we will hold to the evidence of self-saturation, or infinitely divisible reality as a rational basis for "proof" of the infinite. I make this primary acknowledgement and qualification only to

---

my book *Jnana Yoga* as to the necessary place of "objectivity" in the search for absolute truth. The imposed necessity of objectivity actually precludes the possibility of certainty, and while it is appropriate in deciphering between human perceptions what the underlying finite "answer" is, when that answer is an object or discrete truth, we cannot suppose that objectivity is necessarily required in all pursuits, nor erroneously require it in a pursuit of the infinite and an absolute, incorrigible truth (as discussed in *Jnana Yoga*) because it is both damaging to the reasonable pursuit and superfluous to the reasonable apprehension of the solution. "We can't step outside of what is and look back at it." (Dogen, 54)

state that the scientists and the metaphysicists generally ask different questions and we must be careful when translating evidence from one realm to another, though they use similar terminology in some instances. We must understand the words and discussions in the context of their appropriate fields.

Well, science has not proven a finite reality, nor have they proven a non-infinitely divisible reality; almost exclusively the contrary. There is the objection to be made of the Planck length hypothesis, which suggests that reality cannot proceed beyond a certain size (1.6×10^{-35} m). However, one cannot be over-presumptuous on a speculative hypothesis (which may go the same way as the atom went), nor can one assume that the interpretation of the possibility of the Plank limit necessarily applies to *existence* when scientists talk about "reality".

If such a limit does exist, it may be a limit of our technological perception (or our CURRENT AND CONCEIVABLE technological perception), or a limit of the bounds of our conceptual reality. These do not mean that this would be a limit to existence itself beyond these bounds. And as of yet the theory remains unproven and still beyond the horizons of possible testing.

There have always been theories of finitude, but these have consistently been disproven. Obviously it only takes one proof to overturn the possibilities, but the mere hypothesis does not prove finitude, nor does it make it at all likely (as we will show). The Plank limit hypothesis does do one thing in favor of the arguments for finitude; it seems to give them one tiny sliver of hope that their theory might rest on this hypothesis and claim grounds to reasonability. The difficulty of differentiating the bounds of the scientific theory in as far as it applies to perceptual limits, conceptual reality limits, or limits of existence itself still remain in the way of this being a necessarily rational basis for the rationalists who assert finite existence, or deny or disregard the presence of the infinite.

Apart from the supposed Plank limit, science has generally found even perceivable reality to be endlessly complex and divisible. The atom was passed, as were the subatomic particles. We have looked back to the perceptual wall of the residue of the big bang, but that leaves us not with a certainty of finitude, but on the contrary, a certainty that existence exceeds our ability to look beyond it. Similarly the event horizon of the cosmos speaks not to the bounds of existence, but the bounds of reality and life as we conceive it.

Thus the pattern of scientific discovery has tended throughout the ages to show us that what we are looking at is the infinite or infinity itself. It is infinitely divisible, and infinitely expansive. While this cannot at all be counted as a decisive stroke for the absolute proof of the infinite, it does illustrate the fact that evidence for the infinite may indeed be seen before us and that we do have a rational approach to the question of "what evidence would we propose for the infinite?"

As I said, the most decisive force of the conception of the infinite is that its necessity is revealed when examining the arguments for the finite, just as the rational explanation for the nature of the positron was comprehended through the lack of any other satisfactory explanation; it was only then that the beyond-conception became the rational.

Thus, the third question of "is the infinite a reasonable or even evident account based on the evidence we can see or our capacity to gather such evidence as defined?" has already been answered. And I believe it is really self-evident, and even all would-be finitists who operate in science and toy with bounded infinites in their mind make necessary the reality of the one true infinite. A thought experiment I think clearly shows this but we will come to that in examining the case for the finite.

Though we have not yet proven the reality of infinity, we have proven the validity of the discussion and hypothesis on rational grounds. Now we will see if finitists can do the same.

The Absurdity of the Finite

Now we turn to the finite conceptualization of reality. And, though those with much skepticism (or bias) may still hold doubts about the finality and self-evident nature of the infinite reality, let us not neglect an age old tactic of reason, which is to see what is not reasonable and turn to the only thing we are left with[*].

In reality, the real question here is not "what can we say of the infinite?", for we can say very little by definition, but we have good reason for this apophasis as well as for the positive reality beyond our capacities of conception which we can yet begin to see. The real revealing question is, "what is there to be said for the finite?"

---

[*] "When you have eliminated the impossible, whatever remains, however improbable, must be the truth." - Sherlock Holmes (Doyle, The Sign of the Four)

Purpose in Form

The finite is our default assumption. It is our evolutionary predisposition. But common sense does not always make for universal truth. The real truths—the ones with universal reach—are often the inverse of common sense. We had to address the skeptics of the infinite because it is the vogue for the day. But that is all really quite silly for the finitists have literally nothing to stand on.

Beyond the fact that all our observations point to the fact that we are not finite objects, but inexplicable coalescences of mostly empty space that is pervaded by a particularized energy which appears to be expanding and expressing itself infinitely all around, and that everything we think of as an object seems infinitely divisible and inexorably connected to everything else, consider this simple thought experiment: Can you describe a finite existence? What would that entail? What proof could you hope for it? (We need not ask the question of evidence, as we shall see).

A finite existence is the opposite of an infinite one. It is definite, defined, and confined. It has an end; it is bounded. So a finite existence has a boundary. But what is that boundary made of? We don't have to suppose we could see it to see that this is a contradiction.

If there is a boundary of existence, there is a definite end. What is this end made of? What defines it? It is literally impossible to think of a boundary without assuming an outside to that boundary—that is to say a continuing of existence. A boundary is defined, necessarily, not just by what it encompasses but by what it excludes as well. Thus, you can never have an ultimate boundary. This is a very similar problem to the one faced by mind/body dualists; if they are separate, what separates them? Where does the distinction end and begin? And how do the two interact? This is a necessary truth, but we can make it clearer.

The objection may be raised that we are imposing our known paradigm on the edges of existence. We cannot expect the ultimate boundary of existence which makes it ultimately finite to have an "outside" or "other side" in any way that we would expect because that would, as we have pointed out, necessitate further existence. But this is not a highly reasonable claim, though we will give it its due to see it through. Notice, though, that the vague claim is made that finitude and the ends of the universe should, for unexplained reasons, be beyond our grasp or may be expected to be. But this underestimates the universality of reason and the role of humans as universal explainers (See Deutsch). And it gives no clear case as to why this particular

The Myth of the Finite

form of finitude should be different other than it is far off and therefore, supposedly, exotic. So this objection really just rests on the supposition that we must limit our vision in any case that seems out of sight or out of reach at first blush, which is hardly scientific (in fact, it is unscientific by Deutsch's definition). But let us nevertheless explore the argument.

So, we cannot conceive of the edge of finite existence because it is unlike other types of finite boundaries of which we regularly conceive. This is because it is the boundary between existence and non-existence. There is literally no other option here. Any formulation that is not expressly this or reducible to this existence/non-existence scenario is a contradiction, because if there is any existence of any kind or mode beyond the boundary, the argument is false. So we must be talking about non-existence.

Because it is the boundary between existence and non-existence, we cannot "envision" the other side of the boundary, for it does not exist. But there is a problem with this explanation. By juxtaposing existence and non-existence, we still get the image of a bounded space set against the non-existent beyond. But this image is necessarily false since it is viewed from an outside or beyond, and therefore necessarily existent (though hypothetical), source. BUT IT IS ONLY THIS IMAGE THAT MAKES THIS ACCOUNT REMOTELY COGENT.

We must reject this image of this explanation. But, we may be told that, while the image does not apply (just as we cannot hope to imagine an accurate conception of the infinite) there still is the reality. But let us look at this reality. You have existence and you have non-existence. Actually that is entirely incorrect. You have existence and you *don't have* non-existence, because it is not something to have—it does not exist. So you merely have existence. But what is an existence which is only bounded by that which does not exist? It is necessarily infinite! To say that the ultimate boundaries of existence lie on the borders of the non-existent, is to say that they aren't anywhere at all—that they don't exist. If the boundaries were somewhere, there would be a location where the non-existent was located and therefore existed. But because the non-existent is non-existent, there are no boundaries in relation to it.

So what the finitists are forced to describe is a completely unbounded existence which has no ends, no outside, and cannot be defined or described or enclosed in any way*. Thus that existence is infinite. And if anyone is describing an existence which has a boundary, end, or otherwise finitude, it is only ever occurring within the total infinite existence. Thus infinite existence is a necessary truth and an ultimate finite existence is necessarily a contradiction.

We are absolutely incapable of supposing or reasoning about a finite ultimate existence in any meaningful way, and we are given merely in the commonplace operations of our mind a necessary conception of the infinite—any time we imagine a finite space, we necessarily put ourselves outside it. We intuitively know and operate by the reality of the infinite. The spectre of ultimate finitude is only a linguistic conception which is held reasonable by one who considers a finite, bounded hypothetical existence in his own mind, but overlooks the fact he is supposing an outside—an existence beyond that bounded existence.

This is also why there can only be one fundamental existence (ultimately only one true infinite; 'the' infinite as opposed to 'an' infinite, as among a set of infinities) and any idea of a discontinuous existence is flawed. Quantum reality describes the discontinuous nature of the physical universe/reality and it is at odds with age old philosophical conceptions of a continuous universe. "We can speak and think only of what exists. And what exists is uncreated and imperishable for it is whole and unchanging and complete. It was not or nor shall be different since it is now, all at once, one and continuous." (Parmenides, 8)

But whether the old philosophers were intuitively correct or merely fortunate in their mistake does not matter; while it is possible to think about a discontinuous physical universe, or even a discontinuous reality (including the limited, personal consciousness or mind) it is not possible to have a discontinuous fundamental existence. The only "real" or EFFECTIVE boundaries that could separate one existence from "another" would be the boundaries of non-existence, where you had existences submerging into and

---

* "His true name is 'He that is', or, in other words, Being without restriction, All Being, the Being infinite and universal." (Hume speaking of the conception of God as a traditional theologian would put it; readers of *Jnana Yoga* will notice the significance of the conception 'He that is'.) And further, even Hume's conception of a dire skeptic is driven to remark "[the truth of the existence of the infinite being or God] is unquestionable and self-evident." (Hume, 14)

emerging from non-existence; but this conception is misleading because it does not give us a picture of true "non-existence" but rather merely a fertile void, which nevertheless is an existent "nothingness" with which to juxtapose the alternating "somethings" of existence. But clearly the two both exist. Thus there is no way to have multiple fundamental existences, for if there were multiple existences, there would be a more fundamental existent nature out of which the barriers between the distinct existences were built. "Nothing can be completely walled off from the rest of reality." (Peterson, 46) Thus there is only one ultimate fundamental existence and it must be continuous (i.e. One).

Now none of this is to say that scientific speculation about a possibly finite universe is improper—for, as we have said, there is a difference between the scientific term "universe" and the philosophical conception of "existence itself"—nor to say that mathematicians do anything "wrong" in playing with multiple infinities. It is again, merely a difference in category between what the metaphysician talks about and the questions he asks and what the various realms of science theorize, regardless of apparently identical terms. The term "universe" in common use and in history often meant "all that exists" in the same way that the term "world" also meant that. But in the scientific realms the "universe" may be to "existence" as "world" (or "Earth") is to "universe".

This (limited) separation of the questions and ideas of the metaphysical and the scientific notwithstanding, the metaphysical conclusion we have reached most certainly has ramifications in science as well as throughout all lives. There can be nothing more important, in fact, than the certainty in the infinite. In fact, I recommend that all readers pause at this point to reexamine and rethink this first argument and the certainty of the conclusion as much as possible. A lifetime devoted to accepting the reality of the infinite would not be wasted, and so, in many ways, this is the most important section of the book.

The truth of a necessary and obvious eternal existence is always here, but it can be easily overlooked and forgotten, so it is really something quite profound and elegant to realize and begin to accept in one's life. All you are asked to see is that non-existence does not exist. But hearing it and saying it versus really *getting* it are profoundly different experiences. Non-existence does not exist. The infinite is.

Purpose in Form

The Necessary Immanence of the Infinite

Concepts of existence as ultimately finite are inherently unreasonable. The infinite is a necessary truth. But for materialist- and traditionally (dogmatic) scientific-minded people this says little about human life and death. To make any suggestion that conscious life is not finite, regardless of conclusions about abstract existence itself (whatever that means) is the epitome of wishy-washy unscientific nonsense—mere wish fulfillment and sophistry.

The next hurdle that must be made is to point out and overcome the fact that not knowing exactly what we mean by "existence itself" or not completely comprehending the entailments of infinity are the only things that cause people to think of infinity as an "abstract" concept. The infinitude of existence itself means it is necessarily NOT abstract. It is entirely immanent. Recall, the infinite must be self-saturating*. The infinite cannot be a removed entity or concept. It is the base and foundation of everything (necessarily) and it also is entirely present and completely pervades all apparently separate and individual things. These are necessary entailments of the infinite. They are not wishful platitudes.

---

* "He is entire in every point of space, and complete in every instant of duration." (Hume speaking again from the classical religious conception of God; though humanity as a whole understandably struggles with the concept of the infinite, how is it that we threw out all metaphysics as merely superstitious mumbo-jumbo of dimwitted or befuddled primitive minds and missed all the truth they knew about the infinite and its properties?) (Hume, 29)

The Myth of the Finite

There is a diagrammatic way of illustrating this:

Diagram 1:

The set of all natural numbers: 1, 2, 3, 4, 5, 6, 7, 8....

Subset: 2, 3, 4, 5, 6, 7, 8...

Diagram 2:

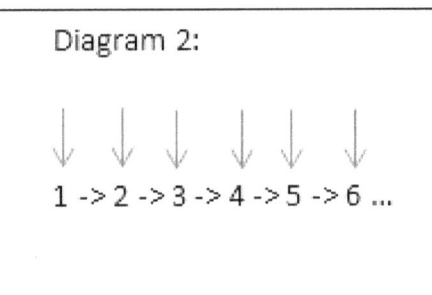

1 -> 2 -> 3 -> 4 -> 5 -> 6 ...

Diagram 1 is similar to one found in David Deutsch's chapter "A Window on Infinity", which contains a much more detailed description and discussion of the mathematical idea of infinity, for those interested. In Diagram 1, both sets of numbers (set 1 & subset 2) have equal amount of terms in them—i.e. infinitely many—even though the second excludes some numbers compared to the first (i.e. number 1). Yet still, both sets have equal amount of terms in them. Such is the nature of infinite sets.

But real number sets—what we are dealing with in this illustration and example—are what are called "countable infinites" (Deutsch, 171). Reality or existence itself is an "uncountable" infinite. Hopefully that is obviously a necessary conclusion (for those who understand the mathematical discussion in question). But we may say that it couldn't be a countable one, since it is not a

Purpose in Form

"line", it is not bounded in any direction. Thus it proceeds all ways and in each part is infinitely divisible. So it is not "countable" in the mathematical sense.

We obviously could not diagram this (go on YouTube and watch some Mandelbrot set zooms for a good visual though!). But take the second diagram. Each number or instance represents a "moment" of existence. The perpendicular arrows represent the presence of the infinite, contrasted to the running arrows which are what we normally think of as linear causal experience (the previous supports or brings into existence the next).

We will get into causation later, but the point is we do not commonly think of each moment requiring the infinite presence and support. In traditional lines of reason, such as the first cause argument, we suppose an infinite, yet we exile it from the line of causal reality or creation and make it merely an abstract concept which may have begun the chain of linear causation and finite reality. But given that the chain itself is infinite, it must take place "in" an infinite "space" or an infinite potential for being, and the infinite, being infinite, must saturate this supposed finite expansion of linear causality[*]. Missing this key point is how people can be unmoved by the first cause argument—they may understand the conception of an infinite regress and even suppose an infinite physical universe, but they don't understand the real implications of an infinite reality[†].

And further, this diagram and conception is inadequate as we have said as it seems to represent each moment as finite, which is how we too often think of them. But since the infinite is a necessary truth and since the infinite requires self-saturation, each moment itself must be infinite as well. So the numbers in the second diagram do not represent discrete entities, they are merely conceptual approximations. Each number in Diagram 2 is not a reduced elementary constituent of a countable infinite set. Rather, though diagrammed like the former, each number is itself AN ENTIRE UNCOUNTABLE INFINITE SET (again, check out Mandelbrot sets for a better visual). Each individual number in the diagram contains the same "amount" of infinity as the entire infinity itself. This is the (THE ONE/THE ONLY) fundamental infinity.

---

[*] "The universal doctrine teaches that all the visible structures of the world—all things and beings—are the effects of a ubiquitous power out of which they rise, which supports and fills them during the period of their manifestation, and back into which they must dissolve." (Campbell, 221)

[†] See Peter Boghossian, Vincent Bugliosi, and Heather Mac Donald, for examples.

Thus the necessary reality that existence is infinite is not an abstraction whatsoever. It is an immanent and living truth, completely present in everything*. I know speaking of the infinite in such terms calls to mind wishy-washy sentiments, or still begrudgingly viewed religious dogma, but these are necessary, logical conclusions of truly understanding what infinity means and entails. And as one can begin to see, it is my case that religious language is amenable to the discussion here because it was religion which first evolved and staked out the (entirely true!) conception of life as infinite.

Conclusion

It is an incredible oddity to me, but a routine one of experience, that one can look over such arguments and, essentially, shrug. Some people are simply not astounded by the reality presented, most likely because they have not been sufficiently disturbed by contemplating the problem and seeming prospect of non-existence.

Richard Muller remarks on a similar issue of the soul saying, "I know I have a soul. You can't talk me out of that… If you tell me that I don't have a soul, that it is an illusion, that you can teach a computer program to act as if it, too, has a soul, I conclude that you don't know what I'm talking about." (271-272) Some people get the issue and you can talk with them about it. Some people just aren't struck by it, and that seems to be as far as we can say, though we would all, on both sides, like to resolve all beings to the truth we so obviously know.

But I think this is also evidence of the shift in our age of being uninterested in or averse to, and therefore undisturbed and unmoved by, metaphysical conceptions. For some reason we not only left them behind, but threw them all away.

For this reason Hume, when considering the classic first cause argument was able to entirely dismiss it and even call it unconvincing, much as Bugliosi reviewed it in his book, *The Divinity of Doubt*, remarked that it could not be denied, and then moved on as if it was still of little importance and no decisive weight. Here is how Hume puts it:

---

* "Every event is alike important in the eyes of that infinite being, who takes in at one glance the most distant regions of space and remotest periods of time" (Hume, 99)

Purpose in Form

> The weakness of this metaphysical reasoning... seem[s] so obviously ill-grounded, and at the same time of so little consequence to the cause of true piety and religion... I shall begin with observing that there is an evident absurdity in pretending to demonstrate a matter of fact, or prove it by any arguments 'a priori'. Nothing is demonstrable unless the contrary implies a contradiction. Nothing that is distinctly conceivable implies a contradiction. Whatever we conceive as existent, we can also conceive of as non-existent. There is no being, therefore, whose non-existence implies a contradiction. Consequently there is no being whose existence is demonstrable. I propose this argument as entirely decisive, and am willing to rest the whole controversy upon it. (Hume, 55)

And further:

> The argument 'a priori' has seldom been found very convincing, except to people of a metaphysical head who have accustomed themselves to abstract reasoning, and who, finding from mathematics that the understanding frequently leads to truth through obscurity, and contrary to first appearances, have transferred the same habit of thinking to subjects where it ought not to have place. Other people, even of good sense and the best inclined to religion, feel always some deficiency in such arguments, though they are not perhaps able to explain distinctly where it lies, a certain proof that men ever did and will derive their religion from other sources than from this species of reasoning. (Hume, 57)

Hume was here talking about knowing the metaphysical structure(s) of God and the world, and he captures exactly the attitudes that I observe—though I am on the contrary side of the sentiment.

For one, in opposition to Hume's claims as a whole that metaphysical speculation is impotent, I can point out the hubris in supposing that something "distinctly conceived" is any sort of reliable criterion. There are so many things we think we "distinctly perceive" and yet are so wrong about. Our perceptions are anything but distinct or definitive. Also, as we have shown, the non-existence of an infinite existence *is* a necessary contradiction. So Hume

The Myth of the Finite

was wrong on both accounts (and indeed about things he said he would stake the entire discussion on); some in depth metaphysical examination and collective criticism would have served well to avoid such errors. And he elsewhere admits to the undeniability of the first cause.

Though the first cause argument does not often seem to move the average person to faith, it undeniably has significance and effect in the world. Just as he himself points out, the analogy to mathematics is apt; how many of you could derive calculus by yourself, from the ground up? How many would be urged to do so? If you can remember how to calculate area based on length and width positioned at right angles, you could approach discovering the area under a curve through Riemann sums (calculating many small blocks of area and adding them up to get an estimate). But if someone told you there was a way to do it much more precisely through working with infinite concepts such as limits and a bunch of other heady stuff, you might understand the utility behind the supposed ability, but you likely wouldn't find calculous as marvelous and spectacular as you should. Mathematicians find the proofs and lines of reasoning toward calculus entirely sufficient and even elegant. They are thankful for these discoveries and all they have led to in our societies. They work with these formulas every day, and find them nearly self-evidently true at this point, even though the majority of people would have a hard time even approaching, let alone comprehending them.

Mathematics doesn't speak to everyone, no matter how imaginative, elegant, innovative, and effective it may be. But how many who have no concern for math in their daily lives and remain completely unmoved by the reality that people out in the world work with and believe in the truths of calculus would object to these truths simply because they cannot understand them or are not interested in them?

Further, mathematics—though their study is esoteric to most people—have direct impacts on our lives through both material effects and comments on the nature of reality and ourselves. We see and benefit from the realities of mathematics beyond our interest or comprehension every day in the progress of the world through technology—computers, space travel, communications, etc. Why should we merely accept what the experts say in this case but condemn the metaphysical reasoning done by professionals in the philosophic field as something unimportant, impotent, or even misguided simply because it does not speak to us?

Purpose in Form

As we will fully show, the effects of differing metaphysical mindsets are clearly demonstrable and significant. If we can see this, what reason do we have for supposing metaphysics should be ignored or dismissed simply because it is something that doesn't appeal to us (for whatever reason)?

In Hume's case, he takes issue with metaphysics and *a priori* reasoning eschewing direct experience and observation—which is a fair criticism; as I stated in the introduction, metaphysics should be informed though observation and experience. Such condemning of *a priori* reasoning and necessity for experience, however, gets turned on its head in the realm of the infinite; "experimental science only has to be introduced to the question of final causes for it to turn into a nonsense." (Tolstoy, 38)

I cannot deny that Hume accurately observes and describes an actual, pervasive, and stubborn attitude of dismissal in people toward metaphysics. But I do object to the idea that metaphysics is of "so little consequence to the cause of true piety and religion". Hume calls to the necessity of personal experience (which I quote elsewhere), and that is truly a necessity. Yet I also believe that the metaphysical conception is a necessary element—one necessary to the collective consciousness' formulations of the attitudes towards life, as well as one which has significant effect (removed and trickling down though it may be) on the individual who is influenced by the collective conceptions of the day (unconscious though he or she may be of such particular influence, or that it comes from a specified metaphysics).

These are exactly analogous to the effects of advanced mathematics, where they are beyond the contemplation of the average person (for interest or intricacy), but they nevertheless shape our physical world and individual world views, consciously or unconsciously. That is to say, as I have made clear from the outset, our metaphysical conceptions are significant and EFFECTIVE throughout life—for society as a whole, and in the individual lives of not only abstruse philosophers, monks, or esotericists, but also for the average individual (though, again, they may be unconscious of the effects and may, on the surface, when directly confronted with the metaphysical discussion, appear unaffected by it).

I hope to show more clearly as we progress how the effects of this conception take hold, that existence itself is infinite, and the infinite is the entire running truth and immanent fact of all existence. To do this, next we must examine how this applies to theories of annihilation or "coming into being", such as are found in the philosophical assumptions of anti-natalism and nihilism.

It would seem a far leap from existence itself being infinite to drawing any conclusions about a human life. And, what is more, we know incontrovertibly that human life is finite! How could we think otherwise? So it seems more must be said than merely contradicting the finite nature of existence itself.

It really is not so. This truth should be all that is needed. But there is a problem of dogma in the way. The materialist conception of consciousness as an emergent phenomenon stands in our way. This conception is entirely unreasonable. It has been scientifically disproven. But the communities aren't talking about it. This is dreadfully unfortunate. Not only am I faced with forwarding outlandish (though necessarily true) explanations like the reality of the infinite, which is hard enough given people's preconceptions, but now I have to take a stand against materialism, which though also necessarily true, will have so many readers simply dismiss the argument already because their dogma says they can. But that is the state of the world and human knowledge and so it must be done. In reality the infinity of existence is the same thing as the infinity of consciousness and very direct and important conclusions follow. But we must here outline the work proving that consciousness is not an emergent, finite phenomenon caused by material substrates.

Key Concept:

The infinite multiverse interpretation and explanation of quantum mechanics- Deutsch brings his preamble on the necessity of explanations to bear on the theories of quantum mechanics and makes the case that scientists are avoiding discussion of the underlying explanations and assumptions of the competing theories. He makes the case that the only viable theoretical *explanation* for quantum mechanics is that of an infinite multiverse. This explanation entails, among other things, the infinite manifestation of parallel universes with infinite versions of "you" (along with all else). This idea obviously supports the idea of the reality of the infinite—infinite potential and infinite manifestation—that we have been discussing and will be referenced going forward. You will have to read Deutsch's book for the full discussion and case made in favor of this theory.

Purpose in Form

Chapter 2: The Myth of Materialism

So many eminent, intelligent, reputable people say outright and in no uncertain terms that we know consciousness is caused by the brain*. How can I suppose to challenge them? How can I hope to not be dismissed on clout alone? Challenging materialism is only something pseudo-scientists and wishy-washy hippies do, right?

But, as Deutsch so astutely points out, knowledge is not justified—much less justified by a personality or academic credentials; clout is only a shade of bias and laziness, but we still have such a hard time with this. What matters is our explanations, our tests, and counter-evidence and counter explanations.

---

* Then again, just as many, of just as high caliber say we have no idea how consciousness or the mind results from brain activity. One's evaluation of the experts and the evidence they present usually only reflects one's confirmation bias. Nowadays, as Murray puts it, there are "endless numbers of tenured academics who can 'prove'" all sorts of ridiculous assumptions (60). Murray was talking about the issue of multiple genders or the unreality of gender, but the point applies to nearly every discipline. Currently people still think of Doctors having some final say in whatever controversy, and that there is a great, unquestionable consensus among the best minds on all important things. But it is becoming increasingly clear that the prefix "Dr."—even when it applies to the appropriate discipline under discussion—is no basis for justification of the things these people proclaim. Doctors and scientists are still people, and just as susceptible to bias, irrational behaviors of all sorts, malice, and outright fabrication as the rest of the population. Jonathan Haidt noted the increase in these phenomena in the recent past as "scientists became 'moral exhibitionists' in the lecture hall as they demonized fellow scientists and urged their students to evaluate ideas not for their truth but for their consistency with progressive ideals." (37) Thus, as a society, we will soon have to confront the reality of epistemology that Deutsch asserts—knowledge is never justified.

Purpose in Form

"The multitude can be and often are wrong" (BNHB, 36).

To begin, we must outline the materialist explanation in its elemental and necessary factors. Materialism is the basis for the assertion that human consciousness is finite and that upon death there is annihilation. If I were to argue that the infinity of existence proved existence after death, that would be uninteresting to perhaps the majority of scientific-minded individuals, because no one (at least, no one we care to listen to) argues that the universe ceases to exist when we die or that it did not exist before we were born.

Materialist scientists believe they know that consciousness is a secondary and emergent characteristic that occurs only upon the aggregation of certain complex structures of organs, and that it dissolves into non-existence when those organs deteriorate completely. Thus, the foundational points of materialism, as they pertain to consciousness and the finiteness of life or experience, are that consciousness is an emergent phenomenon and that consciousness is caused entirely by brain or sensory organ activity. If either of these is proven false, then in the important sense for the questions we are considering, materialism fails as an explanation of the nature of consciousness and experience.

The First Argument (Less Compelling for Those Not Accustomed to Acknowledging and Believing in the Truth of the Infinite)

First I will outline a brief argument in favor of consciousness being an elemental constituent of reality or existence itself, rather than an emergent phenomenon. I believe this argument is true and actually very powerful, but I do not believe it will work on most so-called skeptics[*]. It is, in some ways, too simple and seems like it can be regarded as abstract, rather than immediately pertinent.

I say this not to belittle the argument, I am including it because I think it is necessary and complete and helpful, but because "skeptics" should not take my approach lightly. I have anticipated their resistance, given the dogmas in place, and I will demonstrate next a fully robust refutation of materialism which

---

[*] Again, true skeptics must be skeptical of their own skepticism, as Deutsch points out in his book and I did in *Jnana Yoga*. Skepticism is commonly used as the preferred title for people who merely accept mainstream science dogma and are the most prejudiced about examining other claims. True skepticism is much more open for one is always skeptical of even their own dogma.

The Myth of Materialism

cannot be denied by anyone who is genuinely scientific in their reasoning.

The first argument goes like this: Existence itself is infinite. This infinity of existence is immanent—i.e. self-saturating. As we saw diagrammatically, it is present in each moment, each constituent of existence. Each constituent of existence is itself infinite, as the infinite is uncountable. The manifestation of an infinite constituent (anything within the infinite—which is everything) can only be achieved by the infinite itself—i.e. infinite manifestation must come from infinite potential itself; there is no separate limited cause that could cause an infinite manifestation. That is all to say, infinity is infinite, and its only cause or source can be its own infinite nature. (We will return to causation in detail later.) Consciousness is a phenomenon within existence. Therefore, consciousness is pervaded by and produced by infinite existence[*]. Consciousness is infinite and is produced by infinite existence itself, like all else. Thus consciousness is a property of the infinite and is infinite in itself.

Just as each individual body is infinitely manifested (as supported by quantum theory, see Deutsch), consciousness is also infinitely manifested. Materialism melded with quantum theory (which is silly in itself) says that each separate body in each separate universe causes its own consciousness, and thus retains the limitation of consciousness, even though such limited consciousnesses, as products of bodies, are manifested infinitely across the infinite multiverse.

The real problem here is that materialism should have gone out the window long ago. Materialism is not compatible with so much of what we know about the universe. Materialism (traditionally) claims that physical (matter-based) elements are the constituents of reality. But all scientists know that physical objects are hardly even "physical" or "objects". They are empty space mostly. And even the particles that make them up are bundles of energy. Everything reduces to fluid energy[†]. But materialism has hung on given the utility of our thinking of objects as though they were physical, solid things, on our level of abstraction. This roughly describes their gross behavior and allows us to use day to day objects very well.

So while the ultimate reality of materialism was uprooted, its existence and

---

[*] "There is no being, which possesses any power or faculty, that it receives not from its creator." (Hume, 102)

[†] "Matter, therefore, and spirit, are at the bottom equally unknown." (Hume, 91)

reality was hemmed in to the realm of our conceptions and observations. We see that things behave in ways that look to us like solid objects knocking together, so we continue to describe and think of them as such. And still held within these auspices is purported to be the theory that material interaction in complex ways causes consciousness. Never mind that consciousness seems to be as much an energetic phenomenon (dependent on electrical activity) as a "physical" one. And never mind that brain activity is entirely correlation based but is routinely referred to as causal without any sufficient explanation.

For example, people say that because consciousness is permanently affected by damage to the brain, and we can predict the results of such damages based on where the damage is, therefore consciousness is caused by the brain. But that is only an example of necessary causation for people who already accept the dogmatic explanation that consciousness is caused by the brain. It is only because they refuse to give any credence to other possible explanations that they see this as evidence of necessary causation, rather than correlation.

There is a perfectly cogent explanation of the other side for the same phenomena. Consider this explanation: brain activity is correlative with consciousness but does not cause it. Consciousness has an independent reality from the brain, but manifests in and through a human body through the brain in specific ways. The brain is a precise structure because it is a tool of consciousness for the purpose of entering into and interacting with the physical world. This explanation would equally explain the correlation between areas of brain activity and modes of thought or emotion. Damage to a specific part of the brain would explain impaired function in predicable ways. But none of this proves that consciousness must originate in the brain. This explanation is only rejected for the *prima facie* assumption that consciousness is emergent. Such claims are dogmatic.

As we see, the skeptics still appear to have their materialism to retreat to to refute consciousness as infinite. But if bodies are something existence can manifest infinitely, as quantum theory says, why not consciousness? And if, as I have said, each thing that exists in the infinite (which is infinitely manifested, again, supported by quantum theory) should be considered as primarily supported and manifested by the infinite itself (which makes more sense, since it is infinite, than ascribing to it a discrete, apparently separate cause), then consciousness is a property of the infinite more than of a body. And while this does not prove immediately that the infinite itself is conscious or is consciousness, any more than it would suggest that the infinite is "body" or is a body, it does provide a more reasonable explanation for the infinite potential of consciousness (see Deutsch) than thinking of consciousness as an emergent, secondary, and therefore all the more likely limited phenomenon.

Also, if the infinite has the capacity to manifest consciousness (which it must, again, given that here is consciousness and the infinite is self-saturating, thus present in all elements of existence), and manifests it infinitely, what does that mean?

Is there any difference between having the capacity to manifest and instantiate consciousness and being conscious? Having the capacity to manifest a body is one thing, because a body is an apparently discrete object, and though it is infinitely manifested, it is not a property of being so much. We think of beings in terms of their consciousness. The more they are clearly conscious, the more we think of them as "real" beings. The more there seems to *only* be a manifest body, the less we think of them as beings and the more like automata. So while the infinite can infinitely manifest bodies and objects, its capacity to contain and manifest consciousness seems like it might be a different class of property with different consequences. We are not inclined to say that the infinite is a bodied reality (since the infinite must be unbounded, while a body must be bounded), but many people are convinced that the infinite is conscious, and there is nothing that makes us suppose *consciousness* must be bounded*. We will revisit this question after we become clearer about what we mean by "consciousness".

What Is Consciousness?

There is a problem with the terminology of "consciousness" and its different possible interpretations, which we will address before we eliminate all reasonability for the materialist positions.

---

* Jung seems to object to this: "So far as we know, consciousness is always ego-consciousness. In order to be conscious of myself, I must be able to distinguish myself from others." (CW vol. 17, 326) Thus, Jung's definition of consciousness as fundamentally discriminative makes it necessarily limited. However, our *experience* of consciousness introduces us to a finite consciousness, but there is no question that existence, possibility, and potential extend far beyond our experience—as Jung himself says "so far as we know". And there is always an infinite amount to know beyond what we already do (see Deutsch).

Purpose in Form

When people say "the universe is conscious" and others say "consciousness is an emergent phenomenon", are they referring to the same caliber of consciousness? What is consciousness? When modern westerners and scientists use the word, they often seem to refer to a kind of self-awareness and/or self-interest. As Benatar puts it "consciousness is a function of the cortex." (BNHB, 145) Thus the problem of whether certain animals are in fact conscious is in general a discussion of whether they have consciousness *like the one we do*. Many have sensations, but are they cognizant of a self? That is the question of consciousness for the scientists mostly, it seems. But how does a sensation cause an effect without an awareness of it—without the qualia? And to what does a qualia appear, or what does it affect to impel action?

To most people, even many materialist scientists, there are levels of consciousness. There is a self-awareness which we particularly value and identify with, and then there are more rudimentary awarenesses of sensations and surroundings on a graded scale. But people like panpsychists suggest that there is a fundamental level of awareness, and that awareness is still in some way consciousness, just not necessarily self-consciousness, which it may indeed take a complex cortex-like structure to manifest.

To many, consciousness does not fundamentally mean self-consciousness, but merely "the capacity of awareness". So when we say "the universe might be conscious" or "existence itself might be conscious" or "consciousness might be a fundamental element of reality", we are not necessarily saying that "the universe is a human" or "existence is a complex psyche of multiple sophisticated parts"[*]. This difference must be kept in mind. Again, it is quite possible that, in order to have a human level of psyche—ego, complexes, archetypes, etc.—one must have a structural organ like a complex brain, and that in order to have "emotions" or "sensations" one must have a structural body and conceptions of wants and desires (which require the limitation of form to produce the need or lack). Yet beyond all such forces affecting and impelling consciousness—thus grounding it and apparently limiting it to certain levels of manifestation—there may be an unbounded nature to conscious awareness.

That all being said, we have an impasse; materialists believe consciousness

---

[*] Though see Dr. Jordan Peterson's take on this ("The Primitive Idea of God", YouTube)

is emergent, and likely believe they can claim this whether or not existence is infinite. Others believe consciousness is infinite or fundamental (possibly conceived of as two separate claims—fundamental would necessarily mean infinite, but infinite might be conceived of as non-fundamental, much like a body). Fortunately, we have today definitive scientific proof that consciousness is not emergent.

The Second Argument, Which Uproots the Emergent Theory of Consciousness

The emergence of consciousness is an evolutionary claim. According to the generally accepted modern theory of emergent consciousness, consciousness arose out of a series of increasingly complex species and their developed organs. This provides one crucial test and, ultimately, flaw for materialism and the emergent theory of consciousness[*].

If this is true, then each individual consciousness must be separate from all others, cannot have any affects that reach beyond the physical senses, and cannot have any direct effect on the world. If consciousness is entirely secondary—a limited product of brain function—it can only have effects through the body as it is connected to the physical senses. But today we have robust scientific demonstrations that individual consciousness is not bound by the body, nor even by normal physical and linear accounts of space or time! And we know that consciousness can have a direct effect on the world.

Again with the outlandish claims! And here I cannot possibly do justice to this hypothesis in any non-cursory fashion that could be included. I must insist that you read Dean Radin's book *The Conscious Universe* for full appreciation and scientific (and skeptical) address. That book is a clear, detailed, and scientific meta-analysis of over a hundred years of experiments in the field of so-called psi research.

I know many people may just put this book down here and move on with their lives. But that would not be the rationalist's approach, nor the scientific one, nor the true skeptical one. I'm not saying you have to believe anything on faith here. I'm saying the extent of the evidence and the quality of the

---

[*] To be clear, I am not suggesting evolution is wrong, nor am I suggesting that human and animal consciousness did not become manifested in more complex ways through the evolutionary process of developing more complex organs. I am only addressing the ideas of consciousness being fundamentally a limited by-product of material evolution.

experiments are superb and this is fully detailed elsewhere. I will give a summary of some of the results from the meta-analysis in terms of the level of certainties reached, but the full discussion of the techniques and quality of the experimentation he looks at is really worth seeing.

Opening his book somewhat apologetically, though reflecting some great exasperation as well I'd imagine, Radin acknowledges the popular conception of parapsychology as a mockery of a scientific discipline: "In the midst of all the nonsense and excessive silliness proclaimed in the name of psychic phenomena, the misinformed use of the term 'parapsychology' by self-proclaimed 'paranormal-investigators', the perennial laughing stock of magicians and conjurers... This is for real?" But he continues with assurance of his expertise and the careful study and work that has indeed been performed by real scientists underneath all the misinformation and overly-enthusiastic credulity of many pseudo-scientists: "The short answer is, yes... [genuine] psi has been shown to exist in thousands of experiments... [and] there is no question replication has been achieved... virtually all scientists who have [actually] studied the evidence, *including hardnosed skeptics*, now agree that something interesting is going on that merits serious scientific attention." (xiv-xv & 247, italics in original).

What has been found, which has stumped even the most ardent of skeptics who have actually examined the evidence (as opposed to repeating platitudes of non-scientific rhetoric to pass as legitimate criticism, or even pure falsifications of the actual data) is surmised in the following glimpses at the data on psi effects:

For "dream signaling" telepathy tests, the positive results of many experimental sets analyzed through meta-analysis result in odds against chance of "seventy-five million to one" (71).

In case you are wondering, a statistical outcome of odds against chance of 20 to 1 is usually considered proof that an effect exists beyond reasonable doubt. Let me repeat that: odds against chance of 20 to 1 is the standard for significant evidence of an effect's existence. Keep that figure in mind.

For the "Ganzfeld" sensory deprivation telepathy tests, the meta-analysis of many replication studies by many different scientific laboratories across the world result in positive effect confirmation with "odds against chance of about a trillion to one" (86). Additionally, the magnitude of the effect observed in Ganzfeld telepathy experiments is 10 times greater than the positive effect of

Aspirin in preventing potential heart attacks for those at risk (86). The effect of Aspirin is considered so significant in this mode that it is considered unethical to conduct any experiment which would deprive people of Aspirin when it could benefit them[*]. Again, the effect size observed for telepathic signaling in sensory deprived states is 10 times that of Aspirin's effect.

Though you may surely be skeptical without viewing the complete discussion and analysis yourself, these results should, at minimum, absolutely stop and perplex you. If you have not known about these results to date and you do not find yourself in stunned disbelief mixed with growing curiosity, then you are assuredly caught in a rationalizing and suppressing wave of cognitive dissonance. But we are just getting started. Try to notice immediately dismissive or disassociating thoughts as we continue, and ask if they are truly scientific objections, or excuses appearing in rational form to keep you in your comfortable realm of known territory (i.e. products of dogma and bias).

In reviewing and analyzing all ESP card tests conducted between 1882 and 1939, the meta-analysis shows that a positive result has been demonstrated with odds against chance of "more than a billion trillion to one" (100).

In remote viewing experiments conducted at Stanford Research Institute (SRI) from 1973 to 1988 the positive results were demonstrated with "odds against chance of 10^{20} to one (that is, more than a billion billion to one)" (105).

Experiments testing "Precognitive Remote Perception" (remote viewing through time) result in positive demonstration of the ability with odds against chance of "100 billion to 1" (110).

"Forced Choice Precognitive tests" resulted in a positive effect demonstrated with "odds against chance of 10^{25} to one—that is ten million billion billion to one" (120).

"Dice tossing" mind-matter interaction tests resulted in positive effect with odds against chance of "more than a billion to one" (144).

Testing the effect of mental intention on Random Number Generators has been a very popular experiment with some of the best replications and controls of variables, and it has demonstrated positive results with "odds against chance of a trillion to one" (151).

---

[*] Recall the idea and discussion about a less than 100% effective thing still being significantly effective and worthwhile. Reason is a lot like Aspirin. We are immeasurably better for it, even if its effects are only marginal.

Purpose in Form

This is not an exhaustive list of the meta-analysis' results, nor does it do justice to the rigor of the analysis of the experimental methods and quality and all the effort Radin goes to to address the possible objections (including the so-called "file drawer" problem of unpublished negative studies) and proposed flaws in experimental design or analysis.

Again, you should really read the book yourself. But these claims alone should baffle you at the very least, and—if you're a true skeptic and scientist—motivate you not to suppress the impulse of curiosity and wonder, but to follow it through to be sure this is for real.

Radin includes not only his own commentary and findings, but plenty of sources of study and corroboration from other meta-analysis of data sets, as well as commentary of skeptics. Here are just a few highlights:

From Carl Sagan in a book looking skeptically at all sorts of pseudo-scientific claims:

> At the time of writing there are three claims in the ESP field which, in my opinion, deserve serious study: (1) that by thought alone humans can (barely) affect random number generators in computers; (2) that people under mild sensory deprivation can receive thoughts or images 'projected' at them; and (3) that young children sometimes report the details of a previous life, which upon checking turn out to be accurate and which could not have been known about in any other way than reincarnation. (xv) (Radin does not look at the 3rd suggestion in the book as these are spontaneous cases which cannot be easily tested and replicated.)

On the U.S. Government reviews and conclusions:

> From 1981 to 1995, five different U.S. government-sponsored scientific review committees were given the task of examining the evidence for psi effects... all five reviews concluded that the experimental evidence for certain forms of psychic phenomena merited serious study. For example, in 1981 the Congressional Research Service concluded that 'Recent experiments in remote viewing and other studies in parapsychology suggest that there exists

an 'interconnectedness' of the human mind with other minds and with matter'... In 1985 a report prepared for the Army Research Institute concluded that 'The bottom line is that data reviewed in [this] report constitute genuine scientific anomalies for which no one has an adequate explanation or set of explanations... If they are what they appear to be, their theoretical (and, eventually, their practical) implications are enormous'... [And] in 1995 the American Institutes for Research reviewed formerly classified government-sponsored research for the CIA at the request of the U.S. congress. Statistician Jessica Utts of the University of California, Davis, one of the two principal reviewers, concluded that 'The statistical results of the studies examined are far beyond what is expected by chance. Arguments that these results could be due to methodological flaws in the experiments are soundly refuted. Effects of similar magnitude to those found in government-sponsored research... have been replicated at a number of laboratories across the world. Such consistency cannot be readily explained by claims of flaws or fraud... It is recommended that future experiments focus on understanding how this phenomenon works, and on how to make it as useful as possible. *There is little benefit to continuing experiments designed to offer proof*... The other principal reviewer, skeptic Ray Hyman, agreed." (xvi-xvii, emphasis added)

Well these kinds of quotes could go on and on. The robustness of this meta-analysis, and the rigor of the investigation, study, and proofs offered and the counter positions and objections inspected is truly astounding. Thus I can conclude that the work is nothing short of decisive and definitive for the case of Extra Sensory Perception beyond what can be expected and accounted for by the emergent theory of consciousness.

In looking at the evidence for the realities of remote viewing (through space and time), dream signaling, and random number generator effects, we know that consciousness cannot be confined to the brain and body or limits of the physical senses. Thus consciousness cannot be solely an emergent phenomenon entirely caused by brain activity and therefore separate from other consciousnesses and the physical world itself. Though consciousness certainly manifests and acts through specific, complex structures in the brain, it also has immediate effects on material objects, both near and far, and does not appear to be effected by any such distance. Consciousness also communicates to other consciousnesses without being mediated by the physical body or senses. Consciousness is also privy to information and realities far removed from the physical body associated with said consciousness through both space and time.

Materialism has been dealt a killing blow. Consciousness is not confined to the body and cannot be explained as merely an emergent—and therefore severely limited—phenomenon. This evidence is out there to be seen and should be much more widespread, but because of the effects of human dogma, it is not. Radin covers all this—from psychological reasons for our cognitive dissonances to reviewing academic books and papers (and commenting briefly on the dreadful input of media) which to an alarming degree put forth direct "falsification of data"—in great detail, walking the reader through not only all the overwhelming evidence for psi effects, but explaining clearly why it hasn't been conveyed in any accurate sense to the public.

Again, please read Dean Radin's book *The Conscious Universe* and confront all the evidence yourself. Materialism is false in its core conceptions and cannot be a rational basis for arguments about the nature of life, experience, or existence.

And finally let me clearly iterate that this is the entire extent of the claims about "psi" or "paranormal" phenomena that I am making. I am not making claims about aliens or human levitation, or ghosts or magic, or anything beyond the simple, small, yet definitive conclusion that there are some effects—that we know exist—which uproot and discredit the materialist, emergent explanation of consciousness. These effects—tiny though they may be—are nonetheless there and constitute and effective disproval of the emergent theory of consciousness.

Using these findings as definitive counter evidence for the emergent explanation of consciousness is the only reason I bring the research and discussion of "psi" or "paranormal" fields into play. I will go on to make more of my own extraordinary claims based on theories and explanations constructed off of this philosophic and metaphysical basis, which is justified by uprooting materialistic and emergent theories of consciousness, but none of these are directly connected to any investment in broader "paranormal" research, nor are meant to offer any argument for any of the additional extravagant claims found in such fields. Again, all I am saying is that consciousness exceeds what can reasonably be explained by the materialist model. This has been proven, even if only by very small effects.

Given that individual consciousness is not bound by space or time and not fundamentally dependent on the brain, the question of the finitude of life and the finality of death, now stack up in a very different way.

Purpose in Form

Chapter 3: The Myth of "Coming into Being"

With our new clear understandings of the necessity of the infinite and the reality of consciousness beyond the brain and body, the questions of coming into being and annihilation seem quite different. But it is not self-evident that such rewritings of our preconceptions entirely uproot the antinatalist position entirely. For example, the Buddha was quite aware of the expansive nature of consciousness—both in terms of conscious states that passed beyond the bounds of the body, and in reference to life beyond death—and yet his teachings all center around the problem of suffering. So the suffering of life does not merely bow out when we reframe our basic assumptions, and one still might hold that it would better not to have been born into the world. For example, the Buddha considered all incarnation suffering, and being bound to it for life after life was only eternal suffering. Perhaps these points only exacerbate the problem.

But before addressing the nature of life as it is, let us examine the antinatalist and annihilationist doctrines as they are and see what, if anything can survive the acknowledgement of the infinite itself and the non-material nature of consciousness. Previously, in discussion of the infinite, I took it upon myself to say something reasonable first and then look at the alternatives. I believe now the deck is reasonably stacked against people whose ideas and doctrines had rested on finite life or existence and the emergent, limited nature of consciousness. They can now go first.

Purpose in Form

The Anti-Natalist Dogma

Benatar claims that through the process of birth, one "comes into existence". Before birth, one does not exist. And upon death, he says, we are annihilated. We cease to be. These are no uncertain terms and he says them over and over. These are the core elements of his formulation of antinatalism.

It is only because of one's "non-existence" before birth that one can suffer so inevitably from it; that is the conception on which his asymmetry rests. And it is through annihilation upon death that he rejects ultimate meaning, escape, and hope. The following are statements of Benatar which constitute his faith:

On death: "Death annihilates one—irreversibly ending one's existence" (xviii); "annihilation… [is] the loss of the self." (104); "Annihilation irrevocably terminates the string of psychologically connected states that constitute one's life." (105); "The irrevocable cessation of consciousness is annihilation of the conscious being." (109)

On meaning, purpose, and significance (all of which he equates, or at least acknowledges are deeply connected): "Life has no meaning from a cosmic perspective. Our lives may have meaning to one another, but they have no broader point or purpose." (2); "The evolution of life, including human life, is a product of blind forces and serves no apparent purpose." (36); "Earthly life is thus without significance, import, or purpose beyond our planet. It is meaningless from the cosmic perspective. Because this is true of all life, it is true of all sentient life, all human life, and each individual life." (36); "The universe was indifferent to our coming, and it will be indifferent to our going." (200)

Referencing finitude: "There is no great mystery, but there *is* plenty of horror." (7); "the universe itself has no perspective." (35); "We serve no purpose in the cosmos and, although our efforts have some significance here and now, it is seriously limited both spatially and temporally." (63); "with death we cease to be, but we do not thereby cease to be cosmically insignificant." (94)

To be fair, Benatar occasionally acknowledges that he only "assume[s]" there is no life after death and recognizes that this is only a hypothesis and that what he is proposing is merely the most "plausible" case (136 & 32). He even once wistfully admits "I cannot but hope that I am wrong" (BNHB, 13). But much more frequently he calls annihilation upon death an "indisputable

The Myth of 'Coming into Being'

premise" (179) and his entire philosophy is based around the idea that this outlook is truthful and virtuous, and that we should act on it by not reproducing.

Regardless of the occasional concession, it is clear that this belief is a deeply held faith which directs his actions in life, and which he thinks should drive others. He comforts himself and his readers saying that if one acts on anti-natalism, no one is harmed, so if it is wrong, it won't matter. However, if anti-natalism is wrong, the world looks vastly different to what Benatar imagines, and to suppose he is still right about human life not being worth living and not having human life continue to be experienced is not a detriment to the universe is thus highly suspect. Why should you be so sure that if you are vastly mistaken, you still haven't done anything wrong?

But the real viciousness of his doctrine is in its masquerade as "not-nihilism". You cannot tell from the quotes I have provided how this could be the case, but I assure you he makes the case that it is so. But, in his own words, "saying this and making sense are two different matters." (BNHB, 35) Later, we will discuss in detail why his doctrine is necessarily the same as nihilism and why his argument to the contrary fails. For now, we will focus on the idea of "coming into being" on which his entire belief system depends.

That "Coming into Existence" in This Faith System Depends on the Emergent Nature of Consciousness

The idea that one "comes into existence" from "non-existence" is not a metaphysical claim (it would be pretty silly for Benatar to hold such spontaneous generation of human life as the core belief of his negative world view—using a miracle to show the destitute nature of life). This is a claim based in materialism and entirely dependent on the emergent nature of consciousness.

If we are entirely material beings—nothing more than an aggregate of physical matter which, as a consequence of its complexity and various jigglings and electrical discharges, manifests what we call consciousness—then, since we identify primarily as the secondary consciousness (and even still the body is also finite and dies), we can be said to come from "non-existence" (the absence of consciousness prior to the growth and development of the brain) into existence (complex self-awareness) and then into annihilation (the deterioration and ending of brain function at which time all consciousness ceases). That is the only way it makes sense to explain the claim that we "come into existence" and are "annihilated"—with the conception of the self as the consciousness which is constructed from biological but blind matter and which dissolves after a finite lifetime.

Thus, this conception depends entirely on the materialist explanation of consciousness an emergent property of matter and must be at least somewhat erroneous as we have seen that consciousness is not merely a secondary, emergent phenomenon.

The Dogma of Death as Annihilation

Let us also look at the annihilation conception of death in itself, for it would be unscientific, even if materialism was still on the table. The problem with the absolute conception of death as annihilation is that it is an untestable hypothesis, and it is therefore dogmatic. It is not an unreasonable idea or conception. It at least seems like it could have been the case. But it is forwarded with such certainty; even when people offer possible counter evidence these evidences are ignored, often for the dogma of materialism in general, but also importantly because the doctrine of annihilation upon death is necessarily dogmatic. And then dogmatists claim that there is no evidence for life after death (there is at least some, though the levels of credibility, to the skeptic, are not necessarily high), ignoring the fact that there is no evidence for their side either, and there never could be! Death as annihilation is an unfalsifiable thesis, necessarily.

If death is annihilation, there can be no experience of it. Thus no reports can come from "the other side" because the other side does not exist because it is non-existence. Thus, people who hold this dogma assume that if someone says they died and came back, they cannot really have died, by definition. However, there is, as we have seen from Carl Sagan's interest in the matter, a considerable collection of past life recalls, as well as near death and actual death experiences (the latter where people were clinically dead for some time). And this phenomenon has been known throughout the ages. The vast majority of them report similar experiences.

Materialists had room to explain the continuity of these experiences (regular pathways in the brain firing as the final death throes), but this was taken as a

The Myth of 'Coming into Being'

certainty. People occasionally pay lip service to the idea that they don't really know what happens upon death, but most act like they do (as I said earlier, Benatar himself does this). And, much more importantly, the point not to be missed, is that they forward *their* side of the argument as though it is in line with science—when in fact it is untestable by definition.

At least the view that life continues beyond death offers some hope, in principle, of proof-positive (though it also remains unfalsifiable because proving the inverse, annihilation, requires demonstrating the transition into non-existence, which is not possible). So neither side is strictly falsifiable and therefore entirely scientific—but at least the non-annihilationists could examine evidence. Annihilationists, on the other hand, by definition are closed to all evidence by their preconceptions.

Previously and even contemporarily, only "kooks" took the idea that near death experiences might say anything real about consciousness seriously (or so it was said, at least) because of the common dogmas of materialism and annihilation. That just *couldn't* be the case. To the modern western intellectual, there was no real stock in it, regardless of the amount of evidence or the claims. All were mere anecdotes and hearsay, deserving no investigation because the answer was already known—they must be fabrications or misconstrued hallucinations.

Again we see that all data is "theory-laden" and thus cannot merely be looked at "objectively", on its own. People always approach with their own preconceived explanations, which for the materialists is "death is annihilation"; and either not knowing of or dogmatically rejecting any other explanations prevents them from seriously considering any data to contradict this explanation.

As we open up to the problems with the current explanations of materialist dogma, and learn of other possible explanations within the reality of infinite potential, we are better able to consider what once seemed inadmissible. And there are stronger cases than near death occurrences, though they are less in number and study. As Carl Sagan pointed out, what of cases where a child recalls a past life and can give evidence of, say, where their body was to be found? There are numerous examples like this of people having special knowledge that it is hard to see how they otherwise could have known.

Now, there is an alternate explanation (apart from mere fraud—which surely exists in some cases), but it does not lie within materialism; these do not have to be past life recalls, but could be "mere" examples of remote viewing (which we know exists) with an imagined story of personal connection imposed. But, as we see, materialism is out the window on any cogent explanation of such phenomena. And with materialism gone and doors open to a more fundamental role of consciousness, does that not cast a different light on the near death experiences and past life reports? Might there be something more to these after all?

Up until today (and I don't doubt it will continue going forward, regardless of the attention this gets) scientists and rationalists have dismissed all significant altered consciousness states as essentially aberrations (at most) and delusions and lies more often. Consciousness was "known" to be caused by the brain and therefore death was annihilation, no question about it. Any suggestion to the contrary had to be wishy-washy nonsense, and thus most of it became relegated to wishy-washy reports and fields.

Thankfully, certain areas of psi as demonstrated and championed by Radin did not, but near death experiences and past life visions largely did. I am not making a case that any such reports are entirely true or necessarily reliable. I am just saying that the idea of death as annihilation was based on the assumption of materialism, which is definitely false. And further that death as annihilation was set up to become a dogma in that it was absolutely untestable, so any and all evidence was shunned and ousted from the "respectable" scientific community. But materialism, I hope, will soon fall away and the question of legitimate evidence of conscious experience beyond bodily death should be taken seriously, and what evidence and reports we have should be reexamined and further explored.

While I do not have a host of studies or accounts to report on, I will here provide an alternative to the disproven materialism explanation. And while there are plenty of other problems with antinatalism and annihilationism to look at, this dogmatic conception of death illustrates just how much dogma has grown in our mainstream conceptions, whether endorsed by scientists or not.

<u>The Alternative View of Death Which Does Not Rest on False Premises of Finitude and the Fundamentally Emergent Nature of Consciousness</u>

As we have seen, the assumptions of materialism and the emergent nature of consciousness are false. Conscious awareness is not bound by the body or

The Myth of 'Coming into Being'

brain. So the assumption that it fundamentally comes into being upon birth and growth, and is entirely annihilated upon death is necessarily false.

But there is still room for debate here. We have said that it is true that consciousness is correlated with the brain structure and activity. This is a fact that is essentially indisputable and that people have erroneously taken for causation. But, since the particular consciousnesses which we experience and identify with throughout life grow, change, and die along with the brain, could we not still maintain that we are created—albeit from a rudimentary consciousness—and then die back into this substrate? There would not be a creation or annihilation of consciousness itself *ex nihilo*, but still we know the complex entities which constitute our identities do die, just as they grow.

Is it not a tragedy and a loss to develop a complex identity only to have it dissolved and lost for eternity? This problem centers on the identity of the self; aren't we identical with our psyches? Isn't what we call "I" or "me" that complex proceeding of conceptions, desires, thoughts, feelings, self-awareness, and perspectives? But these questions are not in fact rhetorical. They sound as though they are, and they might be offered by many as rhetorical questions to call the commonplace assumptions about our identity to mind. But they themselves are real questions, real problems. Who are we? What are we? What is consciousness?

The work on identity and consciousness would fill a great library, and the effort individuals have put into pursuing these questions has filled many millennia. I cannot here embark on a book within a book to cover all the possible avenues of questioning that are associated with this topic. It must suffice to say that the identity with one's multifarious psyche is dubious. And there are other explanations, which many have found more fruitful.

One main question which can be posed to those who would assume we are identical with our psyche is: if you are your thoughts and feelings and perceptions, then who is it that is aware of all these things? Generally this is phrased: "If you are your thoughts, then who is it that is listening?"

Those who would wave this off call upon the idea of "self-awareness". We are self-aware beings. We are our thoughts and we are aware of our thoughts. But this explanation really doesn't make sense. Again, in the words of Benatar, "saying this and making sense are two different matters" (BNHB, 35). Thoughts, which are the object of mental consciousness, are themselves consciousness? The thoughts that flow through your mind are hearing themselves? Or your mind is the aggregate of all the independent thoughts which mill around in it and their rudimentary elemental consciousnesses all add up to your overall consciousness? And emotions are the same? All our experience that goes on is made up of self-conscious entities?

When you are angry, what that would mean then, is that there is a body which is pervaded by a perception and an emotion which are basically angry and it is these elements of your experience which are also aware of themselves as being experienced? This is really a bad explanation, if it can be called an explanation at all. Self-awareness is not a property of thoughts themselves, nor of emotions, nor of any of the aggregate phenomena of our psyche. We would never say that it was. So calling upon self-awareness as a vague conception when asked to explain how you are your psyche itself is trying to dodge the issue or make the problem unreal. Self-awareness in fact points to the very fact that you are *not* any of these constituents.

It should be said here, since I am calling the psyche an aggregate and treating thoughts as external objects, that this is a relatively advanced conclusion. Many people have only a rudimentary idea of the inside of their own heads. They think of themselves as one continuous process that has various modes of expression. But that is common sense. Common sense is not an argument. Common sense is so often wrong.

The psychoanalysts believe the description of the psyche (the "mind" as some people call it, thinking of it as one self-contained thing) is far more accurate as a pageantry of sub-consciouses which are independent and vie for airtime as the main determining factors for the action of the body (think of the Pixar film "Inside Out"). "One of the greatest truths in psychology is that the mind is divided into parts that sometimes conflict." (Haidt, 32)

The Buddha also taught that consciousness is an aggregate, and that all its constituents are aggregates. And experienced meditators all around the world and throughout history have come to see that what we identify with in the contents of our psyche are independent from our own true essence; we are not identical with our thoughts, nor feelings, nor sensations, nor perspectives, etc. These things are all passing phenomenon of which we are aware and interpret and interact with and which to some degree influence our actions. But they are not properly called our identity. They are only identified with through error.

Thus throughout the ages the maxim of western society has been "know thyself"—i.e. it is common and harmful to confuse your identity with things

The Myth of 'Coming into Being'

that aren't actually you. This is clearly applicable in the present. Douglas Murray goes so far as to characterize our society as engaging in "a whole series of self-delusions" and says we have reached "a stage of seemingly industrial-strength denial" regarding issues of identity and reality (64 & 77).

The Buddha said all suffering proceeds from ignorance—ignorance of the nature of the self. "Don't overestimate your self-knowledge... What do you know about yourself? You are, on the one hand, the most complex thing in the entire universe, and on the other, someone who can't even set the clock on your microwave." (Peterson, 109) The Buddha went to immense lengths to list all the things that consciousness[*] (or the self) was not. He concluded that there is no self. Anything that we perceive as an object of awareness (which is what we might come up with to call the self) is not the self. How could an object of your awareness be you? And we are aware of our psyche (to a greater or lesser degree). So none of it can be our identity.

Insert years of meditation practice and study for yourself to realize and comprehend these things. These are things that you can come to know and see clearly, but they take time. "Something that seems incomprehensible to someone unseeing might be perfectly evident to someone who had opened his eyes." (Peterson, 106) The psychoanalysts find them clearly evident. And regular meditators are constantly learning how their identity is tangled up in things which are merely objects of their awareness. You can look into it and see for yourself. Meditation is wonderful but this is not a book on meditation. So we have to give an answer and continue with the questions at hand.

It makes no sense to say we are our psyche or any elements of it. We are the awareness to which the psyche appears. Our identity is not any object of awareness, it is awareness itself (many say "consciousness itself", see previous note). But we cannot have an image of our self just as Alan Watts says "we cannot bite our own teeth", nor can we point out our self or turn and look at it

---

[*] Of course he did say that the self was not "consciousness" (at least in most translations) and that consciousness was unreal as well. But go read Daniel Dennett if you feel you can be persuaded to believe that consciousness is not real. We can play the semantics game and say that self-consciousness or ego-consciousness is not real, but the fundamental awareness of infinite life is the real self. We'll get more pedantic about things later, I'm just juxtaposing general ideas at the moment. "The idea of no-self means that we do not interrupt this oneness with our individuality." (Dogen/Warner, 49)

any more than we can "touch the tip of this finger, with the tip of this finger" (*The Book*, 16). This is beyond the limit of objectivity.

But that makes sense. What you ultimately are is your subjective self. So to look at your subjective self would be to look at an object, which would mean it was not the subjective self. So "no appearances can be you" (Mooji, "Remain as You Are"). Our identity is the elementary capacity of awareness itself, and it is this awareness to which the psyche appears for a finite time.[*] Given this new understanding of what awareness or fundamental consciousness (our true identity) is, let us return to the question of whether consciousness is infinite or merely a capacity that the infinite can manifest.

The Case for Basic Conscious Awareness (The True Self or Identity) Being Infinite

Awareness cannot be pointed out; it cannot be meaningfully described (made into a defined, limited object of awareness). To wave one's hand and say "braggle fraggle" draws just as much attention to the reality of awareness as the word "awareness" does. Awareness cannot be "held in the mind" because awareness is what gives rise to the mind[†]. Awareness cannot be observed objectively.

Does the infinite itself not also share these properties? The infinite (as a totality) cannot be looked at objectively—it is known necessarily subjectively just like awareness. The word "infinite" does not capture a reality, but is an apophatic place holder for a concept which corresponds only roughly to a nevertheless real reality. Awareness is also indescribable, but immanently evident in every moment. Awareness is, by this understanding, non-finite (or *in*finite); it can only be known subjectively and is the essence of subjectivity, and any attempts to delineate it (make it finite) end up missing it. The infinite

---

[*] There is an important distinction and often misperception about this awareness being non-self-aware. People in the spiritual communities often say things like "we are God experiencing Him or Herself', and when looked at further these ideas imply that God is basically non-self-aware and uses the creation of limited perspectives to become aware. This proposition is fundamentally untrue, the basic nature of the ground of all being awareness itself, it is necessarily aware of itself. Rupert Spira gives an excellent talk on this particular hang up—see Rupert Spira "God Needs to Our Mind to Know the World"

[†] "Attempting to understand consciousness with your mind, is like trying to illuminate the sun with a candle." (Mooji, 37)

The Myth of 'Coming into Being'

can only be known subjectively, necessarily, and it is the pervading essence of all things.

While one might wonder if the non-corporeal or non-describable nature of awareness is necessarily identical with its being unending/unbounded and therefore infinite (and therefore one and the same as the infinite; since the infinite must be one) in that sense of the word (rather than just merely non-defined), this is not really an objection in that it points to no contradiction or flaw; it is merely a bit of a wonder.

There may be some uncertainty but awareness itself and the infinite certainly begin to look identical in this respect, and as we go on I hope the case will become stronger. This would also give more cogent support to Deutsch's assertion that the human capacity for knowledge generation is infinite, giving that property a good explanation, much better than an infinite capacity miraculously arising out of a fundamentally finite being, regardless of how complex.

So, returning to the question of the death of the organism and psyche, if there is no self in any appearances or occurrences of which we are aware, then the growth or change, loss or death of these appearances (which is inevitable) cannot be a loss of the self or the true identity.

The Buddhists for millennia have contended that it is not merely foolish to mourn the loss of that which is inevitably going to be lost (as we often do), but it is also foolish to think that these things are possessions and identities in the first place. They are merely experiences, like a movie. (Though this is not to say it is bad to play the cosmic fool! Nor that we should be greatly ashamed of our natural and in fact completely necessary ignorance as fallible beings.)

This perspective seems rather harsh to the common human conception, and we will address the downfall of that extreme view of disregard for the limited lives of our forms when it is not balanced by an intimate compassion for our ignorant selves as well. But, regardless of common sense and common sentiment, the point is remains valid that there is at least a viable argument against death as an irreconcilable loss and unjust factor in life, as is asserted by annihilationists and pessimists.

Now the idea of the infinite self is all ooh-ahh and out there. I have had to quickly sketch the craziest of deep realities and revelations because we had to face the question of "isn't it still bad to lose the identity?" which conflated psyche and identity. The alternative explanation was necessary, fantastic though it may seem. But the psyche is not the identity and there is no real cogent way of saying that the identity is the psyche, regardless of however much one feels identified with it. The entire work of Buddhism is centered on uprooting this misconception*, and it is only marginally successful in some people (though that is not, again, to say that it is not effective at all, nor insignificant). Most don't get it. I offered the grand conception as a way of saying there is actually a coherent explanation on the opposing side of the common but ignorant sense of identity—which, all though it makes no sense, without an alternative people would default back to. Don't worry if you can't "see" what I'm saying about the self, that's supposed to take a lot of effort to get. But do try to see how our identity cannot be an object of awareness, something that can be objectively observed.

It does not make sense to say a thought (or anything else) is aware of itself and we are it being aware of itself as well as other things all being aware of themselves. It does make sense to say awareness fundamentally exists, and it is the fundamental capacity of awareness that is aware of all things (it is fantastic, but it is in no way incoherent). The mechanisms for how awareness associates with the body are necessary to make this a clear and complete picture, but they are too much for now. You can read various conceptions (i.e. conjectures) and sketches in Buddhist, Advaita, and other meditation schools' metaphysical explanations, or that of the cabala for the west. It suffices for

---

* For this reason, Buddhism, if they decided to contemplate it, would be considered outright bullying and violence in the post-modernist/identity politics crowd where the identity with one's physical characteristics, perceptions, values, and mindsets is considered sacred and invalidating one's point of view or challenging one's conceptions is considered an existential attack on the individual. "The fearfulness of this loss of personal individuation can be the whole burden of the transcendental experience for unqualified souls." (Campbell, 188) It would be interesting to see how they squared their values of openness to that which is foreign (especially what is non-western and not primarily rooted in Caucasian ancestry), and protection of and champion for those who are oppressed (individuals and cultures)—both of which should favor Buddhism—with an understanding that Buddhists preach truths antithetical to their doctrine of power in your impermanent identity, as well as disseminate a highly effective psychological methodology for seeing for yourself the truths regarding identity. Would they declare Buddhism a religion of violence, as their own doctrine would seem to imply, and become antagonizers of one of the most notoriously peaceful religions of the world, as well as one which has been greatly oppressed throughout history?

The Myth of 'Coming into Being'

here to say that it makes no sense to identify with objects (even mental objects), that the self must be ultimately subjective, and that it is reasonable to think we could approach an accurate understanding and description of how awareness itself (the base of all existence and experience) finds itself believing it is an individual consciousness, experiencing a finite lifetime.

Since we cannot be the psyche itself, the loss of the psyche upon death cannot be an ultimate loss. We are not annihilated in any real sense, we only lose that which we became attached to and erroneously believed we were identical with. Thus, in all truth, the claim that we are irrevocably harmed upon death is wrong. But it is true, as the Buddha noted, that we can suffer from the loss of that which we are attached to, even though this suffering is an error of ignorance, and a finite (and thus passing) experience itself.

The Problem of Suffering

Now we come back to the questions of antinatalism and annihilationism. It is not true that we ever "come into being" from "non-being" because materialism is proven false; particular psyches come and go, but these are not true identities, though we often identify with them. No true identity is ever annihilated because there is only one true identity which is the infinite itself and is thus eternal. "The enduring substratum of the individual and of the progenitor of the universe are one and the same." (Campbell, 239) And while one can suffer from the loss of something to which they are attached, it would be, as Benatar must agree, only through an immense lack of imagination that one could claim that throughout infinite manifestation an eternal awareness could not find anything else to replace such losses, or, more importantly, find more meaningful and less abrasive ways of being than becoming dreadfully attached to that which it is inevitable to lose[*].

Suffering still exists though, even though it (allegedly) comes through ignorance. And while suffering exists in a world, might it not be a net detriment to experience that world and that suffering? These questions, however, are already uprooted, or should be. Only unnoticed habit keeps them around. The questions of "why should we suffer?" or "isn't life too brutal?", etc. all stem necessarily from the underlying metaphysical assumption and

---

[*] Here again the point that fundamental awareness is self-aware is important. See earlier footnote with the explanation from Rupert Spira.

explanation that the individual is a limited, vulnerable being. They all implicitly assume a particular nature of the suffering being and its capacity for such experience—that the individual is essentially fragile[*]. Recall, all data is "theory-laden", and this is the theory behind the observation that our suffering is far beyond what we can hope to tolerate or should be subjected to.

But what if the suffering being is fundamentally infinite? Suffering is a great problem for the finite—or it would be if anything truly finite existed. But once we realize the reality of the infinite, and that consciousness is not confined to the limited form, and that, even when consciousness experiences itself as the limited individual, such experience is only apparent and the true identity always remains as eternal awareness, our lens through which we view our suffering fundamentally changes.

Suffering would be terrible, even if we were eternal beings, if suffering itself were eternal. But the Buddha said "there is a path to the end of suffering", which is an indirect way of saying "there is an end to suffering"[†]. If suffering has an end, any end, it is of no real concern to the infinite. Even trillions and trillions of years multiplied together and raised by a trillion times the power of that number itself would not be a long time compared to eternity or the infinite. So even if that entire time were filled with suffering, it would be but a wink, and the eternal could laugh about it. "For a thousand years in thy sight are but as yesterday when it is past, and as a watch in the night." (Psalms 60:4) So as long as we know the truth—the necessary truth of the infinite and the true nature of the self/consciousness—that "the sufferer within us is that divine being"—suffering is of no ultimate threat (Campbell, 137). The reality of the infinite is the reality of infinite salvation.

And further, because these ideas often seem of no real personal and immediate comfort to the individual (recall Hume's objection), in order for them to take root, we must rethink prescribing even the experiential individual as a fragile entity—i.e. we must examine our metaphysical assumptions about ourselves and the ultimate reality, challenge them, and work to change them and live in the new ones—dying to our old conceptions. "To know eternity is

---

[*] They also inherently assume the importance of the individual, to be worried about its fragility, though they also in contradiction often claim (as with Benatar) that the individual is inherently meaningless.

[†] "How beautiful are the feet of them that preach the gospel of peace, and bring glad tidings of good things." Romans 10:15

enlightenment, and not to recognize eternity brings disorder and evil" (Laozi et. al., ch. 16)

All real and significant suffering and harm depends on the nature of the being who is harmed being especially susceptible or vulnerable to harm—the harm must afflict the being and rise to a serious level. But, belaboring a separate but parallel and illustrative objection to Benatar and antinatalism for the moment, even if we look at ourselves as we normally conceive them—as individual and perishable—it need not be and is not the case that we are so fragile and ill-equipped to meet the brutalities of life in this temporary form. Our individual selves are actually anti-fragile[*]!

Recognizing this and "embracing stress changes how you think about yourself and what you can handle." (McGonigal, xxiii) Thus, separate from all the foregoing metaphysics and the question of infinite or finite, even for someone who believes in the finite nature of life, it is verifiably false to view ourselves as tremendously fragile beings as Benatar does so that all of our hunger pangs and "even an iota of suffering" is some tremendous burden on us (BNHB, 205). Again, that position is theory-laden, and the explanation behind such evaluations is that we are fragile beings. This is false even without exploring the ultimate challenge to our finite nature; though the understanding and reconceptualization of ourselves as fundamentally infinite and the deep connection of the individual to the infinite does a good deal more to explain (and hopefully promote) this anti-fragile nature of ours.

That all being said, and even true, we may still doubt our infinite capacity; and we may certainly doubt our capacity for bearing the experience of suffering at hand. But doubt is not proof. Doubt is belief or faith; doubt is a gamble. And much of our inherited and cultivated beliefs about ourselves are quite wrong when we get down to sorting them out and looking at the implicit, and often unconscious, explanations we hold. Once again, it becomes imperative to "know thyself" to know what suffering truly is and how greatly it affects beings in the world, and thus also, whether life is worth living or worth starting.

This is precisely the question that Benatar fails to address—i.e. who he believes he is and his basic conceptions of life and consciousness; he skips

---

[*] See Jonathan Haidt's work, who adopts this term and greatly substantiates it. Also Kelly McGonigal's book *The Upside of Stress* is highly relevant.

over examining these basic assumptions in detail and builds his philosophy on his biased but, in his view, "most plausible" foundation (Benatar, 32). This is why discussing and examining metaphysics is important. This is why we have to answer these basic questions first.

For a moment, though, let us return to sanity for a breathing space; there is still, undeniably some suffering, and much of it is so horrible, why should we just dismiss it (as if that were possible)? "Pain matters, more than matter matters." (Peterson, 35) Even if one accepted that everything in here were completely and infallibly reasonable and even demonstrated to be true on some levels, it might be reasonable to reject this entire way of thinking since it seems to say suffering is of no concern.

This is one of the main problems with the metaphysical and spiritual conceptions of the Hindu or Yogic traditions (which occurs both in the east itself and in many of the modern circles where it has been espoused in the west) and one to which I believe Christianity gives a better, or at least more explicit answer. I will call this etheric attitude which is dismissive of suffering "The Ethical Problem of the East" and we will discuss the responses to it later, but in short it comprehends the truth of the infinite eternity but not the reality of the finite—"contaminating the principles of the one with those of the other" (Campbell, 196). Erich Neumann calls this being devoured by the spiritual father, which creates "a spirituality that has lost touch with the reality and the instincts" (386).

But I did say that you have to undertake the journey yourself[*]; you have to live the truths to feel their effects. And what is more, suffering is not to be forgotten and the nuances of the true point of view, which contradict and disprove antinatalism, will deal with suffering in a reasonable way. "Your nervous system responds in an entirely different manner when you face the

---

[*]"By what arguments or analogies can we prove any state of existence, which no one ever saw, and which no wise resembles any that ever was seen? Who will repose such trust in any pretend philosophy, as to admit upon its testimony the reality of so marvelous a scene? Some new species of logic is requisite for that purpose; and some new faculties of mind, that they may enable us to comprehend that logic. Nothing could set in a fuller light the infinite obligations which mankind have to divine revelation; since we find, that no other medium could ascertain this great and important truth." (Hume, 96-97) This is very true, though I maintain that many have seen or experienced such states, and that such experience should and can be reliably sought.

The Myth of 'Coming into Being'

demands of life voluntarily. You respond to challenge, instead of bracing for catastrophe." (Peterson, 27) And one must conceive of oneself as an anti-fragile, miraculously capable being* (for which there is great evidence, any past difficulties and negative mindsets notwithstanding) in order to live in this way. But much more on that is to be described later on, when we discuss the appropriate conception of life. Now we are talking about the flawed conceptions.

Antinatalism is not off the hook here. We have entirely uprooted it; it is not compatible with an infinite existence of fundamental consciousness, and even if those points are thrown out as improbable, the undeniable truths of at least a consciousness which is not limited to the body (the refutation of materialism) and the mysterious nature of the self, call for at least an entire restructuring of a counter argument in favor of antinatalism.

One must accept that consciousness is not an emergent phenomenon, and one must undertake the task of defining an identity which can hurtle the challenges of objectivity/subjectivity and stand up to real scrutiny as is found in Buddhist meditation and Advaita schools, etc. And, while taking account of the scientific proof that humans are anti-fragile, such an identity must be still something severely harmed by the suffering of the world in order to come out with anything remotely as negative a view as antinatalism. I do not doubt the infinite imagination and rebelliousness of humans to come up with some florid reasoning which may seem to meet these requirements†, but the question then

---

* "There hath no temptation taken you but such as is common to man: but God is faithful, who will not suffer you to be tempted above that ye are able; but will with the temptation also make a way to escape, that ye may be able to bear it." (1 Corinthians 10:13)

† All such efforts also go to show that when a pessimist dismisses optimistic conceptions of life as merely the product of a biological bias, contrived not by reason as it may appear, but by reason driven to satisfy the human passions, they become the pot, as it were. Pessimism, the drive to negativity, to be dark and brooding, is as much a human passion as is optimism. "I have observed that not the man who hopes when others despair, but the man who despairs when others hope, is admired by a large class of persons as a sage." (Ellery, 238) Optimism is easy to see as attractive. But with a more honest look at the human psyche, one can clearly see its dark attractions as well. And the reality of an attraction and passion driving humans to pessimism is only overlooked through a lack of self-awareness. So the idea that optimists merely look for what they want to see, while pessimists are the brave ones who face the harsh truths (also coming in the form of religious constituents vs. atheists) is not a realistic

Purpose in Form

is not of the merits between the views, but whether you want to merely appear clever, or are you actually interested in the truth?

Though it is dead as it stands, we should look into its previous implications and associations, for there are threats with greater reach hiding within antinatalism.

Key Term:

<u>The Ethical Problem of the East</u>—the spirituality-based attitude that is overly dismissive of suffering, the body and the significance of earthly life, based on the identification of the individual with the infinite or God. (To some degree the Ethics section in my previous book Jnana Yoga may have perpetuated this attitude and so pointing out this misstep and working out the solution are of great importance to both me and my readers.)

---

assessment of the latter being more amenable to facing reality and truth than the former, but only a further contrivance of the very limitations of human reason and lack of awareness of which they accuse their opponents.

Chapter 4: The Myth of Meaninglessness

"A bubble of sense within endless senselessness does not make sense." David Deutsch, 459

The Rational Offspring of Principle of Mediocrity and Myth of Materialism vs. The Fantastic Nature of Fundamental Meaning

The basic thrust of all materialism, antinatalism, annihilationism, and nihilism is the same: consciousness (yours or mine) is insignificant. This is a necessary assertion of all such points of view, and remains true of antinatalism even though it appears to hold the contradictory position that our suffering is bad; and it is what makes them all inherently vicious (and incoherent).

The assertion plays upon the apparently pragmatic and humble realizations concerning the magnitude of life to which we have become aware; it would seem imprudent and arrogant to suppose that our effervescent and apparently finite conscious experience were more than it seems—a momentary flash before annihilation—and even if it were a bit more than that (since we clearly do not understand it), it seems an unfathomably inordinate leap from "miniscule but possibly worth something", to "infinitely meaningful" or consciousness having infinite importance, which is what we would have to mean by ultimate significance, since we have definitively shown that the ultimate is the infinite. This pessimistic view is the Principle of Mediocrity as described by Deutsch.

But a conclusion cannot truly be reasonably rejected because it is fantastic—whether fantastically optimistic or fantastically pessimistic, fantastically self-serving or fantastically self-abating—it must be examined for its explanations, its reasons and consequences, and any supporting evidence and testing.

It would be fantastic to say that all of this is entirely meaningless—but that fantasy leads to nihilism, inexorably as we shall see, and it is most importantly incoherent on the nature of the infinite and finite and does not explain consciousness as we know it.

It would also be fantastic to say that all of this is meaningful—but that fantasy so often leads to delusions of grandeur and the abandonment of reason and science, but we can find the better foundational explanations on this side and there is hope for good explanations to avoid such traps of hubris and inflation. We will also see that there is no real middle ground in this case (other than a performative one) for any real, actual, significant meaning *must* be ultimate (a point which Benatar tries to skirt) and thus if there is meaning at all, it must be infinite; so if we are significant at all, we are infinitely so.

No Middle Way

Benatar tries to neatly divide antinatalism from nihilism, claiming that antinatalism can and does recognize some significant meaning in life. This claim relies solely on sophistry and our tendency to overlook or forget things that are merely given; that is to say, because meaning is inescapable and inevitable, Benatar's claim that life is cosmically meaningless but that local and personal ("terrestrial") meaning still exist doesn't immediately exclaim as the contradiction it is (Benatar, 62).

Because Benatar says his doctrine allows for the local and personal meaning we are all accustomed to, and that he is merely throwing out the grandiose human appropriations of cosmic meaning, without truly understanding what meaning is—what meaning means—and where it comes from, one can be placated and accept this sophistry as reasonable. But what has actually happened, and Benatar does not hide this, other than the fact that he does not discuss and perhaps does not understand the full implications, is that he uproots the foundation of all meaning and says that all life is meaningless, necessarily, and then says that some meaning still exists.

I will discuss and thoroughly show this, but make no mistake from the beginning I am not misrepresenting Benatar's beliefs and work; he says over and over again that "life is cosmically meaningless"; that "the ugly truth [is] that our lives lack the cosmic meaning for which humans so often yearn" (56); that "my view of cosmic meaning is indeed nihilistic" (62); and that "cosmic meaning is beyond the reach of all… we have absolutely no control over the fact of our cosmic insignificance" (193 & 195).

Now Benatar is upfront about this. And yet he also claims terrestrial meaning is significant and considerable in the evaluation of quality of life and happiness. But what he does not do is discuss the all-important question which would make his contradiction clear: what is meaning? Now this is a funny question—"the kind of question only a philosopher would ask" (Bloom, 27)—but it is very necessary to have an articulated explanation—or at least a more clear understanding—to see the gravity of doctrines of meaninglessness and the contradictions displayed unabashed in plain sight in Benatar's work. Honestly, I get the feeling he doesn't really understand what he is saying when he says life is cosmically meaningless.

So what is meaning? Where does it come from? Can you have terrestrial meaning without cosmic meaning? Meaning is intimately tied to consciousness and is largely synonymous with purpose; it is the goal or point driven at, the thing which is sought or sought to be conveyed. Meaning is the perceived connection or understanding underlying a statement, idea, or event. Being so dependent on consciousness, it is easy to see how materialists would be ready to uproot meaning and throw it out as a meaningless byproduct of an emergent phenomenon in a meaningless being. Materialists believe meaning is something like an arbitrary construction, or at most an evolutionary construction of no real significance beyond the electrochemical effects it refers to in the brain of a meaningless organism created by blind and pointless forces.

But here we see the circularity. Only because there is the presumption of meaninglessness of the being and of the consciousness of the individual does meaning become meaningless (and purpose purposeless). Far from being a truly compelling and foundational thesis, the idea of meaninglessness is a *post hoc* thrust of a confused philosophy unable to recognize its own foundations or address its own genesis.

Upon the event of throwing out all metaphysics and religious foundations of western culture, known retroactively as the "Death of God", modern theorists were faced with a problem of what to do and how to proceed. But instead of contending with this problem in any real way, most so-called philosophers looked at the dogma they had been given—that all religion was merely superstition and that man lives a solipsistic existence in an accidental universe—and constructed their "philosophies" based on that dogmatic faith or assumption. Thus they said, "Well since all that is necessarily the case, life must be meaningless and purposeless, at least on a cosmic scale". Meaninglessness was never, and could never be, derived foundationally, because it contradicts itself. That is to say, we cannot explain meaninglessness. It is only the faith based PRESUMPTION of meaninglessness that allows for doctrines containing ideas of "meaninglessness" to propagate and appear rational.

The Meaninglessness of Meaninglessness

Meaning being such a foundational concept, trying to define it and talk about its mechanics is a lot like defining "belief" or "knowledge"—something philosophers have been struggling to do for centuries and have not been successful. That being the case, trying to philosophize about meaning as an abstract concept is not nearly as effective as just illustrating the reality of the word through common sense example.

Consider this: If life (human life and life in general) is cosmically meaningless, then, by definition, human life has no ultimate significance, point, or purpose. We may say that humans experience what they call meaning between themselves and in relation to their local tasks (working in civilization, relating to others, etc.), which Benatar does, but so long as we believe the cosmos to be unconscious and impersonal these local meanings are of no REAL significance, they are only "significant" in the limited perceptions of those experiencing them, and those beings and their perceptions of course are, by definition, meaningless and utterly insignificant.

Incredibly, Benatar even points this out, "If you were created to help your fellow, and your fellow was created to help you, we are still left wondering why either of you (and by extension any being) was created. This purpose smacks of circularity." (38) Benatar also points out that even if we perceive meaning in our limited pursuits that "lives can be meaningless though they are felt to be meaningful... [but] objective meaning is the real meaning and *subjective meaning is merely the appearance of meaning*" (25, emphasis added); and further he says that even if we perceive the meaning in the moment, we must recognize that it comes to an end: "in time, however, those people [you impacted] also die and thus eventually the residue [of your limited meaning] also fades and disappears." (94) Yet, while pointing out these facts considered necessary by his faith, he does not acknowledge the necessary conclusion of those points which is that ALL felt meaning is foundationless, purposeless, and, necessarily, meaningless. By his standards, *all meaning is only subjective meaning* which he dismisses as unreal. Consider that, because meaning does not ultimately exist, all our perceptions of it must be only and entirely illusory, and again, meaningless in themselves.

Thus, though one can make the claim that while life is meaningless humans nevertheless perceive meaning and are frequently enthused by this perception, one cannot claim that this perceived meaning is anything but a lie; and one cannot claim that the experience of being enthused by such a perception of meaning is somehow significant, given that meaning and significance themselves are meaningless and insignificant constructions of the meaningless and insignificant consciousnesses of meaningless and insignificant beings. Benatar tries to have both at once—to recognize cosmic meaninglessness and uproot all meaning, but to retain a belief in and value for terrestrial meaning. But if meaning does not fundamentally exist, from where does our value come and why is it significant?

The whole point of meaning is that it is a connection to an underlying REALITY which goes beyond oneself and one's limitations. Benatar also acknowledges this: "meaning... is about 'transcending limits'." (17) To say that this meaning is preserved by the fact that it is a shared hallucination of the species—it thereby being something that "goes beyond oneself" to the species as a whole—is to not understand the meaning of meaning, even as he himself describes it. Just as Benatar points out, that formulation "smacks of circularity" (38).

Thus Benatar's entire distinction of his antinatalist view from nihilism is based on a nonsensical idea—and indeed a faith based dogma—that meaning can be unreal in every sense, but that we can and should value it because it makes us meaningless and insignificant creatures feel warm and tingly as a byproduct of electrochemical stimulations produced by the false notion of the experience of meaning. This conception is entirely self-defeating and would be laughable if its consequences weren't so grave. For EVEN IF one was willing to grant the nonsensical and inexplicable idea that we should value an inherently meaningless experience of local meaning, one still faces the further contradictions that the consciousness of the being who experiences meaning, as well as those who inexplicably choose to value said consciousness and its meaningless experience, are necessarily insignificant and meaningless.

Benatar states this entirely unsupported and inexplicable faith claim as: "However, merely because a life does not transcend limits in a valuable way does not mean that it is not valuable in its own right or valuable to the person whose life it is… one does not have to transcend limits in order for one's life to have intrinsic value. Because meaningless lives can have such value." (19)

Recall, "saying this and making sense are two different matters" (BNHB, 35). This is why I said that Benatar accomplishes his sophistry by offering common sense something to hold onto though the explanation for why it remains doesn't work. We see here the crux of the error, as well as the entire premise upon which his distinction of his own work from nihilism stands, in that he claims—without explanation, merely stating the faith based assertion—that meaningless lives have value.

Given that the value of life is essentially innate and self-evident, this proclamation gets by easily to the passing reader. But Benatar offers no explanation or theory to his claim that life is intrinsically valuable, and he even goes to great lengths to show how all life is both meaningless and a tremendous negative. If we overlook that all claims are "theory-laden", we miss the fact that Benatar imports this concept of intrinsic value from a metaphysics common in the west but which is completely antithetical to his own and the rest of his claims. What he fails to recognize and follow through on examining is that, by entirely uprooting meaning itself, *he has also uprooted all value and systems of value*. Value is entirely dependent on meaning[*]. If meaning is fundamentally unreal and only subjectively apparent then all valuation judgements and systems lack all meaning and any force for significance or reality.

So while one can momentarily say that local meaning that is experienced should be valued, that phrase can only stand in a book where the author is free unchallenged to bounce off to other points and build off this supposed foundation, apparently separating himself from the quagmire of nihilism, rather than answering the all-important next question of "Why?".

---

[*] And meaning on value, as Dr. Peterson points out (xxxi).

The Myth of Meaninglessness

The answer seems to be, in Benatar's case, "because that's what I feel like" or "because that's what is good to do". But without meaning, what is good? If there is no such thing as meaning, what even is a philosophy? And if there is no meaning, purpose, or significance to life (human or otherwise), what even is the reality (or MEANING) of VALUE? And, even if there is such value for some reason, why should we care given that it's all meaningless anyhow?

Meaning is absolutely foundational and cannot be meaningfully denied. Existential, cosmic, or foundational meaninglessness is a linguistic spectre. And one cannot claim that the "real" foundation of meaning is at the local, experiential level—at least one cannot if they are also claiming to be a materialist and/or believe in any form of objectivity. For if one tries to say that the universe is meaningless but that our subjective experiences create meaning, and that this is superordinately significant over the meaninglessness of the cosmos itself, one is saying that the "objective" reality is insignificant and that the subjective reality is the primary reality. And if one holds this belief, one cannot simultaneously believe that human (or otherwise) consciousness is insignificant—they are by definition saying that subjective, personal consciousness is the foundation of all meaning and significance and is the paramount reality of value.

This idea can appear in many forms from panpsychism to relativism, some seemingly benign and some still quite destructive (and self-contradicting), but for now it suffices to say that I will not endorse any form of absolute relativism, and that the view I am laying out in this book I believe avoids the pitfalls of such a doctrine. Here we are talking about materialism and its progeny, and the assertion of meaninglessness[*].

If one denies meaning or purpose, one negates the reality of their own

---

[*] Relativism in its own way asserts meaninglessness by holding that each experience is equally meaningful and that there are no meaningful distinctions between realities or perceived experiences because there can be no objective arbitration of values between value systems. There are many confusions and contradictions going on in such a doctrine, but for one, when one asserts that another has made a local misconception this is taken as tantamount to asserting the existential meaninglessness of said mistaken individual. In terms of what will be laid out in this work, this doctrine refuses to accept progress and will not die into growth, but remains attached to the imperfect form or misplaced identity. It also assumes there are no foundational values or truths in connection to which others could be judged, but that all so-called truths are merely arbitrary social constructions.

speech, intentions, and consciousness. If someone is talking to you about meaninglessness, ask yourself (and perhaps them if it is prudent to start such a conversation) why they are talking to you then? If meaning itself is arbitrary and does not correspond to any reality beyond the evolutionary construction of human neural and emotional activity, which are necessarily meaningless occurrences according to this underlying faith, why should one seek to share this idea with others? Of what good is that end if there is no such thing as meaning or purpose? And again here are the real kickers for all doctrines which assert meaninglessness that bear repeating—of what value is truth? And of what MEANING is value? Again, these contradictions are not escaped by inexplicably pretending to value the hallucination of meaning within the species, even while asserting that meaning itself is ultimately unreal.

One cannot provide an explanation for grounding meaning at the local level that does not amount to "because I said so". Because humans believe in the meaning and value of truth, at least some will ask "why" of meaning and where it comes from. If it is a foundationless spectre of the human mind then the quest for truth, which comes from the human desire for meaning, uproots the reality of meaning itself. Thus you cannot believe in truth and meaninglessness together. If life is meaningless, so is truth (and then it's okay to lie about the reality of meaning); if truth is to be pursued (as Benatar believes), then one must believe in meaning and cannot accept a merely local account and remain coherent.

In a truly meaningless reality, one who fully accepts this meaninglessness is in nirvana. He does not need to bring others there, because they are meaningless and there would be no purpose to doing so, since purpose is unreal and not meaningful. One has absolutely no duties and all problems are entirely dissolved. Problems only exist because we believe in meaning and purpose. Problems are only perceived in so far as they are obstacles to purposes. That is what it means to be a problem. And without a reality of meaning, neither problems nor purposes are real or worthwhile, regardless of their apparition.

In a meaningless world, even the fact that no one can achieve a full comprehension or embodiment of true purposelessness is utterly unconcerning. The fact that people fill tomes of books and host endless talk shows and lead high profile or even bloody campaigns along all roads of falsehood is also entirely insignificant, because truth is meaningless as well. There is no

The Myth of Meaninglessness

meaning, no point, no significance to any of it and no one would be better off if they comprehended true meaninglessness, nor if they were all crucified or struck down by nuclear winter or sudden caldera. We only worry about truth and who is right and what we and others should be doing because we believe in meaning and purpose and significance; and to the extent that anyone tries to affect any sort of change, they most certainly do not believe in purposelessness or meaninglessness, regardless of the memes their lips mouth.

This also uproots the postmodern idea that there is no truth, only power and groups vying for it. Without truth or meaning there is no power. Power depends on meaning and significance. Most obviously, if no human goals or pursuits are significant, then power is meaningless and unimportant; and this fact does not change if people don't get it and are yet still vying and fighting for things. If human consciousness is insignificant, which is the underlying assumption and assertion of all these meaningless doctrines of meaninglessness, then, not only are all goals insignificant but also all suffering and defeat is meaningless and therefore insignificant. Thus, with nothing to value, nothing to gain, no reality to goals or purpose, no value to any ends attained or favors won or experiences or pleasures stolen or bought, and no significance to any human experience (including suffering) the so called "power games" of people and societies are uninteresting, pointless, and unreal.

One wonders why such scholars are even concerned with noticing such patterns of the influence of said hallucination of power, other than that they themselves are ignorant of the truth of meaninglessness. If one believes in power[*], they must believe in truth, purpose, and significance (whether they like to admit it or not); and if one believes in purpose, significance, and truth, they believe in meaning. Here the wisdom of looking at people's actions rather than their words to see their true beliefs helps dispel the apparent controversy.

Though I really wish I could end it there, I must say that this all applies equally to and is not negated by the belief that we tragically cannot escape meaning because it is programmed into our most basic nature, but that it is actually an unreality constructed by the mindless, haphazard accident of

---

[*] "Of course power exists as a force in the world, but so do charity, forgiveness and love." (Murray, 53)

evolution in a cold, impersonal, meaningless universe.* "You are a randomly united lump of something. This lump decomposes and the fermentation is called your life." (Tolstoy, 40) All these ideas are merely spectres of the intellect that do not refer to any reality. They are the incomplete and incoherent progeny of the theory of emergent consciousness (see previous note) and the principle of mediocrity, which together assert that our consciousness arose by accident and is entirely passing and meaningless. The fear and the despair felt when possessed by such concepts is certainly real, but they do not correspond to any truth and are entirely contradictory, regardless of how seriously they are taken.

Anti-Natalism is Necessarily Nihilism

Any doctrine which asserts cosmic meaninglessness is nihilism, regardless of how it is framed. This is necessarily so. For, though some may fawn playfully with the idea of cosmic meaninglessness while still truly—albeit unconsciously—believing in meaning itself, those who are gripped by the idea and walk through the implications of cosmic meaninglessness will inevitably have to answer the questions: why should I care about these meaningless beings meaningless experience of meaning? And even if I do care because of some biological impulse, or others do, of what significance is that? Such cares, impulses, desires, designs, intentions, and/or purposes are entirely without significance and meaning anyhow. Recall: "The universe was indifferent to our coming, and it will be indifferent to our going." (Benatar, 200)

Without an absolute and irrevocable (i.e. infinite) foundation for meaning one is committed to nihilism. One may fain a middle ground and pretend to maintaining virtues, while "pragmatically" and "humbly" admitting to the cold realities of life, but "what the father hath hid cometh out in the son; and oft have I found in the son the father's revealed secret." (Nietzsche,

---

* Though we are continuing to examine the arguments that stem from the established dogma of materialism and its multifarious superstructure and influenced progeny, I must ask the reader to recall that we have dismantled this ideology at the core by uprooting the idea of emergent consciousness. Thus all these conceptions of meaninglessness and purposelessness and insignificance which proceed from such conceptions are not only contradictory in themselves, as we are showing, but also stem from erroneous conceptions of reality and should thus be thrown out in any case. In Benatar's language, the demise of this theory is overdetermined.

The Myth of Meaninglessness

Zarathustra Ch. 29), and sooner or later one who is more intellectually honest and more moved to action by ideas and what is perceived to be truth will—without noticing the contradiction of believing in truth and the value of acting on it along with meaninglessness—take such doctrines to their ultimate conclusion which is nihilism*. We have seen this throughout history and are witnessing it contemporarily in all those disturbed by the modern nihilism which plagues us and breeds so many of the mass shootings and cultural unrest we are experiencing in the west.

Thus, there is not a nuanced choice in the matter of meaning. If life has any meaning at all, it has infinite meaning. "In order for man to live he must either be unaware of the infinite, or he must have some explanation of the meaning of life by which the finite can be equated with the infinite." (Tolstoy, 54)

The Dangers of Nihilism

Well, this section should be self-evident. What are the dangers in believing that life is meaningless? The absolute best case scenario is a depression corresponding to the degree to which one accepts and sees the world through this belief (even if they call it by the name "antinatalism"). But nihilistic impulses are certainly at the root of many of the horrors of modern society.

> The scientific models built up over the past few centuries imply that human beings are basically nothing but machines… [and] if you watch the nightly news you'll certainly see many people being treated like machines. Machines don't have any intrinsic meaning, and they certainly don't have feelings, or values, or ethics. This is rather a depressing picture, but the scientific world view is the closest thing we have to an accurate account of reality, so perhaps that's just the way it is. (Radin, 286)

---

* "Today or tomorrow sickness and death will come… to those dear to me, and to myself, and nothing will remain other than the stench and the worms. Sooner or later my deeds, whatever they may have been, will be forgotten and will no longer exist. What is all the fuss about then? How can a person carry on living and fail to perceive this? That is what is so astonishing! It is only possible to go on living while you are intoxicated with life, once sober it is impossible not to see that it is all a mere trick, and a stupid trick! That is exactly what it is: there is nothing either witty or amusing, it is only cruel and stupid." (Tolstoy, 31)

Purpose in Form

And those who take these ideas most seriously, who are not overwhelmed by depression and turn to suicide (something Benatar defends as an appropriate response to the nature of the world[*]), only escape the overwhelming sadness temporarily through drugs or through being possessed by an overwhelming rage against the world and against Being itself.

In the modern western world, the common secularist stands aghast at the horrors of mass shootings and war[†] and wonders how people could do this to

---

[*] Both Benatar and David Hume attempt to make a rational defense of suicide. However, in the briefest of responses, both make the claim "I believe that no man ever threw life away, while it was worth keeping." (Hume, 104). This blind spot is so egregious it is hard to overstate. Think about making that claim and what it means. All you need to do is think of one teenager who committed suicide to throw away such an opinion. In 2017, there were more than 6,200 suicide deaths among adolescents and young adults ages 15-24, making it the second-leading cause of death for that age group (Howard, "Suicide Rates Soar…"). Hume, maybe, can be forgiven for lack of knowledge in his time period, but Benatar cannot. One can idly postulate about human freedoms, and be the guy who asks the questions others don't want to approach, but how often does the attraction of being uniquely maudlin push one on the wrong side of such ideas, and looking at it so intellectually, bring one to brashly proclaim things that insult the lives and memories of so many? Yes there are some cases of severe pain and humiliation at the end of life where the question seems fairer, but if you believe that no life ever thrown away had any continuing merit, you clearly aren't a fair judge either. Marginal cases aside, where one weighs the truth of the infinite value of each life against real, unconscionable suffering, the vast majority of suicides in modern times, especially among children and teens are far from good judgements about the worthlessness of life. Therefore one should be far more cautious about supporting suicide, even as an intellectual exercise for only marginal cases. Further, the classic (if not unanimous) assumption behind suicide of one's annihilation upon death has here been refuted, so the entire approach to the question must change. With suicide, one assumed they were ending the dreadful line of cause and effect they seemed to be stuck in and/or headed for. They assumed they were to be annihilated, all experience was to stop. But with the non-reality of annihilation, might this all be invalid? Might death not be the end of experience, nor even perhaps the end of the causes and effects of one's life? ("And their works do follow them" Revelation 14:13) And as we will go on to fully substantiate the realities of purpose and meaning, as with the case for anti-natalism itself, the idea of suicide must be fundamentally reconsidered with the proper conceptions of reality in place.

[†] Obviously many wars are driven by ideologies other than nihilism, and war has been the province of religion and nationalism for most of human history. None of this negates the significant part that nihilism plays in contemporary horrors and the fact

The Myth of Meaninglessness

each other; and yet how many themselves believe that, though we don't think of it much and try not to worry about it, underneath all the hallucinations of our primitive psyches, the world is a meaningless lump of matter in a cold, indifferent universe, and that we suffer here merely to die into complete annihilation?

Whether you like expressing it that particular way or not, those are the underlying metaphysical theories backing most of modern scientific and secular life in western society. And so many hold our "progressive" and "enlightened" worldview in such high esteem and would defend it to the death against any overtly religious or "pseudo-science" dogma, and yet do not see the direct connection these underlying beliefs have to our modern monsters we are dealing with (or rather, mostly refusing to deal with) today[*]. This is an issue we need to confront, and it is long overdue.

---

that nihilism is incoherent and untenable, yet nevertheless part of the common scientific and secular mindset.

[*] Again, it needs to be noted for clarity, modern science itself—from the physics behind relativity and quantum mechanics, to the biology of biofeedback, placebos, and other mental-physical interactions, to overwhelming evidence from the field of psi—does not support this materialistic, positivist dogma of the world. Science has uprooted these conceptions. But our refusal as a society to confront our metaphysics and beliefs—and the reality of our minds and consciousnesses in general—has kept these outdated assumptions around, even in those who know all about the modern physics which make materialism entirely incoherent.

Purpose in Form

Chapter 5: The Myth of Secularism

"The decisive question for man is: Is he related to something infinite or not?" (Jung, MDR, 325)

In a very similar way to Benatar's faith based conception of anti-natalism as separable from nihilism, though seemingly not through as gloomy of a territory, Yuval Noah Harari describes in his book *21 Lessons for the 21st Century* the blissful utopia of secularism and separates it cleanly from all misconception and violence, except what is attributable to human error.

Harari states that secularism is "sometimes defined as the negation of religion", and this leads to only a characterization of what secularists "don't believe and don't do" (207). But, he claims, "Secularism is a very positive and active world view, defined by a coherent code of values..." and that "secularism can provide us with all the values we need" (206-207). In this section, and throughout the book, I am using the term "secularism" in the same way as Harari, and not addressing the specific technical notion of the separation of church and state.

As in most of the book, Harari offers no real foundational discussion of anything, but merely offers you a story that he says is how it is, and paints around that the other images that he says follow in the way he supposes. Aside from the mere shallowness and pandering effect this creates, I find this all particularly annoying given the effort he later exerts to decry all stories (as well as meaning itself). He also pejoratively comments on so called "simple stories", while filling his book with just that! (3-4) Though perhaps it is his

Purpose in Form

sincere belief that humans are not at all universal explainers, but rather beings with poorly developed "hunter-gatherer brains", for whom simple stories are better and "too many facts" get in the way, which motivates him not to care too much about thinking through his ideas, nor explaining their foundations to his audience[*].

In many ways, for its pretention and laundry list of contradictions, I find Harari's book far more irksome than Benatar's—though I realize that Benatar's is the far more overtly dangerous. But what is important here is not how shallow and pandering I find Harari's rhetoric, but the explanations he overlooks and the bad ones he puts forth.[†]

It is important to look at Harari's world view and the problems with it in detail, because this will highlight just how big that caveat included in his supposed utopia is—"except what is attributable to human error" includes pretty much everything.

---

[*] He does make a meager concession at the beginning of the book that his rantings are not to be taken as decisive or complete, merely to get conversation started on important topics, but, in light of all else, this seems only more mere pandering—or at best a convenient disclaimer with which he can evade the necessity to really write something both substantive and effective at reaching a global audience. He claims his mission is global, but his rhetoric and unsubstantiated, borderline propagandistic jargon—from implying that any Christian who supports gun ownership is illiterate toward their own doctrine to insinuating that "pizzagate" was a primary factor in Hillary Clinton's loss in 2016, as well as glossing over her email "debacle"—show he only knows how to talk to other liberals—i.e. to pander (Harari, 241).

[†] Okay so I'm a bit sour here. This is not to say that he does not present good topics or any good ideas in his book. There are actually many good and some great ideas and points sprinkled throughout the book, on all sorts of different topics, you just have to overlook the condescending, authoritative, stereotypical modern liberal slights at all other points of view (and ridiculous lauding of themselves and their ideas) in order to find them. See Jonathan Haidt's research on political perceptions and understandings for evidence showing that liberals, though they consider themselves the party of the highly educated and of erudite understanding, actually do not understand the other sides to political perspectives, whereas conservatives and moderates do (Haidt, 185, 191,193-4, 215-216 & 334). This combination of self-assuredness and constant strawmaning creates an undeniably condescending tone in his rhetoric (to anyone outside of his bubble of agreement that is). However, in the epilogue I take some time to recognize the positive and insightful aspects of Harari's work as a balance to taking him to task as rigorously as I will throughout these chapters. It helps to recognize that people we disagree with or even don't like can be right about some things and do some things well, being worthy of praise.

The Myth of Secularism

The blissful state of secularism only appears blissful in the imagination where all secularists are painted as beacons of virtue, and one either remains ignorant of the fact that minor differences among customs or beliefs in humans can still cause great conflict, or pretends that there is not still significant variation among the secular crowd but that they are clone-like global citizens. However, I do not wish to make a strawman out of secularism. Therefore I will also look at Steven Pinker's vision of secularism which, although within the bounds of his discussion he is far more coherent and cohesive and thus persuasive, still falls short in several obvious and fundamental areas.

There Is No Truly Secular Foundation for Virtue

The first bad explanation and theory which we will talk about now (more later) is that secularism is, as Harari describes it, the most virtuous set of ideals, and that it is even in fact "a coherent set", neither of which are true (207).

Secularism, though he describes it in the most sunny way possible—really conflating "secularism" with merely what it means to be a good person within Western liberal[*] culture—, is entirely bereft of foundations, and when fully explained is, morally, no different from nihilism, as are all systems of thought which are not grounded in the infinite, as we have seen. Harari even explicitly says that meaning does not exist, that all our ideals and purposes are unimportant outside our own heads[†], and even points out the problem of passing the buck of meaning (Harari, 280 & 284). Yet he maintains that the universe is meaningless and that meaning is generated in our minds which he says are a process of our brains, which he claims are but clumps of molecules in a meaningless universe (Harari, 303). Again, as with Benatar, we run into people speaking of ultimate and foundational meaninglessness without any

---

[*] Where "Liberal" refers to the classic sense of tolerance of ideas and others, not the modern American "left wing" connotation.
[†] Though in one of his more curious contradictions he later concludes his book talking about the greatest mystery of consciousness itself... More on that later. But even if that were to relieve him of the prospect of having true nihilism underlie his claims, it would only then be replaced by relativism, which as we said earlier is only a kind of light nihilism as it asserts meaninglessness by refusing the reality of any distinctions between perceptions. Though he rejects this also in considering that "Some Cultures May Be Better Than Others" (Harari, 140). Suffice to say his philosophy is a confused one. Taking a look into metaphysics will help us clear it all up.

effort or real intention to live by or flesh out that impossible idea.

Only those who unconsciously carry the notion of the incontrovertible divinity of the individual and the sanctity of human life (as upheld by the infinite presence which entirely suffuses, knows, and values it) can accept the story of secularism as cohesive and virtuous; it is because they are already instilled with the belief in these divine virtues of the individual that they can consider a doctrine which declares the meaninglessness of life and the solipsism and hallucination of human value benign, let alone virtuous. Dr. Jordan Peterson has covered this point extensively in his criticism of Sam Harris's philosophy. No story, mythology, or explanation can support the value of the individual without having a basis in the infinite, and an understanding of the intimate connection between the "two". And no story, mythology, or purported explanation can coherently speak about ultimate meaninglessness in any capacity, but especially while pretending to retain the notions of value and truth, let alone morality and virtue.

Modern secular intellectuals often appeal to a general conception of humanism as their foundation for ethical behavior toward others. Steven Pinker extols humanism and derides religion, and would object to the claim that religion is necessary and humanism insufficient. However, the doctrine of humanism that he himself lays out is quite clearly non-foundational, even self-avowedly not rooted in any deep understanding, and its corner stone of ethical direction is *still*, after all the efforts made to separate from faith and religion, a statement of faith without any substantive explanation or justification.

Steven Pinker opens his book *Enlightenment Now* "channeling... the ideals of the Enlightenment" in response to a student disturbed by the nihilistic implications of meaninglessness contained in scientific rhetoric (4). He appeals to the student's innate potential and indeed already functioning desire to pursue reason, personal flourishing, and offers the sense of sympathy as a worthy path to follow to cultivate more meaning and flourishing for others (3-4). He calls this "a reasonably credible answer" (3).

Now, I will not be overly dramatic or cynical, this probably was credible enough for the student in question, and it is probably enough for most people to be satisfied and continue with their lives and values, undaunted by further questions of meaninglessness. As I said in the introduction, many people—perhaps even the vast majority—get through life without being afflicted by any sort of chronic existential anxiety or the deep, threatening questions of nihilism. Most people are satisfied with surface level answers and explanations in most things; secularist constituents have their catechisms and religious constituents have theirs, and each sees the faults in the other but is satisfied with their own.

However, to many philosophers and those who *are* deeply perturbed by the daunting questions of nihilism and meaninglessness, the system of humanism is clearly incomplete and laughably shallow. And in this book we are concerned with those depths and combating those very questions and possibilities, without making any assailable assumptions or leaps of faith. So while secularism may have its place and remain "reasonably credible" for a large portion of the population, it must here face, not the popularity or common sense test, but the philosophical, the metaphysical, and even the nihilistic tests.

Many people ask the question "Why should I live?" with much more conviction in despair than the student in Pinker's class appears to. Answering them with "Because of the glory of reason, the potential for flourishing, and the meaning provided through sympathy," is such a poor semblance of an answer—it is actually merely a gamble that the person is not already deeply nihilistic and can be verbally patted on the back through the mild turbulence of the moment—it suggests one is either ignorant of the reality of the question (not understanding the perspective and emotional reality of nihilism) or well aware of their own complete inability to address such depths and content to pretend an answer for their own constituents listening and abandon the questioner as beyond any reach of their system. I think Pinker falls in the former category. I do not think he grasps the depth of nihilism and how truly people are gripped and affected by it.

Secularism, even if we are to concede it can be formulated as a cohesive system as far as it remains within certain bounds, clearly has no answer to true nihilism. To say that life is worth living—or more broadly that human existence has value as a whole—for the pursuit of reason is to answer one who deeply doubts the significance of human consciousness itself with a product of that very consciousness which is already devalued by the nihilist. This answer is still the secularists' strongest argument, and David Deutsch does the best job at making this case. If one accepts the universal reach of reason, and therefore human consciousness, secularism begins to have some claim on the significance of human consciousness.

Purpose in Form

However, the provocation of antihuman rhetoric and sentiment which paints all human action on the world and universe as usurpation and tyrannical, as well as the reality of human fallibility—spun optimistically as "the spiral of recursive improvement" (Pinker, 453)—which puts us far from the ideal of constantly working toward our fellow betterment, but frequently the opposite, still makes this a very hard case for secularists to sell to one already under sway of nihilism and its constant companion of misanthropy.

If we are to try to convince the nihilist that meaning and value are found in sympathy and compassionate action, we are faced with the exact criticism Benatar had of religion (to which his own proposal of terrestrial meaning ironically fell prey as well): "If you were created to help your fellow, and your fellow was created to help you, we are still left wondering why either of you (and by extension any being) was created. This purpose smacks of circularity." (38)

Disregarding the "created" lingo, regardless of our electro-chemically induced fuzzy feelings we get when we help each other, the doctrine of cosmic meaninglessness and the basis of all life in sheer "dumb luck" (Pinker, 19) causing evolution to occur (meaninglessly) in the midst of infinite, pointless chaos, remains underneath all these "reasonably credible" sentiments. Sentiments is all they are. And of what worth are our infinitesimal, mediocre sense-perceptions—whether they induce us to help others and make the world comfortable or not?

Declaring foundational meaninglessness uproots all value systems and discredits the very mechanism by which secularists would suppose to formulate any worthy endeavors; reason itself is ultimately a pointless process growing out of a pointless being. It may have considerable efficacy compared to all the chaos and primitive examples of instinct around it, but ultimately it is merely a refinement of the both selfish and pointless process of gene replication. The only "good" reason would ever have seem to have done would be to elucidate the futility and banality of the whole endeavor, giving the reasoning being the unique opportunity among all creatures to escape this accidental world of immense hardship and infinitesimally meager, though incredibly long-won, gains.

To one who is already positively inclined toward life in general, secularism is probably fine. But to people who are in the depths of despair about life, secularism, if anything, merely reinforces their worst fears—that everything is pointless and that no one even understands them, as the "help" being offered clearly misses the point.

Further, in addition to being impotent against certain levels of human despair and dark philosophy, Pinker's formulation of secularism (actually the Humanist Manifesto III, itself) still contains several fallacies, contradictions, and/or plain old faith-based assertions. Pinker says once outright in his book "life is sacred" (213), and from the intonation of humanist rhetoric, it is clear that this is a commonly accepted maxim. But, the question is, why? What does "sacred" even mean when one is secular? Perhaps "sacred" means that it is part of the highest social contract—life is what we have all agreed to respect and dignify, come what may, because we have decided that it should be so—because this creates the best outcomes for us all.

Well, that doesn't sound very reasonable—and reason is the secularists highest virtue, right? What if one comes up with some really solid reasons as to why human life is not "sacred" and that we don't deserve dignity, and even that these practices *won't* bring us the best outcomes? How does the dogma of sacred life stand up against the assault of reason in a community which ostensibly rejects all dogma and only follows reason?[*] In fact, Pinker admits that the support of human flourishing as described in humanism is a "distinctive moral commitment... that does not come naturally to the human mind," which makes it all the more susceptible to being thrown off by arguments for other sentiments; and then when the community is left with only their maxim that human life is sacred to cling to on faith—how will they handle it when they are the notorious rejecters of faith?

Consider more of the humanistic faith: "We accept our life as all and enough... We welcome the challenges of the future, and are drawn to and undaunted by the yet unknown." (411) Why? Why is our life enough? Why should we accept it? Do secularist even accept it? If you completely accept your life as enough, why should you seek to improve it? How do you welcome the challenges of the future knowing their immensity and the frailty and fallibility of human life and consciousness? How does this great faith in, not

---

[*] Of course, I do believe truth and reason lead to life being sacred, and I think that one will therefore find the better arguments on the side of those supporting human life. I am just pointing out a potential weak spot for a system which supposedly rejects all dogma.

just human *potential*, but human *actualization* come about in those who are also taught we are inept creatures with poorly adapted hunter-gatherer brains?

And let's look at another suspiciously mystical point from the manifesto: "We... animate our lives with a deep sense of purpose." (411) Sorry, purpose cannot be "deep" if you bestow it upon yourself (unless you have a magical belief in your own infinite worth and power). Purpose and meaning by definition are about transcending limits, as Benatar pointed out. To bestow and animate oneself with purpose is to have a very shallow and circular purpose. This also contradicts Pinker's conviction that "there is no limit to how meaningful our lives can become," which would suggest an infinite potential and reality of meaning to be plumbed, which is denied by the doctrine of cosmic meaninglessness[*].

Almost the entire Humanist Manifesto which Pinker lays out and espouses is merely a faith credo with a very intellectual veneer and diction designed to pretend it is not faith based. But the principles are only self-evident and reasonably credible to those already comfortably housed within the tradition, just as the religious catechisms seem to those brought up in religious traditions.

My problem with Pinker's proposal of secularism can be captured in his defense of his foundationless set of catechisms. Pinker's dismissal of the threats of nihilism amounts to: "There would indeed be something perverse about having to justify life itself in the course of examining the foundations of morality, as if it were an open question whether one gets to finish the sentence or be shot." (413) There *is* something perverse indeed about this endeavor of responding to nihilism and antihumanism, but humans can be and often are perverse. And, given your own credo of "distinguishing things as they are from things as we might wish or imagine them to be" we should undauntedly and truthfully deal with the perverse in the most effective way possible, rather than essentially declaring it a blasphemy to broach the subject and wishing it away through high minded sophistry (Pinker, 411).

As I said, Pinker seems to give the reality of nihilism little credence or understanding, and what he may understand he would dismiss as a topic

---

[*] Pinker even essentially admits his own inner belief in God, when he declares his own inner faith in "universals of beauty and meaning" (385). He would probably make some argument as to why this isn't a belief in God, but if you believe in a universe which has meaning fundamentally embedded in it... I don't know what to tell you other than that you believe in God.

beyond discussion or merit of effort. In refusing to engage in this well-known and archetypal arena of human thought and emotion, the system he erects lacks any adequate defense from or answer to the ideas and formulations of nihilism. And, because he bases his system on the story of foundational meaninglessness, he spreads the messages which breed the very demons he is unequipped to face. We will return to this topic later.

Let us return to Harari's misguided conception of secularism, which is much further afield from virtue than Pinker's humanism. Harari shows us how quickly a dangerous level of nihilism can grow in a secular mind when he unequivocally declares that human beings have no natural or innate rights; "the only place rights exist is in the stories humans invent and tell one another… it isn't true that humans have a natural right to life or liberty." (215)

That statement alone should put us all on guard and indicate just how close we are to all-out nihilism and recreating the secular atrocities of the 20th century in listening to Harari's sophistry; regardless of how humble and candid he thinks it is to admit this "truth", and how *in principle* (the limitations of which Harari—in typical intellectual fashion—ignores) courageously confronting the truth, including the shadow, is a good thing. Here already has arisen the very "perverse" challenge to the idea that life is sacred; it is *only* "sacred" in our minds (which are meaningless phenomena after all…); sacredness is mere convention.

Those secularists who don't so willingly put their declarations of nihilism up front often attempt to conjure purpose and value through the circular argument of devoting ourselves to "progress". But take Tolstoy on progress for progress's sake: "To say that in the infinity of time and space everything is developing, becoming more perfect, complex and differentiated, is really to say nothing at all… for in the infinite there is no simple and complex, no before and after, and no better or worse." (36) And in a universe of ultimate meaninglessness, there is no such thing as improvement, for there is no real basis for value—all value is a meaningless hallucination experienced by an insignificant and meaningless being.

So again, we find the problem of not understanding, acknowledging, or dealing with the infinite. If one admits there is an infinity, but still maintains we are accidental beings, and says we should all push for progress, one must face the vision of samsara which horrified the Buddha; eternal progress, eternal striving is nothing but eternal slavery and suffering—it is Sisyphus' eternal labor*. But if any modern westerner can actually read Camus' Sisyphus and extract an actual reasonable explanation of why we should be delighted or pacified to be Sisyphus that does not amount to him saying in heavily perfumed words that that is the noble thing to do, or the rebellious thing to do, or just the downright radical thing to do—i.e. merely appealing to some existing archetypal human desire and value to emotionally charge one into bootstrapping themselves out of worrying about nihilistic possibilities—then I may stand corrected.

As it stands, however, I believe the only true answer to the problem of samsara, the problem of suffering, is the assertion and revelation of the reality of transcendence which is granted through the nature of our fundamentally infinite existence. And if one claims there is not an infinite, first and most fortunately they are wrong as we have shown, but then they must face the nihilism to which the explanations of annihilation and meaninglessness irrevocably push them or those who may be moved to follow them.

And No Redemption, Too

Another problem secularism faces, and another which Harari gets completely backwards, is that it has no legitimate reason to support the progress of humanity, even for the sake of progress itself. Harari says, "If you believe in a quest for truth by fallible humans, admitting blunders is part of the game. This is also why undogmatic secular movements tend to make relatively modest promises. Aware of their imperfections, they hope to effect small incremental changes." (218)

Modest proposals are not the mainstay in public movements, in my observation, though of course the tem "modest" itself is relative to your beliefs and assumptions. But, if we truly take the secular point of view, there is no coherent way to support such slow and modest progress—"the spiral of recursive improvement" as Pinker puts it (453).

Humanity is in a place of great darkness and ignorance, and while optimistic secular proponents of progress might look to human potential to one day pull humanity out of all the terrible messes we are currently in, a secular

---

* "At some point we come to realize that trying to find our sense of worth in life by producing more and more stuff—even if it's *good* stuff—doesn't satisfy us and in fact leaves us disillusioned, empty, and feeling like failures." (Kautz, 79 italics in original)

view of life does not truly allow for such hopes.

If one believes that the salvation of humanity from its own darkness rests in our eventual achievement of a more perfect state, that is all well and good, but we don't have forever to get there, do we? Humanity takes a long time to make progress, and we are still very far from our goals—from being in a state, as a whole, that could be considered a "good" place. So many horrors still afflict humans all over the world every day. "How can a person who is awake avoid outrage at the world?" (Peterson, 151)

How long can we wait? Already all of our history of unacceptably deplorable and hellish conditions is stacked up behind us. Let's say we think as of yet, all that suffering throughout history hasn't made the whole human endeavor a failed cause—that's a big concession, and it's not clear why a secularist would believe that, if one contemplates the reality of all the suffering that has happened already. But if so, how much more can we really take? How long before our continual failure to make sufficient progress and become a species which doesn't commit regular atrocities on ourselves and the world does overcome all hypothetical progress we could make "eventually"?

In a truly secular conception of reality, the idea of future progress does nothing to redeem or make up for all the darkness and suffering of humanity to date, nor of that which is still undoubtedly to come. Of what significance are the future good lives of humans to those enmeshed in suffering today?

Secularists who hold out for some future state of progress are not making a logical assessment of the realities of the world in line with their supposed beliefs; they're just holding their breaths and hoping to irrationally outlast the nihilism and misanthropy which is knocking at their door. As long as something changes soon enough, they can forgive and forget (though, again, it's not clear why within their world view they should, other than it's an irrational drive to stay positive about life—but that's not them being rational secularists, then, is it?). In truth, the secularists need a utopia RIGHT NOW to really justify their desired positivity about humanity. That's probably why secular societies fall prey to utopian visions so easily[*].

---

[*] Also, the utopian visions that come out of secularism stem from a need to place the blame for the "problems" of humanity on an external system which, if only it could be reset, would fix everything. "The idea that we are born in a state of virtue from which the world has unfairly ripped us." (Murray, 250) And that, "if different people had the money, the problems plaguing humanity would vanish." (Peterson, 197) This belief,

Purpose in Form

And, again, these utopian ideal states don't really offer redemption—there isn't any way one can believe good human action and quality of life in the future in any way helps or makes up for those of the past who have since been annihilated and lived lives of horrifying darkness and suffering—they just offer the opportunity to forget and move forward without really thinking it all through. So really, in a truly coherent secular theory, and as we have seen in practice many times, secular movements are driven away from modest progress and toward radical, sweeping reforms, because they lack any form of real redemption in their worldview.

Steven Pinker makes an excellent case for the reality of human progress in his book *Enlightenment Now*. If one is a person swayed by statistics (which, of course, most aren't), and one grants Pinker the benefit of the doubt that he hasn't tinkered with the data or framing (which I am perfectly happy to do, personally), one can have no doubt of the reality of human achievement and progress over the past few centuries, compared to most of human history. It really is a lovely and heartening revelation of the accomplishments of well-directed human effort, and the blessings this has bestowed on us all. And it is a good booster against "the sin of ingratitude" (Pinker, 63).

None of this, however, makes any headway on the case for the secular redemption of humanity, nor the abiding of the horrors of the world. What good is the project of human flourishing to all those annihilated souls who suffered at the foundations of the project? With a purpose only grounded in the self-bestowed quest for more comfort and happiness—pleasant though these be—what do those who died in darkness and suffering receive? Only the far distant future progeny of perhaps some individuals will ever reap any of the greatest rewards of all the work. Of what value is one's sacrifice in this ambitious struggle, even if we assume it will ultimately succeed, beyond

---

though absurd, keeps at bay the problem for secularists of having to contend with the reality that humans are the problem, humans are both imperfect and powerful—thus they have responsibility (though the utopians try to deny it). Secularists looking at a species of effective and imperfect, and therefore dangerous, beasts are forced to contend with their nihilism—why should this species exist? Why should they have freedom? How can we accept such violence and destruction they breed and sow, and still pretend to grant them some unexplained necessary autonomy and inherent goodness? As we will see later, truly looking at the darkness of humanity necessitates a belief in a redemption deeper than anything secularism can offer—an infinite possibility for redemption (i.e. a merciful and intimate God).

buying of a bit more pleasure and significantly less suffering for some future beings whose lives are, in the end, meaningless and purposeless?

And even all the hopeful trends of the graphs Pinker lays out only betray the horrible quality indigenous to all life. "Nature is a war" and "poverty… is the default state of human kind"; "War, scarcity, disease, ignorance, and lethal menace are a natural part of existence." (Pinker, 19, 25, & 4) We may have made significant headway on these problems to date, but we are still surrounded and constantly engulfed. The numbers of horrid deaths and living conditions, even though they have dramatically plummeted, are still astronomical.

The optimist who dismisses nihilism off hand takes this only as a worthy call to action. But those partial to some nihilistic and anti-human sentiments see this only as clear condemnation of the unworthiness of our capacities, and the unjust nature of our existence. What real foundational case does secularism have to justify our abiding a world full of such horrors? Regardless of the shrinking numbers, a world with just one case of rape, genital mutilation, torture, etc. should be unjustifiable for one to whom life is truly sacred. Statistics can help us disassociate and see the hopes for the future. But each number represents such pain, horror, and misery to a sentient human for whom we should have sympathy—how are we to abide when we do start thinking about this side of things and become disturbed by it?

Secularism truly has no answer. They must accept the horrors of the world as they are, but don't have a mechanism for justifying and achieving this other than cognitive dissonance—a powerful and naturally human tool though that may be.

It is only a belief in a merciful God who oversees this absurd finite world, and a fate beyond cold annihilation for those ground up in its terrible mill, that one can stand the necessity of slow progress for humanity. "Do not be daunted by the enormity of the world's grief. Do justly now. Love mercy now. Walk humbly now. You are not obligated to complete the work, but neither are you free to abandon it." (McClure, 235, referencing the Pirkei Avot) No secularist can truly support this attitude within their irreligious belief set.

Secularists hold onto the irrational idea that people will suddenly all change sometime very soon and start behaving much more amicably; but, as Murray puts it, the most likely scenario is that "people will broadly go on behaving as they have done throughout history, that they will continue exhibiting the same impulses, frailties, passions and envy that have propelled our species up till now" (252).

To deal with the world as it is—as it has been and will likely continue to be, and with people as they are and will continue to be—along our painfully slow and recursive path toward growth and progress, you need the intimate connection of infinite to finite that bestows immediate significance, purpose, and mercy in our haphazard and often horrifyingly dark lives.

The Vicious Ideals of Secular Ideology

A final and no less comprehensive blow to secularism as conceived in modern terms is the ideals which are its highest aspirations. Harari again makes the comically backwards claim that "the main problem with secularism is… it probably sets the ethical bar too high." (213) This proposal is laughable.

It is secularism which foists political life—of all things—into the highest sphere of human achievement. If there are no higher purposes beyond human realities, then the overseeing system of mass social intercourse is the highest of human realities. People can follow individual goals and desires, but these are mostly meaningless. Some very few people have outsized effects on society through their innovations, but what through this lens seems consistently most potent in most people's lives and which is positively real and true is the social governance system. How Harari thinks secularism even ideally comes to supporting "an opened-ended quest for truth and compassion", other than by merely importing preconceived notions about what it means to be a good person in place of what he wants to be the goals of secularism, is beyond me—especially since he purportedly dismisses all meaning and stories (of which "quests" would be included) and describes human beings as poorly equipped, dimwitted and deluded beings with no natural rights (213).

It is out of secular ideals that the drive to politicize everything (which madness Murray discusses extensively in his book) has emerged. It is out of secular thinking that the idea that only power games between political groups are real sprung. It is secularism which must answer for making what is perhaps the seediest, most vicious, and banal realms of human pursuit (and almost never "achievement") the virtue to aspire to and the highest goal to pursue.

Politics in any society is doomed to be the lowest on the hierarchy of virtue—the first to fall into corruption and the last to move into integrity—

because politics selects its participants from those motivated by power, and rewards them with more power. Those most susceptible to corruption by power are those who rise to the top through the difficult sieve of getting into politics. Those less motivated by power—and thus less corruptible by it—are not interested enough in the rewards to pursue the hard path to the goals and rewards of the game. Thus politics naturally sorts for people who are easily corrupted by it and therefore becomes quickly corrupted in any state.

Moreover, as Murray points out, in a secular society which imbues politics with the highest meaning, politics becomes laced with "a passion—including rage—that perverts the whole enterprise" even more completely (255). This, in turn, infects the rest of secular society such as the halls of reason and science. "Political ideology undermines reason and science." (Pinker, 32)

Yet secularism sees no higher realities to aspire to than politics and governance of peoples. To think of this arena of human pursuit as the highest possible achievement of humans shows the viciousness of secularism. "The wicked walk on every side, when the vilest men are exalted." (Psalm 12:8) We must, as humans, believe in purpose and significance in our actions and lives which proceed beyond the mere macro effects on meaningless individuals bumping together in more or less harmony.

The Reality of Secularism

Secularism as explained as a miraculous utopia of agnostics and non-believers who turn to the fully complete and cohesive theories of humanism to guide their existence, and the be-all, end-all, catch-all basin for modern ethical conduct and our goals for our future is, as we have seen, erroneous.

Secularism and modern humanism irrevocably appeals to the divine nature of the human individual as a core tenant of its ethics. The divine individual is necessarily a religious concept, not just because it uses the word divine, but because it explains the value of the individual completely and coherently only by appealing to an endowed state of being that makes us valuable by nature of our genesis. Since secularism as a whole pretends to the scientific notion that our genesis was merely a haphazard wiggling of meaningless atoms occurring in an indifferent universe, it has no real ground to claim the value of our being "from genesis" or by virtue of its created nature (since that nature is, by modern dogma, blind and purposeless). But that is all all the easier to overlook

Purpose in Form

because modernists don't like or value metaphysics, and have elected to repress and neglect it.

The only way to truly and completely explain the truth of the divine individual is to appeal to the reality of the infinite and its intimate and conscious connection to each individual (i.e. the property of self-saturation[*]).

The only way to abide with hope in the haphazard but worthy quest for truth and compassion—especially when one leaves behind intellectual speculation in which they get to decree that everyone or even many people will faithfully follow such quests, and confronts the true magnitude and reality of the shadow in the world—is to have a real belief in and mechanism for redemption in life which can surmount the suffering of the world and so many individual lives.

None of these prospects can be supported through an entirely secular worldview. That being said, secularism does have some virtues that we should hope are a part of our future, and though these virtues derive from the foundational virtues which secularism covertly or unconsciously adopted from previous religious systems, it fostered the virtues of tolerance, understanding, and the relatively peaceful mixing of cultures and peoples probably more effectively than any singular system previously[†].

Now I am not a historian, but I do know that relatively tolerant multicultural milieus have existed before modern western society. But, because that is really the one big hallmark of what we should look to secularism to bring us (or to show us is achievable, despite our various faiths), that is kind of a way of saying that secularism has arisen many times in many lands. What we should mean by secularism, and what we should strive to continue upholding that it did very well[‡], is maintaining an open acceptance of multiple practices and expressions of human value, thought, and emotion. Though as rationalists who believe in truth as the highest virtue, we should reject the idea of not believing in an infinite reality and its intimate, conscious connection to each individual—and in that sense we should be in no way "secular", meaning scrubbed of religious ideas—we should practice a tolerance and openness

---

[*] "I am in my father, and ye in me, and I in you." (John 14:20)
[†] The missteps of modern multiculturalism notwithstanding.
[‡] Not infallibly, not with 100% success—not even close—but again, remember, we can be better off through enacting something that amounts to less than the imagined ideal than not using it at all, and we can and should be happy about such marginal successes—just as with reason and Aspirin.

The Myth of Secularism

which exemplars of secularism have shown us is possible[*].

Secularism, as far as it was good, arose from the enlightenment as a byproduct of a movement toward universal acknowledgement and embracing of fallibility. As I have said, though we should believe in the incontrovertible and self-evident nature of infinite existence and the reality of meaning, we should not refuse to explain and substantiate these ideas, and walk any skeptic through the contradictive conception of a meaningless reality. We can hold that these ideas are necessarily true and reasonable and inevitable, but not be dogmatic about it, and never afraid to look into a challenge or seeming loophole.

But further, as we acknowledge fallibility, we must acknowledge the fallibility people have toward fallibility—in that they will not completely accept it and will hold themselves, others, or certain areas quite infallible in many cases, even when they profess an allegiance to secularism, science, etc. This is the attitude of understanding and tolerance, and it should guide us to sharing and examining ideas in a culture of "conjecture and criticism", as Deutsch describes. We should move ever more toward the ideal state where we "let our theories die in our place", which we can only effectively accomplish and embody through moving toward a true understanding of our identities and not being so mixed up in identifying with our thoughts or even our beliefs (Deutsch, quoting Popper, 114). *"Faith in the part of us that continues across those deaths is a prerequisite to thinking itself."* (Peterson, 195, italics in original)

Another point for us to recognize in this vein of understanding our fallible nature is that most secularists and even scientists don't know that is what they are doing or have done. We have unconsciously adopted this virtue of separating ourselves from our ideas and formulating new ideas through conjecture and criticism; and being fallible beings, many will not even notice or agree that is the basis of the virtue in science and secularism even when it is

---

[*] Obviously, as in anything, there are plenty of bad actors who have given secularism a bad name and been plenty intolerant, and even the term and idea of "multiculturalism" is now something taken by an authoritarian, immoral, and intolerant sect which has arisen out of the modern morass we call secularism. Still the modern free society has hosted many great moments of tolerance between peoples, probably more than any society in recorded history, and we should honor this and strive to continue to follow this ideal.

pointed out to them. Thus fallibility is tied to tolerance, and yet it all comes with this paradox that through acknowledging fallibility, if we are to be consistent, we must acknowledge that we and others will do so fallibly and will hold onto infallibility in various ways. So we need understanding and to be able to have patience and play the long game.

Secularism as given—supposedly scrubbed of religion—offers no hope or reason why this should be acceptable; since our suffering is great and we are ephemeral, problems need solving now. Even though the effective way to solve them is through a slow and recursive process, that is not tenable for those who are true secularists and reject beliefs in higher powers or higher purpose—a conscious and intimate infinite—and thus all possibility of redemption.

It is the recognition of the infinity of life that supports the complete reality of our fallibility, our ability to recognize and acknowledge that fact, and the presence of mercy and salvation within this "furnace of affliction". (Isaiah 48:10)

Religion, by definition is the binding to the infinite. "Re-" meaning again, "lig" meaning to bind, gives us the conception putting ourselves back together, of reconnecting to the infinite reality. Take also Tolstoy's masterful words:

> Man may regard himself as an animal living among animals, by the day, or he may think of himself as a member of a family, or society, or a nation that lives for centuries. Or he may find himself obliged (because his reason drives him irresistibly to it) to regard himself as a part of an infinite universe, living in infinite time. And, therefore, in respect of the infinitely small phenomena of life that influence behavior, a rational person must do what in mathematics is called integration: that is, establish a relation to the immediate issues of life, a relation to the entire infinite universe in time and space, conceiving of it as a whole. And the relationship established by man to that whole, of which he feels himself a part and from which he draws guidance for his behavior, is that which has been, and is called religion. And therefore religion has always been, and cannot cease to be, an essential and indisposable condition of the life of rational humanity. (87)

Secularism, taken as it is commonly understood, as a lack of religious commitment, is by definition lacking any clear binding to the infinite. Again, "religion is the bond between man and God... if it does not bind man to the infinite being, it is not religion." (Tolstoy, 88-89) Tolstoy's works *A Confession* and *What is Religion and of What Does Its Essence Consist* really are phenomenal works[*] that chronicle the nearly archetypal experience of a man raised in modern secular forms, an ardent intellectual, confronting his own contradictions and lack of clear purpose and orientation in life, and the inevitable resolution with the infinite, which in turn allows him to see what was once considered the quaint and inferior conceptions of religious life as real living principles which are necessary to life.

So secularism leaves much to be desired in supporting and directing life, and its colloquial nature and acceptance are certainly part of the ground out of which so much of the horrors and nihilism of the day have arisen. But as I have said we can and should retain its truth of the fallibility of ourselves and the understanding and tolerance which open us up as individuals and in society as a whole.

Recognizing our fallible nature is undoubtedly part of our journey in coming to know ourselves, including our connection to the infinite. And further there are many metaphors and literary conceptions which work to introduce one to this infinite reality which enlivens us; so what secularism achieved at its best is the mingling of cultures and religions and their various conceptions and explanations of the divinity of human life, and this remains just as achievable when we recognize the reality of the infinite.

We need not return to being dogmatic or doctrinaire in our society to return to the rational integration of the individual with the infinite. In fact, understanding the infinite more deeply, in the reality of its diverse manifestation, as well as the fallibility of our incarnated selves should lead us to being more open to the multifarious expressions of the divine which arise to guide human life, and life in general, in all its differing expressions.

---

[*] Though throughout each is sprinkled a naïve movement toward communism, which is regrettable.

Purpose in Form

Part 2:

Return to Truth and a Solid Foundation for Life

Three things thus far are certain in life:
-Existence is Infinite
-Consciousness is not emergent
-Meaning is real

    Though it remains less than 100% certain on the surface of the reasoning whether we should definitively declare consciousness itself infinite, the more you devote yourself to realizing these necessary truths as they stand, the closer and more inevitable the conscious experience of the infinite reality becomes, which is the only thing to quell all such doubts. "Were the doctrine of the real presence ever so clearly revealed in scripture, it were directly contrary to the rules of just reasoning to give our assent to it… when [miracles] are considered merely as external evidences, and are not brought home to everyone's breast, by the immediate operation of the Holy Spirit." (Hume, 107) And, "until we encounter God firsthand… all theologies, good and bad, will be little more than the stale crusts of someone else's orthodoxy." (Kautz, 17)

    For my part, based on personal experience and looking thoroughly through the theories and explanations underlying fundamental, infinite consciousness, I believe it is the best explanation we have of the world and life as we know it. It is also a verifiable reality through experience. For that reason, I will proceed as though the propositions "consciousness is infinite" and "the infinite is conscious" are entirely true, though I recognize this cannot be definitively demonstrated a priori, and so has not been.

Purpose in Form

The necessity for us to move beyond the conception of consciousness as severely limited and emergent, however, *is* certain. Our progress from that point to accepting consciousness as a fundamental and infinite reality must ultimately be determined through personal experiences like those sought and promoted in schools of meditation, though reading about alternative theories and explanations of consciousness beyond the materialist emergent conception can help us begin to comprehend and believe, which will then help us see more of the reality already before us.

"*What saves is the willingness to learn from what you don't know.* That is faith in the possibility of human transformation… He identifies with the part of himself that could transcend his current state, and becomes the hero of his own adventure." – Dr. Jordan B. Peterson (218 & 329)

Chapter 6: Purpose in Form

As with meaning in life, purpose in form is undeniable. A handle is a form with the purpose of holding or grasping. Wings are forms with the purpose of flight. Neuropsychologists even go so far as to say that say we define and recognize things by their purpose, rather than their objective form (Peterson, 39 & 374). "We perceive tools and obstacles, not objects or things." (Peterson, 261) But there are also many schools of thought that claim life is purposeless and that form is meaningless. Form clearly exists, but—to them—purpose is not absolute. Yet we can clearly see purpose in form everywhere, so where is the disconnection?

Often the core problem for those who do not believe in purpose or meaning is that they see the "purpose" of a handle—for example—as an arbitrary imposition by humans, which by their definition have no particular value or power within their consciousness—because consciousness is meaningless (the foundational assumption they base all their doctrines on) the determinations it comes to cannot be significant.

Those who do not believe in purpose necessarily do not believe in the significance of their own consciousness. And the greater the degree of meaninglessness or devaluation toward consciousness, the greater the degree of disillusion from purpose in form and therefore life. The problem, as is perhaps always the case, is people not knowing who they are, not knowing their true self. The problem is our muddled and incoherent metaphysics. And in this confusion, the tenets of nihilism emerge again.

The problem also seems to become more apparent when we say, instead of, "here is the purpose of a handle" or "here is the purpose of the car" describing a purpose that we comprehend, and that we invent, but rather "what is the purpose of a tree?" * In cases of natural objects, or in the "objective"† view of man-made objects, what is the purpose? Is there a purpose? Is there a purpose to life itself, to the universe, beyond our imposition of selfish desires and usury?

This is the big question. There is a universe far beyond our comprehension in complexity and size, and if it had any significance at all it would seem to be far beyond us, so our limited judgements of purposes seem only greedy inventions usurping the essence of things for our utility. Why is our perspective significant at all (not to even suppose "right")? Seeing ourselves as disconnected from the infinite and doubting our purposes and significance, for the apparent sake of humility (the principle of mediocrity), we turn back to nihilism (however veiled, repressed, and outwardly denied), despair, and indeed untruth.

The Same Old Issues

So it seems we have two connected issues: the loss of purpose as seen in the questions of whether or not there is a purpose at all, and second, even if there were some purpose, how could we suppose that our consciousness is significant given the immensity we know the universe to be and our incontrovertible ignorance.

Fortunately, however, though the latter problem appears to be the more intractable, it is actually easily answerable. And though the short answer may not seem to address or grasp the underpinning despair being conveyed in the question, it is in fact entirely sufficient; the suffering experienced must be dealt with—as Tolstoy found and related in *A Confession*—in cultivation and

---

* Though Jonathan Haidt points out that even in natural cases, the conceptualization of purpose and design is essentially necessary (227).
† Which, for materialists and secularists, functionally means sterile and meaningless—it is from the imagined perspective of the perspectiveless universe that we hypothesize our "objectivity" and simultaneously postulate the nihilism of a sterile universe. Thus, because a non-conscious universe and the insignificance of human consciousness is presupposed, one must conceive of the (non-existent) "perspective" of the universe to be cold, indifferent, and dismissive of human worth and endeavor. This is not a rationalist's conclusion, it is a self-fulfilling prophecy, a dogma that modern western intellectuals impose all the time, reinforcing the common idea and feeling of disconnection from and insignificance in the cosmos.

Purpose in Form

practice of living in line with the truths we are discovering. Beliefs and mindsets must be embodied and brought into action to taste their fruits.

So to the question of "how do we know our consciousness is significant?" the answer is that it is self-evidently so. There is no way for us to exist or act which does not take the significance of our consciousness as paramount. To ask the question "how is my consciousness significant" is to imply that the answer is significant. If consciousness was not significant then the question would not be daunting and the "problem" it seems to propose would not be a problem. The supposition of an insignificant consciousness is as meaningless as the hypothesis of ultimate meaninglessness—which we have already shown. But, though the question is really answered that simply, let us take a bit of space here to really beat the dead horse, just for good measure.

The claim might be forwarded that we actually can live or act as if our consciousnesses have no real significance, because we have begun to comprehend the vastness of the universe and our own limited nature and this has altered our actions and conceptions of ourselves, so we can take away our surety of an afterlife, or in a proposed God, or we can point out the futility of wars over control of land, etc. Some or all of these may be seen as and argued to be good or right or desirable. But none of this says anything about our consciousness being insignificant. It still very clearly affirms the undeniable significance of our conscious.

It is only because we take our growing conceptions of the immensity of life beyond ourselves seriously (i.e. significantly) that we begin to contemplate our meaning, place, and possible futility. It is only because we can contemplate these and because we take such contemplations to be significant that we care what the answers might be and allow them to direct our courses of action. It is only because we consider our desires and our judgements of what is good and desirable as significant that we can have such a conversation on how to govern our actions based on the changes in our judgements and perspectives. So our consciousness is inescapably significant to us.

Turning the Problem on its Head (Taking the Side of the Infinite and Truth)

Now I can just hear the perennial contrarians jumping on that qualification "to us"; "obviously it's important *to us*, but why does that matter? What if it's not important to the universe?!" But a real and completely satisfactory answer to the question of "How do we know our consciousness is significant to the universe?" is "why do you assume it isn't?"

The problems still stems from that same old dogma of emergent consciousness, which allows one to believe that their consciousness is a meaningless aberration, rather than a real and fully connected and supported part of the infinite universe. This is a bad explanation as we have seen. And, without the erroneous theory-laden filters of meaninglessness and emergent consciousness over our eyes, what real evidence is there to suppose that our consciousness is not significant to the universe? And, if you are despairing of the lowliness of our being in the universe, are you prepared to completely admit a conscious universe or otherwise significant higher power by which you substantiate your judgement of lowness if you are willing to posit that question?

The assertion that our consciousness is insignificant because of the vastness we perceive in the universe and the limitedness we begin to perceive in ourselves is self-defeating. For the ignorance which any true inquirer concludes on our part is so total and encompassing* that supposing to draw from that conclusion the following that "therefore we are not significant" is nothing but inconsistent.

We can claim no significant level of arbitration as to the cosmic significance of anything, even ourselves, if we are taking seriously the assumption that we are profoundly limited, disconnected, and therefore ignorant. Thus, again, it is only because we do assume and must assume that our consciousness (including our perceptions and proceeding judgements) is significant that we come to the suppositions that we might not be significant and life might be meaningless. "Talking yourself into irrelevance is not a profound critique of Being. It's a cheap trick of the rational mind." (Peterson, 87) And Deutsch puts it this way, "feeling insignificant because the universe is large has the exact same logic as feeling inadequate for not being a cow." (35)

So we cannot escape the significance of our consciousness, and our

---

* Especially if we are under the delusion that our consciousness is a hallucination or aberration accidental existence, no significance, and therefore of what real power of comprehension? Why would creatures whose perception arose through a continual test of being "just good enough" to stay alive (as opposed to ideally effective and competent) have any grounds to claim their accuracy or nearness to comprehension of, well, anything?

Purpose in Form

consciousness is one that perceives meaning and purpose, so we cannot escape this either. But it is, I think, this underlying knowledge that we cannot escape ourselves and yet we do not fully understand ourselves—indeed the only thing that we do understand, or think we understand, is that we are things which do not understand, that we are ignorant in some profound way—which causes the turmoil within ourselves, which we cannot not take seriously, which causes us to suppose grand cosmic flaws and theorize about the futility of life, regardless of the futility and incoherency of such endeavors.

That is to say, as Camus perceived, man is disturbed when he confronts the absurdity of life, and it all seems like an endless hell of pointless suffering. But though Camus' reply (and indeed his entire methodology of addressing the problem[*]) is entirely insufficient, we can find better sources of inspiration, address, and testimony[†], and indeed we will try here to walk through an entire address and conclusion to such despair, in so far as one can address the emotion through reason—which again I recognize is only marginally, but these marginal effects are nonetheless significant.

So, given that we cannot escape our own conception of the significance of our consciousness and our perceptions, and that the only bases people have for proposing the meaninglessness and insignificant consciousness are incorrect hypotheses, as we have shown, we are left only with the problem of "how do we know that there is purpose in life at all?", which, given that we do perceive and are even built to perceive purpose, amounts to the question of "how do we know the purpose we perceive is real?" And, also importantly, "how do we know the purpose we perceive is right?"

The first can only be properly answered by following the line of questioning through "what do you mean by real?", which I have done in *Jnana Yoga* and seems so directly linked to the problem of epistemology (what do we actually know and how do we know it?) that it would serve no purpose to reiterate it

---

[*] Benatar comments on the literary nature of old philosophers and how it falls short: "Their style of writing is often more literary and evocative. While it has widespread appeal, analytic philosophers, who are more common in the Anglophone world, have often criticized this writing for being excessively obscure and insufficiently precise." (xv)

[†] "Yeshua said: Whoever searches must continue to search until they find. When they find, they will be disturbed; and being disturbed, they will marvel and will reign over All." (The Gospel of Thomas, Logion 2)

here without also fully reiterating the epistemological conquest. So, for those who the question provokes in that way, please see my book *Jnana Yoga*.

The second question of how do we know the purposes we perceive are the right ones is a valid question but not one that actually stands for any existential angst. The truth and simple answer is that we do not know that what we perceive is right or true, and we may often perceive purposes of others or possibilities for our endeavors which are not the "correct" ones for the situation (as judged by a higher consciousness that would know our "true" path or destiny, which is the really the implication behind such ponderings).

Human beings are fallible. But being wrong about particular purposes is not an immediate problem of metaphysics; it can lead to significant problems on many levels, but it does not stand for any dread of fundamental purposelessness so we will leave it here. We must find particular purposes through our fallible individual consciousness' discernment, and must seek their refinement through the pursuit of reason, within a culture of conjecture and criticism.

If we accept—as we must—that our consciousness is significant, and that we perceive purpose, and that, for our purposes, this perception cannot be any less "real" than the most fundamental aspects of our life and world[*], then we are left with the question of "why would ephemeral purposes of the limited human endeavor be part of the infinite universe?", which stems from the ignorance of what the relationship is between human beings—their consciousness and action—and the cosmos itself—the conscious universe, a higher power, or God.

Religious and ethical systems have almost always (if not exclusively) begun with the given that we—in body and consciousness—are significant and that our purposes, regardless of how seemingly menial, are part of the cosmos. The questions of the significance of the cosmos itself or of why our lowly purposes are permitted to exist were either unaddressed, or addressed only marginally. A very real and completely acceptable reason for this is that these questions are just plain silly.

The significance of the cosmos is as self-evident as the significance of one's

---

[*] Again, I do not deny the skeptic ground to argue here, in fact I encourage it, but that discussion belongs in a full exploration of epistemology and is taken care of in my book *Jnana Yoga*.

own consciousness; it is inescapable. Those who despair at our lowliness, our menial pursuits, our ignorance, and our destruction, must be judging (though many unconsciously) against a supposition of a higher power or potential for our own being of far greater grandeur, intention, knowledge, and benevolence. Benatar himself explicitly shows this when he imagines other fantastic versions of existence—which one can only do given the infinite power of imagination and at least some credulous, albeit unconscious, belief in the manifested reality of infinite potential (i.e. an infinite existence to support such a fantasy)*. Otherwise, if one rejects the reality of an infinite manifestation (and therefore infinite fundamental existence), they must realize that comparing our reality to the figments of our own fallible imagination and becoming depressed about our state by comparison is surely not a satisfactory argument as to the reality of our derelict nature.

Though we can certainly be tortured by the figments of our imagination for a time, eventually these problems are to be solved not by acquiescing to our fundamentally absurd nature and deeming we are fated to endure impossible visions that plague us, but to see through the unrealities that our mind projects and thus rob them of their power over us. For example, as we grow up from being children, we do not remain frightened of the monster under our beds, but we conquer that fear and leave that figment of imagination behind through the process of checking so many times and of knowing and becoming accustomed to the realities of the world to the point where we can let that fear go unheeded.

Thus, one cannot reasonably lament the dreary state of humanity as compared to utopian alternate realities *unless they believe wholeheartedly in the manifestation of these realities*, which draws necessarily on the infinite potential of life itself, as well as human potential; and thus this idea cannot support the solipsistic and dreary world view and conception of human nature that it is meant to.

In other words, the only way to demean and denigrate humanity as it is, is to appeal to and wholly believe in the achievement of its potential perfection (which is, though often unstated and unconscious, always wrapped up with falling into a divine cosmic plan and purpose). As Dr. Jordan Peterson pointed out, when someone says "life is meaningless" that's not what they really mean;

---

* Recall here that the multiverse theory of quantum mechanics, which Deutsch contends is the only viable one, fully supports the reality of infinite manifestation.

Purpose in Form

"when people say life has no meaning what they mean is: 'I'm suffering stupidly and intensely and I don't know what to do about it' – the suffering is meaningful, it's just not the kind of meaning you want." (Peterson, "Bible Series VI").

We must understand the conscious and emotional turmoil that these questions represent and address the problems most proximal to the root-cause to alleviate the particular suffering that those questions represent, which will then allow them to be seen as meaningless and insignificant in their forwarded content; though they were certainly captivating and altogether significant as real representations of pain and suffering in a state of lostness and ignorance. Dean Radin sees the societal problem as such:

> Clinical psychologists know that the feeling of being fundamentally alone quickly leads to anxiety, declining health, and depression. To maintain mental and physical health, not only as individuals but as societies, we must believe and act as though we are living in a world that does have deep meaning and personal value... As science shifts toward a world view that supports rather than denies our deepest psychological needs, we can expect significant beneficial consequences for society's mental health. (327)

Jonathan Haidt also mentions the necessity for a concept and acceptance of redemption in one's own life for the maintenance of optimal mental health (443). Redemption, significance, meaning, and purpose all have their roots in the truth of infinite existence and non-emergent consciousness. Therefore, since we have seen that our present hysteria and ignorance is a direct result of not being clear about the necessary reality of the infinite, and/or not knowing its true relation to the lives of individuals, here we will extrapolate the answers found in religion[*] concerning the apparently menial purposes of man.

Victor Frankl claims that man cannot exist without a purpose—at least not fully, and not for long when up against the worst suffering of life—i.e. not EFFECTIVELY; doctrines not strong enough against the tempest of life in the most extreme iterations will be as houses built on sand (Matthew 7:26-27). The Christian tradition agrees with Frankl; we are taught that God made each and

---

[*] Recall: religion is "that which binds man to the infinite".

every one of us "for a purpose". But, through explorations into Buddhism, especially Zen sects, we may find books or individuals talking about "purposelessness" and the freedom that lies in that truth. Who is right? How do we know? What are the best explanations?

Purpose in Form

Chapter 7: Religious Reading and Interpretation

> "Be not children in understanding… in understanding be perfect."
> 1 Corinthians 14:20

Leo Tolstoy describes his own frustrations with dissecting the religious literatures:

> The question of what I am with all my desires, was left completely unanswered. I understood that these studies are very interesting and attractive but that their precision and clarity are proportionate to their applicability to questions concerning life: the less applicable to the questions of life, the clearer and more precise they are, whereas the more they try to provide solutions to the questions of life, the more obscure and unattractive they become. (36)

Perhaps this is necessary for the one who is perturbed by the absurdity of life (and who is not a jnana yogi[*]), for one cannot steal another's pursuit of the

---

[*] Jnana yogi refers to one who follows the path of jnana yoga—the path of thinking or mind. It is one of the four accepted paths of yoga, the others being Bhakti, Karma, and Raja—devotion or service, action, and the "royal" path which is harder to explain in one word. These four paths also correspond roughly to the Jungian psychological types: thinking, feeling, sensation, and intuition (jnana, bhakti, karma, and raja,

mystery which they were called to undertake. One must find their own way, through their own efforts, rather than being handed a perfect answer which takes away the quest that lies before them.

But the complexity of searching for answers from the world is not just a product of the obscurities and misunderstandings of dissecting esoteric texts. In every aspect of life—religious, secular, scientific, philosophical, literary, etc.—there are people of high calibers, who operate with integrity and are earnestly seeking truth and not seeking to harm others to the best of their awareness. Equally, in each sector of life, there are those who are not only of poor understanding but are non-integrous and who have no notion of seeking truth and display a lack of concern for others, regardless of their words to the contrary. And society runs the gamut in between. People muddy the waters of the world greatly, and if we are looking for answers through what others have said and done, we are without doubt as likely to find people who destroy (consciously or unconsciously) our ideals as we are to see those who appear to uphold them.

If we look at the worst examples of any category of answers to life's questions, we may come to the conclusion that the category as a whole is an evil. Anyone who denies this can only appeal to their own ignorance of the shadow side of their favored arena; and thus their ignorance proves the point in itself. But neither is this to say that all causes which have at least some upstanding citizens must be good in the end.

If we are to take the exemplars of a doctrine or practice as those who have become good people while playing that particular game, we may also fall victim to ignorance—our own or that of others—in that we may look to people who act well for no discernable reason included in their particular field. For example, David Benatar may be a great man on the whole. He may care for others, give to charity in the most effective way possible, look out for his family and neighbors, etc. Yet such acts do not redeem the objective reality that the doctrine he espouses and propagates is one that is wholly evil and detrimental. It is only by our inability to see clearly the roots of our own actions and the incoherencies of all thoughts that there appears this illusion that antinatalism may be separate from murderous nihilism.

---

respectively). Each is accepted as a valid path to attaining union ("yoga") with the divine.

Religious Reading and Interpretation

And we cannot ever entirely remedy this ignorance, for we are fallible and life is infinite. So we cannot hope to use this frame of judgement for or against a doctrine or aspect of life, regardless of how convincing we find it in confirming our preconceived notions of the quality of the section in question. In other words, though "ye shall know them by their fruits" is a nice sentiment, and may work in some cases (and always works *in theory*), it is defeated by human ignorance, in that we cannot in all cases accurately trace the rotten or wholesome fruits to their true main trunk and source—at least not by ourselves, in consistently virtuous acts of clairvoyance (Matthew 7:16).

"What matters is the integrity of the thoughts, not the personalities of the thinkers." (Pinker, 14) We must look at what the doctrines say, what they mean, not just to ourselves—throwing them in a positive or negative light as we prefer ("No true Scotsman…")—but to others of different temperaments. We must look to those who do good and say, "Are they following this doctrine to a reasonable degree? Does it support their actions and world view without an inordinate amount of stretching and buttressing from unseen assumptions and unknown other faiths?"

Equally we must look to those who take the meaning of a doctrine to places of evil and say, "Are they following this doctrine to a reasonable degree? Does it support their actions and world view to an acceptable degree as above?" If we find, through collective examination and much deliberation, those who use the doctrine for good are indeed using a valid interpretation of the doctrine and those who are using it for malicious intent and harm are using a gerrymandered version of the doctrine or otherwise altering its expressions to suit their needs, then the doctrine can on the whole be called good. If the reverse is true then it is bad. And if there are reasonable interpretations which support either side then the doctrine may be neutral or imperfect.

The use of others' interpretations is a key element because it is absolutely true that doctrines have multiple meanings—and that they can have multiple true meanings. If we assume that our interpretation is THE interpretation, we are woefully ignorant. In other words, we are fallible, and we reason best together, in a culture of open conjecture and criticism.

However, while recognizing our fallible nature, we cannot pretend that there is not an objective correspondence between a true interpretation and the text itself, as well as an objective absence of correspondence between a false interpretation and the text itself, even if we can never get unanimous agreement on anything. That is to say there are not an infinite amount of ways to interpret a text or doctrine which hold true and enclose the intended meaning. Life is a complex, difficult, and indeed infinite game. But that does not mean that it is an impossible, hopeless, and meaningless game—regardless of the feelings of despair and frustration its great difficulty brings.

Against Ultimate Relativism

While an extreme skeptic can never be convinced that we know the necessary and actual meaning(s) of a text as the author intended[*], it is impossible to reasonably believe that this means that all interpretations are valid.

If I write the words "petunias are pink" one cannot reasonably interpret that to mean that "dragons exist in alternate dimensions". Even if we are personally unfamiliar with petunias and we question the nature of qualia between persons, we are nevertheless constrained to a limited number of appropriate direct interpretations. Though the number of interpretations increases dramatically as one moves from a statement of fact or perception in isolation, to a large literary story of varying allegory and historicity, the principle remains intact. We can disagree about various interpretations of "God the father" or which "these" Christ asked Peter about, but "God the father" does not become "batman likes cake" nor can Christ reasonably be talking about more than a few possible entities when he ambiguously says "these" (John 21:15).

And beyond ruling out the obviously absurd interpretations, we can further refine our understandings of texts by looking at the explanations for the words that are offered and see which line up best with other contextual elements. There may still be multiple contenders for the "actual" interpretation, but there are not infinitely many, and there is a discernable difference between the true and the false, even though there may be many which fall into the category of "possibly true". And, generally speaking, it would be hard to come to a point where a sentence seemed validly interpreted in two or more ways which directly contradicted each other and the answer could not be found by comparing the interpretations to implications in the surrounding text[†]. Even in

---

[*] This is merely the problem of other minds injected into literary analysis.
[†] This consideration excludes the immense problem of translation, in which such a scenario is not nearly as hard to come by.

such cases though, that quarrel over meaning does not demonstrate that there is no truth, merely that we are not perfect in communication or understanding.

Thus, if we can accept the reality of a true meaning in a text, and we are able to look at various interpretations and the actions they breed, we may be able to determine the quality (in regards to its truth and ethical nature) of any text (assuming it is one which makes truth claims). Or, in a much more reasonable and humble pursuit, we may content ourselves with not judging some text or work as a whole, but rather judging the individual conjectures and claims that a work contains, and discussing and discerning their nature individually. Of course this process is fallible, so there will always be some doubt. But one can recognize fallibility, reject dogma, and practice tolerance, and still not conclude that this necessity of perpetual doubt or lack of closure means that all interpretations and valuations are relative to the point that their adoption is arbitrary and meaningless.

In any point of contention, there will always be holdouts, there will never be unanimous consensus between all humans, especially across all time, and there is always the possibility of learning more and seeing more of what is there; but modern relativism seems to take the naïve position that once we fully understand any given viewpoint, no one who makes a sincere effort can be wrong—everyone is correct in some way, from some point of view; everyone deserves a participation trophy, no one deserves to be wrong; there is no failure, only oppression. But we are all wrong about a great many things all the time. And our lives are all full of failures.

Certainly understanding is a virtue; certainly it is the case that we often dismiss what we don't fully understand and miss truths and valid perspectives that we could see if we were less sure about the finality of our own point of view. And, in some sense, it takes a certain amount of closure and finality to say someone is wrong on some issue. But the world is complicated—life is a difficult game—and these things can all be true at the same time.

It is the case that we never know everything, that there is always doubt; and it is also the case that many points of view and arguments—no matter how sincere the effort made to construct them—are simply wrong. In other words, the reality that we will always be infinitely ignorant, which is a necessity of our finite being within an infinite universe, does not contradict the fact that we are "universal explainers" and have real (and infinite) potential for understanding and effective knowledge (Deutsch, 146).

Purpose in Form

Relativism in the end seems to be a despair brought on by the expectation that knowledge should be justified; that we should have some assurance of finality and infallibility. The despair brought on by the reality of our complete fallibility and the non-existence of any justification for knowledge uprooting these expectations causes the intellectuals lamenting the loss of their beliefs and expectations to declare grand theories of meaninglessness and the lack of truth. But this is not a coherent position, only an intellectually formulated cry of emotional upheaval by those most devastated by the loss or defeat of their desired and expected theories.

That all being said (which was sadly necessary*), there are therefore valid and invalid criticisms of any doctrine or discipline. Some are distorted and ignorant claims rooted in personal prejudice and misconception, positive or negative. Some are valid faults, and some are valid praises.

Popular Examples

One example of an invalid criticism, which is used in sweeping dismissal of all scripture (and there are many like it that are invalid for the same reasons) goes "the bible condones slavery" (and therefore it is bad)†.

Nowhere in the Bible does it say that God loves slavery, or that slavery is a necessary element of life, or that people were good for having slaves. It does

---

* I invite you to also look at Peter Boghossian's pedagogical approach to refuting ultimate relativism, found in his book *A Manual for Creating Atheists*, and Steven Pinker's conclusive argument uprooting it in his book *Enlightenment Now*.

† Or take Harari's sweeping political assertion—and myopic assumption of all-encompassing interpretive authority—where he implies that *obviously* Jesus was a socialist (or would support socialist programs), and a pacifist and would have a problem with people owning guns: "Consider a typical Tea Party supporter who somehow squares ardent faith in Jesus Christ with firm objection to government welfare policies and staunch support for the National Rifle Association" (296). Reza Aslan, an undeniable liberal by any account (and therefore no Tea Party supporter), would undoubtedly have something to say about the clear underlying assumption that Jesus was a pacifist, as well as his view on violence and weaponry, and his affinity for government programs—whether they claimed to be for the people or not. (Or one could see from his scholarship that there is a case against such pigeon-holed characterizations, though given his partisan political descent Aslan might now sacrifice integrity for teamsmanship.) Beware of any forwarded argument, based on a single interpretation of a single quote which entirely supports your political ideas on the point in question and portrays the opposing side as morons missing the point.

Religious Reading and Interpretation

recount many events in a world where slavery was a normal practice and it refers to individuals being blessed and loved by God, even those who had slaves. The letters of Paul which address slavery (translated and framed as "servitude") do not in any way say that God commands slavery and/or that slavery is a permanent and necessary element of creation, but rather focus on how "our unity in Christ must be more important to us than our earthly relationships" and that masters should treat their "servants" well (introductory text to the letter to Philemon, KJV).

It is, therefore, invalid to stretch this into an interpretation which says "the Bible condones slavery". It does not[*]. In fact, numerous times within even the Old Testament, God's purpose is described as coming to "break the yoke" of people's enslavement (Nahum 1:13; Psalms 68:6; Jeremiah 28:2; 28:11; 30:8; Ezekiel 30:18; Isaiah 10:27; and many others). And Hebrew law required slaves that were Hebrew themselves to be freed after a certain term of service, often at most 7 years. It also required Hebrews to shelter a servant fleeing from their master and not return them (Deuteronomy 23:15-16).

And, again, Paul was urging Christians to moral and truly compassionate consideration and treatment for their servants[†]. Drawing on these ideas, Dr. Jordan Peterson makes a compelling argument for how the Bible laid the foundations for the ending of all slavery, as well as many other improvements in universal human rights (Peterson, 186-187). "Christianity made explicit the

---

[*] Passive acceptance of the way of the world or even not doing as much as you should have (either way you may make the case here) are not the same thing as condoning and promoting; this is the lie of "silence is consent" (which is only true in some extreme scenarios—and even then does not rise to the level of holding the meek equally accountable to the malevolent), or, more plainly, "if you're not with us, you're against us". These things would only be broadly true in a static and binary world where all morality was completely known and prescribed and agreed upon by all—where good people knew they were good and evil people agreed they were evil and there were neither grey areas nor areas of multiple conflicting values and risks. Given that zero of those requirements are met by the real world, there is limited applicability to the truth of those statements; though they are appealing and effective for those who want to foment moral (and probably physical) warfare.

[†] Even though, by today's standards, we may believe it obvious that what we consider any reasonable degree of morality and compassion rejects slavery outright—which makes a good case for genuine moral progress, which some people are skeptical of today—we must understand the genuine progressive element these instructions had at the time.

surprising claim that even the lowliest person had rights, genuine rights." (Peterson, 186) "Where the Spirit of the Lord is, there is liberty." (2 Corinthians 3:17) "God hath shown me that I should not call any man common or unclean." (Acts 10:28)

Now one may gripe about the parochial view of the Hebrews and say they should have extended their views to ALL slaves and love to ALL people at that time (rather than having to wait for later cultures to coax these ideas out into manifestation), but that is to have a problem with human history and human ignorance, not the Bible itself, and it does not mean that, though they were ignorant about many things, ancient peoples did not know some things well—or at least get some things right, regardless of their ability to explain and delineate them. "To view the past with some degree of forgiveness is among other things an early request to be forgiven—or at least understood—in turn." (Murray, 179)

Equally, one may erroneously claim in sweeping nature that the Bible is about peace and love. While there is an argument to be made that the true interpretation and reading of the Bible as a whole points to some form of merciful and benevolent conclusion, to say that the Bible is solely "about" peace and love is wrong on at least some valid analyses.

There is, for example, the time David—the future righteous King of Israel—went out to slaughter a neighboring people and brought their foreskins to the current King Saul as a dowry price for his daughter, and Saul had a great pile of foreskins sitting before his throne which he appreciated as a tally of revenge on his enemies (1 Samuel 18:25-27). Saul was not extolled as the greatest king or exemplar of Judaism, but he was not condemned as the worst either; he started very gifted, blessed, and righteous, but fell from wisdom and favor as his covetousness of his own power and refusal to let a new and greater King take his place. David is one of the archetypal Jewish forefathers and Jesus' lineage is traced back to David in effort to assure Jesus' legitimacy as a Jewish messiah. Yet David had no shortage of blood on his hands (among other things). And Reza Aslan, in his books *God: A Human History* and *Zealot: The Life and Times of Jesus of Nazareth*, details a plethora (though I am sure far from exhaustive) of examples of God's vengeful and blood-soaked nature.

The Bible is full of violence. If by "about" we mean "what it contains", then the Bible is about more than just peace, love, and mercy. It is certainly about a

Religious Reading and Interpretation

race of violent, prejudiced, ignorant, and often malicious and cowardly and vicious animals—namely Humanity. If by "about" we mean, what are the messages it seeks to get across, then we come to a more nuanced and contentious issue where on the whole it may be more right to say that the Bible is about peace and love and a merciful God, but at the very least there will be many who offer the possibly valid critique that a book which seeks to impart such a message would do better to avoid the dark methods and subject matter which the Bible uses and contains[*], or to at least go about it all much more directly[†].

There is also the complicated issue of how the Bible is (and all religious are) disseminated, studied, and brought to life in ongoing cultures. Not everyone is encouraged, let alone does, read the book of Numbers or Deuteronomy. People may hear a few quotes from Leviticus, but do not know that it was mostly laying out the rules for the priestly class alone of the Hebrews. And probably many don't even read the more popular sections that are taught, they just know a few quotes from Matthew, Mark, Luke, and John, in who knows what level of context. And there are plenty of literally false interpretations taught out there, even under the auspices of the Churches. Further there is the fact that "a church can preach grace perfectly and offer something else."[‡] (Kautz, 84)

Additionally, consider that the Bible is not the sole informing text of Christianity, just as the Torah is not the entirety of the Jewish cannon of faith, nor the Vedas the entirety of Hinduism. Christianity, though, is a peculiar

---

[*] In the end I think we can say that such a critique, while valid to bring up, is actually mistaken; Joseph Campbell takes up this point when he says of the Bible, "[It is] the utterly sinful course of human history. It's all there—told with love." And, "The sign of the cross has to be looked upon as a sign of an eternal affirmation of all that ever was or shall ever be." (Campbell, 143 & 145)

[†] Though this complaint is also misguided in that it is not a problem with the Bible, per se, but of human consciousness—it is to prefer modern analytical philosophy over ancient allegory; it is like asking to be provided with pictures of people in cars from ancient Rome because you don't like chariots. That is what they had at the time. They didn't have an approach of straightforward analytical discussions of meaning; they had allegory. Wishing ancient people were more clear and direct is, again, a complaint about human ignorance and the development of human consciousness, not about the value of the contents of the Bible.

[‡] "This people draweth nigh unto me with their mouth, and honoureth me with their lips; but their heart is far from me." Matthew 15:8

Purpose in Form

example because this is not readily recognized or admitted in all contexts. The Old Testament makes clear that the Jewish faith was continuously updated and reinvigorated with the emergence of prophets throughout the ages. And in the common era the Talmud and many other Rabbanic and other sources are taken together to inform Jewish life, practice, and faith.

Christianity in some ways claims on the surface that Jesus was the last and ultimate prophet—for he was much more than a mere prophet: he was the messiah—and thus there is no need for anything beyond his life and testimony. But it is nevertheless true that centuries of additional writings, explanations, extrapolations, and even new inventions have built up and formed the Christian tradition into far more than what Jesus lays out in the Bible. Figures like St. Thomas Aquinas, St. Augustine, and even John Milton have greatly influenced, changed, and constructed the Christian metaphysical view and faith. And, indeed, St. Paul himself was the first of these great extrapolators and inventors—pushing the Christian faith to become something more than Jesus the Jew of Nazareth ever set forth.

So to read the Bible, or quote from the Bible alone, and say "Christianity does or does not support this thing" is an entirely incomplete and uninformed endeavor. There are many ideas and practices of the Christian faith that are nearly impossible to derive directly from the Bible itself without being previously aware of and informed by the inspirations of the great saints throughout the ages. Yet these all are valid parts of the Christian tradition (though many Christians would be loath to admit this in certain contexts, because the Bible being incomplete in itself weakens the argument of the Bible as the infallible word of God—see later discussion). And it is simultaneously true that most Christians, pious as they may be, never directly delve into the hagiographies that so greatly shape their tradition; it is mostly the monastics and the priestly class who distill these ideas from the broader dogma into the readings in their sermons and thus the faith and lives of their constituents.

For most people, religious quotes and ideas are cherry picked to support particular points of view, and though they may be appropriately interpreted or not, they may compose the mainstay of one's faith through life. However, we should not take this instance of human ignorance as pretense to judge the Biblical community unique in this disposition; and we can even say there is something about proper about this use of scripture. In the book *Autobiography of a Yogi*, Sri Yukteswar meets with an Indian Avatar akin to a Christ figure who tells him, "be like the wise ant who sifts through the sand and takes only the grains of sugar" regarding taking meaning and truth from a "holy" place (Yogananda, 373). Focus on the actual good and righteous within a larger milieu which may be called by the same names but is not so uniform in spirit. In other words, he is told to cherry pick.

In some sense, this is what is done with scripture and indeed what should be done. Though this also insures, as a corollary, that many in opposition will do the same kind of cherry picking with their attempted criticisms and refutations. While on either side of the issue quotes ideally should not be incorrectly applied or interpreted (used in contraindicated ways considering the context), those general constituents of Christian faith truly need not worry about understanding why we bother preserving the names of violent kings alongside the edict "love thy enemy". Perhaps someone out there has written about the deep esoterics of the line of kings, and perhaps their interpretation is valid and even right, and that is why even the darkest depths of the Bible are holy. Or perhaps you can just read the words of Christ and know the prophets have only ever validly said love thy neighbor, all else is the orthodox conservation of information—be it good or bad—for the sake of knowledge (including our knowledge of our ignorance) (Matthew 22:37-40).

The point of scripture, and what is really important, is that it gives people the answers and structure they need, when they need it. As much as logically minded and analytical individuals might hate it and think it should be otherwise—supposing that we should all be reasonable from the ground up at all times (though that would be unreasonable of them as we can see through reason that this is not how our nature works)—the importance of scripture is not aimed at making everyone in the world literary scholars nor iconoclasts who refuse all claims of truth from authority. Mostly, the point of scripture is so that ordinary people, who aren't going to devote their lives to philosophical and literary pursuits, can go into a place of worship during a time of hardship and they can hear a particularly reassuring or encouraging verse and an entirely biased interpretation of it from a preacher which helps them.

Yes, the preacher is as biased as we all are, and his interpretation may be mediocre at best. Certainly it is ignorant, for he is a fallible being; and the person listening and gaining comfort from the sermon is missing out on a lesson in good old reason and logic; and he probably listens to the sermon as though it comes from an infallible source and has no inkling on the interpretive

Purpose in Form

complexities of analyzing ancient literature.

Academic and "rational" minded modern intellectuals steam at such institutions purveying modern ignorance and lowbrow sermonizing being substituted for the progress of actual thought. We will return to this dilemma at the end of the book in the discussion of the Christian tradition and the Gettier Problem of Knowledge, after exploring what the Christian tradition does get right. For now, let us say that the Western intellectual makes an error of hubris in thinking that the salvation of the world rests primarily in the prospect of all people becoming more liberally academically minded and educated—in all people being remade in his or her image, chasing his or her ideals.

It is certainly the case, as we have said before, that the spreading of the tradition of open conjecture and criticism, and a greater degree of doubt in authority and personal drive to knowledge, is immensely beneficial and significantly effective even though it will never be 100% effective—that everyone will not change their ways and become hardnosed skeptics and rationalists. Still, the idea that the salvation of the world lies in the complete (or anywhere close to majority) elimination of non-intellectuals is a deeply prejudiced and conceited, but widely held fantasy among the modern intellectual class (and probably existed within the class dating back to antiquity as well). "The rationalist delusion is not just a claim about human nature. It's also a claim that the rational caste (philosophers or scientists) should have more power, and it usually comes along with a utopian program for raising more rational children." (Haidt, 103)

There are many problems caused by narrow minded literary interpretations and "doxastically closed"[*] views on the world, it is true, and we shouldn't forget or neglect them (Boghossian, 49); but the chasing of a utopia of a monolithic intellectual reality is a danger as well—there is space in this world for non-intellectual approaches to life, as frustrating as that is to the intellectuals who would solve everything if only everyone would listen to them and follow their lead.

---

[*] This term comes from Boghossian's use in his book where he explains it as: "The word 'doxastic' derives from the Greek *doxa,* which means 'belief'... I use the term to mean that either a specific belief one holds, or that one's entire belief system, is resistant to revision." (Boghossian, 49)

"Deepities"

A critique not as widely spread as illegitimate memes like "the Bible condones slavery", but equally illegitimate, is the intellectually formulated criticism of "deepities" forwarded by Peter Boghossian.

If we take the appropriate understanding of knowledge creation from Deutsch's description, we can see that the accusation of "deepity" is at least severely overbearing and likely a product of mere prejudice. Speculation, conjecture, and pure intuition are all absolutely necessary parts of knowledge creation, and involve reaching beyond the bounds of our current understanding, and therefore formal terms.

Additionally, one can see the issue with the persecution of "deepities" through an analogy with Godel's Theorem. Godel's incompleteness theorems show that bounded systems of consistent ideas always fall short of universal applicability and comprehension, or conversely, that there will always be statements which fall outside the domain of the system, which may nevertheless be true or untrue.

Though there are have been many criticisms of applying Godel's theorem broadly to human thought (beyond arithmetic logic), it is not overly presumptuous to say that Godel's theorem casts substantial doubt in Boghossian's approach, rendering "deepities" meaningless in terms. It does not require us to clarify exactly our proposed basis of axioms for our current domain, nor that we be entirely sure that our analytical logic derives from an entirely consistent system, to note that, even if our system were entirely consistent and ideally defined, we would not capture all there is to know within those bounds.

Godel's theorem has been used to prove the non-mechanistic nature of the human mind, to great criticism. I think the work of David Deutsch describing the conjectural nature of human thought and knowledge creation, along with the support from modern psychology and neurobiology vindicates this notion and renders the use of Godel's theorem in this case a side issue. The creation of knowledge is something irrational, intuitive, and spontaneous at its core, not a mechanized product of preconditioned axioms. But as an inverse to the specious approach of deriving this conclusion from Godel's ideas, we can work backwards in conjunction with Godel's thoughts with more confidence.

Purpose in Form

Given that human thought in general is not necessarily a neat process of clear consistent systems of axioms and rules, and additionally that discovery or knowledge creation requires leaps of conjecture beyond limited systems anyhow, in the pursuit of knowledge creation and truth—even within the bounds of scientific inquiry—we must say things that don't quite make sense, that aren't completely meaningful in the literal analysis of terms we understand.

Even if we had a clearly defined set of basic axioms and rules which made up the bounds of our scientific knowledge, and we were miraculously effective at applying consistent logic to see what was implied and accepted within this boundary of knowledge, it would not be appropriate to say that anything which could not be found meaningful within these terms must be untrue or non-valuable. There are truths which aren't captured by our systems—coherent and effective within their own bounds though they may be.

Thus "deepity" is an illegitimate criticism of religious language and speculation which takes a necessary element in the process of all knowledge creation (conjecture beyond what we know already) as reason for its dismissal. The idea that we should be precise in our speech is important, and it takes a delineated metaphysics and a willingness to discuss this realm to explain and evaluate far-out theories. The accusation of uttering a deepity can only be seen as legitimate in some cases—where one is saying something but refusing to discuss the explanations and underlying assumptions with those who are also willing to enter into such metaphysical speculations (the latter being just as key as the willingness of the speaker).

But to dismiss all conjectures which necessarily proceed beyond our current systems of knowledge as deepities would be to dismiss all knowledge pursuit and creation, and to ignore Godel's proof that any such defined system is limited and lacking in its scope. Further, to limit oneself to accusing only spiritual and religious figures of "deepities" is to overlook the nature of the term "deepity" and the reality of knowledge creation as understood by the rational community—thus to use deepity as a prejudiced epithet is to be guilty of "deepities" yourself; without explaining and understanding the term "deepity" one makes it seem like a legitimate criticism through intellectual prejudice, though the reality of the term is something that negates itself as legitimate criticism and thus has no real meaning in rational terms—"deepity" is a "deepity".

Religious Reading and Interpretation

<u>Taking The Bible Literally</u>

In case it was not already clear from the context, though I see significant utility in traditional scriptural readings which do not necessarily foster the kinds of doubt and inquiry essential to intellectual endeavor, I do not support a fundamentally literal reading of the Bible. God created man to be fallible, shall he have created a book—through man nonetheless—that is less so? In this section it is appropriate to discuss the issue of reading the Bible as the indisputable word of God, not so much because it is something that can be combated directly in this manner of discussion, but more because it is perhaps the most popular scapegoat all kinds of secularists use to keep western religious ideas at arm's length.

First of all, reading the Bible literally is absolutely impossible. Take any section of the Bible where God says he will destroy Israel and its people completely (Hosea 1:6 and many others), or that he will establish a particular throne or kingship forever (1 Chronicles 22:10 and many others), or any such categorical statement. Yet we know he did not.

Or take, for example, how many times he says he will do such and such and then people will *really* know this time that he is the grand actor behind all and all things will be well. Well he does over and over, and people don't get it, they ignore the signs and keep sinning. Is God failing? Is God ineffective? Does God only have one strategy at his disposal? Does he not know what will happen? He is God is he not? So he could have destroyed everyone. He certainly could have made everyone know him in a less round about and error prone way (by, for example, descending from Heaven at Super Bowl halftime in human form and transforming nachos into fish and bread[*]). And he certainly

---

[*] Borrowing this example from Peter Boghossian, who attributes it to Bill Maher (Boghossian, 102). It is significant to note though, that although such claims are made (always somewhat in jest) that even if a grand miracle occurred before the eyes of the nation, that would not create unanimous belief. Atheists often ask why God does not make himself known in more grandiose and obvious ways. Yet Boghossian himself admits that even if he and everyone else in the world saw the stars in the sky aligned to say "I am God, communicating with you", everyone in their own language, he would not take this as sufficient proof (Boghossian, 82). Yet he also rebuffs a priest for not truly taking any evidence against the existence of God, even though the priest gives an example of what might work, though it's clear he wouldn't believe it. The fact is that if an enormous miracle occurred in the world and everyone saw it, we still would not

Purpose in Form

could have said that some people would listen and others would not rather than pretending that doing something would certainly make all people convert on the spot[*]. Was he lying? No, it's just not literal; it's figurative or evocative.

Most directly, if we are to really take the Bible literally, why haven't thousands or millions of Christians around the world plucked out their eyes and cut off their hands in repentance of their sins and prevention of future sins, as Jesus told them would be good to do (on several occasions)? (Matthew 5:29-30; 18:8-9) And shouldn't we all sever our corpus callosum to keep our hands from communicating with each other? (Matthew 6:3) Should we extract our hearts and tear them apart as a true mark of shame rather than merely pulling at our clothes or hair? (Joel 2:13) That is what is literally suggested out of the mouth of Jesus the Son of God and other prophets; why would we equivocate on such proposals? Do we not believe in His truth, and in the reality of the hell which he promises awaits for those who do not? Is this not the literal truth?

Or are we not committed to literally taking the Bible literally, as has obviously always been the case? One absolutely must and does read the Bible figuratively. There are only minor quibbles about whether certain passages may be literal in some cases, and people pretend to say that it is all literal when

---

have harmony. And atheists further wonder why smaller miracles aren't more common, as the Bible claimed they were around all the time. The assumption here is that, were a "true" miracle to occur in the world, we would all hear about it and have it as evidence to bring to the argument. But this is a clearly erroneous assessment of the world. If a miracle happened in the world today you'd never know, because people would ignore it, write it off, and doubt it. No one would report it except for publishers set up to speak to people willing to believe. You don't hear about miracles because you don't believe in miracles (just as you do hear about miracles because you do believe in them). Atheists who are genuine rationalists need to stop asking the questions about miracles because, recall, all-data is theory laden. No one merely "looks objectively at the evidence" (the miracle in question) and comes to a conclusion through a sterile process of reason. That is a bad explanation made by scientists (and believed by many) about the nature of the scientific process. Further, even the Bible says that the disciples forgot the miracles they saw (Matthew 16:9 and Mark 6:52), they doubted the resurrection (Matthew 28:17), and they struggled to comprehend Jesus' allegory and teachings when he was speaking directly to them (Matthew 16:12). So no signs or appearances will do the trick whether in Biblical times or ours (see Matthew 11:18-19 and Luke 16:31).

[*] There are times where God does say people won't listen but to try anyways. I'm generalizing though.

Religious Reading and Interpretation

insisting on certain textual absurdities that benefit them in the moment. Yet they still have their eyes and hands, so no need to take them seriously.

There are so many obvious absurdities about taking the Bible literally—or rather cherry picking parts to insist are literal—that it's really silly to even go over. And I doubt anyone who is reading this could make it this far into this book without already understanding or being open on some level to comparative reading of mythologies and allegory. But still, there are some important points to address in an effort to understand why the literal interpretation is so attractive to some.

Let's take the quintessential literal reading about the creation of Earth. Though the Bible is obviously full of allegory and metaphor (and Jesus even directly says he speaks in parable and coded speech, rather than direct and plain—i.e. literal—speech), in the course of various religious debates some sects have decided that everything must be literal and therefore the magical and dreamlike tale of Eden is a scientific document which accurately records dates, times, etc. from the dawn of human existence and, indeed, time itself (even though accurate recording of time is something we only came to gradually—take the Gregorian calendar for example). Thus, creationists deny evolution and scientific datings of the Earth and believe in a young Earth. Rationalists rally against this and many conclude that Christianity breeds stupidity (oh so rationally of them) and decide that none of it is acceptable in their lives or in modern sensibilities[*].

Why do creationists hate science so much? Well, this isn't the right question. The question one must ask about any (perceived) negative behavior is, "What do I or that person get out of it that keeps it going?" So, what do creationists get out of denying science and insisting on a literal interpretation of the Eden stories?[†]

They get a special kind of talisman. By adopting an adamant faith in an

---

[*] There are, of course, plenty of religious scientists who see no problem with accepting scientific truths and still believing in God the Creator.
[†] Ross Douthat wrote a book detailing the emergence of Christian Fundamentalism in America which probably has much more in depth analysis of several motivations for this phenomenon. It also discusses, from what I understand, how metaphorical reading of the Bible long predates modern insistence on any extreme literalness. I have not read it but I enjoyed his appearance on Bill Maher's show, and offer the suggestion on that basis alone—for better or worse.

arbitrary statement which they imbue with all the power of their God, they get the feeling of devotion and expect the rewards of faith. Essentially, they have created (or think they have created) a cheat code for life. They think they found a glitch with which to mine faith points. They construct an arbitrary test for their faith which they can always win at. Instead of having to face and deal with all the complexities, uncertainties, and therefore trials of the world, they find themselves among the lucky few who have cracked the code; they merely have to profess and enact incorrigible faith in a few textual absurdities, come what may, and they will get everlasting salvation[*]. That's a pretty good deal. And it's a lot like Zen priests who focus on burning incense offerings and chanting (see Dogen/Warner, 5). "Preposterous beliefs are more effective signals of coalitional loyalty than reasonable ones." (Pinker, 359)

Additionally, I can't help myself from posing my preferred problem with the young Earth creation idea; if the Earth is only about 6,000 years old—and the rest of creation (the universe) with it—what has gone on for the rest of eternity?

God is infinite and eternal, so he has always been. But he only *just* created life 6,000 years ago? What's on the other side of that 6,000 year wall in all the "sterile" eternity behind it? Why on Earth (or beyond it) did the infinite God make such a specifically small creation? If he created at all, why wouldn't he create an infinite creation?[†]

To the infinite and eternal, there is no difference between a 10,000-ish-year sized creation and an unending one. An unending space-time continuum does not take up any "more" of eternity than merely a piece of space-time creation

---

[*] Douglas Murray points out a characteristic of zealous dogmatists: that instead of taking contradiction as a sign for necessary self-reflection and reevaluation of their own ideas, they "rush towards contradiction… as anybody aiming at truth [would not]." (58) This is as true of Marxists, as Murray claims, as it is of religious fundamentalists who take contradictions as tests of faith to be doubled down on. Both avoid all personal responsibility for truth and reason and reject the impulse to change—to die and be reborn into a new information; to be re-in-formed. "The refusal is essentially a refusal to give up what one takes to be one's own interest. The future is regarded not in terms of an unremitting series of deaths and births, but as though one's present system of ideals, virtues, goals, and advantages were to be fixed and made secure." (Campbell, 49) "Satan embodies the refusal of sacrifice." (Peterson, 181)

[†] A similar argument applies to reincarnation; if we have/are immortal souls with the ability to incarnate, why would we come just once to the infinite creation?

which only extends 10,000 years (or any arbitrary number). That is the nature of infinity. "Infinity Hotel always has room for more." (Deutsch, 168) So, why did the infinite creator, of infinite power, supposedly just begin creation recently, and what was he doing for all of eternity just on the other side of 6,000 years ago?

In this sense, the Hindu view of the great cycles of creation, spanning billions of years of growth and dissolution before recreation, makes a whole lot more sense when one truly comprehends and believes in the eternity of God. I mean, sure, given that God is omnipotent, I suppose he could create existence in a finite space-time which effectively "begun" what we perceive as 6,000 years ago, but, again, why, and what's going on across the rest of eternity? Just nothing? All in all, I think a finite beginning to creation actually contradicts the idea of the immortality of life and the soul. If life is infinite, then it cannot have a beginning*. But that's just my take.

Now, don't be so hasty to take my words as scorn. Though it is essentially an unconscious drive, this denial of reason is still a fairly ingenious solution to the personal problems of confronting the world. Talismans work. If you can carry around absolute certainty in your God's love and protection from all things and there is a clear, concrete, and unambiguous path to follow to keep those things, it is no wonder why so many people take that path.

Modern intellectuals like to turn up their noses at the stupidity of these Christians, but we must understand that this is a very natural, human, and in some ways brilliant strategy, given the challenges of the world. Life is a difficult game. Now we may hold ourselves and others to higher standards than taking such easy routes out, but, if something is truly difficult, there will be those who fail, and we should not hate those who do fail as if it is an easy thing not to fail; that would be a contradiction of having high standards and thinking they are easily met. "Failure is the price we pay for standards."† (Peterson, 86)

Believing whole heartedly in our own fallibility and enacting all that entails is certainly a daunting task, and one at which we are, of course, also fallible. If

---

* Peter Boghossian takes the idea of an infinite existence to be an effective argument *against* God. This is because he is focused on a literal and narrow interpretation of God as "creator"; if existence always is and was, then there was no "creator" who begun it all. However, if one is seriously postulating that existence is infinite and eternal, one is merely positing the miraculous nature inherent in existence.

† "The law entered, that offence might abound." Romans 6:4

Purpose in Form

you are consistent in your beliefs and you understand human nature as it is, having high standards requires having compassion for those who fall short of them. "Who can have compassion on the ignorant, and on them that are out of the way; for that he himself also is compassed with infirmity." (Hebrews 5:2) More on the difficulty of the world later.

A similar situation occurs with those who believe categorically in the historical nature of Jesus the Christ, the one true Son of God. The figurative reading of Christ tells us that there is God within all of us[*], and that when human potential rises to its greatest heights, the impossible is actualized and heaven unfolds on Earth. "If he [God] is truly infinite and universally active, how can he be said to be more incarnate in Jesus than anyone else?" (Alan Watts, *The Supreme Identity*, 35).

From this position one can see many Christ-like figures throughout history (including Christ himself, the Buddha, many Saints and Bodhisattvas, etc.), and many to come. A reasonable fear some more fundamental Christians may have about this is that it doesn't capture just how miraculous and transcendent Christ was—or the infinite heights of human potential and divinity are; it makes it seem, perhaps more achievable, but it in fact sets our sites on merely the upper levels of the mundane, rather than the incomprehensible heights of Heaven. "For then alone do we know God truly, when we believe that He is far above all that man can possibly think of God." (Aquinas, I, 5, par. 3)

And it's a similar situation with the Theravada Buddhists and the Mahayana Buddhists. It is possible that if one begins seeing anyone who seems fairly erudite with a dash of humility as essentially Buddha-incarnate (or Christ) they will demean the human ideal and thus have a false doctrine. This is a valid concern; we need to be pushed past our perceived limits and not believe perfection is easily accomplished. "Buddhahood is… not automatic, and it is not easy." (Dogen/Warner, 42)

Joseph Campbell, who is no voice of orthodoxy, speaks to the validities of these various approaches, and himself even seems to value more the more traditional and apparently dogmatic conception:

> Jesus, for example, can be regarded as a man who by dint of austerities and meditation attained wisdom; or on the other hand, one may believe

---

[*] "Christ is all, and in all" (Colossians 3:11)

that a god descended and took upon himself the enactment of a human career. The first view would lead one to imitate the master literally, in order to break through, in the same way as he, to the transcendent, redemptive experience. But the second states that the hero is rather a symbol to be contemplated than an example to be literally followed. The divine being is a revelation of the omnipotent Self, which dwells within us all. The contemplation of the life thus should be undertaken as a meditation on one's own immanent divinity, not as a prelude to precise imitation, the lesson being, not 'Do thus and be good.' but 'Know this and be God.' (275)

On the other hand, however, if we believe God was only once on Earth as a human and will only come once more, how close is he really to us? Obviously the Christians believe and say that he is closer than close and that he does live with us, and that such a question is blasphemy; but when part of the Dogma literally says that God only lived as man one time several thousand years ago, that really does seem to separate God from us in some way. "The living images become only remote facts of a distant time or sky." (Campbell, 213)

Additionally it seems somewhat of an issue that God only came into human form in one particular culture and tradition. Why are we so lucky? Certainly it is not for any great virtue inherent in the Hebrews, since God himself was constantly mad at them and ready to give up on them. Of course His censure is a mark of His care, but certainly there was nothing particularly special about Israel over and above all the other cultures and peoples throughout all the world[*].

And if God is universally active and alive in the world (in the Old Testament he says over and over that he works through Israel's enemies—sometimes helping and aiding them—in the book of Jonah he even accepts another people's repentance and offers them mercy), why should we think that other cultures haven't noticed his presence? Why should we think that other religious traditions are not valid, divinely inspired scriptures which talk about

---

[*] The scholarly idea that monotheism is a unique creation of the Levant somewhere around 5,000 B.C. is one of the most flagrant examples of human ignorance and scholarly ineptitude. If nothing else I will gladly lay all my bets on the Rishis and Vedas of ancient India as spiritual equals or superiors to the Hebrews and Old Testament, including in their knowledge and love of the One God above all.

how they came to God in their ways, in their parts of the world? (See previous note) God is everywhere after all, and he is active in all human hearts. Why would we think no one else found him or could hear him?

Doesn't it seem more plausible that the idea that God only favors our particular culture is something created by human arrogance and in-group bias, rather than a reality of the omnipresent God—who is father of all humans and created all beings and cultures as they are—to only choose one culture as his preferred and favorite, leaving all the rest spiritually blind until they can humble themselves to be instructed by this one chosen race on how to be just like them?

> In Christianity, Mohammedanism, and Judaism… the personality of the divinity is taught to be final—which makes it comparatively difficult for the members of these communions to understand how one may go beyond the limitations of their own anthropomorphic divinity. The result has been, on the one hand, a general obfuscation of symbols, and on the other, a god-ridden bigotry such as is unmatched elsewhere in the history of religion. (Campbell, 222)

The other problem with the belief that God has once come and will come only once more is that we thus seem to live in purgatory. There is an acceptance that God is with us and we can chant his name and sing his praises and wait until he returns, but not much more. This is a common criticism that Christianity deemphasizes works in the world and thus allows for a certain level of apathy and neglect of one's duties. "It… strongly impl[ies] that the primary responsibility for redemption [has] already been borne by the Savior, and that nothing too important remain[s] for all-too-fallen human individuals." (Peterson, 189)

Again, looking to what one gets out of the perceived negative belief, it is a talisman effect. They have found the key and entered the code, now they can merely follow the formalities and await the reward[*]. Though the Christ figure

---

[*] To be clear, I believe there are many people who believe in the historicity of Jesus, that he was the sole Son of God, and that there will be a second coming, who are very good people and who work very genuinely to do good in the world. I also think, as I will explain later, that there is very good reason for the emphasis of faith and the Grace

creates a human ideal and gives humanity something to strive towards, in the light of such a judge, humans find ways to put a veil between themselves and Him—by placing him several thousand years away and now removed in Heaven, by saying he was really all God and not human at all, by turning to religious rituals for salvation rather than walking in his image, etc. "It is more worthy of God that He be born spiritually of every pure and virgin soul, than that He be born of Mary. Hereby we should understand that humanity is, so to speak, the Son of God born from all eternity." (Meister Ekhart)

Or, conversely, they find ways to elevate themselves above others as though they are closer to God or have a more privileged access to Him over other peoples and cultures (which denies the omnipresence of God, and thus separates one from having to deal with and comprehend the realities of a truly infinite and immanent God).

The Name of Jesus

Just to harp on a little more, and because I think it will be further instructive, another odd literal insistence is in the divinity of the name "Jesus", spoken in a particular modern language and accent (whatever they may be).

But Jesus' name wasn't even "Jesus", it's more closely approximated as "Yeshua", not that we would pronounce that right either, nor that it was written in those roman characters. If God gave Jesus his particular name because it was so holy and it represents so much, wouldn't "Jesus" as we say be far off the mark and thus not holy? I mean, when I meet a Spanish speaker and I say "Me llamo Roberto", my name isn't actually "Roberto", it's just what they know and say. Close enough, but it's not actually my name.

So what's the big deal about the name "Jesus" then? It's clearly been watered down and mutilated more than once before we even butcher it. Why should our rendition be particularly holy if the literal name is what is holy and important? And, equally, if God so loved the Jewish people and the Hebrew and Aramaic cultures and languages as his chosen and favorite, why should we gentiles think our barbaric English culture and language has any favor with God and captures any level of Holiness or Divinity when we recite the foreign doctrine translated into our barbaric language?

---

of God as the supreme element in life. I just think there are some noticeable pitfalls in the conception that lead some into traps.

Purpose in Form

The only coherent answer is that the literal name is not important, but rather it is the Spirit or embodied ideal that the name represents which is important—and it being a universal Spirit* and ideal, the language and culture is irrelevant as well. This is made all the more clear when, after the resurrection, Jesus is said to shapeshift and take on different forms (Mark 16:12). Thus the form is changeable, but the spirit remains the same and is what really matters.

While that is a perfectly coherent answer, and the appropriate one, it begs the question, "What's the difference between worshiping 'Jesus' and worshipping 'Buddha' if the underlying infinite, universal spirit incarnating in the flesh is what is important, and any culture can find and know God?" Now of course many Christians might object to the Buddha for certain things they think he represents or what they heard he said or whatever, but *if it were the case* that the Buddha represented the infinite Truth and Life incarnate in human form, wouldn't it be the same to invoke the name of 'Buddha' as the name of 'Jesus' since they are both just placeholders for the One Divine? Just sayin'.

But these kinds of questions don't even come into play, really, for those who are living "in the *name* of Jesus" (said with relish). They aren't raising the issues of translations and interpretations, and what effects those have had on their supposedly literal transcript of God's word in their hands. They've got a talisman which says (somewhat mysteriously) that the name of Jesus is holy, and to live in it is good. So they profess wildly, ecstatically, that they believe in the *name* of Jesus. Why the great emphasis on the name? Because the Bible says it's Holy. What makes it Holy? ...That the Bible says it is...†

You see, it's not a question of rational inquiry. It's a way of life, preformulated and prescribed, which results in ultimate rewards and glory‡. We may look down on this, and lament the loss of some applied rationality in the world, but again we must not think that the bar of rationality is some low standard we should all easily meet. We may wish it were otherwise, but that is just veiled disdain for human nature. Compassion for those who fail at the difficult task is the coherent and EFFECTIVE response for one who

---

* "The fullness of him that filleth all in all." (Ephesians 1:23)
† "He that answereth a matter before he heareth it, it is folly and shame unto him." (Proverbs 18:13)
‡ "But in vain they do worship me, teaching for doctrines the commandments of men." (Matthew 15:9)

Religious Reading and Interpretation

understands human nature and the difficulty of reason and progress.

The Infallible Word of God

And here's the other big one, the one that really drives modern intellectuals crazy, and—to be fair—it should. Modern Westernism is built on the belief in fallibility, which Deutsch points out is a tremendous achievement, and it is a core element of what allows us to prosper. So when people in our modern era turn to some figure or source as infallible, we worry they're going to bring down our entire society—they're not acting like "one of us". And it doesn't help that it's toward the tradition we have a history with, one that we don't look back on too fondly (whether or not such a feeling of animosity is warranted or not).

So, yes, as apologetic as you want to get for religion, if you want to stay on the side of sanity and real human progress, you can't consider the Bible the infallible word of God. You can consider it the word of God, whatever that means to you—that it conveys wisdom from God, that it contains the spirit of God, that God works through it, etc. It just can't be literally infallible.

And this isn't just some pet peeve we westerners have that you have to bow to. It's just the straight forward truth. The Bible is not infallible. That doesn't mean it doesn't contain wisdom. It doesn't mean that sometimes the ideas in the Bible you might consider outdated or irrelevant aren't actually good ideas that might help you if you could just humble yourself and be open to them. It doesn't mean that we are smarter than God and that we can arbitrate what is right and wrong perfectly. It just means the Bible is imperfect. We can see this. And we don't have to make strawmen out of the Bible condoning slavery or being about the suppression of women or whatever to do so.

We can talk for hours about how the Bible was constructed. It was constructed by men, and translated and changed many times, by men, for various reasons, including political ones (about as far from Holy as you can get)[*]. That's a classic criticism of this idea, and it's no strawman. You can believe that God worked with man to construct the Bible as it is, but that implies that the text was imperfect and fallible in the beginning (since it had to be changed so much) and that God worked with man to discern the true from

---

[*] "Full well ye reject the commandment of God, that ye may keep your own tradition." Mark 7:9

the false.

Thus, man has the capacity to find the truth in the texts with the help of God, and in that sense *is not the Word more in the mind of man connected to God than in the written page?* Why not have man first consult his connection to the word, rather than this piece of literature*? Is this not what Christ wants when he warns "Take heed that no man deceive you"? (Matthew 24:4) How are we to prepare for deception and the missteps of our faulty perception but by being skeptical and using our reasoning to the best of our abilities—as one would prepare for a thief in the night? Knowing our fallibility allows us to prepare and guard ourselves; pretending that we can infallibly trust the words of scriptures, prophets, or priests is to ignore the Bible itself which over and over again tells us that all these fail. "Believe not every spirit, but try the spirits whether they are of God." (1 John 4:1)

And further, if the Bible were made infallible somehow, at what point does something, under the workmanship of man become infallible? The Bible had to be changed, so it was fallible at one point, and if it is not now, then at some point man perfected it with the help of God. How do we know that happened? When did it happen? And why is that itself not one of the central miracles of Christianity, if it did happen?

Well, back to the issue we discussed earlier, if such a miracle were accomplished by men within the Christian tradition, their status would begin to rival that of Christ, or at least bring into question the idea that subsequent prophets (or saints) are still greatly relevant and required—thus uprooting Christ himself as the only and ultimate ideal and isolated source of wisdom and divinity. The Christian saints, of course, are there and are greatly important and influential, but this sticky issue of the dispersal of divinity and our fundamental role in the revivifying of Truth is skirted by simply not discussing it†.

Moreover, what does it even mean that the Bible is the infallible word of

---

* "Instead of making Christianity a vehicle of truth, you make truth only a horse for Christianity. It is a very operose way of making people good. You must be humble because Christ says, 'Be humble.' 'But why must I obey Christ?' 'Because God sent him.' But how do I know God sent him? Because your own heart teaches the same thing he taught. Why then shall I not go to my own heart at first?" (Emerson, 10-11)

† See my blog post "Our Fundamental Access to Truth" for more discussion of this idea.

God? If it is infallible, is it infallible in its speaking to our minds? Why then does not everyone who reads it understand it perfectly? Why should we need priests or study groups? Why are the saints so greatly revered if anyone and everyone reading the Bible is spoken to in the same perfect way and all "get it" equally? Why are the saints' insights greater than anyone else's?

Well, obviously our comprehension of the Bible is fallible, for we are fallible beings. But then *what good is it calling a book infallible if we are fallible and it is for us?* If we are the ones reading it and employing it, and we are fallible and may misinterpret or misapply it, in what way is the infallibility of the text of any concern or real in any way? Even if we are to consider it Holy and superordinate, we must still figure out in which ways we must surrender ourselves to its commands; the commands are still to be interpreted and extrapolated by fallible means—that is why the greatest and best interpreters and translators (the saints) are so important and so revered and have so shaped our views and faith—so where is there any infallibility?

The reality is the Bible is not infallible, that is plain as day. And it was really never meant to be. Again, "be not children in understanding" (1 Corinthians 14:20) The negative reality of infallibility is a doctrine of control—a way to suppress questions and thought—to maintain power. Western society sees this and reels at it. But nothing is so black and white and the Church is not a wholly evil predator that we must all merely wake up to and see for the evil it is. The positive and reasonable sentiment behind the idea of the infallibility of the text is to not let our intellect run away with itself and make up all its own rules and disregard wisdom from the past that it does not understand.

By holding the Bible as divinely inspired and forbidding the flippant editing or reshaping of the text, one maintains the integrity of ancient wisdom that the naïve and arrogant intellect would surely alter to suit its vision and "comprehension". Dr. Peterson calls this "refusing to subject your faith to your current rationality." (107) This is a wise approach. "Lean not unto thine own understanding." (Proverbs 3:5) But the transformation of that idea into the idea that worshippers should turn off their critical thinking capacities and just follow what the good book says blindly (as if that were possible and no translation and adaptation were going on) is perhaps one of the most clear examples of human corruption of sacred texts and ideas, and of our inevitable blundering fallibility.

Purpose in Form

"In the later stages of many mythologies, the key images hide like needles in great haystacks of secondary anecdote and rationalization." (Campbell, 213) "Discretion shall preserve thee, understanding shall keep thee." (Proverbs 2:11) "The simple believeth every word: but the prudent man looketh to his going" (Proverbs 14:15) "The simple inherit folly: but the prudent are crowned with knowledge." (Proverbs 14:18) Let every man "examine himself" and "think on these things." (1 Corinthians 11:28; Philippians 4:8)

In fact, I would argue that one who reads the Bible, and ponders the events presented and the issues raised, is driven to the conclusion of human fallibility and the inability to rely on scriptures or prophets without thinking and discerning for oneself.

The prophets lie (Jeremiah 5:31; 14:14; 23:16; Lamentations 2:14; Micah 2:11; 3:5; Matthew 7:15). The priests forget their duties (Ezekiel 7:26; Zephaniah 3:4; Malachi 2:1-2). The people get lost and forget the ways of their God, no matter what writings and temples surround them; they fall away and misunderstand (Isaiah 6:9; 17:10; 30:9-10; Matthew 9:34; 11:16-19).

All those commoners who merely listened to their prophets and did what they said, over and over were punished for turning away from God—for *not* thinking and understanding for themselves; for *not* doubting their prophets and their priests' words (Proverbs 14:12; 15:5; 16:2; 17:10; 18:13; 26:25; Isaiah 1:18; 6:9; 17:10; Jeremiah 2:20; Hosea 4:6; 4:14; John 8:39). Think about this flagrant example: "Peter doubted in himself what this vision which he had seen should mean." (Acts 10:17) Even when God grants a vision directly to one of the chosen apostles, the meaning is not self-evident and requires discernment and judgement on the part of the individual.

Further, there would be no need for Christ if the scriptures and teachers were infallible—we would have been given all the tools from the beginning and never strayed from the truth so as to need a messiah. And why would Christ need to return if we weren't still so inevitably wayward?

What, then, are you supposed to do to follow God? You cannot indiscriminately trust and listen to your teachers, your priests, your prophets, or your personal vision for these all may lead you astray, even though the people are reading straight from the same scriptures as always and the visions come from God himself. So, does the Bible not implore us to doubt our teachings? Does the Bible not warn us to take nothing as infallible? Does the Bible not recount story after story of humanity meeting its downfall for being gullible and complacent and doing just that? Does the Bible not show us that our only hope is in individuals revivifying their personal connection to God and reorienting their faith where they have gone astray and helping others to do the same, beyond merely reciting the so called sacred texts in the same way as everyone before them?

In fact, Mark extols us to love God "with all the *understanding*" as do many proverbs request our discernment, judgement, understanding, and knowledge—learning, reasoning, and reconsideration (Mark 12:33 emphasis added; Psalm 50:23; 111:10; Proverbs 2:11; 3:4; 9:10; 12:1; 14:18; 15:5; 25:2; Isaiah 1:18; 17:10; Hosea 4:6; 4:14; 6:6; Haggai 1:5; 1:7; Zechariah 7:9) And Paul is said to have "reasoned" with doubters and to "persuade" them (Acts 17:2; 18:4). Are we then not called to use our powers of reasoning to see the truth the scriptures often obscurely point to? And Paul calls "unreasonable" men "wicked", while praising those who "received the word with all readiness of *mind*, and *searched* the scriptures daily." (2 Thessalonians 3:2; Acts 17:11, emphasis added)

So there is no way a modern intellectual can take the Bible as infallible—it is not part of western tradition, western tradition is about fallibility for all, and the Bible is clearly illustrated as a fallible document when one studies its history and origin and the remnants of older traditions embedded in it. And further, the Bible itself seems to tell us not to take it as infallible by highlighting the dangers people have fallen into for millennia for doing just that. So the idea of infallibility must be a fallible creation by man and the Church, which the latter of course does not escape the universality of fallibility[*].

---

[*] Additionally, take the Pope for example on this. How many times can the Pope rewrite Christian tradition? Given that the Pope is supposed to speak the infallible word of God, how can one Pope correct another without admitting that Popes are flawed and thus not speaking infallibly for God? The truth is, whether we are Catholic, Protestant, Muslim, or Jewish or come from any other tradition, we may say we believe in something's infallibility, but we are always (consciously or not) acting out our beliefs in fallibility by rewriting and correcting certain errors of human interpretation in what was supposed to be and is often still held to be some "infallible" realm of Holiness where human mistakes are prevented by the Divine. We all know it's not true. We could see it if we just looked. But the idea of infallibility makes things simpler, just like our commitment to textual absurdities.

Purpose in Form

<u>Don't Forget the Truth</u>

Now these are all good places to work on some "doxastic openness"[*], but before you all get too wrapped up in other thoughts about how many ways we should revel over Christians' shortcomings, do not forget "the beam that is in thine own eye" (Matthew 7:3).

Those of you who dismissed religions and looked to science, or looked to new age spiritual movements that, like western intellectualism, proposed the purposelessness of form (like nihilism with a little curry powder on top), do not forget what you have done in your distaste for the poor exemplars of religion. In focusing on the shadow of religions, you said "I cannot stand by these people", and you separated yourself and took a stand on the opposing ground of untruth—of finitude, meaninglessness, and annihilation. In your obsession with others and your focus on their shortcomings and inadequacies, you divorced yourself from the incontrovertible truth of the infinite and of meaning and purpose in human life, and you wed yourself to the doctrines of finitude, annihilation, and meaninglessness—a contradictory belief in nihilism and supposed truth and the honesty and care taken to share it.

Those of you who fell away from religion, for whatever reasons, left the truths therein and adopted untruths merely because you didn't like some aspect of the outer practices or trappings of the congregations. Abraham Heschel, one of the leading Jewish theologians and Jewish philosophers of the 20th century, puts it like this:

> Unless we realize that dogmas are tentative rather than final, that they are accommodations rather than definitions, intimations rather than descriptions; unless we learn how to share the moment and the insight to which they are trying to testify, we stand guilty of literal-mindedness, of pretending to know what cannot be put into words; we are guilty of intellectual idolatry. (Kautz, 84)

You yourselves couldn't get past the literal interpretations and the actions of others to see the truth for yourselves. So never let yourself be so haughty as

---

[*] Boghossian's term which means "a willingness and ability to revise beliefs." (Boghossian, 51)

Religious Reading and Interpretation

to disparage the Bible thumpers and feel good about your decision to leave truth behind. I say again, how many of you decry the horrors of the modern world? How many ask in despair why and how school shootings have become so prevalent? And yet how many of you often doubt purpose in life and have tried to teach your kids both honesty and integrity and simultaneously (directly or indirectly) tell them that we are merely an inconsequential accident of the universe which will pass unnoticed and uncared for into the sterile void of dumb space?

All those who have let beliefs in materialism, annihilation, and finitude propagate around them have created this world[*]. Cause and effect. You must recognize the causes you have been putting in throughout your life and into the lives of those around you. Have they been the causes of faith and purpose? Or have they been the causes of nihilism, under whatever preferred veil it may be? "Thy way and thy doings have procured these things unto thee." (Jeremiah 4:18)

Now this is a severe accosting—laying modern horrors at the feet of individuals who are merely a product of the times. But the truth is we do create the world through our actions. That is the truth of purpose and meaning. "The ills attributed to the anthropomorphic abstraction called 'society' may be laid more realistically at the door of everyman." (Yogananda, 536) It is only the upside of nihilism that we have grown accustomed to that tells us we should not have to bear the burden of the horrors of the world around us. The burden of meaning is terrible[†]. But it is also pervaded by grace and compassion of a loving God, and the truths of the intimate connection and love of God for human form and our sinful lives helps make that burden lighter when we really need it.

This book will not be a detailed and dedicated dissection of scripture. In

---

[*] This is not to say that steadfast Christians bear no blame. Christianity has failed to keep up with the times. For the most part, Christianity has not known or figured out how to talk to modern intellectuals well. Their response to the intellectual nihilists has largely been a desperate reversal to fundamentalism. Few bridges across this divide have been successfully built from either side. But, again, we are here to work on ourselves, and this is really not a book for fundamentalists, it is a book for modern western intellectuals.

[†] "Should the feelings chance to become aware of the real import of the world's acts and thoughts, one would know what Oedipus knew: the flesh would suddenly appear to be an ocean of self-violation." (Campbell, 305)

that sense the proceeding discussion may seem superfluous. But I wished to give preliminary guard against the many who simply despise scripture as a rule; who believe religion is either mere superstition or confounding opiate[*]. I will be quoting from scripture and sources who are steeped in the religious tradition in question where I want to establish correspondence with my ideas. In so far as this is done, I believe it is important to recognize the complaints people have against religious interpretations and practice, as well as provide some recourse to their validity.

If there are valid interpretations of Biblical quotes that directly contradict the quotes I use here, which are not directly superseded by the Christian interpretation of laying the New Testament over and above the Old, or the important traditional input of the writings of various saints that sway the matter, then I may be in error claiming that my interpretation or line of reasoning is the definitive message given in the Bible (though it may still be the definitive interpretation adopted by a particular tradition, which may have chosen for valid reasons to favor it over the supposed alternate).

---

[*] In general, it seems to me that the strongest proponents of atheism and those who defend truth in religion aren't even attacking and defending the same things. The best argument against religion comes from Peter Boghossian who does not attempt to apply a literal scientific reading to argue against a literal religious reading, but rather objects to the pedagogical technique of faith which seems incompatible with reason. Boghossian is objecting to the way that people are coached and taught to think (or taught to not think) within religion. He is upset by the epistemology and methodology of reason and suppression of open question and criticism that he sees in the church. He, and others like him, don't like the idea of this area of modern society not cultivating a liberal western, academic approach to reason and thought in all aspects of life. Rational-minded apologists, on the other hand, are often defending or attempting to defend metaphysical conceptions of reality or differing phenomenological points of view on reality, which they see as indicated allegorically in the messages of scripture—bits of deep insight that we have yet to comprehend consciously in our rational minds. Thus, apologists often see benefit in certain attitudes toward life which are founded in a religious metaphysical conception of the world (seeing deep purpose and intimacy with a greater power than is immediately evident) and they believe these benefits should be kept alive, regardless of the source they come from or the ways they are instilled in people's lives. The most astute atheists object to the methods of installing these programs of perception and action because they believe it works against their ideals of making the world more open and rational. Really, the two parties are hardly ever having a real discussion or conversation, they are arguing two separate points of view about two completely different subjects of what is to be valued. I will give a full address to Boghossian's objections later.

Religious Reading and Interpretation

But I do not hold to the generalized claim that a selection of quotes from the Bible which epitomize its positive message are misused and misrepresented even though the Bible is replete with stories of violence, slavery, and all sorts of viciousness. This is perhaps the worst literary criticism ever concocted, though it passes for vogue regularly in much of secular society, often with people who have been supposedly "educated" in the world's top liberal arts institutions; you'd think modern western secular society could have come up with some really valid and foundational literary and philosophical criticisms of religion that would take center stage as this intellectual society's objections to religious dogma. But instead we get scripturally illiterate and invalid memes.

To give a particular example which illustrates the complexity of the issue, I read the King James Version of the story of Joseph for the first time. I could not comprehend what effect this story was supposed to have on me. It seemed to be merely a jumbled record of terrible things that happened, like much else of the Old Testament, and especially the early books. The scripture itself is sparse, and what is there in content is a record of the darkness of humanity—or so it seems. Then I watched the DreamWorks film "Joseph: King of Dreams" and I was brought to tears and moved immensely by the depth and beauty of this cultural story. The same was true of the story of Moses and the movie "The Prince of Egypt".

Imagine also if the same western religion-skeptics brought such a lens to their readings of the Tibetan Buddhist texts. The stories of Marpa and Tilopa— two of the great ancient teachers—are tremendously violent, vicious, and unreasonable. Should we merely read of Marpa's raging alcoholism and Tilopa's abuse of his student and call this a barbaric tradition? Or might there be valid and virtuous interpretations living in the peaceful religions that sprung from these stories, which we do not have the skill to perceive?

The content of the Bible, or any religious document, is only the beginning. What a culture does with it, how they tell it, and what they get from it and how they bring it to life are of immense importance. From these sparse pieces of dark history, the Abrahamic culture has drawn for centuries a narrative of redemption, humility, bravery, love, mercy, and human growth that is inspiring and immensely valuable. You could interpret the stories in a very depressing way—that the world is violent and unfair and that's the end of it. The horror we see is the end of the story and we should be horrified and despair.

But that is not what the Hebrews drew from their experiences, nor what

Purpose in Form

Christians now draw from them. And they take their interpretation to be a key element of their success and survival—their faith is not only based on a reality behind the horror, but that it is in following this faith in Grace that one makes it through the horror. "The problem of the hero going to meet the father is to open his soul beyond terror to such a degree that he will be ripe to understand how the sickening and insane tragedies of this vast and ruthless cosmos are completely validated in the majesty of Being." (Campbell, 125)

In that sense, any interpretation which *only* looks at the Biblical letter, divorced from all the commentaries and documents produced around it by that tradition and the life brought to it through communal worship, is entirely insufficient and invalid in any approach that attempts to speak about the nature of Christianity as a whole. One may read the Bible alone and comment in some arena of literary or historical analysis, but hardly is one qualified at that point to comment on the nature of the living religion which grows out of that text.

One final skeptical query before we move on to see what beneficial truths scripture has undeniably preserved for us—even as our society lost sight of them through "rationality"—is: is it possible that merely devoted attention to a long, difficult, and convoluted text may be a productive endeavor, or at least was for millennia among mostly illiterate peoples? Perhaps looking for the good in an enigma—like looking into a Rorschach card test and seeing only what you hold within yourself—is what creates the good in this case, and nothing more?

Perhaps that is all that religion has been all this time—people finding good in a vat of jumbled occurrences. Or are there actually things worthwhile to be seen in this morass of dark tales? Are the deep questions of life given more address in scripture than a mere mirroring pool for the human mind to fumble about in? Let's take a look at the answers religion gives to the question of man's relationship to the infinite, and how that lines up (or doesn't) with what we can conceive from a modern perspective of the infinity of life.

Key Term:

Deepity – an invalid criticism coined by Peter Boghossian of religious ideas which use terms in ways that are not clearly meaningful upon literal analysis.

Chapter 8: The Christian Ethic – Faith, Works in the World, Purpose, Integrity, and Redemption

"Aim high. Set your sights on the betterment of Being. Align yourself, in your soul, with Truth and the Highest Good. There is habitable order to bring into existence. There is evil to overcome, suffering to ameliorate, and yourself to better." Dr. Jordan B. Peterson (109)

Dr. Peterson continues:

> It is this, in my reading, that is the culminating ethic of the cannon of the West. It is this, furthermore, that is communicated by those eternally confusing, glowing stanzas from Christ's Sermon on the Mount, the essence, in some sense, of the wisdom of the New Testament. This is the attempt of the Spirit of Mankind to transform the understanding of ethics from initial, necessary Thou Shalt Not of the child and the Ten Commandments into the fully articulated, positive vision of the true individual. This is the expression not merely of admirable self-control and self-mastery but of the fundamental desire to set the world right. This is not the cessation of sin, but sin's opposite, good itself. The Sermon on the Mount outlines the true nature of man, and the proper aim of mankind: concentrate on the day,

> so that you can live in the present, and attend completely and properly to what is right in front of you—but do that only after you have decided to let what is within shine forth, so that it can justify Being and illuminate the world. Do that only after you have determined to sacrifice whatever it is that must be sacrificed so that you can pursue the highest good... The word that produces order from Chaos sacrifices everything, even itself, to God. (109-110 & 223)

I think this is a wonderful message and a deep reading in many ways. But I wouldn't say this quite captures the Christian ethic as a whole, nor even its prime emphasis. There are quibbles about what the tradition should emphasize, and what the original teachings do imply on this matter, but the emphasis on faith in Christianity is far greater than is obliquely implied here.

Dr. Peterson's hard work and striving based ethic has been called by Ben Shapiro an essentially Jewish reading and interpretation, since often Christianity is seen as downplaying works greatly. There are differences among the Christian sects contemporarily in this regard, and even more so over the centuries, so this difference is not so black and white. But certainly faith plays an essential element in Christianity which cannot be merely cut out or glossed over. And while I will do my part here to emphasize the Christian texts and teachings which should steer us away from avoiding work in general, in a later chapter I will make the case that there is actually a strong and legitimate metaphysical reason for the emphasis on faith and grace, regardless of the lackadaisical attitude toward mortal labors this may partially promote.

Works vs. Faith

It is a hallmark of Christianity that it emphasizes faith over works. Of course there are scriptural passages which hedge this and they still include the need for works in their doctrine. "Not everyone that saith unto me, Lord, Lord, shall enter into the kingdom of heaven, but he that doeth the will of my Father." (Matthew 7:21; see also 12:48-50; 16: 27; 22:40; Luke 6:46; 8:15; 8:21; John 8:39, Ephesians 4:1 and countless examples preserved in the old testament) But the general conception of Christianity is of being highly faith based (faith based healings, faith based salvation, etc.).

I will not propose here to scholastically or practically resolve the dichotomy

The Christian Ethic

and say that it is definitely one way or the other. But it is interesting to see that even in these extreme examples of abiding by ultimate faith, faith is considered to *do something*—in other words to act or to work. Is it possible that faith is merely another necessary action in the world? In fact, my favorite definition of faith comes from Leo Tolstoy who does not take it to be some sort of gamble or guess work, but says:

> Faith is neither hope nor trust, but a particular spiritual state. Faith is man's awareness that his position in the world obliges him to perform certain actions. A person acts accordingly to his faith, not as the catechism says because he believes in things unseen as in things seen, nor because he wishes to achieve things hoped for, but simply because having defined his position in the world it is natural for him to act according to it. Just as the farmer tills the soil and the seafarer sails the seas, not as the catechism suggest because they both believe in things unseen and hope to be rewarded for their activity (this hope exists but it is not what guides them) but because they regard the activity as their vocation… Faith is man's conscious relationship with the infinite universe, from which he derives guidance for his activity. (97-98)

This is no "deepity". It's a clear statement that your basic views of how you relate to life and whether you belong and have purpose cause you to act in specific ways, different from those with other foundational metaphysical beliefs. I believe Tolstoy unveils a key element of the way we as humans work: we behave in the world according to our basic orienting beliefs and what they dictate. This does not mean we do what we say we will or should, but rather, that our truly held, deep beliefs orient us and guide our actions. Or, conversely, that our actions reveal our deepest beliefs, the ones we truly believe in. Thus Christ rebukes his followers often for their lack of faith, judging by their actions or failures to act—overruling their continual verbal commitments and praises (Matthew 8:26; 16:8; 17:20).

With this lens of understanding for faith and action, we can see "there are no atheists. There are only people who know, and don't know, what God they serve." (Peterson, 225) Even the nihilists have some conception of the world—it being meaningless and cold and grim—and even though they cannot fully embody meaninglessness, this belief means they feel lost and disoriented and hopeless, and they act in accordance with this lack of orientation and the rising tide of suffering. In this vein, here, we will consider faith as a *causal* element—that our orientation toward the basic nature of life causes certain behaviors and attitudes, and that these are necessary in life—and explore the significance of this. In a later chapter, we will look at the nature of faith and its place in the world as challenged by Peter Boghossian.

Another variant of Christian expression that may be construed differently, but will not come to a different point is that Christianity emphasizes Grace over works. Grace may be differentiated from faith in that faith is on the side of the individual person, the conception they choose to take and cultivate toward life, while Grace is an aspect of God. Christianity emphasizes, and indeed is entirely centered around the idea, that God has extended himself into human life and history and it is primarily through that Grace of God—the will and involvement on God's side of the matter—that humanity has any hope of salvation in the first place, and indeed is saved in actuality[*].

Though this seems to remove us further from the idea of individual works, since all can essentially be laid on God, Grace is still an aspect of the world, or is involved in the actions of the world in some way and definitely has a causal effect. Plus there is the recursive idea that God works primarily through the seemingly independent actions of man, which essentially brings us back to square one. One can see why there is ongoing debate on the issue.

What is not up for debate is that in Christianity effects in the world and effects in individual lives are important; salvation, regardless of the name of its primary cause, is the primary concern for human life and it is a certain reality in the world and it can be, and has been, brought about by certain causes.

While the particular cause of salvation is of paramount importance to those in need of salvation, and those who hope for good in this life, there is something deeper underneath the text that is of primary importance to see first of all. And this, I propose, is the root of human belief which is demonstrated in the Bible, as well as pretty much everywhere else—again this is our universal truth: causality.

---

[*] "Something else besides humanity was rescued at Golgotha. It was *everything*. It was *history* itself... The *event* of the crucifixion, as shameful and grotesque as it was, was transformed into a thing of beauty and with it, *every injustice and every heartache we have ever experienced*." (Kautz, 88 italics in original) "God has descended voluntarily and taken upon himself this phenomenal agony." (Campbell, 223)

The Christian Ethic

This reflection on causality is not the content that the Bible centers its story telling on, but it does underlie every element of the text. Well of course it does, causality is the necessary basis of our being and self-conception! Indeed, it is as self-evident as purpose and meaning. But just as we have lost sight of the latter two, and have had to revisit these ultimate basics, so it may pay to take a closer look at our *belief* in causality and how it came about.

The Discovery of Causation and Becoming Effective Causal Agents

In the Bible, I believe the world view sketched out was one of humans who found that those who believed most completely in causality were the most successful or blessed. The earliest stories also likely come down from memories of a time when causality was a new hypothesis—when we first began to put things (including our hypothesized selves) together and realize, well, they actually went together. There is evidence for this in the creation story and the story of the fall; "Adam's waking to the fundamental constraints of his Being—his vulnerability, his eventual death—is equivalent to the discovery of the future… [and his new task to] work… is delay of gratification… [or] sacrifice… The discovery that gratification could be delayed was simultaneously the discovery of time, and, with it, causality." (Peterson, 164; see also Dr. Peterson's biblical lectures on YouTube for extended discussions of this idea.)

The early events of the Bible can be viewed as our discovery of causality; that things happened in a significant order, that events were connected significantly and that we could see patterns in occurrences and begin to interpose new actions (causes) which would create different outcomes (effects). "Our causal knowledge is simply the recognition of constant conjunctions of items or events in our experience, coupled with the expectation that the future will resemble the past." (Hume, xii)

With this hypothesis, we had tapped into causality and began to participate in the fundamental mechanisms of creation, rather than living in the utter chaos of the unknown blooming of existence happening all around us but utterly beyond our influence. Indeed, what "us" was there? "I" only comes about as the hypothesized center around which causal action can be effected. And we found this hypothesis supremely effective. This began the process of human cultivation, and the cultivation of the world, which are necessarily bound together, a theme which we will take up in detail later.

In the Bible, the prophets of the Old Testament are people who ask of reasons and causes, and those who search out knowledge: "It is the glory of God to conceal a thing: but the honor of kings is to search a matter." (Proverbs 25:2) "Come now, and let us reason together, saith the Lord: though your sins be as scarlet, they shall be as white as snow." (Isaiah 1:18) "Produce your cause, saith the Lord: bring forth your strong reasons, saith the king of Jacob. Let them bring them forth, and show us what shall happen: let them show the former things, what they be, that we may consider them, and know the latter end of them." (Isaiah 41:21-22) "To him that ordereth his conversation aright will I show the salvation of God." (Psalms 50:23) "My people are destroyed for lack of knowledge: because thou rejected knowledge, I will also reject thee... The people that doth not understand shall fall." (Hosea 4:6 & 4:14) Thus knowledge of the world was salvation and the ideal combination of courage, will, and humility to search out knowledge, accept reproof and correction from the world, and return to present this new information to society was the path to the favor of God[*]. "Whoso loveth instruction loveth knowledge: but he that hateth reproof is brutish." (Proverbs 12:1)

Unfortunately, two tools described repeatedly in the Bible as used by those of great worth and EFFECTIVENESS were left behind by Christianity and have only been recently revived in the Western world through other sources. These are 1) the commonality of attention to dreams by devout and blessed individuals, and the acceptance of God's presence and significant communication in dreams, and 2) the practice of meditation. These supremely effective tools will be discussed later in connection to their new living sources in the West. One wonders where we would be if their practice had remained common in society, rather than becoming forgotten—or at least relegated to esoteric wisdom practices—for some 2000 years.

God as a Conjecture Beyond What We Know

Now the people of the Bible didn't really know much about the world, did they? At least so we like to think, but let's run with that possible prejudice as our conception for the moment. They knew that they died; they knew that they needed to reproduce; and they knew that the survival of their family and

---

[*] i.e. the hero's journey, as we will discuss later.

The Christian Ethic

offspring depended on the cleanliness, trustworthiness, and numbers of their society. Or maybe they didn't even know these things, but it's what they acted out.

They believed that they could slaughter animals in the name of God and reap rewards (or at least, stave off wrath—which is a kind of reward if wrath is the norm). They believed that they could pray at an altar and receive forgiveness in the name of God. They believed that the proper separating of the fats of particular animals, or the appropriate animals on the right days for the right purposes made their sacrifices all the more sophisticated and effective. This intricate attention to the cause and effect of a sacrifice seems to give modern man evidence that these people didn't actually understand cause and effect at all! If they did, they certainly wouldn't have done all those ridiculous things, right?

But the people of the Bible didn't suppose they understood causation well, let alone fully[*]. They merely recorded and repeated what worked (or what seemed to; we can't always parse correlation from causation on the first go). In contrast, we seem to think our apparently larger understanding of causation can approximate complete knowledge, and thus that we can dispense with a lot of things from the past without giving them more thought, for there is nothing for us to gain from them since we are so superior in every way.

Today, people like to point out that ancient people's reliance on "God" was only a blanket term to incorporate everything they didn't know or didn't understand, and we scoff at this and many have tried to dispense with God as an impediment and even affront to our reason, to our exploration of causation. "'Serving God's purposes' is a placeholder for details that need to be provided." (Benatar, 38) "We give our ignorance the grand name of God." (Harari, 200)

But what could be more intelligent than saying "We don't know everything, but we do believe that there is a great web of causation that works in spite of our ignorance, so when we try to work with and through what we don't know—which is necessary in life, especially in the pursuit of improvement—we will call it 'God'"? "That which I see not teach thou me." (Job 34:32) "Lead me to the rock that is higher than I" (Psalm 61:2) How is it at all

---

[*] "The effects of creation are multitudinous, complex, and of mutually contradictory kind when experienced from the view point of the created world." (Campbell, 259)

intelligent to overview our accumulated knowledge in the modern era, which if understood at all only highlights just how much we don't know and how much the universe operates beyond our understanding, and scoff at the idea of recognizing that an order and purpose unfolds which is much greater than us? Of course the clergy for ages rapped our knuckles and told us so many areas of knowledge were forbidden, so we feel a bit cheeky about claiming all that former territory of "God" for our own. But how can we pretend, if we are at all concerned with truth and real knowledge, that there is still not an infinite beyond us? We are now, as ever, "only scratching the surface." (Deutsch, 175)

Today, some intellectuals believe that we will eventually gain knowledge of everything, so we do not need to rely on "God"; that is to say that since we have learned so much and our reach has extended back to near the big bang and to the horizon of our universe, we can expect to fill in all the gaps and eventually understand the "thing in itself" of the creation; and then our previous ignorance and the worshipped unknown will be proved only to have been a superstition that was holding us back.

This kind of reasoning, if it can so be called, shows only an inability to comprehend the greater orders of magnitude which comprise the unknown unknowns, as well as the leap of knowledge casually proposed from after the big bang, to the big bang itself. This view is epitomized in Lawrence Kraus' book *A Universe from Nothing* in which he constantly derides religion and God and makes sure you know all about atheism alongside the physics you came for, while simultaneously expounding his theory and belief that the universe is a miracle (that it was created from nothing) and that empty space or "nothingness" readily produces these miracles of creation all the time[*].

The idea of knowing everything and not needing a space for the unknown beyond ourselves is rooted in the conception of a finite universe. This has been refuted already with the refutation of finite existence and the proof of an infinite existence. We can and do know that the infinite is, and that therefore we will always be infinitely ignorant. And thus, the universe is KNOWABLE AS A MYSTERY.

Another hypothesis that gives intellectual credence to an oppositional stand

---

[*] Obviously Kraus would object to this formulation for many reasons. A longer discussion of this topic takes place near the end of the book as well as in my book *Jnana Yoga*.

The Christian Ethic

point to this archaic belief in supreme causality that we have been talking about is belief in randomness or chaos. But in such discussions we must distinguish between chaos as "what we cannot understand by our powers" and chaos which is completely causeless—that is follows no order or plan or rule of causation that is knowable to ANY consciousness—something that is fundamentally chaotic or random.

Now the hubris in the latter conception should be obvious, but it too is nonetheless considered part of the acceptable dogma in the modern intellectual world. We laugh at the faith and "superstition" of the past while we posit fundamental chaos—categorically denying the existence of a supreme (or even just higher) intelligence—and suppose that the entire universe can be contained in our own minds because it is finite—i.e. using the intimation of our infinite potential to propose the finitude of existence.

One cannot posit fundamental chaos without supposing supreme knowledge of everything. In other words, fundamental chaos is not a falsifiable theory, it is a faith and dogma—a belief about the core nature of life which extends beyond our knowledge, yet we choose to conceive of it in a certain way which orients our actions and attitudes in life.

If we can reign in our own hubris and properly comprehend our limitations and ignorance, we may in fact (if we are lucky) come back around to a phenomenological view of the world like those living in Biblical times experienced: an unknown world proceeding beyond ourselves outward to infinity—yet one that we are bound up in and experience as causal. We can not only comprehend, observe, and empirically prove *some* level of causality, but we can also use it, act with it, and improve our lives and our understandings, progressing ever higher in knowledge and efficacy. "Improving the world requires an understanding of cause and effect." (Pinker, 47)

From this perspective, we may put faith in an unknown overarching law of causation which is supreme; not necessarily the causation we suppose and posit extrapolated verbatim across the universe, but that there is an order and that things do proceed causally, and that what we have been able to see and come to know in some way is a derivation of this underlying truth[*]. We believe that we would not be able to operate by the miniscule and fallible rules of

---

[*] "The future Laws of Nature will bear as much resemblance to the 'laws' we know today as the cellular telephone does to smoke signals." (Radin, 278)

causation that we have begun to understand, if causation were not true fundamentally of creation; regardless of the accuracy or completion of our map, we do believe that there is a territory, a mapable (though not necessarily perfectly by us) underlying structure.

Working with God (Causation): Working Effectively and Ethically (i.e. Don't Be a Jerk[*])

The pursuit of human life and endeavor as illustrated in the Bible, then, was to dedicate oneself to serving causality and to becoming more causally minded; those who were the most blessed, were those who operated most effectively with causation. Though this modern interpretation of the biblical ethic probably sounds, to scientific ears, far beyond any appropriate level of apologetic—to the point of being disingenuous about the compatibility of biblical ideas with reasonable mindsets, and even fallacious in its attribution of early casual thinking to a time of magical thinking—I will contend otherwise.

First, briefly, from a scientific standpoint it should not be surprising that the basis of causal thinking *evolved* at first crudely in a time long before the notion of a "scientific theory" could even have been conceptualized or discussed. However, as Dr. Jordan Peterson has pointed out regarding Sam Harris and the new atheists, modern so-called scientific individuals like to suppose that reason and science were spontaneous generations of the enlightenment which occurred essentially acausally (i.e. miraculously), and thus could have emerged at any point; and therefore their absence in earlier times, and their only gradual acceptance since their spontaneous appearance, is primarily a tragedy and a mark of human failure, rather than the natural gradual process of human mental evolution.

It is much more realistic and rational to recognize that the enlightenment was a dramatic point of insight and conclusion resulting from (and nevertheless connected to and dependent on) thoughts and methods which were present in rudimentary stages long before and were developed (though certainly in less than theoretically ideal ways) in the traditions preceding the revolution of the enlightenment. The enlightenment certainly marked an inflection point in history, a time when much of the ineffective and even

---

[*] This is in reference to Dogen/Warner's book *Don't Be a Jerk* which I think offers ethical and spiritual advice that is extraordinarily compatible with the Christian faith.

The Christian Ethic

counter-effective dogma of ancient thought was discarded, but it nevertheless was a product of much previous effort and insight, however finely and viciously sieved this had to be[*].

Second, and more briefly, I believe that the view of causality in general as some comprehensible and complete theory which falls neatly into the sterile realm of modern science is overly presumptuous, to say the least. (It is, again, the fallacious theory of a finite universe.) We have successfully parsed an impressive amount of physical and biological causality—relative to human history—and this has occurred within a conception of the universe as an inert mass of mere physical expanse. However, relative to the nature of causality in its entirety—to the infinite—we know nothing and the connections and realities undreamt of that lie within the true depths of "causality" leave room for far more of what we might dismiss as "magical thinking" than modern scientists will care to admit or contend with.

Those objections aside, the goal of Biblical peoples, viewed through this lens, was to become the most efficacious in the world, and the goal of Christian life is to be as efficacious as possible in service to God and the divinity in all humans (that is to say, to be efficacious in a way that is iterable—in accord with eternal life).

The goal of efficacy can be seen clearly as the defining element of human nature and success in the world overall—not just that of Biblical peoples. We have done what is most effective and tested and moved toward the more effective, and it has led us to dominion as a species. Of course we have always been and remain fallible, so that is not to say that we took the quickest or most ideally effective route to our understandings of causality, nor that we will do so going forward. We muddle through as always.

Currently, we fight each other over what will be the next most effective step to take, or whether we should be taking effective steps in one direction or the other (depending on how we are oriented and what we believe is most pressing). But, once again this theme emerges: our muddled strivings are effective and we are better off with them than without them, regardless of our

---

[*] I will give a more appropriate level of praise to the successes of the enlightenment at the end of this book, so I ask the reader, for now, not to view this entire line of thought with animosity for the perceived notion that I look too romantically back at what crippled human progress and speak too accusatory at that which most greatly enabled it.

failure at the ideal.

Christianity (along with other traditions—it is undoubtedly just as present in the Old Testament, though perhaps more subtle) posited that morality was built into causality, that the definition of morality could be apprehended through the study of effectiveness in the supreme sense. This is key because short term efficaciousness could be immoral, but *sub specie aeternitatis* (looking at what was effective across time, over many iterations, and what worked across societies and geographies, etc.) it can be concluded that morality is the superior effector, which shows that it is part of causation.

Thus Christians deduced joyfully that, though there were extreme events (causes and effects) of darkness and viciousness in the world, and that these could certainly propagate, the fundamental structure of reality operated with acute concern for interpersonal compassion, forgiveness, understanding, and benevolence. "If ye love them which love you, what reward have ye? Do not even the publicans the same? And if ye salute your bretheren only, what do ye more than others?" (Matthew 5:46-47) "The wrath of man worketh not the righteousness of God." (James 1:20) "With well doing ye may put to silence the ignorance of foolish men." (1 Peter 2:15) (See also Romans 12:17-21; 1 Thessalonians 5:14-15; 2 Timothy 2:24-25)

The Cultivation of the Individual and Therefore the World: Man Transforms the World by Definition

The Biblical account of humans describes them as working and striving. Not only is it prescribed to man after his fall that work will be his lot, but also the very name of the race of the most blessed people is "Israel"—meaning "those who wrestle with God" or, through our new lens, "those who strive with causation". Man sees the future, he knows danger and evil, and so he works to ward these off. There is always more to do, more to take account of, and more to defend against. "The present is eternally flawed[*]." (Peterson, 94) Those who progress the most, who work the most effectively, do the best and drive humanity forward. Their descendants build off this and move forward more. (Ideally speaking of course.)

Humans that know about causation and the future (i.e. who have knowledge

---

[*] Though an "eternally flawed" arena would be the perfect setting for a fundamentally creative Being.

The Christian Ethic

of good and evil) get to work. We are a working species because of our state of consciousness and knowledge. It is natural and inevitable that humans work, as the Bible stated. But it is also natural for humans to progress in their work, given their knowledge of causation and fruitful and cooperative communities.

"Human beings are world champions of cooperation beyond kinship." (Haidt, 87) Humans—being working and striving and progressing beings by nature—are also necessarily transformers of the world. "All animals are entrusted to their own prudence and skill for their conduct in the world, and have full authority, as far as their power extends, to alter the operations of nature. Without the exercise of this power they could not subsist a moment." (Hume, 100) The Bible acknowledges this also, calling man the steward of the earth.

Man works both on the world and on himself. He finds what is most effective in the world, through action and invention, and he seeks to become more like that, to live more in that way. "He identifies with the part of himself that could transcend his current state, and becomes the hero of his own adventure." (Peterson, 329) In molding himself toward an effective (i.e. successful) ideal, he increases the power his energy output has over his environment; the more effective he becomes, the more power he wields. "We are shaped and informed by what we voluntarily encounter, and we shape what we inhabit, as well, in that encounter." (Peterson, 279) This is all merely definitional.

So long as we correctly understand ourselves and our consciousness, we will accept this part of our nature. "Our actions are part of who we are." (Dogen, 40) Knowing that we are both universal explainers and universal constructors (and the connection between the two), we know that we are destined to transform the world. The Bible recognizes that man has dominion over the Earth because of his consciousness. We can debate the morality of this stewardship, but we cannot pretend that this is an unnatural aspect of our being—some socially constructed and permitted anomalous activity that was bred by the Bible recognizing this reality and implanting it in our culture, creating a self-fulfilling prophecy. No; we, by our inherent nature and consciousness, work, grow, and progress, transforming ourselves and the world alike.

Even if we were to learn more about the long term effects and prospects of our current activity and see as a species that our actions would not benefit us in the long run; and were then to decide to drastically limit ourselves in our transformational activities as they apply to the environment, this would not negate the truth that "the landscape we live in is the product of ideas", because the preservation of natural features would still be the product of our knowledge and actions—though they would be actions of restraining or otherwise controlling our effects (Deutsch, 429). Human consciousness and potential, as it is, has determined that our world is what we choose to make of it—the animals and the environment are under our stewardship and subject to our effects whether we would have it that way or not.

Perhaps the Bible just got lucky on this one[*]; perhaps the proclamation to Adam was just the lusty wishful thinking of primitive man under self-centered delusions of grandeur, but they really only were commenting on the limited world they knew and man's ability to create tools or farms. Perhaps the Biblical people never dreamed of the true immensity of the Earth, and if they had, they would not have dared guess man would have global-reaching effects. But in any case, this prophecy has proven to be true. Man is steward over the Earth, like it or not, and thus the cultivation of the individual and progress of knowledge is simultaneously a cultivation of the society and the physical world. There is no way to undo this fact, just as Adam could not un-eat the apple. To refuse the cultivation of man does not relieve man from his place as steward of the Earth; it merely makes him worse at his job.

> If we wish to take care of ourselves properly, we would have to respect ourselves—but we don't, because we are—not least in our own eyes—fallen creatures. If we lived in Truth; if we spoke the Truth— then we could walk with God once again, and respect ourselves, and others, and the world. Then we might treat ourselves like people we cared for. We might strive to set the world straight. We might orient it toward Heaven, where we would want people we cared for to dwell, instead of Hell, where our resentment and hatred would eternally sentence everyone. (Peterson, 58)

This insight into human nature and the universal reach of knowledge is a

---

[*] We'll take up this line of thought in the chapter on the Gettier Problem of Knowledge.

profound truth that the Bible has carried for millennia. Though there is a great need to discuss the proper orientation of our efforts and the long term effects of our work as our power over the world increases, contemporarily much discussion of those unhappy with the current state of our stewardship seems to center on how we can escape our nature, or convince ourselves that we are not in the position we are.

Any conversation that pretends man is not (whether by nature or right) steward over the Earth or that the Earth in its continued existence is something other than the landscape constructed by human ideas is attempting to deny reality, follow falsehoods, and/or ignore or limit our responsibilities.

God is Dead and You Impotent (But So Are Your Grievances)

Today we face yet another intellectual spectre arising in the confusion of our loss of orientation in the infinite universe: the provocation of "what if it is immoral to be efficacious?" which is tantamount to (and in many instances would not be denied to be identical with) the question "what if it is immoral to be human?", which is really just a variant of "how do we know that our consciousness is significant?"

In order to address this concern, first we must return to the nihilist concern of meaninglessness to cover a point: one cannot believe that the world would be a better place without humans within a belief system that says human action is meaningless, because the value you are attributing to the world comes from a human consciousness, so it is either meaningless, or you are proposing that the human consciousness can make significant judgements; even if you were unwilling to grant that human consciousness was significant, you would have to grant that human action is, even if it is significantly bad (in your estimation… of your conscious judgement…).

Thus those who believe life is meaningless also render their judgements of the moral worth OR WORTHLESSNESS of humanity inert. Therefore, as we have seen over and over again, human consciousness is significant. And given that human consciousness and human action is significant, it is good for it to be properly oriented, because that keeps it from doing inordinate amounts of damage.

Purpose in Form

Bidden or Unbidden, God Will Be Present

Those who believe that there is value in life, anywhere at all, must believe in the significance of their own consciousness. Even those who claim to believe that humans are a disease and that nature without human interference is the paramount of virtue, must hold the belief that human consciousness and human effectivity is significant, because it is making a significant (albeit negative) impact on the world. It remains a pure act of faith and dogma, then, to jump to the idea that, although human consciousness and action is necessarily significant, it can never be good and/or is subordinate to other values and virtues of differing natures ("Spaceship Earth" or the wishes of Gaia, for example)[*].

But it is only through such a faith that one comes up with the idea that human action is immoral categorically—that all human interference with the world is a net detriment. It is incoherent to believe humanity is both meaningless and evil (though it is, of course, incoherent to believe in meaninglessness at all, in the first place). Thus we have a question of which faith should we choose. Human consciousness and human action is necessarily meaningful and significant, this we necessarily agree on. But the question of the day is: is humanity inherently and irrevocably immoral, or not?[†]

Be aware that this is not a choice between humanity being entirely immoral, without redemption, or humanity being absolutely good and never mistaken or destructive. The choice proposed is whether there is no possibility of redemption whatsoever, or whether there may be some redemption in life (and the latter conception might take many forms of varying natures and beliefs).

Surprisingly, today, many people seem to have accepted the former idea as a real possibility. Antihumanist philosophies and catechisms pervade modern society[‡]. A particular catechism that you may spot, or variations on it, goes

---

[*] See Deutsch's book also for a refutation of these ideas.

[†] Increasing recently, the question seems to be becoming about certain races, rather than humanity as a whole. As I will state later, racism primarily thrives on materialism, so the dismantling of that dreadful metaphysics will help with this frightening progression. Aside from that, I think it a waste of time to enter into the debate on this particular question. There are more foundational issues with those espousing such atrocious theories. The conclusions here offered to humanity as a whole obviously transcend and supersede race.

[‡] Any time you hear humans described as a cancer, as I am sure you have many times, this ideology is at work. See *The Moral Case for Fossil Fuels* by Alex Epstein and

like this: "Human activity now threatens the very existence of the human race". But that is literally always true. We depend on our activity to survive[*]. We are always a threat to ourselves. But we are also our own saviors (at least in the physical survival sense).

Given that we are necessarily meaningful and significantly effective, why should we believe that we are entirely cut off from the good without hope? And if that is the case, why do so many people who pretend to espouse this view bother telling anyone about it? Their efforts can only come to evil, right? Even if they could convince us all that this was the truth, would not that act itself—according to their faith—be an evil? For if they, in convincing us that we were irredeemably evil, were to lead us to truth and were to help us in some way or accomplish some other good for the world or universe, that would contradict the doctrine which states that none of our actions can result in good.

> It's time to retire the morality play in which modern humans are a vile race of despoilers and plunderers who will hasten the apocalypse unless they undo the Industrial Revolution, renounce technology, and return to an ascetic harmony with nature... the human species... has never lived in harmony with the environment. (Pinker, 134 & 123)

Again, like purposelessness and meaninglessness, no one believes in a world without redemption, without the possibility for human beings to act for the good. Even the greatest pessimists and antihumanists believe in the power for good that resides in our consciousness. They just believe that that good is achieved through immense subordination, control, and regression of our species[†]. We all believe that we can affect good in the world in some manner.

"How Anti-humanism Conquered the Left" on Quillette for extended discussions and examples; *Enlightenment Now* by Steven Pinker also points out this tendency, though is less concentrated on the matter of what they look like and extended examples of their content and more on the opposing positive points of view.

[*] Recall: "All animals are entrusted to their own prudence and skill for their conduct in the world, and have full authority, as far as their power extends, to alter the operations of nature. Without the exercise of this power they could not subsist a moment." (Hume, 100)

[†] Again, see Deutsch and Pinker for robust refutations.

Purpose in Form

Walking in the Light of the Lord

Thus, given that it is a necessary truth that life is meaningful, purposeful, and significant, and that we as humans can affect the world in ways that can be considered "good". The only relevant question is: "what is the good?"

Well that is a hell of a question, and it doesn't seem to get us any less out of the quagmire to be here above the few steps we have taken. But let us think a moment about what we have concluded. Human consciousness and action is significant and meaningful. There is a fundamental reality of meaning, purpose, and significance in life itself as well as our individual lives. These are all necessary corollaries of the incontrovertible reality of the infinite.

Seeing consciousness as fundamental rather than an emergent phenomenon, as supported by excellent scientific data, helps us to understand and accept the reality of human nature as "universal explainers", as David Deutsch proposes. So, if human understanding and effect is of significant (and possibly infinite) potential in nature (which is possible without overruling the reality of eternal infinite ignorance), then human consciousness and endeavor in the pursuit of virtue *must be a good in itself*. "Who could deny that the very act of bowing to that which has attained the truth is the truth itself?" (Dogen, 132)

But this still leaves us with the problem of deciding on virtue and which path to follow, does it not? Actually, we are only thwarted here by our hastiness to make things complicated. There is at least one virtue which is certain and necessary which can help us—the Truth.

The Covenant: The Discovery and Development of Integrity

Before we move on to discuss the foundational nature of truth and its place in the order of virtues, I must point out the Bible's emphasis on this matter. Most of the Abrahamic story of the Old Testament is centered on the idea of a covenant with God. This covenant with God helped Abraham and his descendants over and over again. Aside from a literal reading that following God's arbitrary commands wins you special favors in the future, one can see that one of the main benefits of the covenant is a development of the will to honesty and thus the principle of integrity of the human being. And honesty and integrity lay the foundations of trust—which has been characterized as the universal currency, that which makes societies flourish.

Jonathan Haidt documents and supports this phenomenon in his book *The*

The Christian Ethic

Righteous Mind. "People behave less ethically when they think no one can see them... Creating gods who can see everything, and who hate cheaters and oath breakers, turns out to be a good way to reduce cheating and oath breaking." (Haidt, 297) However, his evidence and argument mostly supports religion as a motive for integrity and trust within in-groups, not so much between groups. I would suggest, however, that an infinite and universally active God—one who acts beyond the tribe—would begin to bridge this divide as well and encourage integrity in international or intertribal relations.

One can see this perspective in the stories where Abraham journeys to other lands. In other lands, among other cultures and races, he is constantly under threat; he is the stranger. "We trust and cooperate more readily with people who look and sound like us. We expect them to share our values and norms." (245) He is out of place and sticks out. He and his wife might be seized, killed, or taken advantage of. What hope does he have for recourse and defense against injustices when he is a wanderer in a foreign land? He is vulnerable.

Yet many times his covenant with God—his belief in God's intimate presence, connection to, and interest in human life, and his actions to remain integrous with this belief—keeps him safe. "If you abide, truthfully and courageously, by the highest of ideals, you will be provided with more security and strength than will be offered by any short-sighted concentration on your own safety." (Peterson, 173)

Why would a belief in an imminent, active, and watchful God help to build trust *across* cultures and races? Well, in a world where foreigners are enemies and laws apply to and protect citizens or certain races but not strangers, two people who, though different and fully capable of fighting or dealing dishonestly with each other (fearing no legal or social ramifications), both believe in or come to believe in a God who sees all and cares about our actions beyond what the laws of men require allows these two to trust each other—to trust that the other fears retribution for a lack of integrity beyond what society will let slide.

Of course the other can always be lying about their belief in this overarching, supreme God of all. But trust is always a leap of faith when it is first formed—it is always given and can never be earned[*]. When two people

---

[*] "Earning" of trust is a poor phrase. Trust is given and then it is put to the test. When it holds up—when one is not disappointed by their gamble in the other person—the

meet and share an understanding of a greater causal reality which is attuned in some way with a person's moral behavior, they can each be more assured that the other is intrinsically motivated to act with integrity in their interpersonal dealings. This is a significant step up from any average Joe of obscure moral heritage—or who is only concerned with not violating the law of man.

Thus, in developing a belief in and relationship with a personal, attentive, and morally inclined singular God of all, Abraham and his descendants were given a greatly effective tool in building trust. Through the acceptance of the covenant, Abraham accepted the project of developing the integrity of the human spirit—keeping it aware of and connected to God, and putting it in charge of and holding it responsible for governing appropriate action within the physical domain. The covenant was the first step in getting the soul to inhabit form—the human body and world.

We can see this urge to search for underlying and connecting truths between groups if we look at the definition of accountability Jonathan Haidt gives (borrowed from Phil Tetlock), and the requirements he describes which a social system must meet for accountability to lead to exploratory efforts for truth: accountability is the "'explicit expectation that one will be called upon to justify one's beliefs, feelings, or actions to others,' coupled with an expectation that people will reward or punish us based on how well we justify ourselves." (87, quoting Tetlock)

> Accountability increases exploratory thought only when three conditions apply: (1) decision makers learn before forming any opinion that they will be accountable to an audience, (2) the audience's views are unknown, and (3) they believe the audience is well informed and interested in accuracy. When all three conditions apply, people do their darndest to figure out the truth, because that's what the audience wants to hear. (Haidt, 88-89)

One could argue that God fulfills these three requirements of an audience: God sees all and judges actions (1). God's desires and laws are more often than not inscrutable and mostly completely unknown (2). God is all-knowing (3). In

---

trust is strengthened. But there is never any amount of evidence that could be gathered to gain trust. It must be given on a leap of faith and then tested.

this sense, the proposal of an infinite, omniscient, and judgmental God would have considerable influence on one's exploratory thought—pushing one towards understanding and truth.

Many might object that condition 2 is actually not met, since God is often considered to have definite expectations and requirements (the commandments and social laws of the Jews, for example). There is some truth here, to be sure, but technically we are talking in this section about Abraham's journeys and stories that precede the establishment of the commandments or even the Jewish nation, and speculating that this effect may have taken place at that time. God told Abraham very little and communicated with him seldom; and when he did it was often an incomprehensible demand he made of Abraham for unknown reasons.

Throughout the ages after the establishment of the Jewish community and the successes of their tribe, it is undoubtedly the case that this priming for cross-cultural understanding and honest inquiry would have substantially dropped away. It's just a conjecture that it existed back then anyhow. But, even if it didn't, returning to the idea of an infinite and largely unknown[*] God today, who is concerned with all peoples—as Christianity urges—would fulfill those requirements and push us towards exploratory thought and understanding, if these ideas and expectations were articulated and disseminated well enough.

Key Concept:

The Great Mystery- In finding the truth that existence is infinite, and that we exist and act within this infinite reality through our understandings of and interactions with a foundational, overarching system of causation, we were forced to recognize that knowledge of the infinite and its complex machinations will always exceed our comprehension. Thus we can know,

---

[*] "Largely unknown" is a necessary corollary of "infinite" and a comment on our lack of understanding of the entirety of God's mind. It is not a claim that we do not know of God's presence or love for us; He is intimately "known" in that sense of the word.

definitively, that the universe, creation, or life itself is and always will be a mystery. Going forward, one should remember that references to "the mystery of life" or any such phrases are not "deepities" aimed at denigrating and suppressing our nature as universal explainers, but rather matter-of-fact references to the reality of the infinity of life and how it necessarily appears to us as limited beings enmeshed within it.

Chapter 9: Metaphysics of Mind (The Order of Mental Virtues)

"To tell the truth is to bring the most habitable reality into Being. Truth builds edifices that can stand a thousand years. Truth feeds and clothes the poor, and makes nations wealthy and safe. Truth reduces the terrible complexity of a man to his word, so that he can become a partner, rather than an enemy. Truth makes the past truly the past, and makes the best use of the future's possibilities. Truth is the ultimate, inexhaustible natural resource. It's the light in the darkness." – Dr. Jordan B. Peterson (230)

Truth must be virtuous. Our notion of virtue in fact depends on truth, more than the reverse. Truth is perhaps our oldest and most necessary virtue. Anyone who acts with purpose (aims at a goal; strives), who believes in value and meaning (as we all must and do), who lives a life of discernment (the first step in any and all intentional cultivation), necessarily believes in and avails themselves of the effectual reality of truth.

Truth is as foundational as meaning. Just as it is meaningless to talk about meaninglessness, it is absurd to debate the reality of truth. For if "untruth" were the superordinate and definite reality, then *that* would be the true Truth of life. This is not to say that in certain contexts there cannot be multiple or varied truths on differing levels of analysis. It is simply to say that the principle of truth itself is inevitable.

Purpose in Form

How Our Mental Virtues Are Ordered

The necessity to elucidate a metaphysical conception and order runs through all our mental and intellectual striving. Not sticking to this proper order is one of the main problems which keeps sophistry alive and well throughout human existence. People confuse truth with reason, and reason with intellect. The underlying structure of these abstract realities must be known in order to keep these all in line.

Which one is to be sacrificed to? Which one is your God? It has been said since the enlightenment that reason is our new God. Is this acceptable? What are the differences and what is their order? How do we know it is that order and not another? These questions must be answered and this order must be maintained if we are to achieve virtue. We will demonstrate both the necessity for order and the proper order at once in the following investigation.

Truth, not reason, must be our highest goal and virtue in the mental realm. This is because Truth is not purposeful. Truth merely exists. Truth is merely a present reality—a veracity, a standing or shining forth[*]. Truth is not Truth *for* something else. Truth is merely truth. Reason cannot be in the highest place because reason is purposeful. Reason searches and explains; reason reasons. Reason is within the realm of service. The same is true of the intellect. Reason is there for the purpose of finding and serving Truth (ideally speaking, of course).

So how is the order of the subservient realities determined? In what ways do they define themselves and what places are they given? Is reason a function of the intellect or is the intellect a function of reason? This question is odd because it seems to actually give the wrong answer; that is that reason is a function of the intellect and the intellect cannot be a function of reason because reason is not an operational system which drives the intellect, it is merely an achievement of intellect. Therefore reason serves the intellect. But if reason is an achievement of the intellect, is not the intellect in the pursuit of reason, thus a higher goal and reality?

The answer is that both of these perspectives are correct and that they actually reveal the same obvious truth, it is merely that there is a mixing of perspectives, as we tend to ask these questions without being aware of the

---

[*] "The lofty Light which in Itself is true." (Dante, XXXIII)

predetermined order that we are often unconsciously assuming through intuition. One conception looks "bottom up" and says reason is a function of the intellect—the intellect does many things, one of which is reason, but it need not necessarily reason. True enough. But the "top down" conception recognizes that reason is the goal of the intellect, reason is its highest purpose.

Therefore, though the intellect can do many things that are beneath it—it can stray from its purpose—the *proper* function of the intellect is to strive toward reason and ultimately to achieve it. Thus, in "top down" language the intellect is a function of reason; though reason does not compel the intellect or keep it by force from doing anything else; reason ultimately subordinates intellect and that is the proper order. Truth exists, reason serves and leads to truth, and the intellect serves and leads to reason.

But, even though we might say through custom or speaking ideally that this is the proper order, how do we know it is so? It seems to make some sense, but is there not a better order? What of the fact that the intellect need not reason? Why would reason be above the intellect if the intellect was not necessarily mastered and controlled by reason?

This is the proper order because it is the only one that leads to the virtue of truth in practice. If we wish to question whether truth is in fact a virtue, this is not the discussion for us, since we are not engaged in real reason. Anyone who aspires to reason holds truth as their utmost virtue, necessarily, and rightly so. Anyone who, though they may appear intellectual and appear to forward "reasons", suggests that truth is not a virtue or is not the goal of reason is not reasonable and does not ascribe to reason, necessarily.

This is not a debatable subject. If truth is not the highest virtue, then dialectics cannot exist. The search for truth cannot exist. If we doubt truth's worth, we do not know what "truth" means, for it is truth and only truth that gives meaning to all mental efforts. If any say this is not a necessary conclusion (i.e. those who say that this is not necessarily THE TRUTH), we know we cannot trust them because they are engaged in deceit. You cannot reasonably suggest something is untrue without suggesting that there is a truth to be known which clearly supplants that untruth. If you do you are forwarding statements which are self-contradicting, so you cannot have the goal of speaking reason and you must be trying to confound the discussion on purpose.

And suggesting that this is a false binary does not escape the issue and subvert the reality of truth; if it is the TRUTH that multiple varied truths exist and that the idea of a binary option of truth vs. untruth is NOT TRUE, then, as we have stated, there is still the meta-truth to be stated that it is TRUE that there are multiple truths (in some instances). Hopefully this explanation seemed ridiculously superfluous. But it is necessary in this day and age. And it is important. As we have seen, an exact analogy to this kind of deceit is happening within the doctrines and minds of those who forward arguments against the infinite (for truth and the infinite are one and the same at the final resolution).

Thus truth is our highest virtue (in the mental realm at least). All must be in service of truth. But why? Is not reason a virtue? Why cannot reason and truth be the same thing and reason serve itself? This is a confusing question because *reason is only a virtue in that it is an effective path to truth*. Reason has purpose, as we have seen and as is self-evident. If the purpose of reason is not truth, then it is no longer reason.

When we say reason, we mean the proper and complete mental saturation in and orientation toward truth. The light of reason is the rays of truth-light which illuminate before the mind the true ways through darkness. Reason puts the mind in accord with truth. This is all merely definitional. It cannot be another way because that is what we are talking about when we talk about reason. So reason cannot serve itself or anything but truth or it is not reason. So far, anyone who has any orientation toward truth and reason cannot disagree. Any who disagree are engaging in contradiction and thus are lying about their efforts toward virtue and, of course, truth.

But what of the intellect? The intellect is often called the highest human faculty. We love the intellect. It is the intellect that makes it possible for us to reason, is it not? Why should the intellect limit itself to just one of its many talents? Why must the intellect pretend reason is "above" it, since reason is only one of the many things within its operational domain? These questions are precisely why the intellect must be subordinate to reason. Didn't that sound pretty reasonable? Maybe you caught the error, but couldn't you see it going unnoticed? Haven't you experienced so many lines of "reason" or "reasonable" questions just like that where the truth got left by the wayside and the mind began spinning into darkness without realizing it, believing it to be a valid trail of light? Isn't our intellect so clearly fallible?

But, in accord with reason, the answer eventually becomes clear. "It is the intellect that makes it possible for us to reason, is it not?" It is not, in fact. That sounded reasonable. But it wasn't truly. It was a suggestion of cause and effect that seemed directly connected, but it was in fact a complete 180 from the truth.

It is TRUTH which makes it possible to reason. Without truth itself, reason would be meaningless and our intellect could not reason, even if we supposed that it would exist. The reason of reason is always truth. And truth, as the highest virtue in the mental realm, is at the foundation of all. The intellect is the faculty which we possess which allows us to pursue reason. But the intellect does not make possible reason itself. The intellect only makes possible our side of the engagement. Reason and truth are existent in spite of our intellect[*].

The intellect would love to take credit for reason and truth and usurp the throne of virtue, and indeed it tries to quite often. But the intellect is only an organ or the function of an organ of mental existence which allows us to access the realities of that realm. Those realities transcend the intellect itself (see previous note). Because of the waywardness of the intellect, which we have just illustrated quite plainly, it cannot serve itself in a properly ordered being. The intellect CAN upset the order and *try* to live in service to itself, and this does happen all the time—the result is what Erich Neumann calls our modern "sclerosis of consciousness" which is characteristic of our age—but it is always a departure from truth and virtue (386).

It may help to make a distinction between 'Reason', 'reasoning', and 'reasonable'. Reason itself, as when we talk about the virtue of Reason or the light of Reason or the freedom that Reason brings, is the extra-temporal ideal of the intellectual mind—or, more appropriately, group of minds engaged in a culture of collective inquiry and criticism—directed toward truth and the path that that takes. It is the "true route" to Truth that we hypothesize exists from any given point of mental beginning. There are infinitely many conjectures to make in paths of thought, but ultimately only one is (or perhaps a very few are) in accord with Truth and Reason itself. You can take a few steps in the wrong direction, and then turn to the track of reason, and you might say those steps were necessary to the process of discovery, but that is saying that they were "reasonable" or *appeared* "reasonable". That is another issue and doesn't

---

[*] See my extended discussion in the "Metaphysics" section of *Jnana Yoga* on the externality of mind and objective nature of thoughts.

Purpose in Form

change the reality of Reason itself.

Though no one can claim to see exactly all the paths, let alone grasp or master Reason itself, Reason is the impossible ideal we aspire to, and sometimes get close enough to that we are able to find some truth. "reason" is the fallible process we inevitably enact, stumbling along the way and getting lost frequently, muddling through, and depending greatly on the input of others.

What is "reasonable" is what is sounding or did sound like it was in the ballpark of a possible avenue toward truth that we deem worth experimenting along—sending our mental avatars through the gauntlet of communal criticism, and hoping that through enough such sacrifices we may find one that passes through the fire and shows us the way.

Humans must settle for pursuing Reason itself through exploring what appears "reasonable", the fallible process we call "reasoning". "reasoning" consists of conjecturing causal links and walking them through over and over, checking for errors (criticizing the hypothesis). Through arduous efforts in this manner, one hopes they have some skill and a good bit of luck and strike gold, as it were, and alight on a path which may be the very trail of Reason itself. However, such "eurekas" of insight are not always what they seem, and perhaps more often than not only further semblances of Reason, only finer iterations of something that appears reasonable. Life is a difficult game. But there is gold and many people do find it.

These prospects sound dismal amid the infinite darkness. However, there is hope. And there is more hope than we might think. For one thing, the active ingredient of "luck" is not quite as rare or arbitrary as it might seem. For another, it is the case that every single person who strikes gold AND successfully follows it all the way to its source begins to share their findings with others and helps them get to the paths which lead to the ultimate treasure.*

Moral of the Story

Now, in the middle of a book of reason, which has had its far out moments

---

* Here we are speaking in regards to the one ultimate Truth; I am not making the claim that no one ever holds secret intellectual property or truthful information. However, our age being the age of free information does make a good case that this is actually the common practice for the majority of lesser relative truths as well.

and perhaps has already seemed to go quite off the deep end for you, there can have been nothing as of yet to compare to that pile of wishy-washy, fairy tale nonsense—or perhaps in this case inane rationalistic idealism. But I maintain that this is the truth and, though I speak in metaphor, I mean this truth wholeheartedly.

And my tale of seeming fantasy is not done. This is a completely reasonable, truthful, and necessary account of reality. Those who catch onto Reason itself, and proceed through reason into Truth, always share this treasure which is beyond any value or measure or imagination. There is nothing of greater value in existence. The ultimate truth is the definition of priceless, for it is infinite, and it is the very foundation of value. And yet, those who find this infinite treasure come back to offer it to others both freely and gladly. This is because the nature of truth itself is actually free, and Reason leads us to find the truth that life, difficult though it may be, is a non-zero-sum game.

The Truth is, in its magnificence, beyond all splendor, and it is the absolute pinnacle of value, yet it is free, and there is no reason why it should be withheld from anyone. "Freely have ye received, freely give." (Matthew 10:8) The Truth is in service to no one, there is nothing beyond it for it to serve or belong to. Thus, it cannot be bent to anyone's will, just as gold will not mix with anything but gold. Therefore, those who can find it cannot profit from it other than by the joys it can bring to others, and they cannot use it to exploit others without departing from it themselves—for if one seems to have found the truth and yet decides to play at life as though it were a zero-sum game, then they must either have never seen the truth, or they have willingly departed from it.

So, those who know and revere the truth spread it around and call others to the central source. The catch and price is not in the prize, but in the path to it. The only way to get to Truth is to sacrifice all to Truth. You cannot hold anything higher than truth itself or anything on the same plane as truth, or you will not succeed. "If you regard yourself as more important than the dharma, you'll never get the dharma." (Dogen, 127) "For whosoever will save his life shall lose it; but whosoever shall lose his life for my sake and the gospel's, the same shall save it." (Mark 8:35)

Many people sacrifice to themselves. Many consider themselves defined by their intellectuality, so they hold sacrifices to the intellect; many consider there to be no transcendent truth but believe they can still "reason", so they sacrifice to "reason" (which is then but disguised intellectualism). Many sacrifice to many things other than truth. But only those who truly seek truth above all else can find it.

Thus one's inner order must be kept intact and the lesser realities must serve the higher essences in the pursuit of virtue or virtue will not be achieved. Anyone who sacrifices to intellect (holds intellect in highest regard), cannot be virtuous. The intellect is not virtuous in itself, but only becomes virtuous through the service of and sacrifice to virtue. For the intellect and all else that means that they must be prepared to lay down their own nature or their own creations upon the altar of Truth. If they cannot do this, they cannot be virtuous.

Now I have both explained to you the nature of reason and truth and the metaphysical order of the mind, and shown you the light of God as it expresses itself in the Biblical story of the sacrifice of Isaac. Truth and God are one and the same. But the mind is not the only realm in which or by which God can be approached. The mind calls God "Truth", when it is inspired by Reason. When the mind ponders the word "God", it is peering into the ritualistic, traditional, and symbolic representations which, for the most part, do not depend on great machinations of the intellect, though they can be found (as we just saw) to be in accord with Reason.

This understanding allows us to know not only that human consciousness in pursuit of and in alignment with truth *is a necessary good,* but also the proper orientation methodology we must obey. In other words, "The solution to the problems of life is the integrity of the individual" (Peterson, The Divinity of the Individual). "If we each live properly, we will collectively flourish" (Peterson, xxxv)

There is still an enormous battle ahead in sorting the wheat from the chaff in discerning what is true from what is not; and further refining our grasp on truth and reality, and thus our ability to discern. But we can say that human consciousness aligned with truth—willing to sacrifice all to truth—is virtuous and good. Human integrity is the foundation for all other virtues.

This knowledge creates a necessity for action oriented toward truth, where one strives to become conscious of the ideals to which they sacrifice, and to whittle these down to the one—Truth, above all. And these actions we take in pursuit of truth—unless upon finding the truth we see that such experimental actions were in some way antithetical to the truth and should not be repeated[*] given better ways available—are part of that virtue. "It is certain, from experience, that the smallest grain of natural honesty and benevolence has more effect on men's conduct than the most pompous views suggested by theological theories and systems" (Hume, 83). And conversely, "It is deceit that makes people miserable beyond what they can bear. It is deceit that fills human souls with resentment and vengefulness." (Peterson, 221)

Thus we can say that being truthful and sacrificing to the truth is a necessary virtue and should be our highest endeavor throughout all of life[†]. This does not contradict our nature as fallible beings and our essential inability to ever be truly finished with exploring the truth. In fact, *that is part of the truth that is essential to recognize, accept, and hold ourselves to if we are to be successful in cultivating virtue.*

We will always be infinitely ignorant. We know that, for we know that life is infinite. We are fallible. We are broken and imperfect and the pursuits of the highest virtue are the hardest things we can do—as was the sacrifice of Isaac. "People, unsettled by their vulnerability, eternally fear to tell the truth." (Peterson, 51) And yet we must undertake this pursuit, for that is the truth—pursuit of the truth is the truth, and the pursuit of virtue is virtue. "There's only one vehicle, one way to the truth. It exists in the here and now." (Dogen, 229) "I am the way, the truth, and the life: no man cometh unto the Father, but by me" (John 14:6).

In pursuing the truth and virtue, we have found that our best tool for refining our conjectures and overcoming our blind spots is a community and culture of open inquiry and criticism[‡] (see Deutsch and Haidt). By believing in the truth of our fallibility, and sacrificing our conjectured speculations about the truth upon the altar of collective examination and testing, we make our best

---

[*] "Not everything that we might wish to be done (or are glad was done) is something that we think should be done (or should have been done)." (BNHB, 155)
[†] If a murder asks you where his victim went you can lie to him. I don't want to hear your intellectual BS. The truth is the truth of life, not the dead adherence to confines of a finite game created by the intellect.
[‡] Actually, "we" as a society haven't even fully found this out yet. I believe it is the case, but society is not self-aware enough to identify its own core virtues yet. "The very idea of science 'as explanation'… is itself still a minority view." (Deutsch, 263). So recognizing this is still part of our project.

progress toward truth and walk nearest to the path of virtue that our fallible nature allows. But sacrificing all to truth is not an idle claim or sentiment. It takes real sacrifice, and it is really as difficult as Abraham sacrificing Isaac. We don't just have to let go of disembodied ideas, we all too often have to throw away parts of ourselves, our ways of being, our appearances, and even our ideals—symbolized in the early biblical tradition as converting males being circumcised to show their true commitment.

This is daunting and difficult, but it is the only road to progress—rejecting the path or responsibility does not bring one any closer to bliss, in fact it assures the world atrophies and departs from the road to heaven on Earth to some degree. Progress is made of "human accomplishments, not cosmic birthrights." (Pinker, 4) But instead of procrastinating under despair at the difficulties of this game, ponder the possibilities hidden in this conception: "What if it were the case that the world revealed whatever goodness it contains in precise proportion to your desire for the best?" (Peterson, 101) Set out with conviction on the quest for Truth above all and, as Joseph Campbell says, you'll soon find unexpected help along the way.

~Summary of the Necessary Truths So Far

Here we have our starting block: Life is infinite. This is a knowable and demonstrable truth and reality.

Human life and consciousness is meaningful, purposeful, and significant. These are necessary corollaries of an infinite reality and the infinite reach of human understanding (which is better explained and understood through the burgeoning awareness that consciousness is fundamental in nature and is not a secondary phenomenon arising out of matter alone).

Causation (in some form) is a deep and probably foundational element of our reality. We, being both part of it and aware of it, can act effectively through it. Thus, we are connected in some deep and mysterious way to the basic functionings of the entire cosmos.

Given the significance, meaning, and potential of human consciousness and action, we have the ability as individuals and as a species to do good. And while the question of what specific actions and effects may be called good upon what level of analysis are extremely complex and seemingly far from resolved, we do know that truth and the pursuit of truth are necessarily virtues. Thus for humans to pursue truth as their ideal and to sacrifice their fallible conjectures upon its altar (which is a culture of collaborative thought and criticism) is the main flow from which all other tributaries of virtue emerge and return.

From this point we must explore our conjectures. We cannot take necessary steps from this point without taking leaps of conjecture, and then turning back and examining their connections to our fundamental truths and understandings. Thus we will explore from here some conjectures made by traditions of honoring the infinite—some catechisms of faith—which I believe to be common and necessary conclusions that humanity around the world has arrived at and honed over the millennia.

We will look at Christianity and Buddhism for these purposes. There are obviously many other traditions, and I think you could find the truths I will suggest in many if not all of those other traditions as well. But I will use these two religions for our purposes because they appear very different, and most certainly emerged and evolved as separate as we can consider religions to be, but I believe that they still contain the same underlying message in terms of orienting one's Being toward life and how the infinite and the finite are to be related.~

Purpose in Form

Chapter 10: Christianity and Jung – Efficacy in the World and the Cultivation of the Individual in Modern Times

> "I cannot define for you what God is. I can only say that my work has proved empirically that the pattern of God exists in every man and that this pattern has at its disposal the greatest of all his energies for transformation and transfiguration of his natural being. Not only the meaning of his life but his renewal and his institutions depend on his conscious relationship with this pattern of his collective unconscious." – C.G. Jung (Van der Post, 216-217)

The Christian tradition of the western world[*] operates by a certain conjecture of faith which it takes to be true and virtuous. It says that human

---

[*] It is actually fairly obtuse to pretend there is such a unified reality as "the Christian tradition of the western world" given the immense variation of modern Christianity in the west with all its denominations, as well as the fact that much of what falls within that umbrella comes from traditions of Greek philosophy and western enlightenment thought which were written into the Semitic orthodoxies or have been later alloyed in various ways in western minds so much so that it is hard to parse what is generally "westernism" and what has its roots in Levantine scripture. But this is not a scholarly work on the lineages of thought and I am concerned with exploring our ideas as they are; while diagnosing origins is interesting and often important for various purposes, for my purposes here it is unimportant.

life should be dedicated to service of God and each other through love. Christians and the Abrahamic traditions in general believe that humans gain their highest virtues in obedience to God's will. And Christians especially emphasize that God's will is love for all humans, and that it is by Grace that this love and virtue abounds.

In the lens we have taken, we can translate that slightly to say that Christians believe that we should live and act in the most effective ways possible—in ways which are in harmony with the overarching and probably infinite web of causation which is a mystery beyond our comprehension, yet is something which governs our day to day lives and we find it both possible and miraculously beneficial to work with (see, it's easier just to say "God"). We will discuss the matter of the primacy of grace shortly.

Within the tradition as well, as a warning against ruthlessness, cheating, etc. for gains in the short term, Christians believe that acting morally is a part of acting effectively (since God is always watching and is concerned with human moral integrity), and that morality is more than just the following of dead rules[*], but the active love and compassion for man, as exemplified by Christ. Said in this way, the doctrine sounds less offensive to the modern intellectual than the literal readings of allegory (though I do insist that that fault lies in the modern intellectual for not being able to understand and get past their fixation on the literal appearances of allegorical reading, rather than, as they would likely want to have it, on the Christians who may read it only as such).

Within this love for man, along with the basic assertion that man will live and work in the world[†], in the western Christian tradition is included the preservation of freedom[‡] and the proliferation of the human race and its

---

[*] "Let the dead bury their dead." (Matthew 8:22) "God is not the God of the dead, but of the living." (Matthew 22:32)

[†] I.e. the insight that man is a universal constructor—that man is a verb, as Buckminster Fuller put it.

[‡] For those who doubt such a claim: "He bringeth out those which are bound in chains." (Psalm 68:6) "Now the Lord is that Spirit: and where the Spirit of the Lord is, there is liberty." (2 Cor. 3:17) "Stand fast therefore in the liberty wherewith Christ hath made us free, and be not entangled again with the yoke of bondage." (Galatians 5:1) The Bible even appears to contain the groundwork necessary for understanding and proposing freedom of speech and open inquiry for the production of knowledge (though of course there is much else in the text and tradition which works counter to these ideas, and which won out through most of the church's history): "There is a way

stewardship over the Earth (which, as we have shown, is merely a necessary corollary to man's nature—see previous note and chapter 8). Many modern people question how a sovereign God and the freewill of man are reconciled, and people object to man assuming authority over the natural processes of the Earth, but that is not to say that Christianity has no answers to these questions, merely that they are not explicitly self-evident in the original scripture, and many critics aren't too interested in any sort of due diligence, for they aren't yet looking for reconciliation but rather only justifications for their disdain.

The briefest address possible has been given to the stewardship over the Earth, which can be summed up in Jungian terms as, "The integration of the personality is equivalent to an integration of the world." (Neumann, 359) A full address appropriate to the emotional turmoil of the age would take up too much space here and distract from the more foundational issues that we should be concentrating on. The issue of freewill I have discussed at significant length

---

which seemeth right unto man, but the end thereof are the ways of death." (Proverbs 14:12) In other words: we are fallible. "The way of the wicked is as darkness: they know not at what they stumble" (Proverbs 4:14) Ignorance of your mistakes and transgressions breeds loss and evil. "Great men are not always wise: neither do the aged understand judgement." (Job 32:9) You cannot trust merely traditionally ordained models of wisdom and knowledge to direct you right all the time. "The simple believeth every word: but the prudent man looketh well to his going... The simple inherit folly: but the prudent are crowned with knowledge." (Proverbs 14:15 & 14:18) Those who aren't skeptical of all knowledge and instruction get led astray. "He that regardeth reproof is prudent" (Proverbs 15:5) Openness and willingness to be wrong, and the humility to accept correction is the foundation of wisdom and knowledge. "Despise not the chastening of the Lord; neither be weary of his correction." (Proverbs 3:11) Be open and humble. "The knowledge of the holy is understanding." (Proverbs 9:10) Understanding the world of cause and effects, including your mistakes, is the knowledge of God or Holiness. "Whoso loveth instruction loveth knowledge: but he that hateth reproof is brutish" (Proverbs 12:1) Those who are open to these insights do better than those who remain blind. "A reproof entereth more into a wiseman than an hundred stripes into a fool" (Proverbs 17:10) Taking mistakes and corrections seriously makes you wise and you do better in the long run. "He that answereth a matter before he heareth it, it is folly and shame unto him." (Proverbs 18:13) Do not operate by dogma or dismiss by previous knowledge, consider all information and arguments, for you may be wrong. "He that covereth his sins shall not prosper: but whoso confesseth and forsaketh them shall have mercy." (Proverbs 28:13) Hiding from the truth of your fallibility does you no good, confronting it does. "All manner of sin and blasphemy shall be forgiven unto men." (Matthew 12:31) You are free to speak in any manner, against even Jesus himself (Luke 12:10), in this quest for truth.

Purpose in Form

in my book *Jnana Yoga*. Here, we must focus on and not lose sight of the reality of the infinite, and how we are related to it, which remains true and superordinate regardless of one's opinions on subordinate ethical issues. Again, these issues are undoubtedly important—but the foundational truths of our metaphysical assumptions are not uprooted by these whichever way they fall.

The Christian story epitomizes the nature of virtuous life and our path to all things good through the truth and mystery of the Incarnation—the life and story of Jesus Christ. Christ being fully God and fully man gives humanity hope in the intimate and mysterious connection of the infinite to the finite. This is a truth of the world, and an orientation toward Being which we should never lose—the individual and the whole are intimately connected, and even when the individual does not feel it, the whole is intimately tied to and aware of the individual. This is what God's love for man reveals in modern terms—that the infinite is conscious *and* self-saturating. We would be better off in the world if we remembered that and kept our orientation to the world reflective of that truth—i.e. kept our faith intact.

What Christians can hope for in life through accepting this truth and faith is their freedom to be an effective individual, a creator and curator upon the Earth, and to do so fallibly ("sinfully") and not be judged too harshly for their imperfections. "If thou, Lord, shouldest mark iniquities, O Lord, who shall stand?" (Psalms 130:3) It is because of the truth that the infinite is intimately connected to and interested in the finite lives and world of humanity that we are redeemed in our failings and that we are able to pursue our particular destinies, and that we have hope for creating a virtuous world. "Everyone falls short of the glory of God. If that stark fact meant, however, that we had no responsibility to care, for ourselves as much as others, everyone would be brutally punished all the time." (Peterson, 62) "How excellent is thy lovingkindness, O God! therefore the children of men put their trust under the shadow of thy wings. They shall be abundantly satisfied with the fatness of thy house; and thou shalt make them drink of the river of thy pleasures." (Psalm 36:7-8)

Keeping this truth of faith (our orientation toward the basic nature of life) alive in the world would save us from all the antihuman and nihilist notions, movements, and policies going around. It is only because we have lost this orientation toward the basic truth of life that we are consumed by theories of

Christianity and Jung

insignificance, meaninglessness, purposelessness, and finitude of life. Knowing the reality of the connection of the infinite to our finite beings, no one would wonder at the significance of human life, nor wonder if it is a categorical evil to live a human life[*]. One can be ridden with guilt—and indeed people have looked down on and criticized Christianity for seeming to breed a guilty mindset in individuals to their detriment—but one is saved from shame, and that is a highly significant achievement for humanity—salvation from the eternal condemnation of shame[†]. As Murray puts it:

> The consensus for centuries was that only God could forgive the ultimate sins. But on a day-to-day level the Christian tradition, among others, also stressed the desirability—if not the necessity—of forgiveness. Even to the point of infinite forgiveness. As one of the consequences of the death of God, Friedrich Nietzsche foresaw that people could find themselves stuck in cycles of Christian theology with no way out. Specifically that people would inherit the concepts of guilt, sin and shame but would be without the means of redemption which the Christian religion also offered. (182)

---

[*] "I realized that my question as to what my life is, and the answer that it is an evil, was quite correct. The only mistake was that I had extended an answer that related only to myself to life as a whole." (Tolstoy, 60)

[†] In modern psychology, the distinction between guilt and shame is a popular theme and effective tool for teaching and helping clients (though, in some cases, they switch the meanings of the terms, either way the principle and message is the same). Guilt is a negative but necessary feeling which arises and prompts the thought "I did something bad"; it is not a pleasant feeling, but it holds hope for redemption through taking accountability and responsibility for changing one's actions. This negative feeling can thus be a productive impulse toward change. Shame is a pathological negative feeling which brings about the thoughts and categorical judgement of "I am a bad person". Shame cuts off redemption and thus breeds a cycle of negative action—"since I am a bad person, as evidenced by my actions and feelings, there's nothing for it, I guess I just do bad things now…" Kelly McGonigal discusses this in both her books *The Upside of Stress* and *The Willpower Instinct*. "Shaming" people for their bad actions almost always merely drives them back to the negative habits which are their escape mechanisms from bad feelings—even though these are precisely the habits for which you are shaming them. A compassionate approach to helping people grow can and must include some level of criticism of people's unhealthy choices, but one must not forget the necessity to encourage people and remind them that they are capable, and make them feel worthy of and supported in their changes and pursuit of the good.

Purpose in Form

And Jung went to work on this very problem, both by reconnecting people with either their inherited traditions or some other tradition of faith, and by creating a model for human development which implied and relied on the realities of redemption and forgiveness in growth and healing. "For godly sorrow worketh repentance to salvation not to be repented of: but the sorrow of the world worketh death." (2 Corinthians 7:10)

Individuation: The Development of Modern Man in Reliance on God

Greatly influenced by Christian traditions and the other religious cultures that grew in the west (such as Gnosticism and alchemy), and himself saying, "the decisive question for man is: Is he related to something infinite or not?" Carl Gustov Jung proposed a psychological developmental schema of man known as individuation (MDR, 325).

*Individuation emphasizes the healthy development of an ego†—which is more or less the conscious personality—with personal interests and autonomy, as well as a connection to an infinite life beyond oneself through a recognition of and work with the many unconscious aspects of our being as well as the forces beyond our personal being. Through this journey of individuation one becomes a flourishing and all the more effective individual creator, while attuning to and respecting the influence of greater powers and determining factors in our minds and lives beyond our small and fallible personal wants and imaginings. "There's another side of ego which allows us to function in the world. It's that which allows us to create order out of the immensity of life. It's

---

* Please note that it is impossible to include in this book, let alone this brief chapter, a sufficient account of the Jungian school of thought and all the branches it has generated to date. We will look here only briefly at how some of the foundational elements of the Christian tradition play a critical role in particular aspects of the general process of individuation. Anything beyond cursory (and therefore necessarily wholly insufficient) definition of terms like 'individuation', 'shadow', 'ego', etc. will not be found here. This is not a chapter pretending to encapsulate, explain, and/or instruct on Jungian theory; it is at most a shout out and recommendation to look further into the Jungian theories and schools for those who are interested.

† "Ego consciousness, with its discriminative functions… is the organ of adaptation to reality… A higher ego level then [past the juvenile point of ego-selfishness] coincides once more with an integrated personality [as was the case in the preconscious and undeveloped state of psychological unity]" (Neumann, 341 & 348-349)

an ordering principle in life." (Adyashanti)

Jungian individuation, in my opinion, is one of the best codified and developed formulas for embodying the Christian faith and the reality of the incarnation in modern times. This path draws from the truth of the Incarnation—i.e. that the infinite is self-saturating, and therefore the divine is within us and we are and can be far more than we are aware[*]—which is what allows and encourages us to be finite, make personal judgements, and go on our own adventures as fallible beings, not with impunity, but with a promise that the mistakes we make through ignorance alone (rather than malevolence) will not be visited back on us in a manner too unbearable for our souls. "The magic of the sacraments (made effective through the passion of Jesus Christ, or by virtue of the meditations of the Buddha), the protective power of primitive amulets and charms, and the supernatural helpers of the myths and fairytales of the world, are mankind's assurances that the arrow, the flames, and the flood are not as brutal as they seem." (Campbell, 107)

Jungian therapy and conscious development along the path of individuation is accomplished through the encouragement of the individual along their own version of the Hero's Journey[†], and the underlying hope and faith in the potential for each individual to undertake this daunting task and grow from it is rooted in Jung's discovery of and belief in the archetype of the Self, which is common to all and is, among other things, an active principle which brings strength and healing to the individual during and after (and perhaps even through) crisis or trauma.

The Self is our natural ability to grow and heal; it is what allows us to be anti-fragile, if we confront the world in the right way. "The more they afflicted them, the more they multiplied and grew" (Exodus 1:12) It is the living connection to the transcendent and divine ideal (Christ) which exists in us all as a result of the self-saturating property of infinity (the intimacy of God

---

[*] "Even you, just as you are right here and now, have a whole lot of aspects you're completely unaware of." (Dogen, 53)

[†] See Erich Neumann *The Origins and History of Consciousness*: "The hero is the archetypal forerunner of mankind in general. His fate is the pattern in accordance with which the masses of humanity must live, and have always lived, however haltingly and distantly; and however short of the ideal man they have fallen, the stages of the hero myth have become constituent elements in the personal development of every individual." (131)

toward man). "The introjection of the hero archetype, the union with the soul, the foundation of the kingdom that 'is not of this world', and the birth of the king are as much the mysteries of alchemy as of the individuation process." (Neumann, 415)

Many Jungians, I'm sure, may be somewhat offended by the assertion that the Christian Incarnation, specifically, is the underlying key to the Jungian process; though Jung clearly respected religion, many probably like to think of his work as more independent, foundational in itself, and applicable across cultures, etc. But this is more an averse reaction to the title "The Incarnation" and the orthodoxy one associates with it (i.e. the complex they have about anything traditionally Christian or religious in general), than it is about the claim in itself. "The Incarnation" is the title of the Christian story whose moral is the intimate connection between God and man—the infinite and the finite. "The Incarnation" as a title in this sense is only a meme which reminds one that self-saturation is a true property of the infinite, and that this has profound implications for the nature of our entire lives (overall and every minute). And this principle, referred to by the idea of The Incarnation, is necessarily key to the Jungian system.

Think about it; the Jungian concept of the human individual is the hero archetype. And the reality of the hero is supported by the necessary realities of purpose, meaning, and significance in life, and human potential. It is only through our connection to the infinite reality—which is structured with purpose and meaning—that we can hope to live our lives as true heroes, creating virtuously in the world and acting in accord with truth. It is only because Truth exists, and has brought forth a world, that we can live effective lives as individuals. Equally, the connection of infinite to finite, of God to humanity, is a property and "achievement" of the infinite itself, not any creation or grasping of man; the world is set up for us to live out our fallible efforts at being heroes by a power beyond ourselves—we did not create this world, but we find ourselves in it, and though we are fallible, and though it is hard, we are, nonetheless, given the opportunities for success through the hardship in the way the universe is fundamentally structured and connected to us.

In Jungian terms, each individual finds himself in the midst of an adventure of the psyche. We enter into not only a world beyond our immediate control and conception (which is obvious) but also we come into developed ego-consciousness which is ripe for responsibility only after our psyche has endured much unconscious turmoil and reordering. We face imbalance and strife both without and within, necessarily. But Jung believed that against these impossible odds there was hope; and more so that this state of discord and disadvantage was merely the proper and appropriate place for the dynamic soul which is built for and driven by dynamic challenge—our souls are adventurous and thus our broken lives are their perfect playgrounds.

Our ability to live dynamically and grow is rooted in the nature of our soul and its inborn connection to and periodic remembrance of and communication with the Self. The archetypal Self is a permanent reality beyond each individual, and yet the image of the Self—the living connection one carries to this superordinate reality—is contained in each individual and it is what most deeply influences and informs one's life (conscious or unconscious though it may be). The image of the Self, when its machinations begin to make contact with the growing conscious awareness and personality, is that which provides each of us with an innate capacity to heal, grow, and transcend our challenges and sufferings. Thus is the Grace of God—the independent and supreme existence of the Self archetype and its innate and intimate connection to our psyche—the foundational element to one's ability to individuate—to live as a fallible, sinful, yet fulfilled and blessed limited being.

Jung tells us about the Mysterium Coniunctionis—the archetypal (independent and objective existence) of the Self and its innate connection to our psyche, regardless of the apparent discord—the infinite being married to the finite. The Christian doctrine expresses this to us in the story of the incarnation where God descended into man, and suffused human history and human life with infinite Grace, despite coming to full bloom in the deepest, darkest midst of sins. The eternal opposites of the perfect divine and sinful humanity were joined in mysterious union. It is this great union of opposites which creates, supports, and redeems life—each and all.

Thus our entire efforts in virtue, our hopes for meaning and significance, and our pursuit of our own individual purpose are necessarily dependent on and established or redeemed by the infinite connection to reality which exists by virtue of the infinite miracle of existence alone. In other words, in Christian language, God is our savior and redeemer and gives meaning and purpose to our lives; we owe all to Him and have no hope apart from Him, but the good news is he is here and all our hopes are miraculously fulfilled. "I am man by nature, and God by the grace of God." (St. Symeon the younger, The Soul Afire, 303) This is the only rational basis for being able to live an effective and conscious yet fallible and finite life within an infinite universe. This is the metaphysical basis for the emphasis of faith above all else in this miraculous reality—the union of God with man accomplished by preordained grace alone (the natural property of the self-saturation of infinity). And it is this acceptance of who we are and what we are, and how we must live and what we are born into, that is the path of individuation.

Whether the Christian allegory speaks to you or not, the reality of the infinite, and its necessary saturation of, or intimacy with, the finite is the Grace and gift which allows us to live with purpose, meaning, significance, and hope. This is a necessary truth and it is known and lived all over the world. Christians, even though they tend to deemphasize works in their doctrine, work and live according to their individual freedom only through the Grace of God, and if they are good and faithful Christians, they attempt to align their actions and lives with the will and love of God so that a loving, harmonious, and better world may come to be on Earth, that we may see it and finally be able to recognize it as the Kingdom of God, a shining jewel of Heaven[*]. "Walk worthy of the vocation where with ye are called." (Ephesians 4:1)

The reality of God, the reality of the infinite, the Truth of the Eternal is the source of our freedom to be incarnate, to be efficacious—to be limited and striving—and to not be futile, face annihilation and meaningless, or the unmitigated and insurmountable full effects of our unbounded ignorance. "The way of man is not in himself: it is not in man that walketh to direct his steps." (Jeremiah 10:23) If we do not have a knowledge of and faith in the reality of the infinite as an intimate God of existence, then we would be bent and twisted, thwarted images by our own nature. We would be—if we can pretend to picture this impossibility—effective beings who are yet finite and fallible, without any hope of redemption or significance; thus we would be running into all the problems and horrors we do anyhow, but there would be no redemption, no forgiveness, no mercy, and no Grace.

We, as fallible beings in a dark creation without a connection to any real truth or higher power would have no hope beyond merely torturing ourselves along the way to our own destruction. Instead, Christianity gives us the good

---

[*] "One bright pearl" (Dogen, 72)

news that we are fallible beings in a dark creation fated to the torturous sufferings of life along the way to our destruction, and yet there is redemption. Hallelujah! "It is indeed very little that we need! But lacking that, the adventure into the labyrinth is without hope." (Campbell, 18) This sounds like a cruel joke, but that is because one overlooks or poorly values the nature of said redemption. It appears a meager after thought and wishful platitude to placate us to the darkness of reality we see. But our redemption is the infinite. It can appear small consolation, like a mustard seed, but its true nature and worth are immeasurable (Mark 4:31). True comprehension of the infinite reality does offer more than adequate compensation for the grueling experience of finite life.

It is the reality of the infinite which gives space for the shadow (which can loosely be described as one's dark side). It is the reality of the connection between the infinite and the finite that creates a world amenable to our adventurous spirits and harbors our vulnerability and weakness to some extent, rather than a world which crushes our hopes and efforts at every turn for their impotence, imperfection, and all together insignificant limited natures. There would be no hope for the hero if there was not a divine interest in his destiny—if the infinite were not amenable to his desires and efforts[*]—and all the more so when we voluntarily follow our Personal Legends.

In the Jungian conception, the only way to grow and move toward genuine progress (Christians would say the Kingdom of God or Heaven on Earth) is to confront your darkness. And the only way we can hope to confront our darkness is through a faith in forgiveness and redemption. "Be not overcome of evil, but overcome evil with good." (Romans 12:21) Those who do not believe in either forgiveness or redemption, or who do not have a legitimate support within their metaphysics (conscious or unconscious) for a belief in either, cannot adequately look at their own darkness or the darkness of humanity without being overcome and becoming nihilistic and misanthropic[†].

---

[*] We all have some degree of plot armor in our lives, whether we know it or not.
[†] Again, to those who raise objections of secular and atheistic people who remain moral, as we have shown, they retain an inexplicable faith in the significance of the human individual, which is necessarily (though unconsciously) derived from the divine conception of the human individual. They also avoid consistency in considering the basic realities of meaninglessness and purposelessness that their foundational philosophies imply. If one consistently applies the world view of a barren,

Purpose in Form

The darkness of humanity and our own souls is truly immense. It is immense beyond our own personal capacity for redemption or even toleration. Only through the reality of the infinite abiding love of God (the intimate connection between infinite and finite) do we stand a chance at facing our true selves and remaining compassionate and ethical in the world—moving towards heaven on Earth. And it is only by harnessing the power of our complete selves that we stand any chance of making progress at all, rather than being entirely compensated and nullified by our shadows—working at cross purposes with our selves.

Thus the individuation process of approaching one's unconscious and beginning to recognize it is not only based on the reality of the infinite in that it acknowledges our infinite potential and complexity, but also depends on the nature of the world and our own capacities to contain and accept an infinite redeeming and heartening force of forgiveness and grace, which could only be hoped for through the idea that the infinite itself is intimately and consciously connected to, invested in, and caring for the finite. And that is, again, the principle behind The Incarnation which expresses the love of God for man and the infinite redemption this offers to man in allegorical or symbolic language.

Thus it is the infinite and intimate, redeeming nature of God that allows us to grow and develop with the hope of any true progress. It is the infinite which allows us to be directional, driven, purposeful, without forever lamenting all that we would miss and sacrifice through our choosing of a particular path, knowing that we are fallible and mistaken in so many cases along the way, but still hopeful that we may find some real truth in the end and that our lives will have significance in spite of their absurdity of being so limited in such an unlimited universe[*].

It is the conscious infinite connection to the finite which allows for us to be at peace with our fallible nature and the muddled path we have taken and will

---

meaninglessness universe devoid of any reason for the significance of humanity as a whole, let alone individuals, one comes out a nihilist. It is inescapable. Anyone who still acts in ways that reflect the significance, purpose, and meaning of human life, are reflecting a genuine belief in the sacredness of human life which cannot be adequately or consistently explained within the tenants of an atheistic conception of the universe.

[*] "That's what faith is… it is knowing in the darkness that a loving God has a plan that's better than any we could ever imagine. A sovereign God adores us, and for this reason the ending of our stories will be beautiful." (Kautz, 89)

continue to take. And it is the infinite, through the consciousness that we are all necessarily interconnected and dependent, which assures justice and calls for compassion in the midst of this infinite freedom; "Inasmuch as ye have done it unto one of the least of these my brethren, ye have done it unto me." (Matthew 25:40)

Jung's Revival of the Biblical Importance of Dreams

In addition to outlining a psychological schema for modern western individuals to progress in the image of God—to live in line with the truth of the incarnation—Carl Jung also helped to revive the importance of dreams in the modern western psyche.

In the Bible, dreams are an immensely important meeting ground between man and God. It is not just Joseph "King of Dreams" and his dream interpretations which the Bible alludes to. Rather, a myriad of figures receive advice, inspiration, consolation, or purpose through the presence of God in their dreams (see Numbers 12:6; 1 Samuel 28:6; 1 Kings 3:15; Psalm 17:3; Daniel 1:17). In fact, Matthew testifies to the significance of dreams in one's destiny, as well as their service as a connection to the divine, in the story of the life of Jesus and his parents. In the first 2 chapters of the Gospel of Matthew, Matthew lists 5 times Joseph or Jesus was contacted by God or angels in their dreams and given important instructions. And Paul testifies to the reality and veracity of Jesus visiting him in a dream, believing in this wholeheartedly as a genuine direct encounter with the divine (Acts 18:9-10). Through so many iterations, the Bible sets up a conception of dreams as a ready-made temple for finding the presence of God in one's own life. Yet, for some reason, the Biblical traditions did not carry forward this valuation of dreams which was once clearly alive and well in the world.

Certainly people throughout the world over the last two millennia have individually found great value and inspiration—even divine inspiration—in their dreams. And we have scattered reports of plenty of these. But no tradition and unified understanding of the value of dreams emerged and grew in the western world. Nor did one emerge in the East, as the basic philosophy regarding dreams in the east was that one did not accrue karma in dreams, thus

Purpose in Form

they were not an important arena of cultivation[*]. Not until the psychoanalysts emerged at the turn of the 20th century did dreams resurface as a place of massive effective force in one's life—especially for one's connection to the soul[†]. And Jung took to theorizing about and working with dreams more than any other of the founders of psychoanalysis—or at least to a deeper and more expansive place, and certainly one of more divinity as opposed to merely limited personal repressed events.

For this singular revival of Biblical truth and wisdom (which remained dormant though it was right in everyone's faces), Jung and the psychoanalysts deserve the gratitude of Christians everywhere, as well as that of all of the western world, for the EFFECTIVENESS of dream work (or even merely paying attention to one's dreams and valuing them) is profound. This revelation has done humans all over the world immense good to date and will prove a significant force in the course of history moving forward, if we choose to take up the adventure of moving toward heaven on earth.

The Problems with Absolute Purpose and Their Solution

Speaking of dreams is a perfect way to illustrate a problem that arises from connecting the foundational principle of conscious purpose with absolute cause and effect. "God shall bring every work into judgement." (Ecclesiastes 12:14) Is not every effect and every act, then, purposeful and significant? Is not each and every dream saying something of profound importance? Are there not glimpses of the future and one's destiny in every scene?

One encounters this tendency when they meet those swept away by any and all coincidences as necessary signs about their future[‡]. Jung called this the

---

[*] This is a half-truth. It is important to recognize and accept that one is not held personally responsible for the content of their dreams because this content is often frighteningly violent, impudently lascivious, and otherwise disturbing and condemning if taken as a literally accurate picture of one's nature and thoughts. But, though one is not to be held accountable for the extremes of the imagery, that does not mean that this is an impotent or insignificant arena, as was thus assumed throughout the east.

[†] The word "psyche" means soul. And Carl Jung was a champion of both the term and the real conception of the soul. I use the word soul here for that reason, though it is not necessarily precisely the same as the connection between the finite and infinite I have been talking about. I discuss the terminology and idea of a soul in detail later.

[‡] I do think there is a substantial case to be made for the existence of Synchronicity, but over-credulity does not help that case.

problem of inflation, which happens when the ego is overwhelmed by more powerful forces in the unconscious. The problem with this conception of grand significance in all causes and effects combined with one's belief that one can personally arbitrate their meanings is illustrated in the book of Job, when his friends blame Job for his misfortune. K. William Kautz puts it like this:

> *Job wasn't the only one being tormented.* His friends had held to a belief that all of Job's wealth and honor were due to his righteous life. It was a theology that brought them much comfort. They had managed to inhabit a complex world while denying its complexity, and now the entire foundation of their sense of security was exposed as shallow and simplistic. How could it be that a righteous man should suffer? What does that say about God? Is God not powerful enough to redeem? Does he even care? What does it say about their own vulnerability? (13-14 italics in original)

When one believes in absolute purpose, and believes their perception and discernment of that purpose is not significantly fallible, one begins to blame people for their misfortunes. All people struck by tragedy are merely paying for old karma, old sins. "Or those eighteen, upon whom the tower in Siloam fell, and slew them, think ye that they were sinners above all men that dwelt in Jerusalem?" (Luke 13:4) Those born or struck with disabilities had sinned in some way and God is merely balancing the scales; the children at Sandy Hook really had it coming in the cosmic scheme of things...

Regardless of the horrors of life, those who are swept up in the idea of absolute purpose and perfect divine justice (and more importantly the underlying assumption that they can perceive and interpret God's motives and machinations) lay all tragedy at the feet of the victims. They scorn the individuals to keep their conception of God (their mental idol) intact. The Bible warns against this through the example of Job's friends. *"Humility and truth are so interconnected that you can't separate the two without killing them both."* (Kautz, 35 italics in original) The Bible lays some tragedy at the feet of God—while paradoxically still assuring us of his perfection in benevolence and justice. But, paradoxical as it is, this is the *effective* approach which keeps one in line with virtue, even though it poses messy problems for the intellect trying to reconcile its limited images and systems.

Purpose in Form

Whether one is so inflated by the image of God that they cannot function rationally to parse true anomalies from apophenia (or even find the motivation to try), or they are so wed to their idea of perfect and comprehensible (to their minds) justice in life, the prospect of absolute purpose causes humans problems. Steven Pinker in his book *Enlightenment Now* lists "blaming misfortune on evil doers" as part of human nature (5), and illustrates that it has taken us a very long time to consider the possibility that "misfortune may be no one's fault." (24) However, his method for achieving this disconnection between blame and tragedy is achieved through uprooting underlying meaning and purpose in the universe, and denying a personal nature of the cosmos—which he overtly recognizes, praises, and hopes for such perspectives divorced from deep meaning to spread (Pinker, 24 & 439).

Fortunately, there is a simple solution which does not require us to relinquish the necessary principle of infinite purpose, but allows us to act with appropriate humility and compassion, as well as not to suppose we can divine all of God's mind and ultimate purpose through our observation of and conjectured connections to minor happenstances. It is our old friend fallibility.

We are fallible beings. We are not necessarily correct about the purposes we perceive, as we have already admitted. We should take care in rational deliberation, which we can do without turning skepticism into another closed-minded doctrine, and we should not suppose that we can accurately see all causes and effects so as to judge and blame one for their misfortune. There is utility in individuals taking responsibility for their lives and looking to change themselves when they find things to be not entirely satisfactory, let alone gone horrendously amok. And people often, especially contemporarily, err too far on the side of victimhood, rescuing, and neglecting responsibility. Yet, in the truth of effectiveness and virtue, there is no utility in following a rule which puts all responsibility and therefore blame on all victims at all times. This does not help others, the world, or you, in truth. It merely preserves one's intellectual idolatry.

There are always ways we can change to be better, and always more we can do to cultivate ourselves and the world and prepare for the future. But there are misfortunes in life that can overcome even the well prepared. Life is infinite and the effects wrought in the natural world are still often of a magnitude beyond the full constraint of our best technologies and efforts. Life is a difficult game. To look down on those stricken by misfortune and tragedy is to not recognize the truth of the difficulty of life and to not work through compassion—to not be effective, according to the Christian faith. Though fallibility is often the very source of our problems, recognizing and accepting it is actually the solution to a few problems (as it is here) and the first step in approaching the rest[*].

Conclusion

So Christianity gave us the truth of the Incarnation. And Jung played a large role in bringing the lived reality of the Incarnation back into possibility for the western world—reaching many disillusioned and disaffected individuals gripped by intellectualism and its progeny. But what of the objections to this faith? What if we turn to the east for religion as so many disillusioned westerners have? In circles discussing yoga, Hinduism, Buddhism, Daoism and the like there is a plethora of acceptance for "purposelessness", "inaction", "the way of nature", and the unreality, meaninglessness, and insignificance of the world. Let us examine how these so called ultimate truths of the infinite, purpose, meaning, and significance hold up under a different world view and practice.

---

[*] I believe this is also the reason that the Bible is against reading omens and signs. The arts of divination come from the ideas of absolute purpose and the sensing of subtle patterns of energy to determine the future. As the Bible supports an absolute order of cause and effect and purposeful creation, one would think that it should support the idea that deep inquiry and attention to cause and effect could inform one about the future. However, the Bible dismisses and dissuades one from participating in divination practices (Jeremiah 10:2; Deuteronomy 18:9-14; Leviticus 20:6). I believe this is another way the Bible subtly recognizes human fallibility. To trust to signs and get swept up in divination is to trust too much in human interpretation over the reality of infinite possibility. Reading signs and omens may in some cases prepare one for tumultuous events in cases of well-read patterns, but success and reinforced belief only locks one into self-fulfilling loops of prophecy. In disregarding signs and omens completely one may miss out on some interesting instances of precognition, but overall they veer away from being misguided by fallible human proclamations and proceed into a future of unlimited possibility.

Purpose in Form

~So far we have seen that the central idea of the Christian tradition, as it pertains to connecting man to the infinite is that there is an intimate connection between the finite individual and the infinite God of all existence. This fundamental view of the underlying metaphysical reality of life is in perfect correlation with the mathematical conception of infinity as being self-saturating; in considering a conscious infinite nature, one would expect that such infinite consciousness would be able to fully oversee and fully inhabit all of extended existence. "He is entire in every point of space, and complete in every instant of duration… Every event is alike important in the eyes of that infinite being, who takes in at one glance the most distant regions of space and remotest periods of time" (Hume, 29 & 99)

It seems that this conjecture coming from the Christian tradition was a good one, for it lines up well with our metaphysical explanations of the basic truths of reality. We can criticize Christianity till the cows come home (and then some) but this interpretation and understanding of the Incarnation seems to be something they got very right.

To state again: the infinite is intimate with all of finite creation. This is the central message of Christianity found in the story of the Incarnation, translated into a metaphysical proposition.

Now we should look at the traditions of the East to see what they have to say, and if it is any different.~

Chapter 11: Eastern Enlightenment – Moving Effectively Toward the Transcendent

> "Buddhahood, Enlightenment, cannot be communicated, but only the *way* to Enlightenment." - Joseph Campbell (25)

The "Do Nothings" and The Fruits of Recluseship

First and foremost we must address the fact that there are endless western translations, transliterations, and interpretations of eastern thought and religion which range from absolutely abysmal to well-inspired but still wrong (though, of course there are great ones too).

Within the western circles that look to the east for inspiration there are probably more erroneous messages and half-assed usurpations than there are strawmen put up against the Abrahamic traditions. Here we will look at a few examples from author Yuval Noah Harari, who at the very least is guilty of a cursory study and reading-in of what he already believes to be the truth, rather than an actual analysis of the teachings and mindsets of eastern religion. But throughout the last century or so that Buddhism has migrated to the west, many have read it as a "world-denying" philosophy, as well as one of "inaction" and therefore some level of indifference toward the world and human life. Benatar, to his credit, did not try to pull in Buddhism on his side—though many interpretations would have allowed him to do so.

Purpose in Form

> Thousands of years before our liberal age, ancient Buddhism went further by denying not just all cosmic dramas but even the inner drama of human creation. The universe has no meaning, it claimed, and human feelings too carry no meaning. They are just ephemeral vibrations, appearing and disappearing for no particular purpose. That's the truth. Get over it. (Harari, 307)

> According to the Buddha, then, life has no meaning, and people don't need to create any meaning. They just need to realize that there is no meaning, and therefore be liberated from the suffering caused by our attachments and our identification with empty phenomena. 'What should I do?' ask people, and the Buddha advises: 'Do nothing. Absolutely nothing.' (Harari, 308)

Now I don't know how deep into Buddhism Harari considers himself. He talks about having a meditation instructor and quotes a single sutra. But the thing is, though his understanding of Buddhism is so incredibly dreadful, he could very well have a dedicated personal study and widely acknowledged teacher who has taught him all these "truths". Such is the state of westernized Buddhism.

In any case, whether these ideas come from a venerated master or are just the way Harari has heard and interpreted the Buddhist teachings himself, they are dreadfully inaccurate and misleading. It should be easy at this point to see the nonsensical nature of such an idea that Buddhism is based on meaninglessness. That is just the fantasy of modern intellectualism projecting onto an ancient religion with ambiguous and perplexing axioms. But seeing as no theory, modern or ancient, can truly posit meaninglessness, it seems unlikely that this several thousand year old tradition is based on such an assertion—certainly humans are gullible and bizarre, but not to the point of following for thousands of years a doctrine which entirely negates itself. Or maybe they are, but it does drive us to question whether or not this is a good interpretation.

Buddhism does not preach meaninglessness. In fact, go try to find the foundational Buddhist texts on meaninglessness. They don't exist. And any secondary or later texts you find translating Buddhist teachings as meaningless will be as paradoxical as their texts on purposelessness (which we will turn to

Eastern Enlightenment

soon). Harari presents one sutra which is a meditation on form and the transience of life, and he reads meaninglessness into the ideas of transience and the mundane nature of the world. But this is entirely unfounded[*].

First of all, the notion of suffering which Buddhism fixes itself on, is a preoccupation with meaning. Suffering means something. That's why it matters. Second, the entire religion is based off of a set of truths and a particular path of living toward realizing these and transcending them. Truth implies meaning. A specific path and set of ideas over others implies meaning. Buddhism, like all else, believes in meaning. Buddhism talks about the impermanent nature of life and often takes a grotesque look at what earthly life entails, but to read "meaninglessness" into that is merely a projection from the confused modern philosophy it springs out of. The most one can reach for in the case of Buddhism is a disdain for form or earthly life—resulting in the Ethical Problem of the East—though this too is not a correct reading of the texts and ignores many key teachings which point in a different way.

Likewise, Buddhism is not about a lack of purpose in life—though this point is more textually confusing because, unlike meaninglessness, Buddhism does appear to talk about purposelessness—nor does it instruct its followers to "do nothing" in the sense of rejecting care and responsibility in the world and one's own life; again that is a projection of nihilism from the confused minds of modern secularist-nihilists. However, these two confusions of "doing nothing" and being "purposeless" are much more understandable misunderstandings, and they are what we will concentrate on. The idea of meaninglessness, along with assertions of the insignificance of human life and endeavors, are—especially after we have discussed it at such length already—patently absurd. If Buddhism were preaching meaninglessness, it would be wrong.

As far as using religion for wish fulfillment goes, the "new-age" and associated people have at least as many guilty members as does Christianity[†]. But there are still those who have properly steeped themselves in the tradition, and who come from it organically, who talk about purposelessness of life and the illusory, transient, and therefore seemingly insignificant nature of all

---

[*] "A thing isn't beautiful because it lasts..." (Vision, *Avengers: Age of Ultron*)
[†] See Dr. Peterson on the unrealistic assessment from Marx of Christianity as a wish-fulfillment doctrine ("Marxism and Christianity at odds with each other", YouTube)

things. Alan Watts is one who speaks commonly in this vein and seems to validly draw such ideas from eastern scriptures. What can we make of these discussions?

What we must first say (redundant as it may be at this point) is that all traditions, those of the east included, value and strive for truth. And all people and traditions believe in meaning, inescapably, as we have sufficiently shown. The journey of the Buddha is a journey for truth, and he lays out a path for others to follow. The yogic tradition and Hindu beliefs point their followers toward truths. Daoism proclaims truths. These truths are superordinate. They are there whether we believe them or not.

Daoism expounds on "the way of power and virtue"—that is a truth about how the Dao operates *effectively,* though counterintuitively. "Nature does not hurry, yet all is *accomplished*" (Daodejing Ch. 37, common translation, emphasis added). Yoga tells you how to meditate appropriately and prepare your body *effectively* to most *effectively* access universal truth. Even Buddhism, perhaps the most dire culprit of being interpreted to support purposelessness, meaninglessness, and inaction, lays out a particular, most *effective* path to follow and certain truths to WORK toward understanding.

Thus each of these traditions is fundamentally invested in truth itself, the significance of the human consciousness and life experience, and the proper ways of human action, thought, and intention in service to these truths. Just as the Bible does not take the time to explicitly state its foundational assumption of causation, truth, and meaning, the traditions of the east imply and rely on these just as fully and take all of their following steps and directions off this inevitable foundation. Let us look primarily at Buddhism to see this through thoroughly though.

Buddhism, perhaps most often Zen Buddhism, speaks about (or is said to speak about) purposelessness in action and therefore the meaninglessness of life. Taken as catechisms from people who have played a poor game of telephone over from the east, these support all kind of vices and nonsense in western minds that think they are that much closer to enlightenment by purporting these so-called truths. Note that this is different than the Ethical Problem of the East, which believes in meaning and value, but dismisses human form as insignificant—the individual soul and its strivings remain important, but the body and Earth are seen as gross, low, and unworthy of engagement. Here we are looking at a proposal that Buddhism is nihilistic, fundamentally, and thus negates all worth of value, truth, and significance by proposing purposelessness and meaninglessness (which are inextricably tied).

But, one must ask, if there were no purpose in action and no meaning in life, why would there be noble truths and a way of action directing behavior? The Noble Eightfold Path as prescribed by the Buddha specifically includes "RIGHT INTENTION" and "RIGHT ACTION", among the rest of the list which are all irrevocably and self-evidently based in a presumptions of meaning and purpose. If purpose is unreal, how is there a proper way over an improper way? If action is meaningless, why is there one particular path over others? If I am unreal, meaningless, and altogether void of any significance or cause for concern, what does it matter what my thoughts, intentions, and efforts are?

In looking for a confirmation of the modern veiled nihilism, many westerners have put little other than surface level thought into the reality of Buddhist teachings and have merely accepted peculiar translations, which speak to a very different mindset and have their own important contexts, as confirmation of the realities they pretend to believe in of untruth, meaninglessness, purposelessness, and insignificance.

Indeed, the central act of Buddhism, which is also perhaps the most effective practice that the world has yet discovered in changing lives, is meditation[*]. It should also be noted, in light of our efforts in this book, that the Bible is replete with references to meditation as an act that aided its central characters. (See Genesis 24:63; Joshua 1:8; Psalms 1:2; 4:4; 46:10; 77:12; 119:15-99; 143:5; and John 11:6 where Christ was in still meditation for 2 days straight) This fact, along with the biblical importance of dreams, is something that was largely neglected in the development of the organized Christian tradition, which focuses mainly on the effectiveness of prayer[†]. The practice of meditation was relegated essentially to monks. But there is no reason—scriptural or secular—to believe that meditation is something which

---

[*] "You are your own enemy and you don't know it. You don't learn to sit quietly. You don't learn to give time to God. And you are impatient and expect to attain heaven all at once. You cannot get it by reading books or by listening to sermons or by doing charitable works. You can get it only by giving your time to Him in deep meditation." (Yogananda, AumAmen.com)

[†] For a psychological discussion of prayer to the secularly minded, see my book *Jnana Yoga*.

should be esoteric or in some way beyond the reaches of the everyday faithful follower. This is something the east has realized, and—largely because of meditation's revival in the west through its contact with eastern religions—modern neuroscience has newly discovered the undeniable benefits of its effects[*].

Meditation, a subset of which can be called the practice of "doing nothing", is sometimes said to be "purposeless". Yet it is DONE—i.e. enacted[†]—and it has demonstrable effects on people's brains as well as subjective senses of wellbeing. And while meditators of a serious Buddhist nature do not treat it like a mere workout to enhance their physical or mental lives, they do seek a goal; even if that seeking is seeking not to seek and that goal is the gateless gate, they have been told that meditation is part of the particular way to nirvana or moksha, and they BELIEVE (meaningful) in the TRUTH of this path and they ACT IT OUT for that PURPOSE. There is a core Buddhist sutra, for example, called *The Fruits of Recluseship*, meaning: "The things you get out of doing things in this particular way". If that isn't a clear call to and investment in EFFECTIVENESS in life (putting in particular causes to get particular effects) I don't know what is[‡].

Another text, *The Visuddhimagga*, describes all the particular correct (more EFFECTIVE) ways to meditate—it is advice on the proper way to apply the causes in life to get the proper effects. This is no different, in essence, than "following the statutes of God". All systems presume meaning and purpose and they all begin their efforts to influence human life (because they believe it is significant) through suggesting particular ways to change our causal interactions with the world so that the effects we experience will also change.

---

[*] Note: traditions of the east also separated monks and more intensive spiritual tasks from lay people, and meditation is still something that is hard to enact all over, but it is still likely that in the east it is more common to find an average householder meditating than under the Christian tradition.
[†] "Even sitting still for long periods is a kind of action." (Dogen/Warner, 294)
[‡] "Renunciation is not an end, it is the means to an end. The real renunciant is he who lives for God first, regardless of his outer mode of existence. To love God and conduct your life to please Him—that is what matters. When you will do that, you will know the Lord." (Yogananda, AumAmen.com)

Eastern Enlightenment

The Law of Dependent Origination and the Approximation of Causality

> "Everything is intricate beyond imagining… we perceive a very narrow slice of a causally interconnected matrix." –Dr. Jordan Peterson (267)

The Buddha described "The Law of Dependent Origination" as one of the deepest laws of the universe, the understanding of which brought one to the verge of enlightenment[*] (Buddha, et. al., 223). The short summation of this law is that all things that exist depend entirely on the existence of other things which support and create them. This law can be approximated as the idea of ultimate causation which we supposed was underlying the emergent conception of God as the Abrahamic law giver and ordering force of the world. However, there are a few potential discrepancies to sort out, because the words of the Buddha were both general and practical, but focused on only particular instances of causation, and did not lay out a general metaphysical principle nor describe a line of causation back to some creator or big bang as we usually conceive in the west.

When the Buddha described the Law of Dependent Origination, which is akin to causality, he described it in relation to the causes and conditions of suffering for any being as a process of direct and linear causality, as we usually think of it. Beginning with the general question of where life comes from (birth) and proceeding through the conditions of birth and sensuous existence, the Buddha appears to describe a very linear and simple picture of causation. Yet, as the Buddha says to Ananda, this idea is deep and appears deep—it is not to be mistaken for some surface level appearance and comprehension (Buddha, et. al., 223).

The Buddha described one particular line of causal dependence and formation—that of consciousnesses and mind-and-body to birth and death, and therefore suffering. But this exposition of a particular causal chain is clearly dependent on the general principle of causation; thus fundamental causality is implied in the practical example used by the Buddha. Further, the examples the Buddha uses to construct this "chain" of causality to examine and attempt to break—i.e. input new causes, creating new effects—are nebulous aggregates.

---

[*] The Buddha's penultimate vision on the night prior to his enlightenment was that of the chain of causation. (Campbell, 26)

Purpose in Form

The immediate examples of birth and death are generic principles applying to all manners of species (as well as all demi-gods, angels, and demons, in the Buddhist conception). Further, apparent singular principles in the "line" of dependent origination like "craving", "clinging", and "contact" (i.e. all sense perception) are general ideas underlying all manners of infinitely manifested instantiations in different beings and circumstances. So while in the literal text of the Law of Dependent origination, the Buddha appears to describe a distinctly linear and simple exposition of causation, this is a distilled and simplified explanation of the underlying principle of causality, and general directives of where to go to interrupt the processes. But, in terms of how this principle reflects on the wider conception of causality and how it manifests, the Buddha left great room for differing conceptions, of which we may take some time to explore two general approaches.

In the western mind, when we think of causality, we often picture each thing being dependent on one other thing which preceded it and so on indefinitely. But that is a poor resolution picture of what our theories actually indicate. Even in the west causation is more accurately a web of causation, so that lines of causality do not proceed strictly from one thing to another so linearly and separately, but rather each thing that causes another thing is actually dependent in multiple ways on other things. In more concrete terms, I am not only dependent in my existence on my mother, but also my father, and additionally the food I have ingested (and all the causes going into that) and the medical treatment I have received (and all the causes which go into that), etc. So the western conception of causation depicts much more of a web, though we often simplify it by picturing simple lines of causation.

In his teachings, the Buddha also took this simplified approach to expressing the underlying ideas. But, given the generality and simplicity the Buddha took to direct the attention of his students, along with the declaration of the aggregate natures of things like the body and consciousness in the Buddhist system, it is not so clear what the phenomenological and metaphysical conception of causation itself should be, and how closely it need line up with our common conception in the west.

The Buddha generally stated that there was this principle of connected causality—certain things depend on other conditions for their existence, and without such conditions, those connected things do not arise. And the Buddha maintained that the self in all ways (body, consciousness, perceptions, etc.)

was made up of aggregates. This plurality of the self and the necessity of interconnected causes and conditions immediately pushes us to conceive much more of a web of causation rather than a chain, as the literal content of the doctrine seems to describe. But there is another phenomenological approach to describing causality in general which is not ruled out by the Buddha's teachings, and which arises naturally from our long preceding discussion on the infinity of life.

As we begin to conceive of the web of causation as truly infinite, which it is, we move further from any sort of particular, linear causality and toward something more like "field causality". The "web" idea in some way still implies singular, linear, finite connections—tiny and intricate as they may be. In what we might call "field causality", which can easily fit with the Buddha's description of the Law of Dependent Origination, what causes an individual thing is not a complex aggregate of different single entities interacting in complex but finite ways, but rather the entirety of the existent universe acting as an inseparable whole. If we can picture it: a slice of space-time in the universe as a particular field, which then leads causally to the next instance of space time where things are a bit different. Taking any particular thing in the second instance of the universe, we would not say it was caused by individual things knocking together within the first universe in particular ways, but more generally that the new thing caused depended on the entirety of the preceding slice of the universe and all its operation to come into being. This is an acknowledgement of completely infinite interconnectivity.

Though this conception sounds more generalized and the ideas of linear or web causality sound a little more discriminating and intricate, it is not the case that the field conception is the less precise. In fact, I believe the field conception is the more precise and accurate reflection of the reality of causation in general, *as it pertains to the perception of infinity*.

Though in the west we know through experience that dissecting and specifying many of the causes going into the creation of particular objects and knowing these particularities is incredibly helpful and effective in so many ways—and the Buddha too seemed to focus on particular, specified, and seemingly linear connections in his teaching—it is actually a distortion of the reality to specify in the ways that we do, because the reality is infinite, so to delineate it in so many ways is to move further away from the thing-in-itself and more into a mental approximation. This can be seen in the Buddhist teaching by unpacking the terms the Buddha used to create this appearance of linearity and singular causation—each of the terms in the general chain he proposed is not only a general principle underlying infinite manifestation and variation across all life, but are also aggregates themselves in each individual; not only are the examples of birth and consciousness infinitely varied in their manifestations, but birth and consciousness are divisible terms into many different stages and functions even when looking at one example.

In contrast, by conceiving of the entire universe as an inseparable whole, field causality gets closer to capturing the reality of the true infinite interconnection underlying what we call cause and effect, while web or linear causal approximations lose sight of the true infinity and begin to think of the aggregate of the universe as immensely complex, but ultimately finite.

By specifying and delineating the universe in so many ways, we chop it up hoping to make a map out of the parts, but in this construction we miss the reality that the infinite necessitates—there will always be infinitely more parts to put together. Thus we always miss the thing-in-itself; no matter how dense we picture the "web" of causation, it misses the reality of an infinitely dense interconnectivity—an infinite oneness. In Buddhist terms we may say that by exploring and envisioning the complex fullness of cause and effect (the dense web), we miss the truth of emptiness, which is a transcendent shift one reaches. Though the two truths seem deeply akin and appear, from one view, to be degrees along a spectrum, the idea of reversal (a common eastern theme[*]) indicates an inflection point where perception greatly changes and a new understanding is reached that is spoken about quite differently (i.e. a transcendence has occurred).

Another thing that has been entirely missed by modern western society in our dissection of the universe is that causation is not a special property or law implemented below the surface of the infinite, like a rule implemented within a game. We come to this idea from the west in a tradition of building intricately and minutely from the ground up, always assuming our ignorance. The eastern traditions speak in more radical terms of knowledge given their deep development of and trust in intuition. If we first recognize that the universe is an infinite whole—a truth the east has permitted itself to claim more readily

---

[*] Found in Christianity too—it is the source of the maxim "God works in mysterious ways".

than the west—and therefore we know that, in dissecting, analyzing, and specifying the elements and their connections which we can observe, we are merely looking at *some* of the perceivable connections of the universe, then we can understand that *causation is not other than interconnectivity*. Causation is merely the name we give to specified (and therefore incomplete) "lines" of connection that we observe propagating through "time" (which is also a mental dissection made of the infinite whole).

This point is subtle, but it is incredibly deep; it is deep and it appears deep. Causation is not other than interconnectivity. Do not assume that you have comprehended this statement merely because it seems clear to you. If you can make contact with the truth this concept points to, you'll experience the infinite. If you haven't been brought to the experience of that depth, then you haven't touched the meaning of those words. Causation is not other than interconnectivity.

When we contemplate the causal "laws" of the universe, we are not actually looking at specific rules of isolated objects that float around otherwise unrelated to each other. Rather, we are observing one particular way or set of ways in which all things are connected. Causation is the name we give to certain sets of interconnections we observe. When we forget or are unaware of the fact to begin with that our specifications and delineations of the universe, its objects, and "laws", are departures from the greater reality of infinite oneness and interconnectivity, we find it incredible (or, at least we should) that all these apparently disparate things have effects on each other, and we follow an infinite mystery of how deep and wide these effects spread. This slowly pushes us toward the idea that all these things are at least distantly connected across time and space (which, again, are abstractions and dissections themselves). But, if and when we finally get the whole picture, the fact that these things are all interwoven is obvious—that is their nature by necessity of the fundamental infinite reality!

The problem is that when we began to notice causation and take advantage of it, we began building mental maps and models in our minds of particularized connections we found by dissecting the inscrutable mass of the universe dancing chaotically before us; and while these maps were greatly helpful and indeed were true discoveries of particular connections which we could comprehend and interact with, somewhere along the line we mistook the map for the territory and ever since have supposed that the reality of the world is a large expanse of separate objects. We forgot that reality is an infinite field of dancing energies when we payed specific attention to the individual patterns for too long. Now we are essentially evolved to believe the forms within the patterns are the end of the story and that the connections between things are miniscule, subtle, often abstruse and entirely linear and defined.

In becoming conditioned in this way, we grew to thinking that things are indivisible units and that there are eternal, abiding substances on which the changing forms of the world ride and are supported. Rediscovering the infinite is at the same time a rediscovery of the aggregate nature of all phenomena— that there is no abiding indivisible foundation which constitutes fundamental singular links in the apparent chain of causality. Thus, though the Buddha used a linear description to relate the concept to us, and though causality is a real, demonstrable principle, penetrating to the infinite saturation of causality (interconnectivity) is the same as understanding that all forms and substances are conditioned aggregates of phenomena (i.e. there is no self).

Karma, Cause and Effect, and the State of Purposelessness

Karma has been directly called the law of cause and effect* (Dogen/Warner, 66). In that sense, it's a more specific or specialized look at part of the law of dependent origination or the principle of causality in general. It's the eastern term for the idea of cause and effect as applied to human life and volition. It even has the idea of morality or justice built into it, just as western traditions realized the world functioned not only mechanically but also morally (see previous note).

But, in Buddhism, through deeply studying karma or cause and effect, this particular aspect of the law of dependent origination, and seeing that all karma has an origin, an ultimate cause, one becomes freed from karma—so it is said. By looking deeply at cause and effect, one transcends the limitations of absolute cause and effect. What does that mean to the western mind? What

---

* And, indeed, in the Bible, the notion of God's implementation of his rule and judgement (which we have said is largely synonymous with a hypothesis of cause and effect) is strikingly similar to the ideas of karma. One reaping what one sows and being paid back in kind for their sins is a huge theme in the Bible; you'll find statements like "Reward every man according to his works" coming not just out of the mouth of Jesus many times, but on nearly every page of the old testament (Matthew 16:27).

claim is being made and how can we comprehend it? Is this principle also to be found in western conceptions of reality?

Karma, or cause and effect, is of great importance to our hypothesized selves—these limited, external entities (our bodies and minds) that are part of the flow of the world and are buffeted around by all this cause and effect. But when you look at the world of cause and effect, and you see how deeply it is all entwined, nowhere in this infinite web do you find a "self". That is the great Buddhist insight. The movements of karma or cause and effect all involve only appearances and mistaken identities. There are no breaks in the chain, no gaps for a separate effective "self" to slip in and do some miraculous (meaning "uncaused") work on the system. "There is no hard line that divides ourselves from the outside world, or the rest of the world." (Dogen/Warner, 28) The system is fully interconnected.

Looking at this principle from the other side, we would say: since the true self is infinite, it is not an object within the myriad of flowing causes and effects that is subject to their movements. In looking at the ever-changing scenery of the world (which includes the body and mind one is perceiving), one finds only this immense web of cause and effect—of interconnected pieces. "Where men see only change and death, the blessed behold immutable form, world without end." (Campbell, 192) It is from penetrating this reality and comprehending the nature of absolute cause and effect, not as a linear proposition as we commonly think of it in short hand, but as not other than the fact of infinite interconnectivity itself—infinite oneness—, that one begins to see the timeless reality and the lack of an objective self that Buddhism speaks about.

When you realize that all is one interconnected whole, and that actions and cause and effect do not separate things—they are themselves evidence only of the connection between things across time—then you begin to see the "uncarved block" (Daodejing Ch. 37, Muller); you see that there is no time and that there is only one cause, or that there is no cause, all just happens spontaneously together—as One. "Cause and effect are simultaneous… time is illusory" (Dogen/Warner 159)

When you begin to glimpse such a state, you begin to understand the reality of "non-action" and the language of "purposelessness" may start to speak to you. The reason for this is Buddhism speaks directly from and to the infinite perspective—it understands that this is a state where consciousness exists, and

Purpose in Form

one that the human mind can glimpse from time to time.

In Christian terms, though they would be reluctant to admit it, Buddhism has been speaking about and directly to the Christ-consciousness in every individual, and attempting to help their followers seek and make contact with it, for a good 600 years before the historical Jesus ever taught about this infinite consciousness with which he was made eponymous in the west. They might object to this impossibility, yet they forget: "Before Abraham was, I am." (John 8:58) Or, as it was passed down through the East: "Absolutely every element of your body/mind right now was present at the very moment of creation and long before (if a word like 'before' even pertains to such a thing) and will be here forever. Everything you are is connected intimately to the entire universe, near and far, past, present, and future." (Dogen/Warner, 58) This knowledge, this Truth has always been.

Buddhism realized that from the perspective of the infinite—outside time and beyond identification with external, projected identities—the creation of life is seen as "purposeless". This, however, is not a declaration of dismissiveness from the infinite toward the finite, nor is it a statement of meaninglessness of all human stories and goals. It is only a necessary reality that belongs to the infinite itself. The infinite cannot have a purpose. Purpose is, by definition, an orientation toward something greater or beyond oneself. The infinite is all and there is no greater nor a beyond toward which it could be oriented*. Thus the infinite must be "purposeless", not because it is lacking anything, but, in fact, *because it is lacking nothing*. It is because of the perfection inherent in the nature of the infinite that it sees "purposelessness". Purpose is something that can only exist within incompletion and imperfection, where there is a beyond, a more, a better to strive towards.

The infinite is not missing anything, nor does it have anywhere to go or anything to complete given that it is outside all space and time—to the infinite, even all of creation is already complete; it knows all ends. Thus there is no disturbing, no anxiety, no striving, no action. The language of "purposelessness" comes only from necessity of the reality of the conscious infinite awareness. It has nothing to do, properly understood, with commenting

---

* "God would not worry whether he was fulfilling some external purpose... The whole project of transcendence only makes sense if one is limited... it would be incoherent to want to transcend a limit that you did not have." (Benatar, 54-56)

on the worthlessness of the limited lives of humans. One can be told to pursue and contemplate purposelessness, in an effort to get that mind to begin to identify with or recall the nature of the infinite to which it is connected, but that is very different than seriously forwarding a thesis that life is "purposeless" through and through, and encouraging a form of nihilism or despair towards life.

Again, as we have seen over and over, it is impossible to seriously and coherently suggest that human life and consciousness is purposeless or insignificant. One must merely inquire what the jester's purpose is in disseminating their views on purposelessness to see through the charade. Once you are in form, in creation, living a limited life, purpose and desire are inevitable. They are the energies of the world at work—purpose and desire are no less natural, intrinsic, and commonplace than gravity or electromagnetism. They are just variations of cause and effect. We consider purpose and desire very personal, because they seem to arise from within us (or within what we consider to be ourselves), but they are simply part of the unfolding of the world, the play of energy through form. "You are intimately a part of everything." (Dogen/Warner, 58) One has no more power to eradicate purpose and desire than one has to destroy gravity or switch off the sun (in fact, we probably legitimately have more hope for the latter two).

The freedom that is attained from desire, which is aimed at by Buddhists, is not about stopping the proceeding of the world by turning off its energetic proceedings, but merely disentangling the roots of desire from the soil of one's perceived identity. When one is unclear about their identity, and sees their self in all sorts of places embedded in the world, desires seem to ensnare one and keep them rooted, tied down, and begin to suffocate. But when one investigates the truth of one's identity, and finds that there is "no self" in the world, the tangling roots of desire no longer encompass or reach anywhere near the true identity, and thus they no longer are any sort of snare or trap.

In this way, the enlightenment of Buddhism (which is the same enlightenment and salvation as all other true doctrines[*]) does not so much as

---

[*] "The experience of zazen is eternal. It is the same for everyone." (Dogen, 4) This reflects the reality that the infinite truth is, and must be, one. All those who touch the infinite experience the same state, though they may try to translate their experience to others in so many different ways. "Buddhas and ancestors all experience the same state of realization." (Dogen, 213-214) The truth being only zazen or only Christ is merely

destroy all desire (nor does the path to it involve such impossibilities[*]) but rather, in separating the self or identity from the tangles of the world, it leaves the world and the desires of human life space to grow and proceed freely, naturally, along their own course. In dissolving the illusory perceptions of the limited self or selves, desire *as a trap and binding* is undone because the self which was supposedly bound is seen as non-existent. The phenomenon we call desire and once viewed as a fetter (through the Buddhist lens) still exists and proceeds in the world, but its nature is no longer the same as its context in relation to the identity has changed.

In exactly the same way, the redemption and salvation of a human soul in the Christian tradition, where one is reconnected with their infinite (immortal) identity, does not stop them from being human, nor lift them out of the struggles and limited nature of the world; rather, it introduces one to the almighty love and Grace of God, which provides the space and forgiveness to live an imperfect human life. "You do not become a Buddha by having some magical, mystical experience that confers Buddhahood on you, after which you

---

to say the truth is the absolute Oneness of infinity. "That they may be one, even as we are one: I in them, and thou in me, that they may be made perfect in one." (John 17:22-23)

[*] In the technical sense this is not actually impossible, though this technicality actually further affirms that interpreting such doctrines literally is incorrect. In her book *The Willpower Instinct*, Kelly McGonigal shares a case study of a man who through overdose induced brain damage lost his brain's reward system—the seat of the emotion and sensation of desire (130-131). This man was not put into nirvana, but became overwhelmingly depressed. She also cites examples of Parkinson's patients whose reward systems become atrophied—they too are not put at ease but are commonly diagnosed with depression (131). "When our reward system [i.e. desire] is quiet, the result isn't so much total contentment as it is apathy." This bears striking resemblance to those who turn to philosophies of world-denial, meaninglessness/purposelessness, and other variations of veiled nihilism and end up becoming depressed and misanthropic. Even if we are to consider the wisdom of Buddhism and the East and grant that they may still be onto something with the transcendence of desire—that this is not necessarily a poor wording—we must concede that mere extraction of the physical ability to desire from the individual is alone not sufficient to attain bliss; there is something elemental and *purposeful* in the rest of the prescribed path to transcendence—something about the way it is done is significant and cannot be substituted with surgery. This points to purpose and meaning in action, and the significance and necessity of personal cultivation exactly as we have been saying.

can just slack off for the rest of your life." (Dogen/Warner, 42)

Both traditions, of east and of west, recognize that the reality of the infinite does not wipe out the world as something that shouldn't have been, or something that should not continue to proceed. "The first problem of the returning hero is to accept as real... the banalities and noisy obscenities of life." (Campbell, 189) It is the very knowing presence, love, and willing support that the infinite gives to the finite world that keeps our world going. The infinite, far from eradicating the world with all its limited desires and lowly purposes, consciously provides the space (the infinite Grace) for all of these sinful, limited lives to unfold.

Buddhists speak directly about a perspective which is Not Of This World—that of the immortal or infinite self, which sees things very differently than we do through our limited, sequential, and causal vision. In so doing, they speak of "purposelessness" and "non-action", not because life is meaningless and our individual purposes are hallucinatory aberrations, but because the reality of the conscious infinite must be explained in ways that don't necessarily make sense from our perspectives. The Lord works in mysterious ways.

The Buddha did not tell people to "do nothing", as Harari suggests. Though the principle of "non-action" indicates a deep and beautiful reality, it has nothing to do with individuals not putting in effort or suppressing their will (see previous note), or negating their significance; it indicates a state of being where the true identity is remembered, and one begins to see that the body and mind they so identified with are merely natural parts of God's creation, which proceed merely through karma (cause and effect), as part of the same creation as everything else. In this state, plenty of actions occur, but one observes them all from the place of the infinite soul, which is beyond all form and creation (thus can also be called no-soul or no-self, as it is infinite and undefinable—non-localizable).

The Buddha did not say "life is meaningless", quite the contrary, he said life is suffering* and there is a way to end suffering. And Buddhism does not preach "purposelessness" in the sense of discrediting all our efforts and desires

---

* "What profit hath a man of all his labour which he taketh under the sun?... All things are full of labour; man cannot utter it: the eye is not satisfied with seeing, nor the ear filled with hearing... In much wisdom is much grief: and he that increaseth knowledge increaseth sorrow... all that cometh is vanity." (Ecclesiastes 1:3;1:8; 1:18; 11:8) Life is "the furnace of affliction." (Isaiah 48:10)

Purpose in Form

(clearly, given that one of the core tenants of Buddhism is "RIGHT EFFORT"), it merely asserts that the place which is looked for in meditation is a oneness with the infinite consciousness, and the natural state of this infinite consciousness is purposeless, given that there is nothing greater than it or beyond it to strive towards or that it is missing out on. Through describing the quality of the consciousness, one's limited being is (hopefully) put closer in tune with that all-encompassing consciousness—though if one takes it to mean that life is meaningless and the infinite has no cares or concerns for individual beings, one is going further from the truth rather than tuning in with it.

Just as God loves the world through all its sin, in ways we cannot hope to comprehend from our perspectives, and one who dares ask "why?" of God, as though they are on comparable ground to judge as the infinite, gets a scolding and incomprehensible answer[*], the Buddhists talk about the "purposelessness" of the ideal, not because they believe our lives are meaningless and they are really just a sect of nihilists, but because they know of a reality which so far transcends worldly consciousness[†] that it functions in ways that seem counter intuitive or at odds with our own.

The infinite is necessarily purposeless by definition. And, just as necessarily, purpose in form, creation, or limited being, is as real and inexorable as causation. So long as one perceives causation, purpose will exist for them. So long as one perceives suffering, one will perceive purpose—for every problem is but a purpose. This is not a bad thing. It is not a failure to see causation and purpose in the world; it is not a failure to see the imperfection of the world. "Don't worry about being caught up in the world of cause and effect" (Dogen, 74) Causation and purpose are integral parts of the world, just as limitation and imperfection are. To see the world is to see causation and purpose, to live a limited and striving, imperfect life. And to see causation and purpose is to see the world—to be limited and striving.

Part of the PURPOSE of Buddhist pursuits is to ALSO see beyond the world, to the reality of the infinite, to recall the transcendent, which affirms perfection in the midst of all this imperfection. But, just like Christianity, Buddhists are not to disown or destroy the world and to avow the uncreated

---

[*] Think of Job here.
[†] One that can tame the leviathan and do all things than man can't even dream of. (Job 41:1-10)

infinite as the only true and important reality—they are not to abandon the imperfect world in pursuit of the perfect being of God. "[The Buddha] never begrudg[ed] his body or even his life." (Dogen, 231)

The world of cause and effect, of karma, of desire, is a real experience. And because this experience is real, and because there is really purpose in form, there are particular ways to conduct oneself in life—which both Buddhists and Christians realize. The world of form is a world of endless suffering so long as one is ignorant of the transcendent infinite which saturates every moment, but which is missed when one's identity is confused and wrapped up in the world of forms and causes.

But "the Buddha broke past even the zone of the creative gods and came back from the void; he announced salvation from the cosmogonic ground." (Campbell, 276) The Buddha reminds us there is a remedy to this suffering, a perfection underlying and suffusing all this imperfection. And yet "we miss the fact that this transcendence is actually continuously happening throughout every moment of every day. Meditation practice helps make this clearer." (Dogen/Warner, 48) This remedy does not erase imperfection or suffering—it merely lets one know that they are connected to the infinite; it is the same remedy as the Christian who accepts Christ as their own identity and savior. One then can put one's attitude toward the world in proper perspective given the reality of the infinite. One can bear even crucifixion in the world, given the reality of salvation.

It is not by the destruction of the body and the world (which is the only way one would truly end all desires and purposes), but rather by the adoption of a right attitude and way of life for the body and mind within causation, which promotes the possibility for one to find and recall their true identity and connection with the infinite, transcendent reality. "It's all about attitude. What Buddha transmitted to us is really just that, an attitude." (Dogen, 141) This is what the Buddha teaches through the Noble Eightfold Path. Through acceptance of the transcendent, and yet immanent and intimate infinite reality, one accepts and is at peace with the imperfection of the world, knowing that there is a perfection so deep that there is space for imperfection to unfold as it will. There is an end to suffering. Suffering is finite. Life is infinite.

Harari says Buddhism is not about finding a connection to anything; and he is somewhat correct—it is not about connecting to any THING. Buddhism is about disconnecting from identification with all things. But it is certainly not about the annihilation of one's consciousness or awareness or Being all together. The disconnection (of the perceived identity) from things or forms is what facilitates the remembrance or reconnection to the infinite, or that which is NO THING (in-finite).

But overall Harari's assessment and translation of the Buddhist principles is just dreadfully wrong. To say that Buddhism is not about a story, as Harari does, is as nonsensical as saying anything else is not about a story—for even saying "it's not about a story", is itself a story. It's a story of no-story. We don't function without stories. And that's not because stories are lies and we are broken beings who need to be lied to. It's not that the universe is not a story—in fact, I don't think there's a much better description of the universe than a great story (a Neverending Story, as it were)—except for that of an eternal dance or musical composure. Getting caught up in this idea of "no story"* is a lot like getting caught up in the idea of "no self", "non-action", "non-being" or "purposelessness". When you try to bring these ideas down into the realm of human life and consciousness, you get way off track and miss the point.

Buddhism is a story like anything else. And the story of all religions is our journey of reconnection to the infinite reality. That's a story, and it's true. The immediate experience of the infinite is not the same as the story that is told of it, but that does not make the story not true nor irrelevant, nor dispensable in any way (nor is it desirable that it would). The PURPOSE of these stories is, in some sense, to get you to move through them to the reality that is beyond them.

The gold one is seeking, the peace and freedom of enlightenment or salvation, must be sought—through desire and purpose. And one is directed in their striving and seeking by a particular story which orients them. At the end of that story, life does not dissolve; one does not stop living as a limited, mortal being after enlightenment, no more than one stops engaging with the sinful world after being saved through connecting to their immortal soul. One gets to this place of ultimate freedom and grace, and then continues to live in the world, but with a new perspective, a new way of engaging with life (a renewed faith), a new *story*, which comes from an understanding of the infinite transcendence which redeems all.

---

* More on this later.

Eastern Enlightenment

The Same Glorious Foundation

The methods of the east are clearly purposeful and intentional, and clearly invested in purpose in form. They rely on particular effort, ways of thought and action, and, perhaps above all, *discernment*. Discernment implies this over that, a better and a worse, and it implies the crucial and inevitable place of individual human consciousness in determining and shaping one's progress and destiny.

Discernment is the key identifying trait of the human ego which Jungians consider the cornerstone of all personal development and world transformation. Here again, just as we saw in the west, the goal is efficacy in form, pursuits of particular purposes as decided by the significant individual consciousness, and acknowledgement of the divine infinite which is intimately connected to human reality. Even the pursuit of the divine is achieved[*] through ego-discernment of this *desire* and the requisite work and sacrifice of other goals for this supreme goal[†]. In the end the divine is achieved only through itself—we do not create it through our striving—but our striving is part of the path and story here, which the divine has intended.

The language of purposelessness has nothing to do with denying human realities or negating human activity or consciousness (see note). When Buddhists talk about "purposelessness" they are talking about the "just-so-ness" of the infinite creation and reality. "Purposelessness" is, as we have seen, just a required accompaniment of absolute, infinite perfection. So, when Buddhists talk about the "purposelessness" of life, they are talking about the absolute perfection of God. All this talk of "purposelessness" is really identical to Christians talking about the Glory of God. "Reality as it is is a treasure." (Dogen, 233)

Glory is merely a quality that is bestowed on reality through its oneness with the infinite. Glory doesn't "do" anything, it is not made for someone or something to admire or behold (though it can be beheld). In that

---

[*] It is the pursuit and intention that are achieved, not the divine itself.
[†] Even though the desire and work are paradoxical and lead one deep into paradox and require deep transformations that challenge conventional conceptions of what is possible, and this is often translated along the lines of "giving up desire" in Buddhist terms or "hating the world" or "hating the self" in Christian terms—neither of which are instructions we should set out with from the beginning and follow literally; they are products of the paradox that are encountered along the way.

sense, glory is "purposeless". It is not an intentional, ancillary creation of God to amuse himself or us. It is merely a property of the infinite which exists beyond any cause. It is what shines forth by virtue of the infinite merely existing in itself.

The infinite Glory of God is that "just-so-ness" that is characteristic of infinite perfection. It cannot be aimed at anything greater since its own being is the infinite. Thus, all this talk about the "purposelessness" of life, far from being in line with the dreary fads of the day of cynicism and nihilism or quasi-nihilism, is really about the absolute perfection of life and the Glory of God to which we owe all and in which all rests. To bring it down to our level and pretend that Buddhism has some allegiance to the dark and anti-human "truths" of the world that we need to face up to is to entirely miss the perfection of reality that "purposelessness" points to, as well as to somehow entirely overlook the glaring facts that Buddhism, like all else, is entirely and unabashedly invested in human purpose and assumes, like all else, the significance of human consciousness.

Those who gravitate to the terms "purposelessness" and pull nihilism out of Buddhism are projecting their own ideas and desires on the doctrine. So while there are particular phrasings and passages that make Buddhism sound like a "world-denying" philosophy or somehow at odds with the realities of human consciousness—just as there are parts of the Bible that appear dark and incomplete assessments of Christianity that see it as a negative doctrine—in a holistic look at the doctrine, its goals and its broader teachings, one can clearly see that Buddhism is not about world-denial[*], nor does it dismiss the

---

[*] It is true that Buddhism and the Buddha himself recommended all sorts of meditation practices geared toward a certain level of aversion to the body and ordinary human life. Practitioners are encouraged to meditate in graveyards and contemplate rotting corpses. This is intended to bring about an awareness of the impermanence of all things. Contemplations of the putrid are also recommended for monks in keeping their aspirations of celibacy. All of this can be construed in a way as world-denial. But it is not a fundamental rejection of existence that is going on here. It is, rather, a proposed approach of affecting the karma of the individual in the world to become more oriented to a higher purpose. For instance, monks are generally forbidden from secluding themselves from the world. Part of the purpose behind the Buddhist monks' practice of regular alms gathering is to remind him or her that they are a part of the lay world and depend completely on it—they are fully connected to it. They are not above it or separate from it. Thus, the aversion to certain aspects of the forms of the world

significance of human consciousness, effort, or endeavor (i.e. purpose). In fact, Buddhism, just like Christianity, recognizes the mysterious intimate connection between form and infinite formlessness which is the mystery of the incarnation, the divine love for man, and the enlightenment of the individual.

---

that Buddhism promotes are not in any way through and through denials of worldly existence or rejection of the value of human life, curious though they may seem and tempting as it may be for a westerner to interpret them as such.

Purpose in Form

Chapter 12: The Great Revealed Truth of Divine Intimacy

What we have discovered, in two great, historic traditions—which developed quite separately, in vastly different cultures—is that both have (unsurprisingly) taken for granted the necessary truths of life—that human life (and therefore consciousness) is significant, purposeful, and meaningful. All cultures have known this. All people know this intuitively. You cannot really escape it, you can only despair because you think you've lost it (though despair, apathy, etc. all show a care for meaning and an investment in significance and purpose). Today, we are caught in a wave of historical emotional rebelliousness which pushes us away from such reassurances, and makes it the fad to deny them, without thinking through the underlying explanations and assumptions of either side.

Though it is true that today as a culture we are in a state of confusion about these basic principles, it is not, by comparison, astounding that our ancestors knew them. They didn't have the theories of emergent consciousness and fundamental randomness to confuse them so much; and the basic explanations they had (though they came in form of dramatic story, rather than analytical philosophy), which supported these truths, were largely static and given (dogmatic). So there was a much greater buttress against losing sight of these truths, even if some troublesome ideas did come up.

But there are some things that are astounding about what our ancestors knew—or at least held within their belief system and acted out, even though they might not have been able to coherently outline the thesis itself; it is astounding that ancient religions were attempting to point to the infinite and maintain its connection to human life. If we take it as a given that the infinite is connected to and involved in human life, then this is not so astounding—of course God makes himself known and helps us. But that is not the perspective westerners are used to—they are used to deriding such sentiments.

The infinite as an intellectual hypothesis and conception has barely emerged in our minds. And I don't mean "barely" on an evolutionary timescale. It really is entirely nascent. Some brilliant western mathematicians started working with it only within the last 500 years. And there were philosophic western schools speculating about it back through the time of ancient Greece. So its presence as a fringe idea has been around for some two and a half millennia (in western minds[*]). But as a society, we still have no idea what it means (go read Deutsch's chapter "A Window on Infinity" if you think otherwise); even most great mathematical minds haven't begun to comprehend the *reality* the term implies.

As Deutsch says, "Everything physically possible will eventually be revealed: watches that came into existence spontaneously; asteroids that happen to be good likenesses of William Paley; everything. According to the prevailing theory, all those things *exist today*, but many times too far away for light to have reached us from them—yet." (452) Thus, it is no surprise that "many people have an aversion to infinity." (Deutsch, 459) Accepting the reality of infinity is still a task we face in our future.

Yet the tradition of Christianity was developed before this intellectual concept was anything cohesive and broadly influential. At best, from a strictly numerical look at the dates, they developed side by side, but stretching that argument to say that the writers and developers of Christianity were all steeped in philosophical and later mathematical contemplations and insights into the infinite is ridiculous (though some of them definitely were). Equally with Buddhism, the Buddha appeared probably 100 years before we have evidence

---

[*] Similar to the concept of zero, it was discovered first by non-western minds. The concept of the infinite was developed first in India, some 500 years give or take before it would come up in the western world. Perhaps it is less surprising, then, that the East has so much sophistication in their traditions dealing with and speaking directly of an infinity of life.

The Great Revealed Truth of Divine Intimacy

of explicit ideas about the infinite arising in India.*

How, then, did Christianity develop an idea of God who was "entire in every point of space, and complete in every instant of duration" and "Being without restriction, All Being, the Being infinite and universal"? How did they perfectly lay out the reality of infinity in their idea of God and posit the idea of consciousness transcending space-time? Was it really all just Christian monks and scholars being close with all the intellectuals of their age and borrowing from the burgeoning conceptions in mathematical minds of the concept of infinity? Is this all thanks only to people like Leibniz?

The story of the Incarnation says otherwise. Long before mathematicians in the 17th century began seriously developing the ideas of the properties of the infinite, the Christian tradition developed a story whose allegory contained the key to such mysteries. In the story of Christ, we hear the lived and revealed (i.e. first experienced and lived out, intimated in story and intuitive, visionary inspiration; not preconceived by the intellect and hammered out logically before being worked into a fantastic narrative) truth of the infinite reality.

In the story of Christ and the idea of the Incarnation, Christianity brought forth the experiential reality of a self-saturating, conscious infinite and how it was involved in the life of each individual, and the purpose of mankind as a whole. They called it God. They had no notion of infinite sets and their necessities of self-saturation. They did not know that God was infinite, or that The Infinite was God, since they did not have that term. They knew, through inherited allegories and visionary experiences, that God was a higher power—then even the Highest power; and yet he was also close, also compassionate and merciful.

---

* These figures are based on western anthropological scholarship. They are probably inaccurate as Eastern philosophy through the Upanishads and the Vedas were at the very least poking at the idea of the infinite and the transcendent. Yogic practices and philosophies date back much further than this and are perhaps the origins of man's serious conscious interaction with the infinite reality and his conscious potential. Equally, as it pertains to the origins in Western culture, insights into the reality of the infinite can be found in the allegories of Sumer and Ancient Egypt alike. So the intuitive knowledge—at least—undoubtedly precedes the intellectual formulations. "Very often, during the analysis and penetration of the secrets of archaic symbol, one can only feel that our generally accepted notion of history of philosophy is founded on a completely false assumption, namely that abstract and metaphysical thought begins where it first appears in our extant records." (Campbell, 227)

Purpose in Form

What our ancestors woke up to slowly, which we still are moving toward comprehending (incredibly fallible though the process certainly is), is that life is infinite. And that is very different than the modern intellectual speculations of a dead but unending sprawl of disjointed material manifestation with which atheists suppose to uproot the idea of God. The reality behind an infinite life is something still far beyond our intellectual comprehension. But lived human experience, intuition, and insight is ahead of our intellect (as should be expected, to those who do not fully worship the intellect). And the living reality of the infinite burgeoned definitively in the religious stories and ideas of Christianity and Buddhism[*].

Buddhist and Christian stories both spoke of an ultimate redemption to the suffering of the world, without whitewashing and ignoring any of the suffering. They both insisted that this redemption was available to all people, and that it was somehow connected to our consciousness, as well as dependent on our attitudes and our lived conduct. And both traditions found that the process by which this redemption was reached in humans, and therefore the purpose of all human life, was not through disavowing the world and body—ascetic practices in the wilderness or throwing one's physical form away—but by full conscious inhabitation of form (the human body and world) [†]. This means deeply accepting the limitations, putridity, and suffering of life, and being able to fully be with it all—to be fully present for the crucifixion of your life. "The happy ending is justly scorned as a misrepresentation; for the world, as we know it, as we have seen it, yields but one ending: death, disintegration, dismemberment, and the crucifixion of our heart with the passing of the forms that we have loved... The myths do not deny this agony (the crucifixion); they reveal within behind, and around it essential peace (the heavenly rose)." (Campbell, 19 & 247)

---

[*] And certainly Hinduism—especially the yogic branches—before them both. Judaism is somewhat more murky. As Aslan details, much of Judaic history is the Hebrews and Semitic tribes worshiping limited tribal gods, and merely asserting hopefully—zealously—that they are the best. It was from this devoted monotheism that the idea of the One infinite reality was able to arise—as the infinite must necessarily be One. But it is unclear when this shift actually occurred—even whether it preceded the advent of Christianity or not.

[†] "The Incarnation is the symbol that the spirit has to fully inhabit the body." (Peterson, "Mysticism, Spirit and the Shadow")

The Great Revealed Truth of Divine Intimacy

Attention to, investment in, and *ENGAGEMENT*—in other words INTIMACY*—with the world is perhaps the more primal principle than even effectiveness—though we discovered its value through searching for effectiveness in our efforts—for it is what underlies all effectiveness. This is your life and lot: you are thrown into the throes of form anyhow, and looking after your affairs, cultivating and pruning your efforts, leads to them going better, but, in order for you to pay adequate attention to the full spectrum of your life, you must have the strength to watch yourself die slowly and painfully to achieve full, most *effective*, intimate engagement life. "For he hath not despised nor abhorred the affliction of the afflicted." (Psalm 22:24)

You must have the courage of spirit to meditate overnight in a graveyard, to confront all the horrors of life and still strive for its growth and cultivation. "This deed accomplished, life no longer suffers hopelessly under the terrible mutilations of ubiquitous disaster, battered by time, hideous throughout space; but with its horror visible still, its cries of anguish still tumultuous, it becomes penetrated by an all-suffusing, all-sustaining love, and a knowledge of its own unconquered power." (Campbell, 22) You must accept your fated nature and willingly, consciously, lovingly pick up your cross and carry it to your end. That is what full inhabitation of form takes, and that is what redeems and transforms life. What can achieve such transcendence of suffering so as to be entirely with it, fully engaged and intimate, we call Love.

Thus it is love—this transcendental gift of the infinite—the Divine love for man, the intimacy of the infinite with the finite, the transcendence which is omnipresent throughout life and the infinite redemption it offers through all horrors—which transforms life. It transforms individuals in their conduct, reminding them of a greater order of causation which is interested in moral

---

* Engagement with life is something modern secularists and intellectuals would not object to hearing. Nor would it surprise us modern disenchanted individuals as a necessity for growth and success. You must face your problems; you must devote your energies; you must work and strive. That is all quite obvious (though some don't like it and think it should be otherwise, there is no doubt it *is* the case). But what does the word "engagement" mean other than "an intent to become intimate with"? Becoming intimate with life is the key to life. For true Life—the source, the wellspring of life—is to be found in the intimacy of the finite and the infinite. One's committed and devoted effort on their end of the engagement brings one to the union awaiting in the allegorical bridal chamber. "When the bridegroom leaves the bridal chamber, that will be the time to fast and pray." (Logion 104, The Gospel of Thomas)

integrity, and in so doing, starting at the lowest level*, with the individual and all their darkness, love attempts to grow and change the world. "In the last analysis, what is the fate of great nations but a summation of the psychic changes in individuals?" (Jung, CW, Vol 9, pt 1, pg. 47)

It is the cultivation of the individual which is the purpose of our lifetimes; and it takes the knowledge of an infinite redemption and transcendence for us to truly work with that process and fully inhabit our form (our bodies and the world†) and allow our consciousness to witness all the horrors therein. Individuation is the path of the rising consciousness of the Divine which transforms the life of each individual. And this cultivation of each individual is the only stable process which truly leads to heaven on Earth. "The behavior of Buddhists makes the Earth manifest itself as god and ripens the Milky Way into delightful cheese." (Dogen, 54)

Divine Intimacy is the living solution to the mystery of life. It is not an intellectual solution that dissolves the infinite mystery. Rather, it is the metaphysical orientation or core of the appropriate faith in life that we must keep conscious and aware of and strive to grow towards and embody. "No man knoweth the Son, but the Father; neither knoweth any man the father save the Son." (Matthew 11:27) In other words, stated inversely, he that knows the infinite (the Truth of life), knows the intimate relationship of infinite to finite (as father to son); and no man knows the reality and true worth of man (man as the Son) save he who sees him of infinite worth—through the eyes of the Father.

This is the foundation of all ethics and morality which recognize the divinity of the individual through their intimate connection to the omnipresent infinite. All other so-called ethical systems either borrow abstracted notions that can only be explained from this basic metaphysical conception, or are founded on nihilistic conceptions of annihilation, meaninglessness, and finitude. The reality of the infinite and its intimate, conscious connection to the finite individual is the necessary basis for all ethics, as well as the source of all purpose, meaning, and salvation. It is both the basic truth of our nature and the

---

* "It dwells in lowly places that all disdain." (Daodejing, Ch.8)
† "When Zen people say the 'body' they generally mean the entire physical world by extension." (Dogen/Warner, 40)

The Great Revealed Truth of Divine Intimacy

basic mystery of life; there is this truth that at our core lies what is knowable as a mystery and miracle.

In the next chapter, we look to nail down this idea by clearly indicating the necessary yet mysterious connections between the infinite and the finite which we observe from our end, and the peculiar and specific ways the transformation of individual lives and consciousness is achieved.

Purpose in Form

Chapter 13: The Great Mystery that Divine Perception Is Dependent on or Connected to Physicality

"The ways that lead to conscious realization are many, but they follow definite laws." C.G. Jung (CW, Vol. 17, pg. 197)

In way of definition, concerning the title of this chapter, I have begun to use Divine as synonymous with The Infinite or Infinity. I believe that the case has been made sufficiently that they are interchangeable for our purposes. I also use the term "physicality" here as a synonym for how I have been using "form" throughout the book. This is to emphasize the peculiarity of the concept we are going to discuss. Why should the Divine Infinite be involved with mundane physicality—what we think of as dead, gross, and inert? Yet we see that it is so. That is our topic for exploration.

This mysterious connection between the infinite formlessness of no-self and the finite proceedings of form and creation is a paradox common to both the east and the west. And it is that very truth we have been talking about—that the infinite is intimately connected to the finite. "'All things are Buddha-things'; or again (and this is the other way of making the same statement): 'All beings are without self.'" (Campbell, 127) From a popularized perspective of the east, a spiritual idealism where all form and matter are merely illusions

Purpose in Form

("*maya*"), it is very curious, to say the least, to suggest that the infinite nirvana is connected intimately to the particular forms of limited, mundane life[*]. Yet, this idea runs entirely through eastern doctrine, just beneath the surface (or directly on the surface but overlooked), as it is a necessary truth of the world.

In the west, this idea—though still a paradox—is more openly accepted; it is the miracle and mystery of the Incarnation itself—that Christ is fully God and fully man; somehow the infinite and the finite are intimately tied, for reasons and by mechanisms beyond our comprehension. Why does God care for humans and humankind? Why is God close and merciful and compassionate, rather than distant and uncaring? We don't know why—other than the "answer" of "Love" (which is no real answer for it is but the title we give to the mystery called "Love")—but we do know that it is so. The Divine Transcendent and the mundane physical world are married in reality, in ways we habitually over look and forget. Joseph Campbell calls this "the paradox of the two worlds in one" (197).

It would be quite easy and comforting for spiritual idealists of east or west to say that Divine Perception or Experience (the vision of God) comes entirely of its own, is of the formless and is the formless, and is of the causeless and therefore is uncaused. From this perspective, the forms which "induce" or promote this experience (meditation, prayer, etc.) are merely conveniences for our own handicaps of belief in form—i.e. illusions, since all forms must be.

In this conception, all is in the hands of God, thus our actions are mostly meaningless, but he tells us to do some things so we do without knowing quite why. Or, stated in eastern terms: nirvana is the only reality, all else is illusion; all form and phantasmagoria of life is but *maya*, we meditate to pass through it and destroy our illusionary and fettersome desires and purposes. This attitude breeds the Ethical Problem of the East. "If they think their souls are immortal, the loss of their body is no big deal... an immaterial soul is unmoved by the earthly incentives that impel us to get along." (Pinker, 429)

---

[*] Or, that is the case for about half the misinterpretations; the other half fall on the other extreme, where mundane life is perfect exactly how it is, and no cultivation is necessary. Dogen thoroughly derides this notion, and it denies our reality as Beings who are universal explainers, constructors, and verbs. We'll counter this idea a bit more thoroughly later.

The Great Mystery...

But this is a very obvious dogma. It dismisses the facts of reality for its preconceived conceptions of the way reality should be. It is necessary to conclude based on experience (examining cause and effect within the "illusion" of creation) that Divine Perception depends on or is intimately related to form or physicality. This is particularly curious as the divine is that which transcends the finite arena of form. Why should our experience of it be so intertwined with form itself—requiring particular causes, which happen within the field of the limited phenomena, occurring between finite things, to bring us to the causeless and infinite, which is already everywhere without distinction?[*]

Why must we cultivate and discern this from that, choosing a particular path, to produce a perception of that which is omnipresent? It doesn't make sense to one who approaches the question with a faith that says the infinite transcendent is necessary disconnected and beyond all form (which it is). But to those willing to see the mystery and let go of our rigid, limited conceptions we can see that it is so—that the infinite transcendent is also connected to form and limited action and striving and desire in particular ways.

Divine Perception, often called mystical experience[†], is indeed perception of the formless and infinite. Since it is an experience of the infinite, it is necessarily subjective—one experiences their identity with the infinite. One

---

[*] "The truth is everywhere all around us, but if we do not practice, it doesn't show itself and we can't experience it." (Dogen, 2) In fact, the entirety of Dogen, the great Zen Master's work could be seen as an exhortation of this mysterious truth—that the infinite is omnipresent and always with us (just like eternal salvation), and yet we must go through particular finite actions and work in the physical world in order to reach this omnipresent reality (just like we must act in certain ways to find salvation). In other words, the Divine Infinite is intimately connected to finite form, and finite form is important and has significant purpose to the Divine Infinite. "[There] are standards of action that exist prior to recognition." (Dogen, 22)

[†] Not to say that everything that has ever been called a mystical experience was a direct and clear perception of the infinite reality. Many altered states get treated as mystical yet only muddy the waters. The Buddha described painstakingly all the false states of altered consciousness that were to be transcended. But the infinite is what the mystic seeks and thus is the true mystical experience. "No matter what the world thinks about religious experience, the one who has it possesses a great treasure, a thing that has become for him a source of life, meaning, and beauty, and that has given a new splendor to the world and to mankind." (Jung, CW, Vol. 11, pg. 105)

cannot experience the infinite objectively—for in standing apart from it, they assure that what they behold is not infinite. The infinite unites all, including your own "personal" consciousness, necessarily, so the Divine Perception is a subjective experience of infinite oneness. The spiritual idealist takes this absolute basis of all experience and holds tight to its omnipresence and is satisfied. But there is more to be seen (as always).

The spiritual idealist ignores the "path to" the formless, deeming it as unnecessary and misconceived—only a product of human attachment to illusion. In their mind, one is already formless and has only ever experienced formlessness and that is that; the infinite is always infinite. This is the path that Christ did not take in the desert, of throwing his body off the cliff and dismissing the significance of form and pretending that the indisputable truth of God's omnipotence and omnipresence would allow him to transform the desert into an oasis and wash away all earthly difficulties. (Matthew 4:6-7)[*]

This is the demonic nature of spiritual doctrines which dismiss form and "seriously" preach purposelessness and meaninglessness as a truth on the level of human stories to be applied to human life. It is a disdain for physical incarnation and the material world masquerading as a highly developed spiritual state. This is what I have called the Ethical Problem of the East, given its tendency to manifest through eastern doctrines (or new age systems borrowing selectively from eastern doctrines) and because Christianity has a direct (though allegorical) refutation of it. "Is not life more than meat, and the body than raiment?"[†] (Matthew 6:25)

The tautological truth that the infinite is infinite is not so helpful within the world of form; and in pretending to forget or not recognize the experiential reality of form, of finite within the infinite, the spiritual idealist rejects the world and simultaneously refuses to affirm the connection between the infinite and the finite. Just as Satan in the desert encouraged Jesus to accept his infinite reality and forsake his bodily form as unimportant, the spiritual idealist denies his own experience and attempts to forget the reality of individual experience.

---

[*] "Christ does not casually order or even ask God to intervene on his behalf." (Peterson, 183)

[†] Contrast this to the *Bhagavad Gita* where God tells Arjuna that the body is only raiment that can be lightly discarded.

The Great Mystery...

This is what Christ and the Buddha and Bodhisattvas reject; to them, the first shall be last and the last shall be first; the eternal King of kings and the liberated beings are on Earth to wash the feet of the sinners and serve the world (Matthew 20:16; John 13:13-15).

If we do not hide from the reality of creation and we look into the real experience and its particular character[*], it seems undeniable that certain modes of form are prerequisite to the experience of Divine Perception, of union with the omnipresent, of being and becoming what you already are[†].

Perhaps the most crucial and basic element of limited causal reality is the intent, the search. In the end the search must be laid down too, but have we ever known of any that have achieved these realizations without first wanting them, seeking them, or at least having done some work (consciously or not) which allowed the states to manifest themselves? Even in cases of apparently spontaneous enlightenment, like that of Ramana Maharshi (who achieved enlightenment apparently out of the blue at 17), do not turn around and recommend we await divine intervention without care; Maharshi wrote a book for seekers, inviting them to engage in the pursuit and cultivation of this experience.

This intent and drive to growth and cultivation is the seed which manifests the rest of the particular path in whatever way suits the practitioner best. But it seems certain that achieving Divine Insight or Perception requires an intention to seek it and then some set of practices or actions appropriate to that intention. Thus there is the Noble Eightfold Path of "right intention" and "right effort", or the injunction to seek God first and above all and to walk in his statutes. "If we could attain the truth just by being told we're already Buddhas, then why hasn't everyone who ever heard such a thing been enlightened? ...Gautama Buddha wouldn't have taken the trouble to expound his teachings if it were that easy." (Dogen, 10)

It is of course true that the achievement or culmination of formal practice is almost always paradoxical—that it comes unsuspected, in a moment of

---

[*] i.e. bring our conscious spirit to fully inhabit and engage and be intimate with form.
[†] "We need to do some work to truly become what we already are." (Dogen/Warner, 59)

seemingly unbecoming form* as to what has been desired, as a thief in the night—and that these moments are ultimately gifts of Grace. But this does not at all prove the quest unnecessary, nor the forms impractical or unproductive.

Of course we never leave the seat of all existence and experience—we have never, never could, and never will—the infinite will never not be infinite. Thus the infinite is always with us by its own nature. So seeking and practice has nothing to do with the reality of the presence of the Absolute. But seeking and formal practice has almost always accompanied Divine Perception or insight which is the brief alteration of the limited organism's perception—the rising of mundane perception into the divine. Even if it is up to God in the end whether or not He will bestow any vision or revelation, that does not mean that effort and intention are not helpful or *effective* in bringing the possibility closer to actuality.

Divine Perception is what is sought and what should be sought. For we must know and accept that we are fallible and limited in our conscious perceptions. The knowledge (and requisite faith) that we are never separate from the divine even in the darkest depths of hell does indeed provide respite—a tiny annulment which in its placement is immensely powerful and fully Divine—but this knowledge is intimately bound with (even dependent on) Divine Perception which is sought and periodically achieved. How would we be passed down such a faith if some of our ancestors had not gleaned some insight through experience?

What I am getting at here is that your perception of It is part of It; your rising and falling perception is as divinely ordained as your physical path, and the two are connected (though they might function in harmony or juxtaposition). Your perception is not the same thing as the infinite unalterable perfection of eternity; your perception is part of your temporal adventure. There is just as much striving and toil required in cultivating the field of your perception as in the field of physicality through the cultivation of your form.

The "achievement" (or gift) of Divine Perception comes along a certain path of a particular journey for a particular purpose. And the gift of this

---

* "The loathely, underestimated appearance of the carrier of the power of destiny." (Campbell, 43)

perception allows one to greatly affect form. The Divine Perception is intimately related to and indeed inextricable from form. It allows one to do much more within form—that is to say it changes or transforms the forms it occurs in, further proving this connection, rather than it being a call to disregard and further disavow forms. In fact, it is Divine Perception which shows us the power of attention brought into to form (and the requisite Love required for this process of embodiment). Divine Love for finite life (humanity) is the message perennially given through Divine insights throughout the ages.

Thus, the reality cannot be adequately explained—as the spiritual idealist tries to do—as the center of the Divine Experience dissolving the illusion of form and uprooting all causes, reasons, and purposes. In the discussions of purposeless and the enlightening experience of the absolute, as they propagate in circles greatly influenced by the spiritual idealism of the east, this rejection of a definite conclusion is uncommon and perhaps blasphemous (even though they would all also tell you to meditate or otherwise engage in the cultivation of form—of limited causes—which depends on discernment and discrimination and all sorts of conscious activity and effort—i.e. right effort). To speak so openly and explicitly of this side of the equation that there are obviously particular causal inputs of form which help to promote the experience of the Divine Reality—i.e. to point out the mysterious connection between the infinite and the finite, the divine and creation—goes against the tradition of talking about mystical experiences as the Absolute itself—which would mean they must be uncaused and thus unrelated to form.

The Absolute is indeed uncaused and the deep mystical experience is the subjective experience of the identity with this uncaused infinite existence, and during this experience one does perceive all form to be uncaused (or to have only one true cause), and through this the world becomes dismantled from what you had thought it to be. "Purposelessness" and infinite glory unfold before you bursting out of the veiling horrors you had thought to be the procession of samsara—the sprawling, inert, and heartless material universe.

It is proper in truth to recognize that Divine Perception is not merely a thing that humans cultivate and produce reliably all on their own, but rather that Divine Perception depends essentially entirely on the infinite presence of God, in the same way we must recognize that Reason depends wholeheartedly on the reality of Truth, much more than the mere existence of an intellect. In that sense Divine Perception is indeed entirely bestowed by Grace.

But just as we saw the curious connection between works and Grace discussed earlier, it is improper to make a distinction (to create a separation) here between the reality of the infinite presence behind (and in fact saturating) all forms and the reality of the observable patterns of the world that certain causes support the transformation and transcendence of the individual perception. There is a core mystery of the connection of the infinite reality to the finite reality and particular causes within it. We cannot explain it, but we know it is so. This is not an avoidance of explanations which Deutsch condemns as seeking to avoid criticism, for we have a perfectly cogent explanation for why this cannot be explained; we know life is a mystery. Knowing this, it is unsurprising that the core connection between infinite and finite—the miracle of creation itself—should remain a mystery.

Through acknowledging this reality that the particular causes within finite life are significant and distinct, we understand that there are indeed divinely ordained ways of being and action which promote deeper unity with the infinite—which are more divine and sacred than others. Thus again is our discernment clearly necessary (though still undoubtedly fallible), and our consciousness proven significant and purposeful.

Karma and Meditation

It is said in eastern religions and philosophies that one must "get rid" of their karma to achieve (or experience) enlightenment. And "karma" (though it is defined in many ways in different contexts—here meaning the bad stuff you want to get rid of) is said to be the fruits of desire and especially intention (i.e. the particular causes you are intentionally affecting in the world). It is said that there are particular practices and attitudes which "uproot" old karma and prevent the planting of new karmic seeds.

But this formulation also leads to a silly conception that the way to cultivate oneself is by attempting to become more unconscious and less in control of one's own actions. If taken literally, one thinks that karma is produced by desire and intent in action. Thus, in order to not create more karma, shouldn't one seek a state of thoughtless and unplanned action? The more spontaneous and irrational one becomes—the more one avoids planning, intention,

The Great Mystery...

precision, and discrimination, the less karma one will incur?[*] Why don't we all just get our prefrontal cortexes removed, then, and act "only on instinct" (as Obi-Wan recommends)?

This idea is absurd, for we do not escape cause and effect or habit and consequence in our evasion of conscious attention; "without rules we quickly become slaves to our passions." (Norman Doidge, from introduction to *12 Rules for Life*, viii). There is certainly merit to talking about spontaneousness in connection with the experience of the causeless, as well as part of a calculated effort to uproot doctrinaire tendencies within the ego; and there is merit as well to emphasizing the importance and purpose of the irrational elements in life, in learning to trust one's intuition for example and not try to make everything in life merely an obstacle course for the intellect. But it is absurd to believe that the highest spiritual direction from the east would be to get rid of your consciousness all together and act completely on the whims of the moment, which are no less caused and conditioned than our deliberated intentions.[†]

First of all, within the noble eightfold path one is directed to have "right view" and "right determination" (or right intention) which are both clearly conscious mental attitudes to cultivate. Also, the goals and directions of the rest of the path (right conduct, right speech, right livelihood, etc.) all clearly depend on and require an active and discerning and discriminating mind.

---

[*] "Drop wisdom, abandon cleverness,
And the people will be benefited a hundredfold.
Drop humanity, abandon justice,
And the people will return to their natural affections.
Drop shrewdness, abandon sharpness,
And robbers and thieves will cease to be.
These three are the criss-cross of Tao,
And are not sufficient in themselves.
Therefore, they should be subordinated
To a Higher principle:
See the Simple and embrace the Primal,
Diminish the self and curb the desires!" (Daodejing, Ch. 19, John C. H. Wu translation)

[†] This conception certainly does exist and is not helped by the popular conception of meditation as "turning off your mind", but there are better conceptions there that are more subtle. Certainly many eastern influenced peoples and even so called gurus will tell you that this is the way. But it is not.

Purpose in Form

How do you know what is right to say without understanding so many things about the context of the society and the person you are talking to? At some point much of the social understanding does become unconscious habit, but it only gets there through cultivating conscious attention toward it, and still there will always be sticky situations where great care in attention and discernment is obviously necessary. Thus it is absurd to say that the eastern philosophies overall encourage you or expect you to turn off your mind and become unconscious, even though many readers and even teachers draw that message out of the texts and conversations they take at face value (and it is arguably directly asserted as a legitimate path in the *Daodejing*—see previous note).

Secondly, there is the problem of the metaphors around meditation that drive people in this way. Meditation has often been described as quieting the mind or quieting the thoughts, which has often been taken to mean turning off the mind and getting rid of the thoughts[*]. The desire and intent to control the mind or thoughts is itself just another thought being clung to and adding noise to the mind. The ideas of quieting the mind and thoughts are approximations and metaphors but become inaccurate when one believes they are instructed to grab the mind and pin it down, or that only by "checking" on the mind and finding it silent does one know they have achieved meditation.

These ideas and efforts directly inhibit meditation and the quieting of the mind, because they inevitably direct one to interfere more with the mind and make the "problem" worse. Alan Watts describes this method as like trying to smooth rough water with a flat iron ("The Mind", YouTube). Though there are many kinds of meditation, the general practice is one of developing space from or non-reaction to (equanimity towards) ones thoughts, which allows the mind to run itself out if that's what it needs to do or settle down if it is overly agitated.

In any case, meditation is certainly something taken on with purpose and intent. Even if we do it to get beyond the mind's habit looking for purpose in everything, we still do it for that reason and purpose and because we believe that that state of being more in touch with "purposelessness" is more beneficial or EFFECTIVE for ourselves. At most, if one is greatly wed to the discourse around purposelessness as found in the east, we can agree that that term is

---

[*] See Sadhguru "How do you stop the mind's chatter?" (YouTube)

commonly ineffective. Either it has the effect of directing one to put less effort into cultivating their lives, which is not good, or it gets people hung up on the purpose of purposelessness and keeps them spinning in questions and analysis when they should be meditating and cultivating.

If the idea of "purposelessness" works for you, great, keep meditating. If it confuses you or you feel it is directing you to disown your consciousness, chalk it up to a poor job in translating and understand that all philosophies which are in any way positive and coherent are ones of discernment and cultivation of the human body and mind; this can be seen clearly enough through all the rest of Buddhism and yoga.

Zen vs The Intellectuals

"Please avoid theoretical and philosophical discussions, and focus your questions on matters related to your actual practice" (A sign that hangs in Harari's teacher's meditation room; Harari, 321)

First, I will say that there is something very right about this advice. "Inopportune questioning can confuse, without enlightening, as well as deflecting you from action." (Peterson, 158) You do eventually have to get down to doing the work (being *effective* in the right way), and the sooner the better. The rubber has to meet the road. Tolstoy found just that—as he relates in his work *A Confession*—eventually you have to try acting out the faith to see the fruits of the work. But Tolstoy did not, and seemingly could not, get to this point without thinking many things through first. And in the east they are well aware that there are different kinds of people, with different paths of work and learning (see also 1 Corinthians 12:8-11). Jnanis[*] are not as well served by cutting off their strings of thought before they become over long. Jnanis have to think themselves out eventually.

What is more, in defense of the sign itself rather than its message as a general principle, the sign Harari talks about is in a place and the rule applies to this place during a certain time. You don't come to meditation class to discuss philosophy, you come to meditate. Just as if a physiology major went

---

[*] Jnana Yoga is the path of thought to union with the divine. A Jnani is a follower of this path.

to the gym and just wanted to talk about different kinds of workouts it would be annoying, one who goes to meditation class and knows all the theory of meditation, but won't meditate is missing something.

But that is not to say that thought has no place in life, nor that knowing the metaphysics of mind and the theories of consciousness does not actually enhance and inform meditation—as knowledge of the body gained through study may allow one to exercise all the more effectively. In fact, in the words of a Zen master, "theory and practice are the same thing, expressed in two different ways." (Dogen, 73) And further, "we have to think, and plan, and limit, and posit, in order to live at all." (Peterson, 221) Someone who tells you that in the search for truth there is no place for thought is either a wise master who wishes you would just get around to the business of finding out for yourself already—of DOING the tests and the work, rather than talking and supposing about it forever—or they have no faith in the mind, no faith that human consciousness is indeed an aspect of the infinite and contains infinite potential[*]. The latter are cynics who teach about what is impossible, and forward deepities to cover up their cynical and nihilistic explanations, and who mistrust the Jnanis who go out and achieve that impossibility. And the cynics are in the vast majority to the masters.

Being a Jnani myself, I do not like the pretense of being told or having others generally told not to think. First of all, I cannot control whether I think or not any more than you can, or any more than either of us can control if we breathe. I and many others are compelled to think. Those who think the only way to truth is to "shut off the mind" and follow the road of meditation can be excused for their inaccuracies of speech insofar as such imprecision of thought does not get in their way and their karmic or bhakti work goes well for them[†]. But this sort of person who can accept the edict, "refrain from thinking and only meditate" (insofar as it is taken as a general instruction which applies beyond the meditation room where it was posted) are probably no different than those who can be raised under the catechisms of Catholicism (or any other religious dogma) and find contentment. Thought is not their way and they see it as getting in the way—they mistrust the intellect (and there are truly as good

---

[*] They do not believe that humans can be categorized as "universal explainers".
[†] Karma and Bhakti reference the other paths of yoga—accepted pathways to divine experience.

and valid reasons for this as there are to mistrust the intuition). There are people like this, and this is not an insult. There are valid and worthy paths for them. But if one uses such a rule to eschew true discourse and the search for truth (especially one who writes a book full of examples where a good deal of additional thought, criticism, and refinement would be a welcome thing) then they are quite out of their element and confused in their own philosophies (and, again, some more diligent thought might be exactly what is needed).

To appeal to reason, expound on thought, and encourage education and analysis, as Harari does, then to equivocate, saying that thought gets in the way and too much precise thought about reality and metaphysics and the like are misguided hindrances, is to be of little of faith in human consciousness—to be dawdling in the mires and bogs of the mind and encouraging others to do the same. While the ultimate reality must be experienced and it cannot be apprehended or defined or confined by the mind (or anything else), and while even the Jnanis must get around to some kind of meditation and/or cultivation of the physical form eventually, there are paths of thought and ways of mind that lead to such an experience, and that lead to the desire for meditation and faithful living.

And further, to pretend that the world would be well served to give up on its mentation, or that this is at all a practical possibility or effective urging are all sophistries and pomposities of Zen minds that are all Zen and no mind. Of course the truly Zen ones would laugh and not object to such an accusation, but those with some level of mental karma can understand the need for and benefit of mental honing and directing as much as the need for physical and spiritual honing and directing.

So, yes there are some who are not served by mental practices and who get lost in them, and there are some whom mental processes have served for some time but have now become an impediment, and all these (and everyone else, to be sure) would be served by getting down to the actual practice and experience of life as it is. But there are many who are compelled to a path of thought, whose minds drive their lives inexorably; and their mental demons, be they dark sides of truths or mere specters of intellectualization, must be confronted and defeated in this realm in order for them to progress.

And that is all merely spiritually speaking. The case for the honing of mind

Purpose in Form

for the benefit of our material lives is cut and dry*. Conjecture, criticism, and sacrificing all to Truth is the way to make heaven on Earth (for of course assessing the world as it is on the material level includes the need for us to meditate and to expand our awareness and address all our spiritual and emotional sicknesses, for all are connected and One in reality).

---

* See Steven Pinker's book *Enlightenment Now* for the full bombardment of evidence in this case.

~So we can see that the eastern ideas for connecting man to the infinite and orienting him are really the same as in the west: that there is an intimate connection between infinite and finite, between God and man, between emptiness and form. In fact, the Buddhist Heart Sutra, which is considered to be one of, if not the most important sutra (much like the Incarnation is the heart of the Christian tradition), says plainly "Form does not differ from emptiness, emptiness does not differ from form." (Dogen, 32)

In both the religious traditions of the east and those of the west, one is expected to act in certain ways and develop their individual character in proper ways to move closer to this infinite reality and experience. The infinite cares about the expression of form and its growth and cultivation; the infinite is invested in the individual lives and purposes of the finite. This is a mystery, but it is true, and both Buddhism and Christianity have found it to be so and taught it for thousands of years. This is the understanding we must retain in our lives which is the gift of religion.~

Chapter 14: A Modern Religious Story

"Schism in the soul, schism in the body social, will not be resolved by any scheme of return to the good old days... or by programs guaranteed to render an ideal projected future... or even by the most realistic, hardheaded work to weld together again the deteriorating elements. Only birth can conquer death—the birth, not of the old thing again, but of something new... there must be—if we are to experience long term survival—a continuous 'recurrence of birth'."
Joseph Campbell (referencing Prof. Arnold J. Toynbee's work, 11-12)

No Story?

Yuval Noah Harari's last chapter of *21 Lessons for the 21st Century* is quite peculiar. In so many ways it contradicts the majority of what he has said throughout the book, and not least the penultimate chapter in which he declares the ultimate reality of meaninglessness and the non-reality of any stories. He does of course admit that we need stories, but he also claims that truth is his highest value; and while it would make sense to say that one who wants to be truthful would tell you that the reality is that no story is true but still talk to you in a story because that is necessary, it does not make sense where the value of truth comes from if all is meaningless. And this is just the beginning of the contradictions, though perhaps points to the core of them. And I am really giving him an enormous benefit of the doubt here given that he was not in the least bit explicit about taking such a tact and leads off the book saying "clarity is power" (Harari, xiii).

So let's really clear things up. Several of Harari's words on the experience of meditation are actually quite profound. But others are not and are full of blatant misunderstandings, as has been shown extensively already. My guess is that he may be trying to borrow wisdom; he knows a teacher or particularly blessed individual who has related to him some profound experiences through a story, and Harari liked it and adopted it into his own conceptions, beliefs, and hopes for himself. This is just a guess. It is also possible that Harari himself has had a moment of insight or two. Maybe more.

But if that is so he is missing the skill to translate those experiences into a cohesive set of thoughts and perspectives, and/or to bring them to bear on all the rest of the junk going through his mind. It is for this very reason that the Buddha extensively listed all the differing mental states and levels of perception and insight which were *not* the final state; one is not to be swept away and persuaded by grand pompous visions and believe they now know it all and can arbitrate on the misconceptions of the world.

I do not say this to belittle Harari. He's just wrong and a lot of his misconceptions need to go—thus we must dissect and sacrifice them upon the altar of truth with the tools of applied criticism. While there are a few grains of seemingly great truth in his stories about meditation, the flood of half-truths and erroneous, unexamined theories around these and throughout the book are deadly. This is the problem with his conception that "simple stories" are better; it leads him to not bring his explanations and underlying assumptions out front so they can be clearly seen as erroneous (Harari, 3). He would do better to realize there are no explanationless theories nor theory-less data. And he would be helped by getting rid of the intellectual arrogance of looking down upon human stupidity and pitying their poor "hunter-gatherer brains" (Harari, 233).

One must understand the universal reach of human consciousness and our nature as universal explainers. One must have faith in people, or one ends up pandering and filling their supposedly globally oriented text with slights and tones that work at cross purposes to their agenda. In other words, without the appropriate faith one is less EFFECTIVE than they practically could have been. Even if one wants to present as simple a story as possible to be more effective across a wider spectrum of people—not just something people of a

A Modern Religious Story

philosophical mindset can get into[*]—one has to really hammer out the underlying philosophy first, so that the simple story is as reflective as possible of the adamantine truths informing it. Making a simple story but ignoring the prerequisite work is the exact recipe that would lead to the disastrous conclusions flooding Harari's book.

And it is not sufficient to play the Zen master card and pretend that because all formulations are empty, none are closer to the truth or more effective at conveying it or pointing towards it; especially not while also espousing the highest value of truth, and calling for more education for all. As we have seen, in all cases, if you are writing a book, if you are concerned with suffering, you are engaged with purpose and meaning. It cannot be otherwise. If in that book you write about how life is truly meaningless and how nirvana consists of accepting and enacting meaninglessness, you are declaring your work unimportant and ineffective. For even if you are right and this is true, then your inaccuracies are as insignificant as anything else and your efforts were no different and no more meaningful than a monkey playing with a typewriter. In this case there is no problem, nor of course is there a problem with me here criticizing you, for my words do not matter, nor does my nearness to truth, nor my mental or emotional perturbation at your erroneousness and inconsistencies. Congratulations, we are all saved through meaninglessness.

But if we are to be serious, and if we are to take seriously "reality as it is", rather than the stories we think of it or life as we think it should be, then we must consider the reality of purpose, of meaning, and of truth (Harari, 318). And if we are considering the world as it is, then we know that the effectiveness of expressing clearly and being as coherent as possible about the truth is of profound affect and importance (even if, like Aspirin, it is only marginally effective when compared to a hypothesized panacea). So it is of profound importance to get our stories right, to make them point out most accurately the truth which they seek to convey. So first we must clear up the ideas about truth and stories.

First of all, as we have demonstrated, the value of truth is inseparable from the reality of the infinite. And the significance of the truth, its correspondence to reality, and effects on people and the world are only real given the reality of

---

[*] A real advantage that Dr. Peterson's *12 Rules for Life*, and many other good books to be sure, have over this book!

meaning. Meaning, purpose, and significance are all necessarily real; we all necessarily believe in them; and their reality is necessarily infinite. Our understanding of what it means to believe in them and their infinite reality may be incomplete and incoherent, for we are fallible and ignorant, but these realities remain incontrovertibly. So much for that, we have covered it all in great detail already.

Secondly, one must be very clear about what is meant by "fictional" when referring to all "stories" as "fictional" (Harari, 287). Given the air and context of the book preceding and surrounding these claims—especially the paramount value of "truth", the disparaging of religion, and the urging toward the dropping of our stories (though paradoxically claiming we need them)—I cannot believe that by "fictional" something other than "unreal" was meant. This is supported by the quote "To the best of our scientific understanding, none of the thousands of stories that different cultures, religions, and tribes have invented throughout history is true. They are all just human inventions." (Harari, 285)

But there is a great problem in analysis that has been entirely skipped in order to get to the point of playing the arbiter of truth and reality and separating the wheat from the chaff. What do we mean by true? Applying the "scientific understandings" and expectations of truth to biblical stories is exactly what Christian Fundamentalists do. They read an account and expect it to be "scientifically" (though infallibly and authoritatively) reporting on reality. It is no better to read the bible and look at it scientifically and come up with a negative review than it is to do the same and come up positive. We should not be concerned whether the Christian story is scientifically accurate in all its details. We should be concerned with whether the story conveys truth and how effectively it does so.

Moreover, *of course stories are all human inventions!* How could it be otherwise? But the sentiment is enclosed in that one key word "just"—qualifying the entire notion as unimportant[*]. They are *just* human inventions. The implications behind that dig reveal what is at play here. The underlying assumption behind that phrase is identical to that of all nihilists under whatever coverings: *human consciousness is insignificant*. That is why human creations are condemned as unimportant. That is why our purposes are believed to be

---

[*] Much as all perceived synchronicities are "just" coincidences.

meaningless. That is why we are dismissible, and ultimately contemptable as a species in modern minds (and why Harari believes none of us really have any rights (215)). Our consciousness—all our ideas, perceptions, and feelings—are insignificant and meaningless. So who cares if we made up stories? Of what good or use could they possibly be since the whole enterprise of our lives is worthless anyhow? It is the nihilism that has grown under and through so much of modern western intellectualism rearing its head again. We must begin to see this underlying motivation and faith in all these varied formulations.

Fictional stories are not "unreal" as in non-relevant and non-valuable. Fictional stories have specific purposes and can be tremendously, even infinitely, valuable. So to dismiss the Christian story as "fictional" and equate that with "untruth" is to fail miserably at understanding literature. It is to want literature class to be biology, and for the same rules to apply. The Bible is a work of literature, a work of art, and "artists use lies to tell the truth" (*V for Vendetta*). The question is not "is the biblical story, when analyzed under the criteria of a non-fiction, scientific work, of passable merit?" The question is, what truth does the Bible tell through its story? If that truth is really a deep truth and is valuable, then it is a good story. Likewise with other "stories"—i.e. mythologies—that absolutely contain truth—to analyze their surface-level content as objective, scientific reporting on the construction of reality is to be either severely deluded or duplicitous.

Thirdly, we must seriously consider the urge to drop all stories. Even if we are to agree in principle that your own nature is "not a story", why should that mean that the meaning of life cannot be conveyed in or alluded to in a story, or even that this is not the most *effective* way of doing so? Harari does not consider this distinction at all. Though the questions of your own true nature and the meaning of life are indeed intimately tied, *they are not precisely the same question*; so to dismiss the value of stories because they answer the meaning of life with a story while your own nature cannot be a story is a non-sequitur. A better explanation of why this causes problems would have to be given.

And further, though there are undoubtedly many cases of understandings and conjectures gone awry, engendered by any given story (even the best of ones), one must also tackle the practical problem of "what is the other option"?* And this is where Harari must admit defeat, because he himself not only most clearly illustrates the inescapability of stories through his actions, but also explicitly admits to their necessity. So it is entirely unclear why he supposes we should or could drop our stories, or why he mentions the whole "problem" in the first place.

Stories are inevitable. So is ignorance. Thus it is true that "all stories are incomplete" (280). But that does not mean that we can or should abandon stories. Nor does that mean that stories are bad. Nor does it mean that some stories are not more accurate than others. And, just to reiterate, none of this rests anywhere near the domain of stories or the reality that underlies them being meaningless (regardless of what people's stories might say to the contrary). The incompletion of our stories is merely a necessary corollary of the reality of the infinite—the knowable mystery of life itself.

It is also not the case that good stories don't have to touch the universal, as Harari so authoritatively proclaims (280). Certainly no one story can be made to appeal to all people (especially across all time), but the truths they convey must be the underlying truth of the infinite existence and its intimate connection to our individual lives. If your story doesn't reach to the ultimate and orient you to the fundamental reality of life, then it's not as useful a story as it should be, as we need in our times (and in all times).

We need religion—we need stories that connect us to the infinite and orient us positively toward the adventure of life. If our stories remain finite and don't bring us into contact with the ultimate, they are shallow and of incredibly limited worth. If they do indicate the intimate presence of the Divine in each and every individual life, they are of infinite worth (assuming they do so in a memorable and EFFECTIVE way).

Perhaps such a heap of misconceptions about stories themselves and humans' proper relationship with them is why Harari's work is so far from consistent and reasonable; of what importance is the story really, or the facts, since it's going to be gravely mistaken anyhow? Why bother with the facts and reasons if humans are all stupid? *Why try if we are fallible and will fall short of*

---

* Douglas Murray also points out this mistake of intellectual idealism (hubris) and urges us to always ask the question "compared to what?" when presented with arguments as to how our systems are failing when compared to a perfect, but non-existent, ideal. (251)

A Modern Religious Story

the ideal? We're all already screwed anyhow and there's no real possibility of redemption, so what good is any real effort? Beware the nihilism of intellectualism.

The Beneficial Heuristic of the Soul and its Dualism vs. The Inevitable Truth of Monism

Harari is right that stories are never complete and cannot be the end of the road. The story is a directive; the experience or attitude they attempt to convey is the point of the story, and is where the truth lies. When we talk about realities through stories, we inevitably invoke ideas which aren't precisely accurate or true. They're just part of the story. But as the reality that ultimate stories point to is the infinite, and therefore necessarily beyond direct expression, as it cannot be defined, some inaccuracies and metaphors must come into play in the story. We have a need to reach beyond our current intellectual capacities (as we always will, no matter how much it grows); and stories have proven to be an effective tool for doing just that—for capturing in allegory or image far more than we can specify or comprehend[*]. Let's consider a few of the main ones we are bound to encounter, and which we will use in constructing our own modern story.

Especially in modern times when encountering the dogma of materialism, which twists one away from the truth of lived and intuited reality, it seems necessary to declare oneself as a believer in the spirit or the soul—I am more than just a body. And there are of course a plethora of traditions testifying to and explaining the metaphysical reality of the soul. You may find those who learn from the east and believe in the *atman*—that it is this eternal soul that gathers and is plagued by karma. You may find yourself in new age spiritual discussions of astral realms and astral bodies, which have all sorts of diagrams and theories about other planes of existence and (often) their superordinate reality and significance. Or you may be in the Christian community and be told of an immortal soul.

---

[*] "Because there are innumerable things beyond the range of human understanding, we constantly use symbolic terms to represent concepts that we cannot define or fully comprehend. This is one reason why all religions employ symbolic language or images. But this conscious use of symbols is only one aspect of a psychological fact of great importance: Man also produces symbols unconsciously and spontaneously, in the form of dreams." (Jung, Man and His Symbols, 4)

Purpose in Form

All over the world we find people believing in the soul. Recall Richard Muller's proclamation: "I know I have a soul. You can't talk me out of that." (271). Carl Jung believed in the empirical reality of the soul. The two hold outs are modern western intellectual secularist-nihilists, and Buddhists. The former's belief system has at this point been entirely dismantled.

Buddhists, at least technically and scripturally*, do not believe in a soul. Buddhism, in large part, distinguishes itself from its parent tradition of Hinduism through its rejection of the concept of the *atman*. Brad Warner, in his translation and commentary on Dogen's work, puts this historical and philosophical distinction as follows:

> The word used in early Buddhist writings for the concept of self is *atman*. Atman was an idea propagated by many Indian philosophers and is similar to the Christian idea of the soul. It starts from the sense of "I am" that all of us experience. This "I am" feeling is taken as evidence that there is a permanent abiding something in us that remains stable and constant throughout the changes we experience. Thus the soul you had as a four-year-old child is the same soul you have today. This soul is different from the body because even though the body clearly changes, the soul does not. Many philosophers further extrapolate that the soul survives the death of the body. This makes sense if we accept the basic idea of the soul. If you believe that the soul remains unchanged while the body ages, it follows that the soul is not the body and therefore follows that the soul could go on even after the body decays and dies. The Buddha completely rejected this idea. First of all, he noticed that what we refer to as the soul or atman *does* change. Our personalities do not remain static throughout our lives. We mature internally as well as externally. The Buddha did not accept the idea that body and mind were two different kinds of substance. (47 italics in original)

Who is right and how do we know? In this case, the truth may be that we do not know. Materialists would writhe at such a lack of definitive negation in

---

* You will find discrepancies and oddities in the actual practices as they vary across the world and are often mixed with traditions of animism in the East.

this case, but they should be busy sorting themselves out as their belief system is completely unfounded and outdated. Speculating after-death realities is specious either way you swing it—that is, toward a soul or no soul; annihilation has been soundly refuted.

Indeed, the Buddhist tradition is quite meticulous and is a different species of faith than westerners are used to—it is all about personal inquiry and discovery. But in the case of the Buddha, when he declares that there is this absolute certainty after his death that he will not be reincarnated, that he has eliminated his karmic soul, I cannot help but think that this is no different than Jesus prophesizing his resurrection. There are people who believe in both, certainly. And I have my own views and beliefs in both. But, from the standpoint of humble human ignorance and rational inquiry, certainly they are both fantastic proposals that would rely entirely on the listener's act of faith (in the sense of believing what you do not know and what cannot be proven) to assent to either.

That being said, Buddhism does have some strengths in this case. They have an explanation as to why they doubt the *atman*, and it is something one can and is encouraged to look into. Christianity merely has a given dogma that there is an immortal soul in each of us that was created by God. There is no upfront detailed theory and explanation which differentiates the idea of the soul from the Holy Spirit—though they do seem to be distinct—nor how we share ultimate identity in Christ but also have an individual immortal soul. Why does man need an intermediary soul between himself and God? What is this middle man? And if our true identity is the Infinite reality of Christ, is this not superordinate to the individual soul?

This avenue of questioning is uncommon and not the genesis of the soul theory, I think. The soul comes about in our conceptualizing other worlds or the heavenly afterlife. We think of bodies in worlds so we create this second, etheric body to house the experience of that next life, or that eternal life. It is a description which comes about through necessity of the image, or the story one constructs. There is even well-accepted scientific evidence which suggests we are biologically driven to conceive of a soul and our dualistic existence (Bloom, "Religion, Morality, Evolution").

The reality of the Soul, I think, is a lot like the reality of the Christ. To some it seems to matter a great deal whether Jesus the Christ (as distinguished from Jesus of Nazareth) lived in empirical human history. Equally, many fret over or fully believe in the empirical reality of the soul. Some, on the other hand, affirm the resurrection of Jesus the Christ without hesitation, and without thought that this is necessarily an empirical claim about a physical body of a man from Nazareth rising after its death. The Resurrection and the Soul are true elements of their stories, and they point to truths. The quibbles about historicity and manifested realities are, to some, inconsequential and in fact quite unrelated questions. They are category mistakes.

For the time being, I will call the soul a reality in this sense—it is a necessary part of a true story. That is to say, it is at least a beneficial heuristic. It conjures a reliable image in the mind. It fits with our stories and conceptions. So it can be used effectively to communicate some meanings and concepts which are beyond our current intellectual sight. And, before one gripes about this as some kind of lie or trick, let me remind you that it is necessary for us to reach beyond our current conceptions.

We must grope beyond our conscious limitations. We must conjecture out of our imaginations in the quest for progress. Working with ideas that lie beyond rationality is, thus, part of rational inquiry. It is part of the process of knowledge creation. First you must gather all the grain before you, undoubtedly you hold some chaff, but only by picking it all up and looking through it do we begin to discern. Stories, even ones with many empirically false conceptions, bring realities to us to examine. Stories are our most primal conjectures, and we have found they have the farthest reach into our unconscious where we must seek.

So when we talk about life beyond death, or reality from a higher dimensional perspective, we almost always run into two discrepancies with intellectual theory, two imagistic implications which do not fit with the reality we are supposed to be describing. These are the image of the immortal Soul and the language of dualism.

Assuming that the Buddhists are correct and that there is no immortal soul, we still run into the necessity for the image. For example, even though Buddhists themselves reject the idea of the soul, they also believe wholeheartedly in all sorts of other worlds and lives that we as individuals have and will experience. What connects these experiences and "other lives" if

A Modern Religious Story

not an overarching soul?*

Well, though an on the ground investigation of the individual reports of personal belief within Buddhism wouldn't necessarily show it, Buddhists *don't* really believe in reincarnation and "other lives", even though their teachings and stories are full of this conception and many of their followers all over the world would speak and act in many ways indicating they do. They do and they don't. Just as one can believe Jesus Christ was resurrected but the historical resurrection is at least somewhat doubtable, even dubious. It's a question of what level of inquiry is being imposed, and what story is appropriate. And we can't always keep these straight. Life is a difficult game.

Equally, no matter how monotheistic your religion (or how much you philosophically ascribe to monism as the true nature of metaphysics) you will speak in dualist terms. You may believe in an infinite God, but you will often think of him and describe him as finite—either walking around inside his creation in an embodied form, or being outside it, separate and removed from it, or ascribing to him a particular gender, etc. The stories necessitate this dualism. This is what Joseph Campbell called "the paradox of the dual focus" (246). It is painstaking to speak in non-dualist terms, and even then the appearance of achieving non-dual descriptions is a limited veneer. Additionally, non-dualism as a linguistic approach only appeals to a select group of people†. Dualistic stories appeal to massive groups of people—they have far more reach—even though they may contain the same underlying message of truth.

Stories are like Trojan horses, which may smuggle in ideas beyond the

---

* And inversely, Christians believe in an immortal soul but don't explicitly accept the reality of reincarnation, even though the Bible directly states that this is at least possible and happens sometimes given that John the Baptist is Elias reborn (Matthew 17:12-13). But further than mere hinting passages in the scripture, the reality of an immortal soul, I think, necessitates the reality of reincarnation just as the reality of an infinite and eternal God negates the idea of a young Earth/finite creation. The deeper realities described in the scriptures uproot these parochial points of dogma. To believe in an eternal God and an immortal soul is to believe in an infinite creation and the reality of reincarnation, Christians just haven't bothered sorting out these metaphysical issues as a whole so they think somehow reincarnation and infinite creation are contradictory to God's truth, rather than necessary realities which reveal God's Infinite Glory.

† For those interested, I recommend the works of Rupert Spira, Adyashanti, and David R. Hawkins.

borders of our intellectual comprehension. They make us vulnerable to be sure—as the story of emergent consciousness and a dead universe has smuggled nihilism into our midst. But this permeability also allowed the conception of the living infinite to propagate in our midst, before the intellect had begun to wrestle with even its diluted mathematical reflections. Stories allow us contact with our unconscious, in which we may find demons—as we have—but also in which God is to be found (or, at least, the image of God, as Jung would say it).

So stories won't always be completely coherent with an intellectual delineation of concepts and realities that come out of them. Sometimes this holds us back, as when we cling to the literal interpretations of allegory and fret over contradicting the creative imagery that we hold as empirical fact. But equally it can push us forward and take us beyond ourselves. So stories are necessary. And they hold infinite potential—for good and evil. As our conscious rational capacities grow, we will have to sort out more and more from the images we are given what accords with reality and what can be proven to be inaccurate. In that vein one might think that we should do away with the concept of the soul, much as some religious groups are attempting to operate under strict non-dualistic language (fallible as their process may be).

But it is my take, as I said earlier, that this existence or non-existence of the Soul is something which is still beyond our capacities for verification. It is, ultimately, a faith claim. It has its purpose in the place of our stories. And there are stories which challenge this. But I see no reason to think that we are close to a place of effective arbitration on this matter (even for oneself, rationally speaking). We know reality is infinite. We know consciousness is not annihilated on death. But we have not begun to know anything beyond that perceptual barrier of death. Far be it from us, then, to say there is certainly no overarching soul[*].

---

[*] Personally, I do lean toward the Buddhist conception. I think it captures the nature of infinity. But one has to get really technical and far out to start to comprehend the actual claim that is being made in the Buddhist rejection of atman and assertion of "no-self" or no-soul. This book won't contain any additional chapters on the mechanisms of reincarnation vs. the claim of an infinite life minus a soul and without reincarnation. And, though I have seen great truth in the Buddhist conception, I truly do maintain a skeptical position on the whole. Just as I think it may be the case that we find the Buddhist conception to be correct in a deep manner through experience, I also would

A Modern Religious Story

Curiously in this realm, the materialists have the more coherent base of metaphysical monism and are on somewhat of a right track in that they believe their essence/their entirety as persons is subsumed under one integrated (that is, interconnected, inter-effecting) whole. They do this by rejecting the soul. They believe in mind (for the most part), they just find it to be a different manifestation of the same primary essence, which they take to be the "physical" reality. They achieved a seemingly unified metaphysical theory. The only problem was, it wasn't a metaphysical theory at all, it was a physical one. And their metaphysics is all screwed up. We must do away with the dogma of materialism, but we should not lose the underlying, intuitive push toward monism in our metaphysics.

In the common clash between secular materialists and modern non-materialists, this has almost always been attempted by simply adopting completely different philosophies and terminology—materialists have been extolled to "just feel the spirit, man!" Or they have been dragged to aura readings or reiki healings or given drugs, all to try to get them over to the "side" of recognizing a supposedly different and separate aspect of the self. This story of the supposed dualism of the individual would not only be hard to comprehend, let alone believe, because of the deep dogmas of materialism, but also because of the positive intuition that the truth must be a unified conception. Where is this Soul? How is it part of me and yet not the same as my body? How is it affected by my life, yet not of this world? Dualism creates problems and is seemingly antithetical to the truth of the oneness of infinity.

Buddhism, again, has something going for it. "Buddhism teaches that body and mind are not separate things... mind/spirit and body/matter are

---

not be surprised to discover that God has created immortal souls which inhabit all of creation. Nothing is beyond the infinite and we will never exhaust, let alone comprehend its possibilities, nor its workings. So I keep an open mind on the matter as a metaphysical reality. On the level of attachment and illusion, however, I think the concept of no-soul can play an important role in opening our eyes to the insufficiencies of an immortal experience of sequenced incarnations, no matter how varied they may be. The Christian tradition supports this, though opaquely, with its insistence on Grace over works (I have discussed this extensively in my book *Jnana Yoga*). Buddhism also pushes us to the idea that we have to transcend the pursuit of "good karma" or works and the rewards of etheric heavenly worlds. Buddhism pushes us to the unknown, unconscious infinite over the seemingly concrete, and seemingly wonderful, immortal (or unending) but individual (i.e. limited) soul. At least that's how I see it for now.

undivided... There is no hard line that divides ourselves from the outside world, or the rest of the world... The physical world as mind is still the physical world... what we conceive of as mind is an intimate aspect of all things... and... we are so deeply connected with everything around us that we can say there is really no separation at all." (Dogen/Warner 8, 17, 28 & 100). Both Buddhist ideas and pedagogical approach will be useful as we progress in reaching modern materialists.

But for the most part, the conceived center of the controversy, as it stands, in the critical discourse between science and soul, has continued to be portrayed as the materialist monists and the "spiritual" dualists. But, materialism can be entirely refuted, and needs to be by all materialists who believe in truth and progress. Thus the doctrine of the physical human body as the be-all, end-all source of one's being is verifiably false. Consciousness is not emergent. But if we reject materialism, do we lose monism along with it?

No. Dualism is just part of the stories. We need to remember that. Dualism likely runs as deep as causation. It is part of our biology. But it is not impossible (nor I think incoherent, though we are a long way from being able sort it out) to speculate about reality beyond causation—especially linear causation. Non-linear and non-casual reality is something far beyond our current conception. If we were to try to describe it in some way, we would undoubtedly end up using some causal and linear language. Just as with God we use dualistic and limited spacial-temporal language, for example. Or just as, when we believe in an infinite Oneness of reality as a metaphysical truth and necessity, we yet use the language of dualism between the Soul and the body or the Soul and the world.

This has all been a preamble to a new story. And it is a way of saying, don't look at this story as a set of empirical claims. Don't ask me about the varying "claims" within of dualism vs. monism, immortality vs. eternity. Don't expect this to be an intellectually constructed, perfectly consistent map of the territory. It's a story. It may sound highly intellectual and thought through, and even appear largely consistent. But it's still a story. I believe it's a true story. But a true story is not a story that contains only verified true truth claims. The truth of the story is in what it leads or points to or reveals, and I hope this story will be an effective directive toward the infinite.

A Modern Religious Story

Our New Story

Here is a story of infinity and our connection to it—a religious story that those in the modern age with intellectual sensibilities might like better, though it is, of course, the same, as the truth always is and always will be.

It is important to note that this is a religious story, not the proposal of a religion. This one story fulfills only the 1st function of mythology outlined by Joseph Campbell of binding and orienting man to the infinite and intimate mystery of life. A religion fulfills all four functions and has a great deal of societal rules and decorum built in. I am not creating a new religion here, just offering a new story that may help orient the modern mind to the infinite while it plays and perceives the game of limited form. "New wine must be put into new bottles" (Mark 2:22)

This story is called "The Game Theory". The story plays off some modern trends. People like Elon Musk and Neil deGrasse Tyson have publically speculated that we may be living in a simulation. People love The Matrix and Ready Player One. There is a massively popular YouTube channel called TierZoo which teaches biology, zoology, and evolution from the perspective of life as a video game; and there is the popular trend of referring to Trump's presidency (among other things) as evidence that our "show" is in its "final season" (with peaking evidence in the chaos of 2020). The upcoming movie "Free Guy" also plays on the popularity of this trend—regardless of its eventual performance and perception, some writers and producers have clearly noted the interest in the theme and hope to capitalize on it.

Game theory itself—the study of mathematical models of strategic interaction among rational decision-makers—is an important modern development. Steven Pinker calls game theory a key modern concept with "deep implications for morality and meaning." (386) Dr. Jordan Peterson speaks of life as a series of games. And people have been relating to the complexities of the world and dealing with the collective conscious (or unconscious) of others by calling them "NPCs", which is a game reference and also grows out of the speculations in the air of life being a simulation. We relate to and understand games very well.

Set Up and Parameters

The story is that the Infinite plays the game of limited life. The One Infinite is the constructor of the platform, the writer of the program, and the player behind each and every character (and is the hardware and screen itself on which all is run and appears). But, though this set up seems nonsensical and as though it would be pointless ("purposeless"...), the game is non-trivial. "The game is important. If it wasn't important, you wouldn't be playing it. Playing a game defines it as important." (Peterson, 213) And it is not written to be broken down by all the characters knowing how to hack the rules and play without concern for difficulty or consequence.

The characters don't know "they" wrote the game—or, rather, that underneath their programmed consciousness, deep at the base of their unconscious, they are connected to that infinite consciousness which wrote and designed the game. The characters have limited consciousnesses and take the game very seriously. In this sense, since this right here, right now, is part of the game, I am a character like M'aiq the Liar. I am breaking the fourth wall (or attempting to), though this fourth wall breaking is also an inherent part of the game, included by the programmer.

The story is told about a direct confrontation between the infinite programmer beyond the game—lovingly perusing its creation—and a particularly disturbed character within the game, who cries out for answers. The character doesn't know the infinite can hear him, nor that it would care. But the infinite does hear and does have compassion, but it doesn't know quite how to respond to the character's question because their paradigms are so different.

Hopefully through this story one may begin to understand how a compassionate infinite can abide and even support this dark world of suffering; hopefully we can move toward an understanding that our own projected conceptions and expectations on the infinite are not the accurate frames of judgement that we think they are, and we may be opened up to a far more expansive conception of the nature of this game of life. "He shook his fist at a rumored God—only to find Him to be light years beyond the comfortable reflections of someone else's need for security." (Kautz, 19)

Within the game, those who share this planet and seem to play the same game—who exist within the same sphere of general parameters—would mostly agree that this game is *difficult*. Life is difficult. What "difficult" necessarily means is there is a high failure rate. It means there is failure all around. Failure we can call "suffering needlessly" or suffering without knowing redemption—suffering without hope or apparent purpose or justification. And the difficulty is evident even to those who succeed, for they suffer through the quest and see and hear the others who do not succeed, and thus suffer all the more; whether they have yet evolved a compassionate response to those they see or not, they still see the suffering.

Those who are suffering ask why, why do we suffer? And the infinite, immersed in watching the gameplay—both from above and through the viewpoints of each and every gamer—, ponders because "why is suffering necessary?" is actually an odd question, though it seems so important and valid to the characters within the game. Because the question comes from a place of such profound ignorance, it is formulated in such a way that it seeks an inaccurate answer; it comes from within the game, within the bonds of ignorance that make possible and real the suffering, and it is a question entirely of that realm. The REAL answer, the answer in accord with the truth of the infinite is "because you made it so—you elected to enter into suffering—*you wanted to suffer*" (or at least you were willing to).

But that answer is not precisely appropriate because the "you" in that answer does not address the individual who asks the question, it addresses the hero and empowering Self within their unconscious with whom they do not readily identify—who they have forgotten and neglected. The individual who asks the question does so with the deep, clear understanding that they *do not* want to suffer—that suffering is bad. So is that really "the" answer or the best answer? Is it the most *effective*?

Other answers seem equally problematic, for if we concede to answer directly the one who is ignorant, we enter into his ignorance and the answer is of an ignorant nature. If we say "because God wills it", then the individual is left with the inevitable conclusion that "God is bad. God torments his creation for his pleasure". Within the game, this answer is horrifying, and seems unjustifiable and unreconcilable with our necessity to retain a notion of an ideal which we call God. But in Truth there is nothing wrong with the conclusion "God torments his creation for his pleasure", because God's creation is not separate from God and therefore the torment is only ever applied to God himself and his pleasure also belongs to all of creation. Because the truth is "it's just a game", this is fine.

But the Truth of the compassion and mercy of God has been found superordinately important to know within the game, so we veered away from

Purpose in Form

such Abraxion-esque conceptions.

The truth is if you wrote a game you would fill it with challenge—and challenge is difficulty. And if the game you wrote was one with similar parameters to those under which our game occurs (feelings, bodies, etc.), then you would create a world much like this one, with all its suffering and horror. And, honestly, you'd probably create one harder and darker; one that would push you more fiercely to manifest your warrior and champion traits. And if you didn't—if you made a game much easier than the one you currently are engaged in, one not so enmeshed in difficulty and suffering—not many would play it, and any who did would get bored quickly—including you. But none of this absolute truth helps the individual who suffers—or at least very often it does not.

If the individual has no concept of a higher reality, and cannot let go of his own limited existence and interests (which are two sides of the same coin), then the vague claim that there exists an eternity beyond suffering, and that the infinite is so free that it plays games such as ours for pleasure is not at all comprehensible and is consequently unhelpful. Or at worst it is *analyzed*; and the being in suffering alights on the imperfections of the metaphor and assumes that because God plays these games for pleasure, God must be incomplete or unhappy in himself and therefore unhappy and imperfect! Thus God himself is of no use and existence is flawed and futile and tragic to the core!

So it is hard to know what to say from the infinite to the finite; but this is only a reflection again of the fact that the game is difficult. If it were easy to explain, and everyone could comprehend, it would not be difficult and it would not be this game!

The realms where everyone can understand the Truth are heavenly realms; they are not necessarily "easy" realms where infant souls are introduced to the idea of play at low difficulties, but they are more broadly realms where the suffering of life is lessened because the strength and courage that is engendered from the source of the infinite pouring into the game comes to the forefront of the majority of the play; some of these may be the infant, easy realms, some of these are the realms of the "professional gamers" who are all playing a non-zero-sum game within their competency level.

But that is not to say that "professional gamers" only appear and play in the heavenly games. It is just to say that a heavenly realm would be characterized by the lack of direct infliction of unnecessary suffering upon each other (no one playing to kill the others and/or steal their things), combined with the skillful playing of the game which produced a high success rate in the broad play.

The realms where no one has a clue what any of this mumbo-jumbo of eternity, infinite, or higher powers are about are the realms of hell. Perhaps they are realms where everyone who was attracted to that particular game at the same time happened to all be biting off way more than they could chew (which a way of saying "the difficulty was set too high" without absolving the element of personal responsibility). Or perhaps the game parameters themselves are set up to require zero sum play, and the kind of actors attracted to that kind of game are the ones who deserve to live in them; or perhaps that is the way that the players have chosen to play, that they think is best, and they have consistently chosen this across time so that now their game has deteriorated into the hell it is.

This game is somewhere in the middle. But it is not "in the middle" in the sense that the difficulty is only set to moderate. It is that there are some people who (even if they were considered, in some realms, professional gamers to begin with) took on a difficulty that was a real challenge to them and in this iteration they have failed, and they will continue to incarnate and fail many times before achieving a new level of mastery. But there are also some people here who are competent in this realm, and some that are exceptional. So there are circles in this realm where hells manifest, and there are circles where heavens are maintained, and there are great swaths of overlap.

The Rules: The Law of Eternity and The Law of Sacrifice

That all being said, some people know exactly what I am saying; and some kind of get it; and some are on the verge of getting it and can move into an understanding through this. For those I will describe two sets of rules of which we must play both at once. These rules are the attempt at a most effective answer to the question of "why is there suffering?" That is not the question they answer, however, for as we have seen, a direct answer is problematic. We seek to answer this question by answering the next best question of similar kind: "what can be done about suffering?"

"Why is there suffering?" is a way of objecting to the game itself. But you

Purpose in Form

chose to play for a reason; and although you no longer remember that choice, the reason for that soular amnesia is included within the difficulty of the game. "What can be done about suffering?" comes from a place of acceptance of the game, a willingness to play in accord with your inborn purpose in electing to play the game in the first place. The former question is just a tangle of ignorance and a cry of pain. It should not and cannot be addressed for its apparent intellectual content. The latter is something we can work with through reason and direction. So that is where we must turn.

Each set of rules is concerned with the alleviation of suffering, which, for most is the "goal" of the game. It is not the particular goal, but the general or archetypal one. Alleviating suffering may look like taking a promotion and starting a family, or it might look like devoting your life to prayer or charity, or any other of the infinitely unique though commonly human paths found in this game. That cannot be specified for you. But we all are oriented toward completing the game in such a way that allows us to say "that was great!" rather than "NO! THAT WAS SO FUCKING STUPID! SO UNFAIR! DUMB FUCKING GAME!" which obviously means you'll be playing again... (Not that the one who enjoyed it won't play again, but he or she is in a state to freely and joyously choose to play again; the other is compelled to play again, and is in a state of frustration and attachment that does not necessarily put him or her on a track to do any better.)

A graceful completion of the game depends largely on playing in a way where we aren't suffering needlessly, or at least where we aren't needlessly suffering excessively. Too much needless suffering equates to a frustrating game (i.e. the reality that you are not playing with the skill you believe you are capable of and you are engaged in the challenge of progressing to that level).

Thus the rules of the game in broad terms of alleviating suffering are helpful to know and pay attention to. In case it wasn't perfectly clear already, these aren't rules that are impossible to break; they are not the edges of the map. There are no such rules in the game of life. It is a game of infinite and terrible freedom. These rules are merely ways of imputing consistent causes to get consistent results geared toward one's goal.

One set of rules says that suffering is created by ignorant action, and that therefore suffering can be addressed through skillful or enlightened action (you might say "intelligent" action but the intellect alone cannot conquer life, so that is a bit of a colloquial misunderstanding). This rule for suffering can be called the Law of Sacrifice, or the way of sacrificial action or duty. Through trial and error humans have learned that this game cannot be played on a whim—or at least that they cannot sufficiently discern between a "divine whim" (i.e. true intuition) and all the other noise of thoughts that appear to their inner faculties. Thus the reality of ignorance creates ignorant desires which produce suffering, but which are nonetheless present and attractive and captivating. So there is a necessity to let go of many desires and the conceptions which generate them. This is the Way of Discernment, which has been called the Statutes or Commandments of God, or the Noble Eightfold Path, or acts of "good karma".

As the ignorant conceptions we all have are not differentiated from the self—which is perhaps the core of the ignorance, but it is also the necessary condition of the game as the true self must by and large be confused with the individual incarnated character—this letting go of these concepts is experienced as a sacrifice or a loss. That is to say that in order to enter into a finite game, we must possess a love or desire for the finite experience. Given that precondition, we will necessarily value and desire the finite expressions we meet and acquire within the game. Even though these are impermanent illusions (from a certain point of view), we are necessarily invested in the illusion, or we wouldn't be playing the game. Thus we grieve the loss of illusions while we are in the game, but we must make these sacrifices, unpleasant though they seem.

Within the game, this action of sacrifice of the unskillful or unwise (though it seems precious) for the pursuit of the wise and skillful, results in an overall experience of less suffering and creates an upward trajectory for the characters—and their society as a whole, if largely applied. This rule of sacrifice can be used both to help the suffering of the moment (deal with anxiety through creative endeavor or exercise, for example) and to mitigate in some ways the onslaught of future "bad karma" that would perpetuate or increase suffering.

We have found that "you get out what you put in" and by putting in skillful action and making the necessary sacrifices, you seem to get more a more beautiful path. It would be somewhat impossible to say that "what bad karma is destined to come your way is averted through this", because we can never know "what would have happened", but we do know that the journey, even if it is exactly as it was "going to be" either way seems to become sweeter when

Purpose in Form

we effectively engage in beautiful action and sacrifice.

This first rule is the "more finite" or the more "game oriented" of the two rules. But it is completely necessary and only untrue in that it is incomplete in itself, which is a necessary fact about all uttered truths in the finite world.

If you are in this world, you have been sacrificed. You are limited, and you must be a certain way or set of ways, which means you—so long as we are talking about the limited, experiential "you"—will not be infinitely many other ways. You must make choices. There is no such thing as "not choosing" or "not doing". Therefore there is sacrifice at the core of your nature since, in Truth, everything is you and belongs to you. You are inevitably sundered and split here, and that is the sacrificial nature of the world. The rule of sacrifice says, the more you accept it, and the more wisely and willingly you engage in this basic way of the world, the more you will enjoy the game; for it was your basic purpose in playing this game to be sacrificed, so you might as well do the thing right and not try to get away with as little loss as you can. Rather, dive in, and make daring choices which, though still founded in love, make you ever more particular, but ever more apt to the purposes that call to you. Become the Phoenix that dies again and again in order to live; one must die to habits, mindsets, goals, expectations, desires, and all sorts of things in order to live a fully beautiful and successful life.

The second rule is the "more eternal" or the more "transcendent" of the two rules. Though it makes little sense and seems contradictory, this rule is still not complete by nature of its instantiation in the game. This is the Law of Eternity or Nirvana. The rule of eternity states that eternity is. It is merely the truth of Truth. It declares the transcendent. It is the lion's roar. That is all it needs to do.

But in way of "explanation" we may say that the rule of eternity calls to the mind the image of God; or deeper, it dredges up from the well of the soul the resonance with the divine. The truth of eternity cannot do anything as words alone. No matter what I state here, the effect is not contained in the formulated words but in the reality of the connection of the soul to the eternal; the intimate connection of the infinite with the finite. And the magnitude of the effect is determined by the level of consciousness attained by the individual—the degree to which he or she can be aware of this reality and consciously feel the resonance emerge in and creep through his or her being.

The rule of eternity is the idea of salvation, of your sins already being

A Modern Religious Story

absolved, or at least that they will be absolved by something beyond you. Eternity itself is Salvation. The fact and truth of eternity, the more it is consciously known to the individual, brings great relief from suffering, both in the moment (when the resonance can be achieved or is granted) and throughout life (by making possible the reality of faith). It allows for one to say calmly "this too shall pass", rather than to mouth the words and be disappointed two seconds later that "the spell did not take effect". The Law of Eternity is the Resurrection of Christ within the individual soul; it is a Great Remembrance which breeds a knowledge that we are each the kind of being who can bear this great sacrifice, for we are all united with God already and always, and this knowledge imbues the willingness to live and act in the light of this Truth.

To many, it seems that the truth of eternity is in fact the only law of life and the only True mitigator of suffering. This is almost not untrue. But no law in the finite world is complete. The problem lies in the fact that you are having a finite experience. This is undeniable—or rather, denying this fact does not actually help. Denying it has no desirable effects. Accepting finitude, even if you call it an illusion, and working with it does have desirable effects. And what is found in this finite experience is that you cannot be in complete, unending consciousness of eternity and also play the game.

To be here in this game means to at least have periods throughout life where that consciousness is dim at best; and more often than not the experience of this game is that the periods where this consciousness of eternity is even dimly guessed are the fleeting minority. Most even say that they know nothing of this experience. The reality of the game is that there will be times when, even if you have had many visions, even if you absolutely know the truth of eternity, you will suffer great darkness and be almost entirely engulfed in despair and sorrow. In these moments, saying "this too shall pass" does not ring the way it used to, and the experiences you will and do undergo will be such that you will say that you cannot bear them—or ask "Father, why have you forsaken me?"

Of course you have not been forsaken, and you can get through; and going through such experiences teaches you better about the limitlessness of your being and your anti-fragile nature. But what this all means is that sometimes the truth of eternity just doesn't help in the moment. This is an experiential fact. The one who is at some point in their life conscious of the law of eternity will be better off than the one who never makes such a connection consciously.

Purpose in Form

But it will not be that you will suffer less in these moments, it will only be that you won't give up. So the law of eternity always helps in the long run, but doesn't always help in the moment. That is the nature of the game as it is.

To some people it doesn't matter. Some people believe the law of eternity is all that is needed. Maybe they are right. Maybe it works for them. Or maybe it just has so far. Or maybe they have overlooked the ways in which they have practiced the law of sacrifice when it came down to it. But to many people, the reality of the game is, well, part of the game. And that means that the reality of the suffering in the moment is such that it cannot be simply ignored without change (i.e. sacrifice) for the sake of the suffering individual—ultimately illusory though he may be.

The truth of sacrifice is a powerful tool to alleviate the sufferings of the moment, and seems to pave a way toward a sequence of experience where those deepest of torments are not experienced so often. But, as the Buddha emphasized greatly, the law of sacrifice or good karma is not the way to ultimate attainment. And as Christ said—this perhaps being the one thing they mostly clearly agreed on—works alone will not save you. One cannot hope to spend eternity only generating good karma and remaining in heaven, or even in an ever upwards game of ascending through heavens. You do not reach eternity by continuing far enough in a straight line.

The Buddha taught both the rule of nirvana (or eternity) and the rule of sacrifice. The Buddha said "life is suffering", which called to attention all those who know they are playing the game and seek to do it better. The Buddha gave them hope and faith—made these real and effective tools in their lives—by declaring "there is an end to suffering" or "there is an eternity which makes all suffering throughout all time null". But the Buddha's words are often taken to mean something that is entirely contradicted by his steadfast case that you cannot get to nirvana or eternity through the accumulation of good karma.

People believe that when the Buddha said "there is a way to end suffering and that is the noble eight fold path" he was saying that the effects of the karma generated through following the path would generate or create the state of nirvana or eternity, which otherwise had no existence beforehand. This is not and cannot be the case. Eternity is uncreated by definition. It is causeless. If you were to create it through action, it would have a beginning and therefore an end, and thus not be eternal. You cannot bring it into being because all

A Modern Religious Story

being already rests in it and is suffused by it.

Probably a more accurate transliteration of the Buddha's words would have been "there is a particular path along the way to the inevitable end of suffering which is more beautiful to walk than others". The Buddha first gave the absolute declaration of eternity (that there is an end of suffering), and second invited you to make the finite ride full of joy by describing the "way of proper being", which is only another way of saying "the way of proper sacrifice", or, shall we say, "the way of properly enjoying being sacrificed". The mysterious way of playing the game knowing it's a game, and yet still being fully engaged in it.

So the game of incarnation has two rules by which it is played, and you must play by them both at the same time. There is an eastern principle which says wisdom is letting the yin dominate when it is time for the yin to dominate, and letting the yang rule when it is time for the yang to rule. But it cannot be dictated to you which rules apply when, nor will it even be clear to you which is appropriate for the moment. They are both always true, and they are both potentially effective always. But sometimes you will make the wrong decision; such is the nature of the game. For life is a difficult game. There is no way to play this game such that you can apply these laws so well that they will utterly dissolve the immediate experience of all suffering. There is a minimum necessary level of ignorance to engage in the game of limitation; and thus there is an inevitable measure of suffering.

The rules of eternity and sacrifice are only there to help you make your sufferings as few and bearable as possible. There is no panacea here. No absolutely effective tool. For life is a difficult game, and the want for a full remedy or a cheat code is the want to escape this game of life; this comes from the one who asks "why is there suffering?" and still objects to the game. The one who accepts the game must accept that it is a difficult game. They must accept their fallibility. The only way to uproot ignorance completely and never suffer is to never play the game.

But when you aren't playing the game you know the infinite redemption of eternity, which always is, and the full knowledge of which is why you voluntarily elected to play the game in the first place. It is only the character within the game who asks "why does suffering exist?" or "why does God permit suffering?", and that question is precisely as absurd and erroneous as his very existence, his perceived separate identity. It is experientially real and

Purpose in Form

meaningful, but in the end it is quieted by the reality of Eternity. Thus rather than directly answer the question, we can only remind him of the laws of sacrifice and eternity. Which is to say, "Have faith! And remember that every little thing is gonna be alright; but if you find yourself desiring a more beautiful path or playground, come this way!" Yet the way is strait and narrow, and few find the gate, for life is a difficult game.

Part 3:

Sticking to the Strait and Narrow

Thus far we have accomplished quite a bit. We have discovered some eternal metaphysical truths, we have revived purpose and meaning in life, we have found the principle proposition underlying all positive ethics and values. But there are still a few powerful intellectual questions that must be addressed, not because they in themselves pose any direct threat to the metaphysical necessities we have unveiled, but because they are common preoccupying possibilities, nagging thoughts that might delay the process of accepting and integrating these great and virtuous religious truths.

So we must hem up these stragglers—cutting off the misconceptions on either side to ensure our journey remains on course; and in the process we will see all the more the necessity and truth of what we have already discovered.

It bears repeating, however, that the problems discussed in these final chapters are ancillary at best; were these addresses to fall short in some way of resolving the problems satisfactorily, this would in no way destabilize or uproot the necessity of the truth of the infinite, the necessary connection of the infinite to the finite individual, and the resulting affirmations of purpose, meaning, and significance in life.

We will begin by addressing the intellectual darling of pantheism, and why it cannot take the place of more anthropomorphic stories that are contemporarily seen as parochial.

"We cannot invent our own values, because we cannot merely impose what we believe on our own souls… We rebel against our own totalitarianism, as much as that of others." – Dr. Jordan B. Peterson (193)

Chapter 15: The Problems with Pantheism

> "The symbols of mythology are not manufactured; they cannot be ordered, invented, or permanently suppressed." – Joseph Campbell (2)

There are many problems with pantheism, lofty and ideal as many intellectuals make it sound. Reza Aslan touts pantheism's advantages over the obscure panentheism—which is the belief or doctrine that God is greater than the universe and includes and interpenetrates it—as 1) not seeking to humanize God (where panentheism leaves room for a separate body of God beyond creation) and 2) affirming the infinity of the universe rather than supposing a finite universe within an infinite God (165-171). He also supports pantheism over a traditional Christian God for the same reason of dehumanizing God from Christ's form, and emphasizing God's oneness.

If forced to choose between pantheism and panentheism, I would choose the latter, unlike Aslan. I have a different understanding of what the view of a "beyond creation" accomplishes than Aslan supposes is the chief factor in pantheism. Additionally, I do entirely believe that creation itself is infinite and I do not support the belief in a finite universe; yet I still believe panentheism is the better option. For one thing, there can be infinities which are greater than other infinities (or at least so say the mathematicians), so it is not necessarily a question of supposing a finite universe and infinite God beyond; it can be an infinite universe without ever exhausting the infinite potential of God.

But more importantly, it is a question of emphasis. Alan Watts objects to pantheism because, according to pantheism: God minus creation equals zero (or null) (*Behold The Spirit*, 126). Even if we understand the universe to be infinite, and therefore still affirm God's infinity, the doctrine of pantheism, in some way, reduces God. Part of the problem is that we often say "the universe" and hold an image or conception in our minds which is more reflective of "the physical expanse which we know or know the beginnings of".

Even though "the universe", as Aslan points out, means "all that exists", which is technically the same as God (existence itself), we have great trouble in remembering just how much we do not know. The universe (all that exists) is far more than the physical, observable reality which we believe we know[*]. And on top of that, the reality we think we know compared to the infinite reality which is (even if it were only physical!) is infinitely smaller than we think. These sound like the same point stated inversely, but there are two distinct points to be made: 1) There is far, far (infinite) more to know about reality right in front of us—not just out beyond out sight—than we do. And 2) even if our conceptions were correct and there was not infinitely more to the observable reality right before us that we do not see, the expanse beyond which we can see is so infinitely greater that we do not know anything at all.

These natural human attributes and tendencies (namely: our necessary infinite ignorance and our tendency to think we know a significant amount, regardless of what we know about infinity) cause pantheism, in practice, to be a reductive theory of God. Panentheism on the other hand emphasizes that there is always a beyond beyond, which we cannot grasp. It emphasizes the knowable mystery of God and pushes his nature beyond our conceptions, while pantheism tends to subtly suggest that God is within our conceptions. (Here we will leave behind the term panentheism and forget about it; it was only part of a brief comparison discussing what Aslan brought up. Going forward we will only be discussing pantheism and the anthropomorphic religious conceptions.)

This problem is quite plainly seen in Spinoza's theories where he declares out right, with all the appearances of steady logic, that God is amorphous, distant, and uncaring. And Aslan exhibits the same tendencies, purporting

---

[*] This is precisely why Peter Boghossian believes that proposing an infinite reality or fundamental existence defeats God—because we fail to fully comprehend the reality entailed by "infinity".

The Problems with Pantheism

belief in a God without form or will. Both Spinoza and Aslan miss the intimate, and self-saturating nature of the infinite, which is a necessary reality and points to a personal God—a God "at hand... and not far off"—above a removed and dehumanized one (Jeremiah 23:23). This is something very easy to miss because the infinite is so mysterious and so beyond our comprehension that it ends up doing things that we would not imagine. But Christians know through faith and wisdom that "God works in mysterious ways", and Buddhists believe "every single thing we encounter—including ourselves—goes beyond our ability to conceive of it." (Dogen/Warner 40) Meanwhile, pantheists believe they have calculated the truth on their own and comprehended it, thus reducing God to something that they can supposedly intellectually delineate—which is to abandon the infinite, subtle as it may be.

More problems with pantheism arise clearly within Aslan's claims and statements of faith. He believes God has "no will" and "no form". But he also believes that we are the image of God and God is everything. What, then, is form, if not God? And if we have an image, does not God have an image? How is God our essence, but not our form? If God is everything that exists—and form exists—then God must be connected to form or possessing form in some way. And further, since Aslan rejects a "beyond" creation for some formal or formless God to dwell in, God must be within and suffusing creation—yet he is somehow unformed?

The only consistent way to answer this problem is to say that form is unreal and does not exist. To say that God's form and image is only the totality of existence, so that we are included in it but do not nearly reflect its totality is to miss the truth of the self-saturation of the infinite, and thus the fractal or holographic nature of reality, and to contradict the proposition which Aslan affirms that we are made in the image of God. Thus one either reduces the nature of God and claims exclusions to his domain, which abandons infinity and thus God, or one must claim that form is not real. When one claims that form is not real and all our experience of it is an illusion, one falls prey to the ethical problem of the east of denying the reality of the finite. This prospect is not tenable, or at least does not encompass the whole truth, as we have seen even the Buddhists and Yogis recognize that purpose in form and cultivation is necessary.

Thus, form must be accounted for, and if form is real, then God has form, even under pantheism. And as one comprehends the true nature of the infinite—its self-saturation—one begins to see that form is not only the "sum-total" of creation, but also the individual "parts". They are all reflections of the same infinite presence. Thus a close and personal God is a necessary reality, and we are made in His image, and though we have undoubtedly made gods in our own images throughout the ages, this does not mar the necessary truth that we are made in the image of God; the image of the infinite which necessarily saturates our being and is not separate even from physical form. Those who try to make God fit into their image or their expectations only create a false god. But those who see the Truth expressing itself in human form, know that we are made by that Infinite Reality and reflect its structure and nature.

Moreover, if, as Aslan claims, God has no will, then the same sort of questions arise: what is our will? Is our will not God's if God is all? If there is no will in God, then is there no purpose in creation? If God is not directing or intending any of creation, much less any of our lives, and thus doesn't care, why are ethics meaningful? Again, the only cogent answer Aslan can give is that our will does not exist and/or does not matter. If it does matter, it must be meaningful in some way and the results must have value. If they have value, that reflects a purpose. And value, purpose, and meaning all must be foundational—infinite. Again, pretending that *we* give our wills and purposes meaning relies on the divine nature of the individual and the attention and care of a personal God. Without these, secularists and pantheists can pretend they stand for these things, but underneath their premises are unsupported and they really forward nihilism by their claims of an uncaring infinite or an inert finite existence.

So if our will is an illusion, or existent but purposeless, then we must be ultimately nihilistic in our ethics (even if we choose to reject despair and act as though this was not our conclusion or underlying truth). But, knowing the truth of the infinite presence which is All and Each and Every, by nature of the necessary self-saturation of the infinite, we understand that our wills are real, our purposes are significant, and that God does intend and intimately involve himself in and care for his creation. So while pantheism appeals to the intellectual in appearing to preserve the true oneness of God, and in fashionable rebellion against the perceived childish or whimsical nature of a personal God, it actually drives one far closer to nihilism than necessary, at best, and does not offer a tenable and cohesive answer to the questions of meaning, purpose, and form in general. In being a highly valued intellectual

The Problems with Pantheism

gambit, it dismisses the profound mystery of life which is a knowable truth.

Looking at perhaps the chief intellectual concern in this case of the oneness of God[*] one can step back and correct the simple mistake. The scripture and wisdom which declares God One and indivisible above all should not crudely and literally be interpreted as denying God's presence within creation.

Indeed, pantheism as Aslan describes still doesn't even answer this point. He says God's oneness is preserved by the pantheistic notion, yet he also says we are all God and God is all of creation. So how is God the all and sum total, and yet fully suffusing a variated creation? The pantheistic response must be that all separation and variation is an illusion and unreal—thus running into the ethical problem of the east and missing the intimate connection of God to form and the clear and necessary purpose in form that even eastern doctrines cannot escape. Or, if God is the sum total of all and yet form and variation are real, then none of us are in fact made in the image of God since we are only odd appendages constituting a miniscule fraction of his ultimate form. Either way, God is separated and distant from the finite, and the oneness that is supposedly preserved still seems to be missing something.

God's eternal oneness and indivisibility is a truth that states the reality of God remains indivisible EVEN WITHIN CREATION. "For the One who has become many, remains the One undivided, but each part is all of Christ." (St. Symeon the Younger, The Soul Afire, 303) God is indivisible not because he remains removed from creation or because creation is in fact unreal, but because God's infinity is a miraculous enigma and mystery which allows for a differentiated creation full of form and purpose and individuality without ever escaping the oneness of God. This necessary mystery is taken by intellectuals as an affront to reason and intellect, for they believe they should be able to entirely conceptualize and grasp the infinite with their intellect—proving that they have no real comprehension of the reality referred to by the term "infinity".

But perhaps a more clear way to illustrate the oneness paradox—though it should not be mistaken as a complete solution to the mystery of divine intimacy—is that separation is impossible within God and nothing in creation

---

[*] Though one should not underestimate how much pure rebellion and dogmatic opposition to the perceived shadow of Christianity motivates the modern intelligencia in their atheism, nihilism, and pantheistic chimeras.

is separate either from God or the rest of creation—i.e. all is infinitely interconnected—but separation and variation or differentiation are not the same, or can be meaningfully distinguished in this manner. Separation is an illusion of finitude; it is the manifestation of ignorance. Differentiation and variation is the truth of creation and form and is fully meaningful. One can talk about trees and mountains and people and flowers as different entities of creation meaningfully without suggesting that they are separate and finite. Supposing separation is believing that existence is non-unitary, which is impossible—thus God is eternally One and indivisible. But talking about differentiation, thus form and creation, is perfectly meaningful and true within the infinite oneness of God which provides for and intends all these things. But again, though pantheists might try to avail themselves of this intellectualization, they run into the problem of how or whether we are made in the image of God and to what extent we each possess divinity while they try to maintain an aloof and impersonal God.

In pulling unidirectionally toward one conception of God, pantheism satisfies the desired intellectual purity of the scholar, but misses the intimate and mysterious reality of the Glory of the Infinite. Christianity, on the other hand, does not give us a singular conception of God, though it maintains the Truth of God's eternal oneness. It lets the paradox be. Christianity describes for us a trinity of equal conceptions of God which together pull us close to his mysterious reality which is necessarily beyond our conception. But by meditating on these conceptions and holding them each equally real and true, we circumambulate the infinite reality which they cluster around, and we may become saturated by its presence in these images and thus receive some Grace of a vision or faith beyond rational conception (as the vision of the infinite must be).

God the Father in Christianity testifies to the God seemingly removed and beyond creation—the sum-total God and the watcher beyond all limitations, including space and time; yet it reminds us that he, as a "father", is intimately related to his creation and that he cares for it deeply and closely. God the Son as Christ reminds us that God is not only ephemerally present with us through our lives, but walks with us and lives with us and as us—he not only observes our sufferings but fully embodies and experiences them. He also gives us an ideal to look to and strive for, calling us to cultivate ourselves and the world to create heaven on Earth—to know that purpose is meaningful and that our lives are worthy beyond imagining, and thus our deeds carry great importance. God the Holy Spirit reminds us of the God within us, calling us, inspiring us, and living as us (not just removed in others and memory). This is a God that is formless and all-penetrating which is yet sensitive to our humanity and guides us compassionately. Through this trinity we can be called to orbit the mystery of God's reality and not stray too far into idolatry of limited conceptualizations (even if they use the term "infinite" in their doctrines).

Try as you might to deformalize God and recall your ignorant projections from him, unconsciously you will reduce him to an intellectual conception, a limited entity. Thus He is not only the removed father or the effervescent Holy Spirit, but also the incarnate Son and the intimate Father and Spirit. But when you think God is ONLY human (as Aslan fears is the downfall of Christianity), the eternal Father and the active Holy Spirit are there to push you to break free of your dark and ignorant desires and strive for more—and really, the enigmatic nature of Christ himself pushes us to question what is right and to discern our divine impulses from our ignorant actions (like whether or not we should revel in our desire to punch a child in the face…).

While it is certainly true in practice that many people who call themselves Christians have humanized God in their minds and excused themselves from striving and ignored their own faults (though this also happens from dehumanizing and etherealizing God by making Christ's nature completely unreachable and thus separate from practical life), it does not seem to me that scripture in any way supports this attitude. Christ unequivocally calls for love and mercy in the face of persecution and tells us all our actions are directed toward and done unto Him, our savior, regardless of the form we see before us. We all fail to turn the other cheek and fail to see Christ in our enemies every day. If we do not listen to the Bible's exhortations to be very conscious of our failings (which we can only truly be through knowing the true mercy and glory of God) and strive for better, then we cannot so much fault the tradition and teachings as merely the ignorance of man, which pollutes all paths, true or false.

I cannot say it is always better to conceive of God as a trinity, for that would be to suggest there is a conception of God which captures his infinity. The general notion of pulling away from rigid conceptions is a good one, and it is emphasized constantly in the Bible through God's iconoclasm[*]. But if we follow this impulse to move towards a singular, disembodied conception, we have not found the truth, but merely followed another path away from it—trading in the idolatry of the trinity for the idolatry of pantheism and intellectualism. There is no perfect formula, but Christianity does allow space for a dynamism in our conceptions that seems more useful than a static notion of God—dress it up as perfect as we may. Whether we understand and practice this well is another issue—not one to ignore, but not one that should cause us to abandon the true wisdom within the doctrine.

The final issue that I feel it is necessary to point out in Aslan's formulation of pantheism is his complete disregard for the problem of consciousness and how it plays into his theory. Being closely involved with and tied to mainstream western intellectualism, Aslan seems compelled to avoid the issue, and may indeed believe it is a non-issue. But it is a fundamental issue.

For any pantheist, for whom God is All, does this not include consciousness? Does not God create or manifest consciousness in creation as all else? So in what way is God not conscious? And if God is conscious, and one accepts a view of panpsychism or closer to it, how is God impersonal? How can God have the capacity for consciousness and yet not care for or intend our consciousness? The position of a pantheist who rejects consciousness of God makes no sense and only stems from the dogmas of modern western intellectualism like The Principle of Mediocrity and the dreadful hypothesis of entirely secondary and purposeless (random) nature of consciousness (and human life in general). It is from these demonstrably false dogmas that such conceptions arise, taking incongruent assumptions as their bases and thus coming up with a formulation that so clearly begs the question of consciousness but refuses to address it.

The pantheist clearly falls prey to the argument outlined earlier: if God is infinite (all), and consciousness exists, then consciousness is within the domain of the infinite, necessarily. Thus the infinite creates, and therefore necessarily contains the capacity for consciousness. So why should we assume the infinite is not conscious or that consciousness cannot be created and manifested in infinitely many ways? Moreover, as we have seen that

---

[*] "God... often asks for intimacy by exposing the false foundations of everything that makes us feel safe and warm." (Kautz, 11)

consciousness has been proven to be not a secondary phenomenon and to transcend space and time even as it exists in ordinary humans, the basic assumptions of an unconscious universe and the random and inconsequential nature of consciousness should be revisited and reexamined with great skepticism. Thus the pantheist cannot adequately start from these positions and must address the issue of consciousness and how it factors into their theories again from the beginning. And once they do, they must wrestle with the issue of how they seek to keep God amorphous, aloof, and unconcerned with individual consciousnesses, while he is, by definition, at least capable of consciousness, and must be, by nature of the infinite, FULLY present and whole in each moment and area of space and time (and beyond).

Between the requirements of a necessary capacity of consciousness and a necessary complete saturation of all, it seems impossible to rationally deny a conscious and intimately present God throughout the entire universe—which seems to clearly imply an entirely personal God, seeing as humans are part of the universe with which God is entirely present always, and of which God is at least capable of being fully conscious. And since God is entirely aware of all things as well as conscious of himself, in what way should we suppose that God is removed from intimate personal knowledge of us? As we see, though Pantheism is posed great problems and hides internal contradictions even within the normally accepted paradigm, when we turn to the truths we must begin to accept of the self-saturation of the infinite and a non-emergent consciousness, Pantheism completely crumbles.

Pantheists could resort to Deism and claim that God voluntarily distances himself from creation and removes himself from an intimate relationship with created beings, though the potential certainly exists. Thus Deists must claim, that while God did create intentionally and consciously, he then removed himself from creation either for a set amount of time—until some planned stage—or unendingly. This would apparently preserve their desired conclusion of a removed God.

The problem with this is that it is a conception from within time and it applies the conceptions of time to God. God's intentional and conscious involvement with creation, which Deists grant, "at the beginning" is no different from his involvement with creation eternally, for God is eternal. When God created creation, he created it end to end. To suppose God created an evolving creation which he does not know the end of is to suggest that God is not beyond time (or that there is a border of "non-existence" out of which the future continually pours and which God cannot penetrate—as we saw earlier, such conceptions of non-existence and the non-unitariness of fundamental existence are absurd).

Thus, while Deists may believe that God takes a predominantly non-interventionalist role throughout creation, that is only a metaphor and story which attempts to address and explain the common (but false) human perception of God's absence. God's necessarily intentional creation means that he has intimately involved himself in every aspect, every moment of creation, whether merely observing the continuing line of causation with intimate acceptance and approval ("not intervening" with what he "set in motion"—which to God is no different than "directly created", since he made[*] the laws of causation as well) or diligently fine tuning all aspects of the procedure; the difference is only in semantics and the images created in human minds.

The necessary reality of God's infinity is that he is intimately present in and conscious of all creation at all levels—i.e. (as it has always been known) omnipresent, omnipotent, and omnibenevolent (i.e. compassionate, or conscious and caring[†]). Thus all conceptions of a "removed" God are only metaphors and cannot be rationally intended to literally mean God is "separate" from creation—that would imply spacial limitations to God. It is merely a metaphor which seeks to explain the reason for the darkness of life and the lack of miracles and wonder we seem to encounter constantly. In that sense, God as "non-interventionist" is not meaningfully distinct from "God works in mysterious ways".

---

[*] Don't worry, we will turn to the metaphor of the "creator" very soon.

[†] As I have demonstrated in *Jnana Yoga*, the consciousness of God is identical with love and the highest order of compassion by necessity of its nature as eternal and self-knowing. The so-beloved critique that this trinity is a contradiction I deal with at length in *Jnana Yoga*. It is false. It is mere hubris. The forwarded contradiction is not disproof of benevolence but mere doubt of omnipotence—for if God is omnipotent then he possesses the power to make you see him as benevolent—to change your perceptions. "Something that seems incomprehensible to someone unseeing might be perfectly evident to someone who had opened his eyes." (Peterson, 106) Holding onto one's limited perceptions and resulting judgements as categorical and inescapable condemnations of God is only self-aggrandizement and disbelief that God operates within you, and that ignorance is where the supposed contradiction comes from. Consider first, "perhaps it is you current knowledge that is insufficient, not life itself." (Peterson, 99)

Chapter 16: On What Is Meant by "Certainty" and Other Epistemological Issues

Throughout this book I have declared many things certain. I have also declared it a certainty that humans are fallible beings. And I previously wrote a book of epistemology that uprooted all certainty in formulated theories and knowledge. So here it is appropriate to clarify what I mean by "certainty".

I stand by my previous book on epistemology; there is only one absolute epistemological certainty and that is the existence of the infinite—the incorrigible tautology that existence is. All other so called knowledge is fallible. We are fallible beings and we should never forget that. So I say, colloquially, that it is "certain" we are fallible beings—even thought this is a conclusion reached by a fallible being, through fallible processes, and so can never be concluded absolutely certainly. I do not begrudge the skeptics. I am an extreme skeptic. Skepticism has many merits and is something we could use more of.

It is also true that people who ascribe to the ideal of being a skeptic are fallible about this process as well, and what often passes as "skepticism" is just

Purpose in Form

a form of defending and upholding a modern orthodoxy. If you are to be truly skeptical, you must see it all the way through and do the thing right. That is what my book *Jnana Yoga* is about.

A third truth is the one that Hume points out in lampooning his skeptical character Philo, asking him if he will really be confused about whether to exit by the door or the window. Skepticism is useful, and people can be skeptics. But a skeptic won't, each morning, wonder if the mechanism for starting his car has changed overnight without him knowing it. He will put the key in and start the engine and not be the least bit surprised or shaken in his skeptical attitudes that the car starts as usual and all the world proceeds as normal (and this remains true even though the skeptic can overrule the ideas of "probable" knowledge, as I demonstrated in *Jnana Yoga*).

Skepticism has its place, but it is not a moment to moment practical solution to living life. It may exist in the background. A skeptic may be less perturbed by anomalies that crop up, because he has less concrete beliefs and infallible expectations, but he, like everyone else, develops habits and tendencies by which he lives that are not deconstructed each day and rebuilt from the ground up, making sure everything is still how it used to be.

In the same vein, a skeptic does have his or her own language and unique conceptions and attitudes; and these come out when the time is appropriate. But that does not mean a skeptic cannot have a normal, colloquial conversation with any average person they meet. For example, when someone tells me a story about what they did the other day saying, "I went...", I do not butt in and challenge them to define this hypothetical "I" they seem to believe in. On the contrary, I tell them about whatever interesting thing *I* did recently. This does not change the fact that I am a skeptic about the nature of a unified self-identity which is wrapped up in the body-mind and involved in action. It's just a different mode of operation.

No skeptic escapes some level of normality. No skeptic fully embodies skepticism all the time. It is not only impossible to do, it is also a silly—and ineffective—endeavor. Skepticism has an important and significant effect on life, and this is optimized when it is kept to operating within its proper domain and not interfering with too many of the habitual norms of day to day life; otherwise the skeptic is more properly called "the neurotic".

Therefore, I have no reservations about calling things certainties in this book. For our purposes, when I say certain, I mean that these things are as certain as the existence of causality, the objective reality of the sun, or that my body is constantly accelerated toward the body of the Earth. As I have said, causality is a hypothesis, and I believe that existence probably proceeds beyond causality—it is certainly the case that existence proceeds beyond *linear* causality, which is how we normally think of causality. And, with a more expanded view of consciousness, there may be some doubt as to the true "objective" reality of the sun. Further, there is currently a significant and mounting collection of evidence for the severe limitations of gravity—even the possibility of entirely transcending its effects—in the reliable military reports of UAPs which fly in patterns not physically possible without cancelling the effects of gravity. The skeptic always has room for doubt in everything we call "certain".

From the point of view of a true through-and-through skeptic, all of our colloquial certainties are superstitions. Thus, one skeptical of all sorts of metaphysics and religious language could challenge me on my declarations about the certainty of purpose. I will grant you this challenge and discussion, but then I will expect you to apply this skepticism consistently.

As I have said, our perception of purpose is fallible. We cannot be sure whether the *particular* purposes we perceive are divinely ordained or are products of mere selfish endeavor. But we do know that we believe in the underlying reality of purpose itself—this we cannot escape. We would not be skeptics if we did not believe in the significant effects and therefore purpose of the skeptic approach. We take this foundational belief and orientation as certain. The skeptic may raise issue with taking a fundamental assumption of our imperfect consciousness as certain, but that comes from doubting the significance of our consciousness, which comes from the story of consciousness as an emergent and secondary phenomenon, which conveys the self-defeating faith of nihilism.

Our foundational beliefs have effects in our lives. We may not notice how deeply they influence us and how significant the effects of a correct orientation are when we never end up doubting them, but if we ourselves have experienced life through the lens of nihilism, or have paid close enough attention to those who have, then we know just how significant these different faiths are. When we accept our foundational and inescapable beliefs of the significance of our consciousness and the reality and significance of purpose in life, we encounter much less turmoil, suffering, and chaos—or at least, when we encounter all the turmoil, suffering, and chaos that we do, we are not driven to nihilistic suicidality or murderous rage at the absurdity of life.

When we come to believe, through the influence of some story, that the basic nature of our own being is fundamentally flawed and misaligned, we experience life as a curse. We cannot actually change the fact that we consider our consciousness significant, and that we see purpose everywhere and follow it (even if it is the purpose of telling people purpose does not actually exist), but we can be tortured by the thought that from the very genesis of our being, we are mistaken.

When we come to believe that we are mistakes of the universe, unintentionally formed through haphazard, blind chance, and that all our worth, values, instincts, perceptions, emotions, and ideas are mere hallucinations that we are inescapably programmed to chase (even when we come to believe they are lies), we find that the suffering of our lives increases dramatically. Not only are we plagued with such doubts and such despair at our cursed nature, but then all the other hardships and inconveniences of life take on a whole new meaning. They are no longer obstacles to our purposes, capable of being construed as challenges, which push us to grow if and when we face them willingly; they are now merely acts of cruelty and torture inflicted by the cold, hostile, unconscious universe. We can be hypnotized into thinking all our purposes are lies, and this belief (though false) has its effects, but nothing can take away the significance and reality of our suffering. Our suffering can only be exacerbated or ameliorated by degrees.

These are some of the effects of our underlying and most foundational beliefs and assumptions. These metaphysical orientations are not scientifically derived theories—they are faiths conferred by a story. The scientists have never derived the theories of meaninglessness, purposelessness, or annihilation foundationally. If they tried to, they would recognize them as absurd beliefs with negative effects—including being at odds with the belief in the virtuousness of the truth and honesty (which is the supposed reason people give for spreading such nihilism). These beliefs, these orientations of faith, were conferred through the story they constructed of secondary, emergent consciousness created by mere chance playing out across an infinity of space-time (without comprehending the total reality of "infinity").

This story was the narrative constructed to underlie the more contemporary observations of the reality of evolution. In seeking the origins of evolution and creation, the scientists entered farther and farther into speculative territory (sincere effort and genuine belief they put into the task not withstanding). They reached back some 3-4 billion years and supposed the origins of life and consciousness in the haphazard wigglings of inorganic materials. This was intended as a scientific hypothesis, to be sure. But one cannot escape the fact that it is also a line of creative storytelling and *a priori* philosophic reasoning—and much more the latter two than the intended former. One cannot actually hope to prove or disprove this thesis based on material evidence. It is only falsifiable through philosophy—through the refining and dissecting of the theory. It is an *a priori* endeavor which science so often pretends to shy away from.

In any case, this story was accepted under the title of a scientific theory. And this story was believed, to a greater or lesser degree. But what was further unknown was that this story was not even a foundational story, as it seemed to be. Underlying this story is an entire set of faith-based or metaphysical assumptions which were, through the acceptance of this overlying story, firmly cemented in the scientific dogma (certainly they were vastly prevalent already, but this story grounded them and reinforced them, making them truly foundational). These metaphysical beliefs, this set of faith claims, underlying the scientific story of creation were: the universe is finite[*] and causation is meaningless, insignificant, and possibly fundamentally random or incomplete. These assumptions, this underlying faith, laid the path for science to become fundamentally nihilistic.

Our fundamental beliefs and orientations toward life itself are based on stories, not scientific or philosophic reasoning. That is because our fundamental beliefs are about something which extends far beyond us and exceeds our comprehension; we are oriented toward something that we do not

---

[*] Many would object to this claim and say that science believed in or posited an infinite universe—for that is the only way that the infinitely unlikely miracle of self-replicating particles coming into being against all odds really makes any sense. However, the materialist-influenced conception of what an infinite universe entails is so far removed from the reality of the true infinite that, although they used the word "infinite", the principles and conceptions they forwarded alongside that term showed just how limited and sterile they viewed this "infinite" expanse. Thus, though the content of their language claims otherwise, an understanding of their theories clearly indicates they believe in a finite universe (even if they do not comprehend this level of their mistake).

fully understand. Since we do not and cannot fully understand that toward which we must take a position, we must accept a basic, fundamental faith. That is not a speculation that I am hoping you will accept which will then cause you to pick up a faith. It is a statement of the reality that you, by definition, inescapably, have a faith. You are oriented in some way toward life. You can tell yourself all sorts of superficial stories about how you understand things, how you came to realize things, how you are different or whatever you want; none of it will change the fact that you have fundamental orienting beliefs on the nature of life and existence and your place in it. These comprise the basis of your faith. And your faith deeply affects all aspects of your life (whether you are aware of it or not) including your basic perceptions.

We will get to Boghossian's objections to the epistemological conception of faith, but Tolstoy's category of faith is necessary and good. A religious faith (that is, one that affirms our connection to the infinite) keeps us from going into the underworld of absolute purposelessness, for example. This religious faith actually allows us to function as western scientists. It is only because we can be firmly faithful in the existence of purpose, significance, and meaning, while recognizing that we are fallible and may be wrong in so many ways about the particulars we perceive, that we can investigate our errors without becoming nihilistic and/or misanthropic through being fooled into doubting purpose, significance, and meaning themselves.

What keeps a scientist interested in pursuing knowledge and creation? It is a basic *belief* (not fact or empirically derived theory) in purpose which has not yet been eradicated by the nihilism creeping through other levels of his system. What allows the deeply skeptical scientist to stand on top of all other past scientists' work and continue progress rather than doubting the reality of everyone's discoveries and claims and theories that came before? Why does not every skeptical scientist start from the level of knowledge of primitive humanity and try to work out the basics of Copernicus through Newton first (redoing all experiments and reworking all the details), then all the way back up to where we are now, to make sure there haven't been any grave mistakes? What motivates this faith in other people? How can any biologist trust that a spectrophotometer measures and indicates what others say it does without investigating and testing for himself all sorts of laser physics and physical chemistry, and building the apparatus for himself from the ground up? Would one really deny that these are valid skeptical doubts, extreme though they be?

There must be some basic trust toward life and others for movement and action. If you pretend to be the ultimate skeptic in the realm of religion, and argue that we cannot be certain of the purpose, meaning, and significance of our consciousness, then I must ask you to deconstruct all the theories and apparati of science yourself, start all pursuits of knowledge from scratch, and reconsider each time you leave whether you will exit by the door or the window. "Life is short, and you don't have time to figure everything out on your own. The wisdom of the past was hard-earned, and your dead ancestors may have something to tell you." (Peterson, 158)

Faith as a Negative Epistemology

So far we have looked at how faith is good and necessary in life, when faith means one's basic metaphysical assumptions and orientations toward the nature of life and how those direct our attitudes and actions through all manners of life. This level of faith is entirely compatible and, as I have just argued, necessary for a scientific, skeptical approach to knowledge in which we recognize ourselves as fallible beings.

Peter Boghossian, however, defines faith as "pretending to know things you do not know" and takes issue with its presence as an epistemological approach in modern western society (24). This is the best objection that modern atheists really have about religion. Although Boghossian and others are certainly justified in a personal aversion to such epistemology, and though it is true that western rationalism as a societal norm is at odds with authoritarian dictation and/or submissive acceptance of knowledge claims, I believe the scope of his approach and his goals for the "street epistemologists" atheist movement may be misguided.

But, to reiterate and be clear, although I will spend the rest of this section taking issue with and arguing against what I perceive to be some of the assumptions which guide the goals and principles in this particular atheist movement, Boghossian is absolutely correct to state that many people (perhaps even a majority of people) take a faith-based approach to epistemology at least in some arenas of their lives. He is correct that this kind of faith is entirely contrary to the ideals of a western rationalist society and the enlightenment. And he is correct that a more thoroughly developed rationality in our society would bring many good effects with it, and that encouraging a rigorous and open epistemological approach driven by curiosity and freedom of inquiry (which will undoubtedly often come across as aggressive or overly confrontational) is an effective way of encouraging the growth of this rationality which is of great value.

I do, however, believe that his vision for a movement is at least partially influenced by the kind of modern intellectual utopianism that we have discussed in relation to secularism. And I believe that through a more realistic and rational assessment of the world and our values in life, the scope and perhaps methods of his project might require some adjustment.

Let us recall two contrary perspectives on effectivity of any given thing in question. Some look for or hope for 100% effectivity, and are disappointed with anything less. Some can be pleased with or even ecstatic about quite a small effect (relative to the ideal of 100% effectivity). We must ask to which camp (pessimistic idealism or optimistic realism, respectively) the vision and quest for a rational society belongs. If the primary vision of modern rationalists (be they atheists or not) is motivated by the belief in the actual possibility of their 100% effectiveness in converting people to rationality, we must be very wary of their pursuits. If they are far more grounded in reality and have realistic expectations and goals, then their efforts will be much closer to a force for good in society.

It would be easy for any proponent of the rationalist or atheist movement to wave off these apprehensions as trivial, and declare that of course they are all perfectly reasonable in their goals and expectations. But if that is your position, it only makes me all the more concerned. The unconscious drive toward utopia, which inevitably entails deep systems of controlling others, all of which is supported and justified by an underlying (and, again, often unconscious) disdain for either humanity or certain groups of it and their beliefs, is not to be overlooked or underestimated. And intellectuals are especially susceptible to this drive. That is a fact we must face as a society that values and encourages intellectualism in many ways.

So my questions for the movement toward a rational epistemology, and each individual in it, are: What level of rationality do you believe exists in society already? What do you believe is the optimum level of rationality? And what percentage of increase in rationality (and in what time frame) would you consider as a success for your movement? The answers to these questions (assuming we trust the honesty of them revealing their true plans and assessments) will be quite telling.

Each question is entirely open-ended and speculative. There is no definitive study to draw accurate data for direct answers to these questions. For one thing, therein lies a massive problem of defining and measuring "rationality" as so many people (oh so rationally) would most readily define rationality as the adherence to or acceptance of certain particular beliefs—of course Boghossian would object to this and hopefully his street epistemologists have been imparted enough zeal on that end to not fall prey to such a trap. But still, it remains an issue; I mean, how many people who would consider themselves rational even know what "epistemology" means?

But anyhow, the answers to these questions, speculative though they may be, may reveal underlying perceptions of the would-be rationalists, which would shed light on their true motivations and ends. (And one should not take this literally as an investigation of one person to another, it is equally important and informative to examine one's own true ideas and motivations in any case—to discover their unconscious attitudes and drives, many of which may come from their shadow.)

The lower one estimates the current state of rationality, in answer to the first question, the more we should be concerned or at least curious about the possibility of an underlying attitude of contempt or superiority pushing this intellectual attitude. This is not a cut and dry conclusion. To be clear, I would not rate the rationality of society very high, certainly not a number in the majority (we would discuss the question of analyzing individuals as a whole vs. parsing out individual decisions made by individuals all over, and coming up with a sliding scale of how many people are rational how much of the time). My argument is not that rationality and diligently skeptical epistemological inquiry is already flourishing, thus this movement has little to do. I am merely interested in the complexities of the situation which I think are not captured in the vision of promoting wide spread rational epistemology evangelism.

The higher the answer to the second question, again, the more we need to be concerned about the arrogance of this rising intellectualism. Many might say the more rationality the better, especially if we are talking about rational epistemological inquiry, rather than some dogmatic conception that rationality is community which agrees to a set of beliefs. But I believe there is a strong case against this idealized notion. The basic summary of my position is that life is not just about being an intellectual—that there are valuable pursuits in life and ways of being which have little or nothing to do with the rigorous development of the intellect and the subsequent movement toward reason. The fact of the matter is, regardless of how much virtue you see in reason and its products, devoting yourself to the cultivation of reason takes a tremendous amount of dedicated effort and constant work. To pursue reason, one has to already have chosen the intellectual path in life.

Now, many intellectuals will take what I just said as some sort of pejorative about people who are less educated or have a lower IQ, but that is merely their own projection, revealing their own prejudices. It is almost a taboo in intellectual discussion to suggest in one way or another that not all people can or will be significantly moved along the path of intellectualism and/or rationality. It is very similar to the taboo about talking in detail about race-based differences in IQ or athletic performance, etc. One who hears the question fears it will go to a racist[*] place, or that it will be overheard and taken as such, and so the topic is avoided. Equally, if intellectuals hear you talking about how not everyone is an intellectual, they think *you* are making prejudiced assumptions about people or groups of people. But it is only because the intellect is so full of itself, so convinced it is the singular pinnacle of virtue and value, the only hope for the future of humanity, that it is horrified that you should suggest it is not a universal gift given to all, which could be unlocked in everyone if only we had the means and the tact.

But, aggrandize itself as much as it may, the intellect is not the only valuable capacity in life, and reason is not the only virtuous pursuit. We humans, being limited beings with limited time and energy, cannot pursue every avenue of life in a single life time. Some will be intellectuals, and those would do best to strive toward reason through a skeptical epistemology. But it takes a lot of wasted time to be a thorough intellectual, as Yuval Noah Harari points out; "It usually takes a lot of training to calm the mind and make it

---

[*] Actually, conveniently for me in this book, racism thrives primarily within the materialist paradigm. With the discrediting of materialism, and the elevation of a universally endowed, infinite conscious potential, (notice I say "conscious" potential which is not at all the same claim as "intellectual" potential) we will wave goodbye to the mainstays of racism along with nihilism, and move toward a more perfect union of peoples which Dr. Martin Luther King Jr. dreamed of where "everybody will talk about God's power and human power." (Murray, 254)

concentrate so it can start observing itself methodologically and objectively… [and] if you want to go deeply into any subject, you need a lot of time, and in particular you need the privilege of wasting time." (Harari, 225) Those who end up being intellectuals must find a lot of time to waste. This means that they must either have been born into an extremely privileged[*] life, or have reached a point of privilege at some point. Intellectuals, like Buddhist monks, would do much better to realize fully their complete dependence on lay citizens (non-intellectuals) and broader society. It takes wide spread success and stability—which is always hard worked for and hard won—to have a plethora of philosophers lying around and theorizing.

There will always be others who will not be devoted intellectuals, but may do all kinds of other valuable things. Thus, the question of "what do you believe is the optimum level of rationality?" also asks, "what percentage of the population do you believe is and/or should be intellectual?" The higher the estimate, the more aggrandized (and probably conceited) the ideal of the intellect has become, and likely the greater degree one overlooks their dependence on and the inevitable necessity for continuous labor and maintenance which supports their leisure[†].

A higher proposed goal also may reflect a lack of the ability and virtue of

---

[*] I use the term "privilege" here to make a point, as it is something cooked up by academics and intellectuals themselves, but it is really a dreadful notion which cannot be sustainably used for social judgement, nor practically and accurately measured in even a single individual. "One person may have 'privilege' from inheriting money. For another person this same privilege may be a curse, giving them too much too early and disincentivizing them from making their way in the world." (Murray, 87) The proper term for speaking about the benefits one has experienced in life is "blessings"—for the proper attitude is gratitude, not envy and covetousness. "Let us walk honestly, as in the day; not in rioting and drunkenness, not in chambering and wantonness, not in strife and envying" (Romans 13:13)

[†] Moreover, even in a future where automation has given everyone the possibility of such leisure, one may find intellectuals incredulous of people who do not choose to spend their extra time becoming more intellectual—for to them this is the pinnacle and even sole virtue to be had in life; beyond the begrudging possibility of merely recognizing the current environment-mandated dependence on other values, it is essentially eccentric to propose within most intellectual circles that other pursuits outside the intellectual sphere are of inherent value. Steven Pinker, to his credit, combats this perspective (though I think his system is not as steadfastly amenable to such sentiments as he suggests); "It's presumptuous to pass judgement on how people spend their lives." (255)

tolerance, which seems to have been steadily eroding for some time now; in a society where differing thoughts and (in certain cases) customs and beliefs are considered violence, it becomes more socially acceptable and thus easier to demonize people with contrary beliefs and principles. When it is generally accepted that society and the world is fundamentally categorized as warring intellectual and relative belief groups striving for zero-sum power, then tolerance of opposing parties can be viewed as mere complacence and a moral failure in living and letting live; one must be converted or be at odds—with us or against us—as social groups look forward to the inevitable future when these conflicting points of view must turn to physical battle for supremacy.

Though for the most part the atheistic and scientific circles have seemed less infected by postmodern/neomarxist views, the practice and views of "street epistemologists" will show whether they have preserved the virtue of tolerance (which they would rage for if not extended to them) or have become conquistadors for their ideology. There is still no clear right or wrong answer, no immediate give away or accurate judgement—though I would think anything close to a sweeping majority of proposed conversion is cause for concern.

The answer to the third question may indicate many underlying conceptions. It hints at how reasonable these rationalists are in their expectations (taken in conjunction with answers to the first two questions). It hints at whether they are optimists or pessimists (true progressives and humanists retaining their unconscious roots in infinite redemption or utopians). And it may give an idea as to the underlying sense of urgency they see in the quest—their level of zealotry—which gives one some inkling on the methods they may take and the lengths they will push them to. How deeply do they know infinite redemption and salvation? How much does the horror of the world propel them to attempt to reorder it as soon as possible?

These are important questions to ask of the reformative epistemological movement (and for them to explore in themselves). They need to face the upfront reality that not everyone is an intellectual, not everyone will be inspired to follow or grateful for the quest of rigorously devoting themselves to the intellectual pursuit of ironing out all of one's thoughts and theories into a coherent notion of where they stand. And the atheistic thrust of the movement means, in light of what we have shown thus far in the book, that pushing people out of their faith will disorient them in their relationship to life and open them up to the serious threat of nihilism. It cannot be naively assumed that everyone who one successfully shakes off their original faith (authoritarian or non-fallibilist as it may be) will also successfully convert to a stabilized modern quasi-nihilist that modern intellectuals take as an acceptable moral position today. Street Epistemologists, therefore, are not conducting a lighthearted quest which poses no significant threat to those they involve. They should be acutely aware of the risks they are pushing people towards and, in my view, first work on themselves and their own beliefs on the infinite and proper orientation toward life.

Of course, that is an ideal. They aren't perfectly aware, and they won't be. The movement is fallible and the people are fallible, of course. And this is not to say that "look, its more dangerous than you realized, therefore you need to stop". None of this contradicts the reality that creating more "doxastic openness"[*] in individuals throughout society will be an effective good, both for many individuals and for society as a whole. It is an effective approach. And the desired effect of promoting curiosity and cultivating a properly rigorous epistemology (at least in those who are genuine intellectuals and will benefit and grow from it) is a good one.

But there is a legitimate dark side to this quest and possible movement. One being that we are all fallible, and so we cannot accurately adjudicate who is a true intellectual whom this water of rational and skeptical epistemology will invigorate, and who it may affect but only to bring them toward nihilism and despair, without also giving them the tools to disarm this "antidote". The other major one, of course, being that the atheistic branch of this movement contains many seeds of nihilism in their faith and foundational stories. And they sow these alongside the impulse for doxastic openness as they go.

On that note, we turn to one of the last bastions for atheist rebuttal against the traditions of faith—the notion of a creator and the metaphysical inconsistencies this seems to imply.

---

[*] Again, Boghossian's term which means "a willingness and ability to revise beliefs." (Boghossian, 51)

Purpose in Form

Chapter 17: Creator, No Creator? One Cause, No Cause?

"Emptiness in Buddhist terms doesn't mean nothingness. It means every single thing we encounter—including ourselves—goes beyond our ability to conceive of it. We call it emptiness because nothing can ever explain it. Reality itself is emptiness because we cannot possibly fit it in our minds." (Dogen/Warner, 40)

God or Emptiness?

Sam Harris calls a creator God an unfalsifiable thesis. An extra-universal embodied deity who created the universe like some kind of genie, who is by definition beyond detection is indeed an unfalsifiable thesis. But that is not the real question—at least it is not the important one, the best formulated one. The real question is whether there is an infinite source or not, or, more simply, a source. Whether or not life is infinite. And this is neither a falsifiable nor unfalsifiable thesis because it hardly qualifies as a question, it is self-evident. It is a (perhaps the only) proven thesis.

It doesn't strike me as particularly important that the dualistic conception of an extra-existent being, standing metaphysically apart from the rest of all existence, who brought it all into being from the void, watching it from an outside perspective, may be literally untrue (or at least conflicts with our current conception of what infinity is and entails). What does seem significant is that infinity exists, and that the nature of the infinite is not such that there is merely an unending extension of a random array of meaningless material objects, but rather that there is an intimate connection between the "whole" of infinity and any "individual" point. Recall, "He is entire in every point of space, and complete in every instant of duration." (Hume, 29).

Insofar as one admits the existence of infinity, regardless of one's purpose of uprooting a particular metaphor for God, one has, in my estimation, abandoned atheism and affirmed the existence of the One Eternal Infinite which is the ground of all Being. Rejecting the title of "Creator", then, seems of little importance. The only way this concession of the infinite is not seen for what it is, is through the attachment to a dogmatic material conception of the world—i.e. supposing infinity is merely the continual addition of unending finite objects across all space-time. This is necessarily a misunderstanding of what infinity entails given that the material, "finite" conception of the world is only true from the human level of perception and abstraction, and that infinity must include all other (infinite) levels of abstraction and analysis, under which reality is vastly different than a collection of material objects.

The remainder of the emergent conception of consciousness arising from materialism also lends itself to not grasping the reality one proposes when one accepts the infinity of existence. One keeps at arms lengths the necessary entailments of infinite mental realms or planes of consciousness, as well as the foundational consciousness which is infinite itself, by still holding onto the parochial conception of the universe as only an unending assortment of material objects and our consciousness as entirely separate from the rest of the universe, and absolutely accidental and unintended by it.

In that sense, when one proposes the infinite nature of existence in order to argue against God (against the literal interpretation of the creator standing metaphysically apart from creation), one does not actually concede or propose a truly infinite existence—they use the terminology and part of the conception to their benefit, but they do not hold themselves to consistently consider all the entailments of the reality of infinity. This is the argument I just made about the foundational stories of science and evolution assuming a FINITE existence, regardless of their terminology to the contrary. The influence of this mistake (and the inability to recognize it) is broad and needs to be systematically rooted out.

To give this argument it's due, let's look at another formulation of it. What we call "empty space", Lawrence Krauss shows is actually an infinite sea of creative energy potential. So the claim that Krauss makes against the metaphysical assertion of God does not precisely rest on him claiming that the universe is a miracle (at least so he would argue)—it's not really creating something from "nothing" as though causation is miraculously violated. Rather, what Krauss forwards, and the same concept underlies Boghossian's position, is that *something exists* (that *existence is*) fundamentally. This does entail the infinite. But at no time was there nothing (meaning "non-existence"). So something was never *created* from nothing. Thus there can be no creator, and existence is (so it seems) not a miracle.

But if everything around us is a sea of infinite creative energy, and if one remains doxastically open to the reality of all that entails (and it entails literally everything*), atheism isn't looking too hot. So, the pedantic intellectual reels at the literal interpretation of religions—but cannot themselves see past them—and exclaims that a creative universe which can manifest creations from its own potential excludes the need for God. But to think that all conceptions of God are the external image imagined in literal interpretations where God sits outside the universe and thus becomes superfluous under this conception is simply profoundly ignorant. "Buddhists don't believe in a God who stands outside the universe and makes it work. Instead, the universe itself is God." (Dogen/Warner, 277)

Additionally, as we have seen through examining the real implications of Infinity, and as was emphasized in the chapter on pantheism, the realities of a personal God as well as the always infinite and inexhaustible potential beyond all (still also infinite) manifestation lend support for the traditional conceptions of God. The infinity beyond infinity is just part of the nature of infinity. And the fundamental nature of consciousness—that the infinite itself is conscious—means that this beyond beyond, often called the formless, is yet conscious. So if there is a consciousness which proceeds beyond all manifestation, is there not an infinite presence "outside" of this infinite existence? Or, at least, can we not see that we cannot rule out this possibility?

Once again, it is the lack of comprehension of what Infinity entails that supports all these atheistic and nihilistic notions which suppose to build their theories off of what they call "the infinite". Insofar as they are atheistic or nihilistic, they are actually conceiving of a finite existence, even though they

---

* Recall, "watches that came into existence spontaneously; asteroids that happen to be good likenesses of William Paley." (Deutsch, 452)

use the term "infinite" in their description of their theory—which is the only thing that gives their theories apparent consistency.

In short, one can say with equal reverence for the miracle of life that "there is only One God" or "there is no God"; that "there is One Creator" or "there is no Creator"; that "there is only One Cause" or "there is no Cause"; and they come to the same tautological point that infinity is infinite and uncreated. Existence is a miracle.

Infinity is a necessary conclusion. You can look at all extended formal existence (i.e. Creation) and wonder at the fact that this is all a single spontaneous (uncaused) existent infinity, which yet does not exhaust the infinite potential and mystery all around and beyond beyond; or you can look at the same infinite expanse of existence and marvel at the fact that there is this One Infinite generative power, this Infinite well or void of potential, the necessarily uncaused presence of which gives rise to all of this.

The central wonder of God is not that one need fixate on the "first" link in an infinite causal chain. The central wonder of God is his Infinite (uncaused) nature (Glory). Getting rid of the literal conception and image of a figure standing over and above the void and creating it from without is only to follow the directions of God himself where in the Bible he tells people not to worship idols! That image is an idolatrous conception of the infinite reality which cannot be defined.

> Yeshua said:
> If flesh came into being because of spirit, it is a wonder.
> But if spirit came into being because of flesh, it is a wonder of wonders.
> Yet the greatest of wonders is this:
> How is it that this Being, which Is,
> inhabits this nothingness? (Logion 29, The Gospel of Thomas)

What comes of relativism?

With a growing conception of the true nature of infinity, and the rising significance of the subjective consciousness of each individual, doesn't this territory seem ripe for the continued growth and supremacy of the relativism which plagues our society and, as I have said, effectively brings one to a state of nihilism in equivocating and thus invalidating all discernment (or at least all interpersonal discernment)?

Creator, No Creator? One Cause, No Cause?

Not to suppose any argument against the theory of relativity[*], but can we not see relativism as merely the inverted (and myopic) negative view of the necessary reality of the infinite and our fallibility? Relativism supposes we can make no judgements—it takes a pessimistic view of our natures, or at least that our own power has utterly consumed us, and thus was too much for us—for each is justified from *some* view. But, although we can concoct infinite intellectual rationalizations, that is not the question at hand, nor the true assertion of relativism.

Relativism tacitly declares that there is no ultimate underlying structure against which to verify two vying perspectives. Dr. Jordan Peterson, and traditional scientists all around, say otherwise—that we put ideas to the test and see which ones play out well in the game of life over time and reiterations. We test their EFFECTIVENESS. "We must allow the world to tell us whether our ideas are correct." (Pinker, 393) Relativism not only defeats itself in uprooting all purpose—by disconnecting us from any hope of something beyond our own hallucination[†]—it overlooks the fact that some things are more effective than others. We can and do know this.

Relativism is an unfortunate universality made out of the difficulty and disagreements of the world. Relativism thrives on reasonable doubt, of which there is always some. We are fallible, we see different things, we approach things differently, there is so much variation that we often appear to be acting totally at odds, with entirely different and incompatible motives and rationales. Relativism sees—in probably a true act of understanding—the rationales for both sides and declares them equal (they were, after all, both contrived from the great logos inhabiting human kind). There cannot be a single formulated law or description which dictates the appropriate actions in life (or about any other objective realities), nor even a cohesive set of such rules.

Relativists, springing from the intellectual class, find this abhorrent, for (so they feel) there should be truth in life and we should be able to agree on it; but they see the vying formulations of the world and come to the conclusion that there is not. What they have overlooked, however, is that life is not for the

---

[*] Though we know it may very well be wrong in some fundamental way: "We know that both of the deepest prevailing theories in physics [relativity and quantum mechanics] must be false." (Deutsch, 458)
[†] Recall, purpose must transcend our own limitations.

Purpose in Form

intellect (at least, not for the intellect to conquer). Life is not about being completely defined and nailed down, taken care of, finished. Life is infinite. There is always infinite more. The intellect is undoubtedly useful, effective, and powerful, to a certain extent—but not to an ultimate level, as it wishes and believes.

Though we cannot formulate a single, perfect edict nor set of rules for life—even pertaining to a particular situation (for we are fallible and may see that situation where it is not or miss it when it is here)—, that does not mean that there are not laws of life; though one cannot conceptualize and formulate the way through, one is expected to reach the destination. The intellectual balks at such a reality, thinking that unfair—those aren't the rules that it would put in place if it were in charge. But, as the adage goes, life gives one the test first and the lesson after; life is a difficult game.

Life asks one to perform, and doesn't give one the theme, genre, or melody to go along with. But there is success and there is failure. This is the game we have been playing as humans for millennia. This is why we have retained the Bible—God expects *something* of us, though we didn't know that for a long time, and we still hardly know what it is (and still widely doubt it as such). We have purpose and there is truth. We cannot say what it is and we speculate fallibly, and there is no end in sight. Relativism looks upon this and calls it eternal damnation—there is no ultimate truth (thus no meaning, purpose, good, or value). Those with faith (traditional scientists here included) believe in a reality beyond the ego of the intellect. Reality is not ultimately hell, it is just dismally difficult and mysterious—it is infinite and we finite.

We are ignorant—perpetually. To the intellect that is condemnation, for the intellect wants rulership and victory—it wants a finite reality (without realizing it or knowing that this is foolish). But to those not possessed by the intellect, who know life is about more than mental projection and dissection of the world, this is merely the arena of the game: infinite prospects for growth, experience, love, and joy, hard won though they be.

Relativism applies the wrong explanation to the observed true phenomena. It is true that life is infinitely complex and difficult and we are fallible to the core. That does not mean that all hope is lost and that we know categorically (which would contradict the unreality of truth) that there is no truth (and gone with it are all hopes of progress, goodness, and redemption). It merely means that we play a difficult game. Relativity is one of its complexities, and the immense varieties of human perceptions and attitudes can be understood deeply and empathetically (a testament to the virtue of understanding only if it does not lose hope and fall into relativism from there), though they appear to clash on the surface. And many times we may have no idea how to resolve the clash, though we can understand the underlying values and approaches intimately (and even if we came up with a resolution, certainly not all parties concerned would agree to it). This is the difficulty of life.

Relativism asserts the problem that all judgements are made from systems of value. And yet, there is no (that we know of) underlying factor for judging value or systems of value. One judges another's values through their own values. But each set of values makes sense through its own lens (or at least can be rationalized to the extent that it appears so). Therefore, relativists claim, no person can judge the value of another's values. All is mere bias.

As we have seen, however, all believe in the realities (and value) of truth, meaning, purpose, goodness, and effectivity. And what is effective in the world can be tested. The world—i.e. life itself, the infinite—can be the judge. We are fallible in interpreting its judgements, to be sure. But it qualifies as judge for the case in question as it transcends parochial attachments to one's ego-centered and intellectually formulated ideas.

Those who doubt the moral integrity of the underlying structure of the game, wondering if it is genuinely set up to give favor to not only the most effective but also moral actions across time may come up with many examples; they may find evidence that they think points to the immorality of life. But all data is theory-laden. What is lacking is not evidence for either side; it is an explanation for the basic metaphysics of life. What is missing from relativism is faith in the divinity of life—of intimacy of the infinite with the finite—of the omnipresence of infinite consciousness and its connection to the construction, organization, and integrity of life itself.

Though relativism seems to spring out of the hypothesis of infinity, it actually springs out of the Principle of Mediocrity. It limits our conscious potential and believes our consciousness insignificant and has no inkling that it is in any way connected to the infinite. Thus, once again, we see this theory of "infinity" missing the entailments of an infinite interconnectivity and self-saturation. Once again, it is a fundamental theory of finitude masquerading under the terminology of infinity.

It is because the reality and all the entailments of Infinity are barely nascent in our consciousness as humans, and that our groping conceptualizations and conjectured formulations are so woefully inadequate (as would be expected in such a state of incipient awareness and fallible nature), that we appear to find such ideas supporting all sorts of variated growths of nihilism and atheism that have sprung up over the last few hundred years (and especially the last fifty).

But if we continue to remain doxastically open to the realities of Infinity which we may comfortably admit we do not know fully, being aware of our fallibility, and we willingly bring our conjectures (even our cherished and unconscious metaphysical ones) to the altar of truth for the festival of sacrifice through collective criticism and open inquiry, we will move towards an understanding of the Living reality of Infinity, and away from this nihilism which has grown in our midst. We will see that the ancient, barbaric, and flawed stories of our ancestors—who had neither well understood or applied rationality nor science to help them—described far more accurately the reality of Infinity than we do through our best mathematical and scientific postulation to date.

Chapter 18: The Christian Doctrine and the Gettier Problem of Knowledge

"The great, corrupt edifice of Christianity still managed to make room for the spirit of its Founder." –Jordan B. Peterson, reflecting on the insight of Dostoyevsky (191)

Though Christianity has had its share of intellectual supporters and apologists, for the last several hundred years it seems that the fashion of deriding religion—primarily Christianity as the most salient token to the western intellectual—has progressively grown both in quantity of those chiming in as well as the airtime such coverage gets on public media.

Now there are many understandable reasons for the animosity intellectuals feel. My intention here is not to dissect the cultural progression of combating ideologies. I have already addressed some of the main legitimate questions or criticisms of the Christian faith (meaning orientation toward the foundation of life). While there is a reasonable discussion to be had concerning these foundations of faith, as I have said, each challenge aimed at uprooting the infinite and its entailments, which are well illustrated in the Christian Doctrine, falls short of being sufficient reason to abandon this underlying truth.

Though there is certainly space for inquiry and criticism, I believe that a greater amount of the dismissal of and indeed disdain for Christianity comes not from honest intellectual inquiries, but from a rejection of the shadow projected on Christianity. Most western intellectuals are simply raised in the modern dogma of looking down on religions, but perhaps especially on Christianity. There are reasons there that are forwarded, as we have seen, but the true brunt of the position, I think, is founded on an image of the Christian as an imbecile—or at least a slave.

In the minds of modern western intellectuals, Christians are generally viewed as both foolish and unreasonable, and often, if we are honest, evil—a plague on society. They are fooled into believing in a cult. They are unreasonable in their arguments and assumptions and requirements of others. And they are so often seen as aggressive proselytizers that they are thought of as bereft of understanding and tolerance for others. All in all, their faith seems to be the antithesis of the "tolerant secular" ideal that modern western intellectuals aspire to be (or at least, they once aspired to be so, and we should hope this virtue continues as a paramount of modern society).

Of course, like all projections, this image is distorted, one sided, and not representative of reality. But at the core of this situation rests a peculiar instance of the Gettier problem of knowledge, which puts the modern quasi-nihilist in an awkward position.

The Gettier problem of knowledge illustrates that knowledge is not merely "justified true belief," as epistemologists had for so long described it, but must be something more (or different entirely). One of the classic illustrations of the problem is done by imagining passing a farm property. As you pass at a distance, you notice certain features of the property—in this case certain animals that appear to be sheep. But that's not how you say it in your head. You don't think "those animals appear to be sheep but might not be"; you think "oh, there are some sheep over there". From this sighting you conclude that there are sheep on that property.

What you do not realize, however, is that what you saw was not a herd of sheep; you saw some Bedfordshire Terriers (which are dogs that look a lot like sheep). However, additionally, and also unknown to you, there are actual sheep on that same property, removed from your sight. So when you concluded that "there are sheep on that property", you actually had a "justified true belief". You saw what you thought were sheep, and thus you believed there were sheep there. Your belief that there were sheep was factually correct (true), and you had a reasonable justification for your belief—you took what you saw as evidence (as we all do all the time).

From an omniscient 3rd person perspective on the problem, however, we

The Christian Doctrine and the Gettier Problem of Knowledge

would hesitate to say you *knew* there were sheep on the property—we wouldn't grant that your "justified true belief" (which we once thought of as the definition of knowledge) counted as knowledge in this case. You were not informed in the "correct" manner to make your conclusion given your mistaken observation, and you were only right by some odd instance of luck.

But stating exactly what that "correct" manner of justification is and being able to assess it correctly in all cases, and thus redefine knowledge more accurately proves immensely difficult. This famous problem of knowledge shows us that when we speak of "knowledge" we do not merely mean "justified true belief"—we are concerned not only with the justification of knowledge, but the *proper* justification of knowledge. Yet we are not sure just what the rules are for proper knowledge justification are, given that we are always completely fallible.

Deutsch's epistemological theory turns this on its head saying knowledge is never justified, but that conjectures are made and then evaluated. Knowledge is not bestowed with its truth through its origins or method of retrieval, but rather through commitment to the subsequent testing in a community of rational criticism of our various conjectures—whether they come from observations, expert testimony, or dreams of immortal beings—and a rejection of believing in final conclusions on any matter. Knowledge is not, as we had for so long hoped, the concrete and definite products of thought which we can hold onto forever. Knowledge is an effervescent title given to the set of best-performing conjectures in the continual testing grounds of a large and intellectually diverse culture of criticism. Gettier-type problems will continually arise, but the more robust and integrous our system the less likely we are to be greatly damaged by them.

This is by no means a dominant or widely accepted view of knowledge, however. Most are still looking for proper justifications in some way or the other; most modern so-called scientists (and people who "believe in science" all the more so) merely reject the dogma of religion and accept the dogma of what their favored arenas and inclinations within the sciences say. "An endorsement of scientific thinking must first of all be distinguished from any belief that members of an occupational guild called 'science' are particularly wise or noble. The culture of science is based on the opposite belief... science is not a list of empirical facts." (Pinker, 390-391)

Science is not not a dogma because it is a magical entity which could never be dogmatic because it is against dogma; science is only not a dogma when the people practicing it refuse to behave dogmatically—or are reliably called out for it by their peers when they do. And, what that essentially means is rejecting justified belief and accepting ultimate fallibility. Someday a significant portion of the science-minded population may live up to this high truth and difficult standard, but like anything else that will take the long (and fallible) journey of individuals everywhere taking responsibility for themselves and doing the hard work of personal change.

In the case of the Christian tradition and dogma, however, I believe the Gettier problem plays out in a different way. As we have seen, the Infinite is an existential certainty*, and this has immanent and personal consequences in each individual's life. The metaphors of a personal God with an intimate relationship to the life of the individual, the divine incarnation and sacrifice, and the reality of a salvation given, not attained, all map precisely onto the implications of an infinite conscious existence. Even to the most cynical anti-religionist, the fact that Christianity's central tenants give an accurate interpretation of the metaphysical and moral issues of Infinite Existence must be a striking example of attaining to the "justified true belief" requirements of knowledge (assuming that those cynics have accepted the necessary reality of the infinite, the self-saturating requirements, and the non-emergent nature of consciousness).

Boghossian, for one, would object harshly to the justified portion of Christian knowledge. However, Christians merely take the Bible and their preacher as experts, and they listen to expert testimony. Do we not all read books by experts and then claim to be informed of knowledge? This seems exactly analogous with the fallible perception of sheep. Sure, one could say that we should all be skeptical of all our perceptions all the time, but that is ridiculous; if you perceive a bus coming at you at high speed, you're not going to wonder "gee, is that a bus or do I just mistakenly perceive it as a bus?", you're going to jump out of the way because you know a bus is coming at you.

We could be skeptical that we saw sheep, but we probably won't. We could be skeptical of the doctrines in the Bible and the qualifications of it or our preacher as an expert source, but many people won't. And yet, they still end up with some true beliefs and knowledge (even if it is in allegorical form), and

---

* I have also proven it epistemologically in my book *Jnana Yoga*.

The Christian Doctrine and the Gettier Problem of Knowledge

ones that are importantly effective against the nihilism that has proven superior to the secular philosophies (including humanism) which only pretend to escape its grasp. Is Christianity so bad then?

While most anti-religionist intellectuals would love to sit in a high chair and laugh at the incomplete "knowledge" of all those simpleminded, overly-credulous Christians, or harp on their lack of intellectual efforts in scrutiny, or the authoritarian pedagogy of their priests, the Gettier problem does not shake out as much of a "problem" in this case; and while many people feel that all the devout and worshipping peons around the world are merely deficient in their reasoning or intellectual capacities, it does not look so superior for a person of intellect to be espousing a falsehood as a reactionary position to those who believe in the Infinite Truth, merely because they don't like the fact that said truth was disseminated from a source or through a certain methodology they dislike and view as antithetical to reason.

Now of course there are many other reasons intellectuals have problems with faiths and those who follow or claim to follow such doctrines. I am not making the claim that the sole grounds for grudges on the part of the intellectuals lie in their feelings of intellectual superiority to the halls of worship. But what is undoubtedly the case, regardless of the understandable nature for the grudges held by intellectuals, is that their animosity toward the organizational problems or the hypocritical actions of many who are terrible examples of such faiths has led them to stand off against a deep truth about reality and espouse a falsehood in the name of greater reason.

This would be a noble stand if 1) truth were subservient to reason and 2) this Infinite Truth were any lesser order of truth. Unfortunately for the intellectuals, reason is only virtuous in that it is a reliable path to Truth itself. Truth holds the ultimate virtue. And, while it is important, *if one is to be a thoroughly reasonable intellectual,* to follow a particular style of exploration and path to all relative truths (one of fallibility and a culture of criticism), the acquisition of the eternal truth of the infinite seems to be of a different order.

Surely it is good to have some dissidence so as to develop a fallibility-tested path of reason to the infinite; that is to say that there are many intellectuals in the world who would never be satisfied with the path of Bhakti Yoga (of devotion). The demons of the mind are often quite reasonable, and it takes superior reason to uproot them. So there is undoubtedly a need in this world for an intellectual route to God (or to Truth)—which is the path of Reason.

Purpose in Form

However, it is not at all the case that this intellectual route is the only one, nor the necessary one, nor the superior one. All true intellectuals must eventually walk this path and defeat those demons of seeming reason; but what of those who are not so intellectually motivated? What of all those despised-by-intellectuals masses who are able to accept the Infinite Truth of existence and purpose on "mere" faith? Are they in any way worse off? Are they wrong? Are there any conceivable consequences for not having any more than (debatably justified) "true belief" in this case?

Two possible objections come to mind: 1) that all Bhakti Yogis will be reincarnated at some point in an intellectual life and will then miss the undeveloped line of pure reason to God, and 2) that the prevalence of revealed or "given" doctrine is a breeding ground for dogma within which many who might otherwise behave morally are lead astray in the name of the Divine (this is Boghossian's fear).

Behind 1) is merely the prejudice that intellectuals are better than non-intellectuals[*], as the precise inverse can be stated as well; all individuals who theorize about God, will one day be born into a body and mind not suited for intellectual pursuits—or given a purpose and passions that do not lead them down the intellectual path—and their ability to intuit, submit to, and serve the good without spinning in thoughts for decades will be put to the test. Not all people are intellectuals and that is not a bad thing. Life is about more than intellectuality and there are many things of value beyond the scope of intellectual life.

2) Sounds reasonable but is merely a fear of the shadow. Intellectuals have their shadow too. If we got rid of the Bhakti path and had only the Jnana Path, how many would be allowed to get lost in the mires of sophistry and uncertainty in the name of "finding out for yourself", who otherwise could have lived happily and righteously in the light of revealed scripture and faith? Certainly dogma is a threat, and certainly we need a culture of criticism within society. But not everyone is an intellectual and not everyone should be; this is a truth that is quite obvious in light of the knowledge of the infinite, but that the intellectuals have missed in their haughty doubting of the self-evident.

---

[*] "The rationalist delusion is not just a claim about human nature. It's also a claim that the rational caste (philosophers or scientists) should have more power, and it usually comes along with a utopian program for raising more rational children." (Haidt, 103)

The Christian Doctrine and the Gettier Problem of Knowledge

It seems that throughout time intellectuals have thought, in one way or another, "hell is other people", and especially that it is the sheep who are so unlike unto that blessed race of thinkers which they were thankfully (but also meaninglessly) born into (Sartre). The dull and the simple have been looked down upon for holding the entire race back in countless ways. What intellectual has not, in all honesty, had the fantasy that they would be the ideal ruler of the world—that they would set it aright—if only everyone would listen to what they know so well? "It is one curiosity of academia in recent decades that it has found almost nothing it does not wish to deconstruct, apart from itself." (Murray, 53)

But how often has the intellectual class destroyed life and society? It was intellectual elites in India who decided, through their so-enlightened reading of the scriptures, that the castes were fixed for life and entirely discredited any idea of personal change or growth in life. It was an intellectual who, though he never held a job requiring physical labor, decided that everyone should be rewarded equally merely for the fact of being present, and that a society could be maintained and even thrive when the unequal rewards for greater striving and effectiveness were eliminated—for they were only the results of greed (though, of course, wanting rewards for nothing was not).

It was intellectuals who decided that life could be explained by a haphazard wiggling magically (but also definitely not magically!) beginning to make more of its own pointless self, and purposelessly changing through mere random error from there. It was these intellectuals who "achieved" the death of God, ignored the reality of the infinite, and fostered a modernity of nihilism and despair that has left countless people in society with nowhere to turn but drugs, suicide, and vengeful anger and mass killings. Hey, I'm an intellectual too. There's nothing wrong with being an intellectually driven person. But let us not miss our own shadow, and our necessary infinite ignorance, and pretend we are the world's saviors and can, on our own (or even as a class), walk the one true path perfectly.

Going back to our own projections: take even the most annoying preacher or proselytizer, what have they gotten wrong? They are coming to share with you the message of eternal life (of which you must hear the spirit not the letter!). So maybe they're not a great teacher or expounder; so what if you think them unenlightened? What is wrong with their faith? Consider it this way: what if a man came around to tell you that you had a heart in the center of your chest? Would you scoff at him and say, "What makes you so sure? Have you ever cut open your chest and looked? Get out of here you false physician!"

So what if he has not physically seen his own heart? Likely he has never even had a sonogram or other images taken and seen it. Most likely, he only has read about others who have examined the human body and trusts what they say is there—for it has been found to be true time and time again. Perhaps all he goes off of is this expert testimony and the beating he feels with his palm. Is this man worthy of dismissal? Has he failed in some great way by not becoming a physician? Does he not have the right to say he has a heart, and that I have a heart?

Now how is the Christian any different? He relies on expert testimony—those who have done the introspective surgery and even undergone the operations to find out—and the pulse of truth that he feels when he is taught to look for it within himself (the Holy Spirit). Why is he to be dismissed? One may object that it seems less people have tested the reality of eternal life than have been shown to have a heart. But how many tests would you need to see or hear about to believe you had a heart? More than a few? And, as we have seen, is the fact of life eternal not the most obvious truth? Is it not the only certainty? Is it not something that can be reaffirmed every moment[*]? Even if that only to you feels like a faint pulse—something you hadn't noticed before and have not been taught to remain conscious of—does the explanation and the testimony line up, and when you do feel that pulse, even for the briefest of moments, are you not assured?

Take another example of a professional sports player who attributes his game to God. How many dismiss this sentiment by simply telling themselves how he doesn't know better to say otherwise—it's just a trained piety, a platitude—so they let it slide. But in what way is he wrong? Certainly there remains a personal issue of growth if he says the words, but inside he thinks himself the greatest and has no true humility. Just as with a priest who goes

---

[*] "They ask me whether I know the soul immortal. No. But do I not Know the Now to be eternal? Is it not a sufficient reply to the red and angry worldling, coloring as he affirms his unbelief, to say, Think on living, I have to do no more than you with that question of another life? I believe in this life. I believe it continues. As long as I am here I plainly read my duties as writ with pencil of fire; they speak not of death. They are woven of immortal thread." (Emerson, 15)

around pointing out all our motes but overlooks the beam within his own eye (or the sexual abuse in his own church, say).

But why should we assume that a professional athlete has no grasp of the transcendent? A lifetime training and perfecting one's body to play to its fullest potential and beyond, while yet being constrained by rules, is a perfect ground for the blooming of transcendent vision. "Flow states" are often associated with high intensity sports performances and these are at minimum low intensity visions of the no-self reality which, when brought into sharper focus and experienced in complete awareness, is the all-consuming fire and beatific vision of Eternity. Why should we assume these athletes are merely mouthing platitudes from their moderately pious upbringing? And, once again, even if they are, how are they wrong? Are they not speaking the truth when they say "all glory is to God" and they express their gratitude for his presence and blessings in living this game through them?

So, as I said, I think the modern intellectual who is upset about the pious devotees only possessing "true belief" (though perhaps before reading this they would call it "false belief", or just "belief") has found perhaps the one place where the Gettier problem does not apply. It is not as universally important in the case of faith in the Infinite and Eternal to attain to such an attitude through the "proper" channels of connected inquiry and logical discovery as it is with all relative knowledge and truth.

Instead, in this instance, the modern western intellectuals' projections of fear and inferiority retard him from approaching and attaining the great Truth and Good News contained in the Christian doctrine. It holds him back from experiencing the Holy Spirit, singing hymns next to lines of imperfect sinners just like him, who yet feel what he does not—and he largely disdains them for it, creating a story of their poor character to distract from his own misery, confusion, hopelessness, and fear. It keeps him shunning the idea of the perfection of man, and the necessity of purpose that goes with it, and moving away from heaven on Earth, that he might be excused from the terrible burden of looking at one's true self and deep darkness, which he fears because intuitively he knows it is too deep for him alone to conquer—all the while telling himself empty words about the human spirit or the value of a bitter truth, without any real underpinnings for such a spirit or value or truth itself within his dearly held conceptions—the limited creations of his own mind.

To continue the illustration of this point, let us grant that all of Reza Aslan's

Purpose in Form

scriptural analysis in *God: A Human History* of the historicity of the texts and the evolution of the ideas of God is correct. The Bible is full of discontinuities, the terminology and conceptions don't line up. Sometimes they speak of a plural god, sometimes of a parochial tribal deity, and sometimes of a unified Infinite Oneness. There are lies and fabrications, and there is ignorant doctrine.

Humans evolved haphazardly in their thoughts from worshipping parochial wizard-spirits to conceiving of an eternal God that survived and even planned his own defeat in battle—but they only came up with this transcendent vision through pure cognitive dissonance and stubbornness in not wanting to accept that their god had been wrong all along. Through this grand process of fallibility—from the conquering tribes fighting for their gods, to the First Council of Nicaea where ancient intellectuals fallibly formulated a *post hoc* unified theory under threat of death—somehow the idea of an infinite God emerged.

What does this cynical view of our bumbling and unconscious path to the Truth do? Does it negate the reality of the infinite? Does it make the Truth of the Incarnation invalid? Should we throw out all our fumblingly constructed ideas and force ourselves to restart to do it in a way we find more agreeable to our desired perceptions of ourselves? Or should we rejoice in the Truth of the Infinite which arose miraculously in our ignorant and fallible evolution?

The modern western intellectual to whom God is dead is thus a hollow and empty spirit, unable to truly divorce himself from truth, value, purpose, and meaning, but convincing himself of their impotence and unreality every day to avoid the process of discovering and reorienting himself in line with the truth that is born in him and eternally with him beyond his control or hope of imagination. And it is only once the western intellectuals are prepared to bury their hubris, and to die to themselves, to their own expectations, and acknowledge the necessary Truth of the Infinite—that God is Eternal, undying, omnipresent, and has never left them and is ready to forgive them—that is, only when they are ready to accept, rather than earn, conquer, or create, the love of God—that they will know peace, grace, and fulfillment and be legitimately able to begin productive, meaningful, and worthy work in the world[*].

---

[*] Not so say that atheists or secularists have never or cannot do anything of value, but that they will always be carrying a shadow and in many cases, far more than they

The Christian Doctrine and the Gettier Problem of Knowledge

It is not this way because I belong to a dogma which says it is so, and we want to destroy intellectuals and humiliate them before granting them clemency. It is this way because the infinite is. That is the reality to be found. The existence of the infinite is infinite and eternal (obviously), and this is a miracle at the heart of all existence, which allows for and abides all our darkness and foolishness, and we come to it and make peace with it only through humility and acceptance of a Grace far beyond ourselves, regardless of what brand of sin has been our personal favorite.

A Long Line of Sinners

Christianity is not a community of angels, nor of infallible humans, no matter what any proponent might say or believe; nor are they so much holier than thou, regardless of what outsiders (or even constituents) might feel. "I am not come to call the righteous, but sinners to repentance." (Matthew 9:13)

Christianity is a group for sinners who seek salvation, for the imperfect to know the perfect Love which is given to man beyond all hope. Christianity is for the harlot, the tax collector, the leper, and the uncircumcised Gentiles. Just as Buddhism is for the thief, rapist, and murderer[*]. Never let someone tell you otherwise. *"There is something lacking in all of us* and that is precisely why grace is offered." (Kautz, 83 italics in original)

Thus again I ask of all you intellectuals: Christianity being made for the imperfect, for the fallible, for the scandalous[†], should we then expect its reputation to be untarnished or its constituents to be models of virtue? Or its dogmas emerging through *their* interpretations to be perfect renditions of the divine? What is the recognition of universal sin but the admission to ultimate

---

realize, they will be spreading that as well; the Christian absolutely also carries a shadow and often spreads it. But the Christian has the *hope* of facing their shadow in full and knowing their mistakes most fully, while the atheist will always either repress some aspect of their shadow or allow it to consume them given their inability to appeal to Infinite Grace. And the more fully one knows themselves and their shadow, the more effectively they can work on themselves to mitigate these effects, thus move all the more effectively toward the reduction of suffering.

[*] In Buddhist literature, including early cannon material, there are stories of thieves and murderers receiving the Dharma and even achieving enlightenment (or Arhathood, depending on the tradition). And in the Jatakas, the stories of the Buddhas previous lives, the Buddha himself is a rapist in one of his recent incarnations.

[†] "We are all scandals." (Hillman, "C.G. Jung & The Red Book")

fallibility and inherent dependence on the infinite? And what is redemption by Grace but the truth that the infinite is and does uphold us, though we cannot fathom why? Of course these have been made into other things and used for control and manipulation, but that is merely confirmation of the ubiquity of sin and highlights the continued ineffable glory of our salvation through it all.

Chapter 19: On Tolerance

> "Bless them which persecute you: bless, and curse not... recompense to no man evil for evil... If it be possible, as much as lieth in you, live peaceably with all men... Avenge not yourselves... Therefore if thine enemy hunger, feed him; if he thirst, give him drink... overcome evil with good."
> Romans 12:14-21

Must Love NPCs

> "Reality itself has made regular people into its causes and conditions." –
> Dogen, 166

Our equality in sin and the infinite redemption offered to all alike beg the question, "Why can't we all just get along?" If we are all saved, why aren't we any better at relating or working together?

It is the case that there are false doctrines of the evil stranger—or false applications of the truth that strangers harbor threat—that turn us against "the other", while we overlook the evils of ourselves and our brothers in fear of the aggrandized enemy at the gates. But there is also this great evil doctrine that we can all just agree to agree or disagree, and that dissention between humans is manufactured from the outside—probably for profit or control—or that,

Purpose in Form

even if it is indigenous, any serious conflict could be easily avoided if we all just made an effort. And there is the third evil idea that accepting the invalidity of the latter means we are a species condemned to violent conflict between ideology groups vying for power. Where is the middle way?

There will be people who look at other groups and object to their basic programming of xenophobia (and any and all the other "-ophobias"); there will be people who look at certain groups and are incensed by their lack of appreciation for social order and the realities that create wealth and abundance[*], especially as, in their brainwashed ignorance, they push for sweeping changes that threaten these hard won realities on multiple fronts at once. "You have to be pretty damn reckless to be leaning this hard on so many untested heuristics your parents came up with in untested fields that aren't even 50 years old." (Eric Weinstein, found in Murray, 4) And there will be many—some from either camp, and some outside both and understanding some of both—who look at all the strife between groups in our society and exclaim in exasperation, "Can't we all just get along?!"

No, we cannot all just get along. Or rather, *this* here and now *is* us "getting along"—you're looking at it! We muddle through as always. Many will think this a remarkably pessimistic and vicious declaration, in such a contrast to what I hope has been the clear optimism of the rest of the book. But things are not always what they seem[†]. Life is a difficult game and "all things take place by strife" (Heraclitus, 241).

We do not, cannot, and will not get along because we are fallible and life is infinite. "Human beings will never disagree any less than they do now, and that is a very good thing." (Deutsch, 351) To believe that all conflict is a product of avoidable bias and ignorance is to believe naively that the game of life is easy and that ignorance has a shallow root. But ignorance is a necessary, foundational element of the game.

As finite characters submerged in an infinite universe, we are irrevocably ignorant. Ignorance is not something of our creation, not something that does not exist until we are corrupted by a system or exposed to greed. Ignorance is a fundamental part of the miracle of creation. Ignorance is a miracle of God.

---

[*] "Order is… safely inhabitable, even by the naïve." (Peterson, 37)

[†] Another great truth that arises from beyond the intellect and is kept alive by traditions of wisdom much more than intellectuals.

On Tolerance

Ignorance is one and the same with limited conscious existence—the game of life. Ignorance is not trivial. And there are infinite avenues which it may take to stir up chaos.

In an understandable moment of frustration, one throws out this exasperated phrase, "Can't we all just get along?" It is expressive, not cognitively meaningful. Take a moment to think about it, "Is it possible that we could all just get along?" In that moment of thought people all over the world, including children, are being raped, murdered, and abused. Can you get along with a rapist and murderer—especially your rapist or your child's murderer? No. We cannot just get along. That's not how it works. "When they shall say, Peace and safety; then sudden destruction cometh upon them." (1 Thessalonians 5:3)

We can make progress though, for progress doesn't depend on us getting along with 100% effectiveness. In fact, progress in part depends on us disagreeing, even though our disagreements are part of us not getting along (degrees of seriousness in the conflict varying as they will)."Some degree of conflict among groups may even be necessary for the health and development of any society." (Haidt, xx)

For years I had felt that balance was a virtue and a deep truth of life, but I could not put into words why—it was simply an archetypal virtue I was aware of. Then Dr. Jordan Peterson put words to it for me, and it seemed so simple and obvious. Balance is necessary because no answer is perfect and works forever; in other words, we are fallible and life is infinite. And, especially on the biological and cultural levels where we try many different ways to get things right, balance means disagreement and conflict to some degree.

What is painfully obvious from a biological and evolutionary perspective (and the intuitive wisdom of traditions have also told us this) is that we are blind creatures—the blind leading the blind. We may personally believe that we see the right way but, no matter how impressive our intellectual credentials, nature knows not to put all her eggs in our basket. Thus we have secular and nihilistic academics, transhumanist scientists and technofanatics, religious dogmatists, new age spiritualists, and everything in between.

Life diversifies not just to spread and search (competing if necessary) for resources (including truth) in the present, but to prepare for the unpreparable—to survive by any means necessary the unforeseeable difficulties of the future. That means some people and groups need to be on the fringes, enacting different modes than are generally accepted in society.

Purpose in Form

Perhaps the transhumanists will turn out to be the fittest, rewarded for their disregard of outmoded beliefs in the sacredness of the body and the perennial fears of new technology; or, perhaps, the strictly Kosher Jews will survive do to a sudden and severe epidemic brought on by shellfish and pork, and the transhumanists will be wiped out by a solar flare frying their circuits and any who survive will be left with underlying genetic deficiencies that had been considered irrelevant given technology.

In any case, the balance and success of life in the long run outweighs the strife between groups this necessitates in the present—or at least, it has until now; the threat of mutually assured destruction reveals the difficulties brought about by the "what has worked until now is good enough" blindness of evolution. This is simply another difficulty of the game. Understanding this, we may have compassion and even gratitude for the great balance of the world appearing as strife. Though, that is not to say we should not seek to criticize and correct aims and values that we think can be shown to cause more suffering and not be in accord with truth—though we should remain doxastically open to learning something new, even when we are on the attack.

We will never all agree. And there will be no agreement to all agree and live peacefully forever. We will constantly disagree and this will cause conflict. And, this gives us a relevant rule of thumb, in line with what we have been exploring with utopians and hopes for 100% effectiveness: you'll never get humanity to all act together no matter how good the cause—even if we are invaded by a hostile alien species, there will be a significant amount of alien sympathizers (many of them also antihumanists, to be sure); thus, if your cause requires or presupposes all humans joining you, and it can't work or be worthwhile even if you only get a minority, it is probably better to reconsider your goal and expectations than to pursue coercion and claim "if you're not with us, you're against us" (which will only make your movement less popular and appealing anyhow), or to decide that the human race is evil and hopeless and turn to antihumanism or nihilism.

"Presence of group centered belief makes conflict with other groups inevitable. In the west, we have been withdrawing from our tradition-, religion-, and even nation-centered values, partly to decrease the danger of group conflict. But we are increasingly falling prey to the desperation of meaninglessness... [because] loss of group-centered belief renders life chaotic, miserable, intolerable... and that is no improvement at all." (Peterson, xxxiii)

On Tolerance

We cannot give up our basic orienting beliefs, nor our fundamental values; thus we will conflict with others on some level. And we will naturally group and live with others who share our values (the only way to stop this natural tendency being a draconian system of centralized housing and socializing controls), so we will experience conflict as group conflict.

But this does not mean the world of human conflict is or must be a static reality. Steven Pinker entirely discredits this claim in his books *The Better Angels of Our Nature* and *Enlightenment Now*. Progress on violence and conflict is possible. For one thing—I will leave the majority of statistical and data driven concerns to the masterful expertise of Pinker and focus on the philosophical issues[*]—we have developed and promoted the value of tolerance (the cause of which Pinker traces back to the proliferation of open markets) in modern western society beyond any other society in history. Tolerance means agreeing to disagree—to some extent. It means valuing peace, trade, and flourishing over an honor and dogma driven crusade to eradicate wrongthink. It means feeding your enemies and blessing those you curse you.

However, in some defense of root-causism, the erection of tolerance—achieved as it was by a proximal address of symptoms (i.e. introducing people to peace and showing them how they can flourish if they work and trade across ideological borders)—may have indeed been only a Band-Aid suited for the short-term address of social symptoms, but incomplete in the long run when put up against the moral dilemmas of ideological difference.

On the one hand the rise of modern "multi-culturalism" (ironically) seems to be eroding the value and practical reality of tolerance. As Yuval Noah Harari notes: "Some cultures may be better than others" and some level of shared and agreed on—and therefore conflicted over and sorted out—central cultural values in a society must exist (140). In fact, Pinker himself knows that things like reason and fallibility are "non-negotiables" (8); so how do we deal with those trying to negotiate these—when their numbers and influence are growing and if they keep doing so?

And on the other front, aside from sheltered and academic-bred nonsensicalism, issues of global tolerance, as championed by Pinker, face

---

[*] Though this might be characterized as a form of "root-causism", it is at least a form which leans in the direction of progress and believes in addressing such roots, rather than resigning in self-fulfilling pessimism (Pinker, 169).

serious threat in light of international moral lapses beneath the veneer of magnanimous agreements on altruism. For example, how is the United States to respond to the internment and abuse of Uighurs in China? Drastic economic sanctions seem a viable tool, but they also drastically increase the chances of war, as Pinker acknowledges. But is mass internment and human rights abuse not something we have thought reasonable to justify war, if necessary? There is obviously a line to tolerance, and times when being "tolerant" in the face of "different opinions" (as the NBA recently described Chinese views on censorship, imperialism, and (tacitly) the Uighur issue) is in itself a moral failure (Blum, "NBA Commissioner Announces…").

Yet in many areas of our society the progressive *intrusion* of morality—the insistence that everything political be a case of basic moral belief and principles—is what is promoting civil unrest and driving us closer to mass violent conflict; mounting as many cases of moral transgression and lapse as possible (i.e. interpreting everything in moral terms) wins the more vigorous emotional buy-in of constituents, but this stoking of passions is the quickest route to violence[*]. For that reason I am not even sure the example I gave above regarding Uighurs is an appropriate line in the sand. It may be more appropriate (though seemingly horrifyingly callous) to leave the wrath up to God. Life is a difficult game indeed.

Between movements dismissing tolerance as a moral failure in a society where it is clearly not (and whose existence as a movement is only retained by the incredible tolerance of our society), the seemingly diminishing voice for tolerance in the world, and the actual challenges to the limits of tolerance that are faced today, how can tolerance maintain its status as one of our chief virtues? Pinker provides all the necessary data for the lauding of tolerance and all it brings with it, but how can we assure that it is enshrined as an adamantine pillar of our world—something to be inexorably returned to even if we must descend into war in some extreme cases in spite of it?

Tolerance must have a foundational case for its existence, not just a proximal implementation and efficacy. Luckily, within the foundations that we have discovered and explored in this book, tolerance can be rooted and fully embraced as a core virtue. Tolerance can be practiced in the deepest points of

---

[*] "We should aspire to a world in which a politician appealing to someone's empathy would be seen in the same way as one appealing to people's racist bias." (Bloom, 49)

darkness, dissention, and disagreement because of the truth of infinite Redemption. It is knowledge of and faith in Salvation which supports and enacts the most forgiving level of tolerance. (Even when we also recognize that many preach salvation and grace and offer something quite different in their actions.)

Just as Salvation and Redemption allow for the true abiding of humanistic progress through the unconscionable darkness of our world—which is but a general tolerance of the world—they apply equally to the particulars of the world—including all the ignorant, misguided, and in some cases evil people who we would otherwise love to eradicate or explain away and dehumanize (often as a precursor to the former) as "NPCs". In other words, though it has been hard for modern intellectuals (those who still believe in humanism and progress) to see it, the essential fundamental faith in Salvation and Redemption (along with meaning, purpose, and the rest) are the enlivening forces behind the "Better Angels of Our Nature"[*].

With these infinitely robust foundations for tolerance, we can accept the true difficult and fallible project of human flourishing. We can exercise tolerance as much as possible—though we will undoubtedly fall short or wait too long in many cases, as we are fallible. We can accept these mistakes as we accept our own fallibility and ignorance. And we can try to not let this acceptance become complacence toward progress, and fighting the good fights when necessary, as the acceptance of faith-based salvation should not excuse us of works in the world and moral development. We have no perfect formulas, and we wield a double edged sword. Life is a difficult game.

But, in the name of tolerance and progress and the knowledge of its wonderful fruits and its divine justifications, we can, in some cases, let go of our identification with our higher level beliefs (or the language and images in which these are formulated), ideas, perceptions, emotions, or character in question, and we can begin to accept the sacrifice of these elements in the

---

[*] Though, indeed, they had to reject and excise dogma and other forms of doxastic closure (i.e. infallibility) from their midst and graft on reason (i.e. true, unfailing faith in the spirit of logos in every man, fallible and wayward as it may be) in its stead for us to truly flourish. Now, through their imperfect self-diagnosis and surgery they have metastasized growths of nihilism and anti-humanism that hobble their pursuits of true virtue. These must now be cut out at their roots and replaced with the wholesome roots of connection to infinity—religious faith in Tolstoy's sense.

social arena of collective criticism. This disillusionment from identifying with things that are not us, and corresponding move towards our true Self, will be effective in lightening some of the conflict. Steven Pinker notes that "identity-protective cognition" is the cause of people having a threat-response toward challenges of their ideas (377 & 379).

Recognizing and being grateful for the tremendous improvements made in human life through western liberal and enlightenment values can also quell some of our aggressive and destructive drives to remake the world into an immediate utopia. And deeper faith in our beliefs in tolerance and progress can allow us to abide some level of the utopians and other authoritarians, rather than giving into the impulses of our aggressive righteous minds. But we are fallible and life is a difficult game. We will not all even attempt this journey, let alone all be even moderately successful[*]. And with our different rates of progress, we will run into others at different levels who will trigger us all over again and bring out projections and complexes we thought we had taken care of or gotten a hold on.

In our journey toward progress, the movement will be slow and disorderly (non-linear), for the causes we put in will be fallible (in their content and application). Thus our effects in this endeavor will be minor to moderate at best. But, like Aspirin, that is not to say the effects are insignificant, meaningless, and unworthy of praise and gratitude. Far from it. All of our efforts toward progress, toward understanding ourselves and governing ourselves compassionately, moving toward heaven on Earth, even though we do so only marginally, are infinitely significant, wonderful and praiseworthy purposes which we should be glad to dedicate ourselves to. Only the utopians (who are most likely utopians for the driving fear and unrest of their underlying nagging nihilism) need 100% effectiveness to be satisfied. Those who know the infinite, who know redemption, who know the Game Theory of life, can be contented with our inevitably slow and fallible process, and know that "conflict in the created world is not what it seems" (Campbell, 246).

The road ahead is long and we are still very much deep in the darkness;

---

[*] "But Iluvatar knew that men, being set amid the turmoils of the powers of the world, would stray often, and would not use their gifts in harmony; and he said: 'These too in their time shall find that all that they do redounds at the end only to the glory of my work.'" (Tolkien, 36)

there is no sign of the horrors stopping anytime soon. Life is a difficult game. We need to be prepared for that journey—the difficult one, the adventurous one—not to expect the world to all just get along. We need to know that purpose, truth, meaning, and redemption all transcend this world full of violence, rape, terrorism, greed, war, sickness, and all other forms of suffering. There is an end to suffering says the Buddha. There is Redemption and Salvation through Christ, say the Christians. The Infinite is, say I.

The Gift of Repentance

> "If you repent with your whole body and mind, you'll receive immeasurable help from the Buddhas. The power of repentance dissolves wrongdoing."
> (Dogen, 143)

Douglas Murray devotes a section in his book to the question of forgiveness in the modern age. "How, if ever, is our age able to forgive?... Is there any route to forgiveness?" (Murray 176 & 181) These questions and this problem have been asked more and more frequently over the last decade. The first time I heard this issue brought up, it was by Maajid Nawaz in his appearance on The Rubin Report. Forgiveness is a virtue, and it is obviously connected to tolerance, but it also appears in the post-modern age that we have neither a reliable, defined route to it, nor an incentive to bestow it, nor a valid foundation for it.

Murray does his best to lay out a secular, social argument for the necessity of forgiveness among individuals. He credits most of these ideas to Hannah Arendt who outlines an argument beginning with observations about our limited knowledge in the world which line up perfectly with the requirements we have been laying out for our state as limited beings in an infinite existence. "We can never really know what we are doing" Arendt concludes. (Murray, 177) And this is compounded with the reality that our "action processes are not only unpredictable, they are also irreversible; there is no author or maker who can undo what he has done if he does not like it or when the consequences prove disastrous." (Murray, 178) That is to say, we are fallible yet effective! And, "Only one tool exists to ameliorate the irreversibility of our actions. That is 'the faculty of forgiving'." (Murray referencing Arendt, 178)

Purpose in Form

I will make an additional point on the use and power of forgiveness, which brings its clear necessity beyond that of mere interpersonal regards, using the traditional religious notion of forgiveness and repentance. "Only the penitent man shall pass." (*Indiana Jones: The Last Crusade*) Penitence is a mark of one who is holy or virtuous (i.e. pursuing God or Truth), not because he scorns his own being, knowing human existence to be so necessarily sinful (even though this may be so) that he regrets his station, but because he is growing—becoming better than he was, and thus looks back on himself and finds fault through the vision of his new knowledge over his previous ignorance.

Thus, it is necessary for those who have grown and made progress in life to repent because they will see the errors of their past, which they cannot change. It is not repentance because they are unworthy; rather the worthy repent because they have become worthy through action and growth. So, without a modern route to forgiveness, nor a valid foundation for seeking repentance, we cut ourselves off from the possibility of tolerating significant growth in ourselves, which is the only hope for the progress of humanity and the world.

Containing this capacity within yourself—as something possible to achieve between yourself and God—is all the more important as well, given the unwillingness of others in this age to offer it. In times where mistakes and moments of fallibility are seized and weaponized against you; and further, even moments of uncertainty and hesitation on any matter—" attempts to weigh up the facts"—"can be repackaged as moral transgressions or even acts of violence," where can people turn who have no faith in a personal connection to the infinite? (Murray, 110) In a time when we must rethink so many of our assumptions, doctrines, actions, and even desires—given that "a great amount of thought often necessitates trying things out (including making inevitable errors)"—what hope and freedom do we turn to to encourage us to expose our fallibility and seek our own correction, if that correction is to be bestowed and judged by an insatiable and unforgiving crowd? (Murray, 109)

Repentance is not primarily a shackling doctrine imposed by the Church to make you feel bad about yourself and thus be dependent on them for your stability, even if it has been used as such; repentance is an effective tool for striving courageously toward growth and the cultivation of virtue. If you are closed off to the possibility of repentance—because you reject the idea of redemption, and/or any and all dogmas of the Church as superstitions—you are closed off to an extremely effective and almost universally necessary tool for maintaining your growth. Without repentance one is significantly more vulnerable to being overtaken by their shadow.

Those who undertake the adventure of cultivating themselves should keep the tool of repentance handy, so that they can maintain their virtuous course and not be shipwrecked by their shadow which catches them unprepared.

All in all, it does seem that Christianity got some very important and foundational things right, and this we cannot dismiss as a lucky Gettier issue and pretend their methods are ineffective or disposable—especially when those most eager to do so reject the necessary reality of the infinite, and all meaning and purpose with it! These ultimate foundations of virtue must be things we carry with us into the future if we are to sustain progress and faith in humanity.

Purpose in Form

Chapter 20: The Problem of Personified Evil

> "The moment you know that jerk-type action does not exist outside your own conduct, that is the realization of the truth." (Dogen, 152)

While I have favored the Christian doctrine for providing a direct answer to the ethical problem of the east, I do think Buddhism has one particular strength that is missing in the mythologies and ideologies in the west. Throughout ancient cultures across the world we have viewed the world in hierarchies of power, almost always with central authority, or at least symbolic sovereign heads of power. We were almost always ruled by kings, judges, popes, etc., so this makes sense.

This tradition has been challenged and has begun to change across the world, beginning with the ideas of a radically decentralized government arising with and out of the Enlightenment in the west. But what appears to be quite unconscious is the fact that we view central, identifiable individuals as pinnacles of power not only on the side of good and sovereignty, but also on the side of evil[*].

For all the questioning of God, the devil has been brushed aside on pretense, merely as a superstition. But this deeply ingrained myth cannot be so easily eschewed. People across the west tend to blame leaders and identifiable systems of power for evil all over the world, even in their own lives. There is always a scapegoat, always one singular entity responsible and behind all the

---

[*] As I noted earlier, Steven Pinker notes and speaks about this tendency.

misdeeds—or even misfortune; one who it all comes down to and who, if they were to act differently, would have changed all these things that should not have been.

This is unsurprising, though ironic, for as we have seen it is the rejection of God, and hence ultimate redemption, that drives secularists toward a greater *need* for the devil. Without the infinite love and redemption of God, one cannot look fully at the darkness of humanity and their direct responsibility for it without becoming nihilistic. So the would-be atheists and secularists call upon some conceptualized form of the devil to lessen the guilt that they must lay upon humanity; responsibility for the horrors of the world is foisted upon oil companies, Christians (of course), religion in general, lack of education or "proper" education, the military industrial complex, the Illluminati, etc. Of course these all beg the question, for anyone who asks must see, one pass of the buck and it's just humans all the way down. But we retain these scapegoats and obvious abstractions because they are required for the health of the unstable psyches we have constructed.

In any case, one way or another in the west we have the Devil[*]—a personified notion of evil, of separate origin than human creation (and therefore responsibility). Buddhism on the other hand—aside from its more allegorical interpretations focusing on *Mara*—proposed originally that the cause of evil is ignorance. And in this way they more or less uprooted even the notion of "evil". There may be a metaphysical distributor of ignorance (*Maya*), but in practical life ignorance is not a dominion of evil, ruled by a central devil. Ignorance is diffuse and personal to the individual.

In the west, *someone* is always to blame for all the evils of the world; there is a central do-badder (or group of them) who needs to just be eliminated and the world will finally go right. In its best formulations and understanding, the good Christian understands that he himself is the devil, he is the crucifier (and the crucified); "But what if I should discover that the least amongst them all, the poorest of all beggars, the most impudent of all offenders, yea, the very

---

[*] This entirely separate source of evil opposing the force for good of God actually has its origins in Zoroastrianism, from which Christianity inherited some ideas and imagery. The Christian tradition generally speaks in these categorical light vs. dark terms of Zoroastrianism, whereas the Bible itself is more equivocal on the issue, given its recurring insistence that evil is all the work of God (in some places) and in others it is of Satan or "the tempter".

The Problem of Personified Evil

fiend himself, that these are within me, and that I myself stand in need of the alms of my own kindness, that I myself am the enemy who must be loved. What then?" (Jung, CW, vol. 11, pg. 339) "The line separating good and evil passes not through states, nor between classes, nor between political parties either, but right through every human heart." (Solzhenitsyn). But almost always it is projected and some outside center of power is to be blamed for evil. And secularists have—willingly or not—inherited this nearly universal tendency.

The east, on the other hand, proposed the diffusion of power in regards to evil long ago and has been cultivating it for millennia. In Buddhism, the cause of suffering is ignorance. And ignorance is in oneself, and in one's mother, and in one's child, and in one's neighbor, and in one's boss, and in one's coworker—not just in one's ruler or congressman (or more likely someone else's!). Of course people can, will, and do ignore this fact and still project ignorance as something only existing out there or in "those people", but the mythology and requirements of Buddhism actively push one away from this projection.

Christianity has become a conception of God vs. Devil in cultural practice, but as Alan Watts points out to attribute evil to anything other than God is to deprive him of his infinity (*The Supreme Identity*, 119). Christianity does recognize this off and on. And, to the greatest point, Christ himself, when confronted with the greatest evil and sin, did not say, "Father, remember that the devil has tempted them!" He said, "Father, forgive them FOR THEY KNOW NOT WHAT THEY DO!" (Luke 23:34, emphasis added) He said, "remember their ignorance". Christ pointed to the ignorance of man as the source of evil, not to some external interference. This is a testament to both the Bible being the word of God—in that there is still such great truth to be found therein to instruct us further—and to the fallibility of our dealings with this text—in that we continue to miss all this truth and follow less effective paths of interpretation and thought in our ignorance.

Regardless of the utility of the term "evil", having a cultural doctrine that diagnoses clearly the underlying root of all evil to be personal ignorance is a fantastic achievement—one that should be cherished and cultivated in the west—and mysteriously arose in the east which was not the hotbed of individualistic thought in our history. The devil no doubt will remain as a common character of allegory and myth, as a tool used to call attention to malevolent attitudes or perspectives—well-dressed by the intellectual tongue though they be—but knowing beneath the figure head of the devil is a more definite and final metaphysical cause of evil changes our attitudes—especially our tendency to project—and gives us a more direct course of effective action in life for combating evil (rather than declaring holy metaphysical war on an eternal demon).

As we turn our focus toward working effectively against ignorance, we must be careful not to import our old habits of projection and merely rename the devil "Ignorance". We must accept the diffusion of power of evil, and we must accept personal responsibility for our own share of ignorance. We must tend to the beams in our own eyes first. And perhaps the most effective personal misunderstandings to begin work on is this lingering notion that would make ignorance synonymous with evil.

We like the idea of evil, we are used to working with it, so (if we must change) we want to merely transpose the words ignorance and evil and call it a job well done. But the point of all this is that evil is a high-level abstraction we came to after much observation and thought. Evil is above mere "bad things" (like hatred, meanness, stealing, etc.), it is the concentrated essence of badness, where even badness is an abstraction. The concept of ignorance is also an abstraction and the product of refined thought, but it refers to a low-level, proximal reality, whereas evil refers to a removed metaphysical actor of lofty and eternal nature.

Even if evil is not to be seen as synonymous with the devil (the devil being a further abstraction), evil is at best reducible to the grouped and labeled products of a particularly sinister grouping of active complexes in an individual. We look out for these patterns of motivation and behavior and call them evil. But ignorance is not the later product of our complexes or motivations, though complexes, projections, and inflations can certainly increase the noticeable ignorance. Ignorance is the foundation of our nature; it is the soil out of which our psyches and all motivations and perceptions grow. Ignorance is a necessary fundamental reality of the game.

In a way, this does seem to lead us to just another devil—an eternal reality which exists prior to ourselves and beyond our permanent eradication. However, there are some important differences. The devil is evil because he despises humanity, and he wants to take advantage of their lowness and imperfection to make them sin, to spite God's love for them and convince God that they are unworthy. This foundational conception pits the devil as an adversary of man and all his evils are products of our weakness as a species not living up to God's intended purposes and expectations. The concept of the devil as the genesis of evil spotlights our failure and makes all our weakness his strength—thus our weakness is to be hated.

The concept of ignorance as a foundational requirement of the game of life, on the other hand, says that ignorance was a necessity in our creation. This great weakness, this cause of all suffering and strife, was a known and intended element of our genesis. Far from being some twisted reality which is taken advantage of by greater beings for sadistic pleasure, our ignorance is divinely ordained. It is part and parcel of the gift of life. Our infinite ignorance is put in place for the divine purpose of our infinite adventure—the journey of our spirit. It is true that this necessary reality leads to horrible and terrifying deeds. But this is not because we are some sort of mistaken miscarriage of the divine, left behind to be raised and tormented by unholy forces. It is merely because life is a difficult game.

Thus in the conception of ignorance as the root of suffering, God retains his infinite nature (rather than being usurped and rivaled by the devil), so we have a consistent metaphysics, and all our evil actions are known and accepted hazards of gameplay. Though they are easier to see as cruel and unusual punishments, implemented by an eternal sadistic figure, our malevolence is part of the purpose of our lives; something our heroes are here to contend with as part of their adventures. That should give us much comfort—and the more so the deeper we reconnect with our faith in purpose!

As we take back ownership and personal responsibility for the evil of the world, we must call more deeply and more faithfully upon the reality of infinite redemption and the divinity of the individual; we must also use more diligently the gift of repentance. And we need to identify more strongly with our transcendent spirit, and less with our habitual tendencies (thoughts, actions, desires, etc.), so that we can willingly sacrifice those which do not serve our highest purposes. "Becoming more and more like Christ means surrendering all those things that we cling to for safety." (Kautz, 66)

We need a deep faith in the infinite conscious saturation and connection to life to allow us to most effectively face and work with our darkness. We must meet ourselves where we are; we must have the courage to look at our true nature. That is the first step of progress: knowing and accepting where you are, so that you might plot an *effective* course to where you want to be. Taking this first step is tremendous, so let's close by looking at how it is accomplished.

What Looks Willingly at the Darkness?

What courageous vision or divine center in man can look upon the true nature of the world and fully accept it? What is it that can look upon the face of the abyss and not be overcome? What is it that can fully enter this tortuous game and not be converted? What can hang upon the Cross and not be lost? What can walk step by tiny step of man through the dark paths of all his lives and future, and not get frustrated with his slow and wayward pace? What is the best player of this hardest game?

It is Love, the softest of things. Love itself is that which can endure all dismemberment of fully knowing and inhabiting the psyche of man. All-transcendent Love is the only *effective* approach for reaching full embodiment—full incarnation. It is only through knowing the intimate presence of Love and learning to serve its mysterious purposes that we can come to see the full nature and purposes of our finite characters.

Thus we began with doubt and reason in search of Truth, but inevitably we are driven toward Love. Love is the truth of Truth, and it has been there all along. What is doubt but the infinite courage to be married to the lively enthusiasm of curiosity? What is reason but the divine and proper vows of this marriage—those which uphold their fidelity and ensure their continual service and sacrifice upon the altar of Truth? The Truth to be found (or beheld) is the Infinite existence. The Truth to be lived is Love.

Conclusion:

<u>Looking to the Future and Acting in the Present—Effectively</u>

"Feeling compassion for the future, we need to value the present." (Dogen, 88)

What a storybook ending. But we need to be a bit more analytic than that for our purposes—for this book, as much as it tries to escape it through intellectual pomposity, is about practicality and effectiveness. This is precisely in accord with Tolstoy's frustrations mentioned earlier; "These studies are very interesting and attractive but... their precision and clarity are proportionate to their applicability to questions concerning life: the less applicable to the questions of life, the clearer and more precise they are, whereas the more they try to provide solutions to the questions of life, the more obscure and unattractive they become." (36).

In our imprecision we can say broadly that life is about Love. How wonderful. But let us not believe that answers any particular questions or difficulties—especially those between people. "Just feel the love, man," does not give one a remedy for all quandaries. You may be told that we must act with love for our children and society, which means we must take away weapons from our citizens. You may be told that is what Jesus would do. You may be told that we must love freedom and cherish our hard won independence and preserve it into the future, so that our children and society may flourish, which means we must honor the principle of citizens retaining the tools to defend—violently if necessary—their precious rights. You may be told *that* is what Jesus would do. You may think love is leading you to adultery or polyamory. Others may say love is about monogamy and commitment. Some may say love is tough love. Some may say love is all-suffering and all-accepting...

Merely accepting the necessity for Love in life does not lift the spell and end the game. It is just a further necessary truth that Love underlies the game itself—it is what supports the game continually and what brought you into it in the first place. You played the game because you loved the possibility, the stories, the adventure. Infinite Love for the finite is simply a metaphysical reality. Accepting that reality and acting in accord with its truth—fundamentally orienting yourself with it, accepting it as your faith—is merely the first effective step to take toward infinite problems.

Faith in Love does not make us infallible (or the phrase "love is blind" would never have taken hold), and thus does not guarantee success at any point. It is not 100% effective, for it does not seek to create incorrigible people. It does not seek to change the nature of the game. Thus it is love of the world *as it is*—not love of an ideal that one thinks the world should and must become, and must be hastened towards so we can move on and forget the world as it currently is—that is the key to progress.

It is ironic, for those who dream of bright futures seem such energetic and willing tools of progress, but it is those who deeply love the world and accept it *as it is*—those who would die for the world as it is, with all its darkness and sin—who are the true wheels of progress. Those who are willing to be here and now, to look at what-is directly and work directly with it, are the ones who will make *effective* change. Those who cannot stand the world as it is, and are in a panic over all its faults, shortcomings, and horrors, will only ever be working through their inaccurate projections and assessments—they will make miscalculations and naïve, desperate plans.

It is not those who believe we are on the brink of doom and fear we will soon meet our ultimate failure that will truly move us forward. One of reason knows we are always on the brink of doom and must make change and progress to overcome it (see Deutsch). It is those who have faith in redemption, who can take up a quest against the odds and remain steadfast in the face of the storm, rather than consumed by complexes of zealotry or despair, who will be the constructors of heaven on Earth.

Step one toward progress is accepting a basic faith toward the world of Love, hope, purpose, and redemption. We need to clean up our metaphysics.

Conclusion

Step two is putting faith in action and starting to iron out all our own conscious and unconscious resistances. Earlier I made a shout out to the Jungian process of individuation as a wonderful codified tool brought recently into the western world for this purpose, but a more basic and fundamental tool, which can help Jungians and all others alike, in line with what we have been discussing is mindfulness meditation[*].

Meditation is—through this lens—the basic process of increasing one's faithful and loving consciousness in the psyche[†]. An infinite, loving presence—a completely compassionate consciousness—is the only effective meditator. It is the background to which all perceptions may appear freely. Meditators practice becoming or expanding this presence within themselves, chasing the goal of being undisturbed by (completely open and loving toward) any thought, image, or feeling. In pursuing meditation, one pursues the knowledge of this compassionate consciousness which can be fully present with all things as they are.

A mindful attitude cultivates the space for our rationality to function more effectively in tense situations—when that space between stimulus and response is so tight and hardwired that it reduces our chances for freedom. Meditation is the effective tool for increasing our freedom, for bringing our awareness to our unconscious habits, motives, and preconceptions, and giving us the opportunities to interpose new causes in our lives which will surely bring about new effects. Increasing one's open, compassionate, conscious presence through all moments—deepening one's intimacy with one's own finite life—with the tool of meditation, lays the foundation for growth in purpose, virtue, and efficaciousness. And whether moved by such philosophical mumbo-jumbo, or by the modern neuroscience and psychological studies of the beneficial effects of meditation, one is benefitted by accepting such a practice.

Life is a difficult game, and this is as far as I can take you. You have the recommendation to clean up your metaphysical room—your basic orientation toward life, your personal faith—which we derived through extensive, and I hope sufficient and effective, reason. And you have a vague, possibly inspiring, vision of Love and redemption. A practical next step toward fully

---

[*] This is not a particular endorsement for any school called "Mindfulness Meditation", it is about meditation and/or mindfulness.
[†] See my post "The Visudhimagga" for extended discussion

Purpose in Form

incarnating these realities is suggested as beginning a practice of meditation. But you may not meditate. You may do yoga, or psychoanalysis. You may start a garden, or begin painting or composing. Whatever you do, my recommendation is to begin consciously cultivating in your life. Ken Wilbur in conversation with Brother Wayne Teasdale once said truthfully, "We just don't know why human beings transform." ("The Mystic Heart 6") In the end we can observe the reality that people do make progress and see what happened to them and talk about patterns. It seems that some arenas of change and practice are better than others, and any activity and effort is better than none. But life is a difficult game, and many people fail at what worked for others.

We cannot prescribe a perfect path for you. But we do know there are highly effective arenas of change, which one can enter and engage in. Then the mysterious alchemy of personal transformation may take place. Bring into your conscious life the symbolic acts of purposeful growth in some way, and the pruning that goes with it. That is the best bet, and that is all we have. The concepts in this book are not intellectual principles to be nodded at, this is not merely a mesmerizing glass bead game; these are bloody ideas begging to be incarnated. If you make a sincere enough go at it, then you may make contact with the living force behind the apparition of these ideas and images, which will sweep you on your wu-wei.

Progress: Going from A to B

There is one final issue to address here too. It is a problem easy to state and with a quick solution, but its significance is not to be overlooked. Dr. Jordan Peterson states from a neurological perspective we perceive the world as a place in which to move from point A to point B, and that the majority of our positive emotion is to be found in the pursuit of goals ("No Goal, No Positive Emotion").

Yet today, helped by the disillusionment and depression of thoughts of meaninglessness and purposelessness, and the antihuman notions of the inherently evil nature of our efforts, people wonder why we have to work, why we must strive, and they believe their lives would be fulfilled if they merely had all their (ever-expanding) "rights" met magically and they were relieved of all required responsibilities. Kelley McGonigal talks about this same mindset as the common aversion to daily hassles and the erroneous belief that there is

Conclusion

some ideal, stress-free version of your life out there waiting for you (69). "Beloved, think it not strange concerning the fiery trial which is to try you, as though some strange thing happened to you." (1 Peter 4:12)

This modern western intellectualized depression loves what they hear in the statements from the east of "just be yourself"; Alan Watts preaches this a lot, but even Dogen (though he also preaches against it) mentions it "[you're] already a person who is 'it'; [you're] already a person who is of the ineffable, unnamable *something* of the universe" (Dogen, 262). And they feel personally attacked and shocked by the uncouth notions, mainly marketed by conservative Christian types, that one is here to work and serve. "To ask that God's love should be content with us as we are is to ask that God should cease to be God. The love of God necessitates growth and maturity in us... it doesn't stop at mere benevolence but rises to the level of a searing flame, burning off the dross and refining the gold." (Kautz, 18)

So there seems to be this dichotomy of ethics. But, though you will find less of an emphasis in Watts (who died of alcoholism by the way), Dogen of course and others of the East are not averse to work, nor under the delusion that man is here to be served and live lavishly in the name of happiness. "Meaning... in the great stories of the past... had more to do with developing character in the face of suffering than with happiness." (Peterson, xxvii)

Once again, the western intellectuals have projected their own desires onto the eastern philosophies and heard what they want. But in reality there is no discrepancy between the statements "be who you already are" and *"there is something lacking in all of us"* (Kautz, 83 italics in original).

Once again, the problem is ignorance of the self. The self, in so far as it is spoken about within causation, is a verb, as coined by Buckminster Fuller. The self is an actor, a doer, a creator, *a player*. Playing the game is why we are here. Our being is a playing, a doing, an unfolding. Our lives happen. We are growing and developing beings. We are a becoming. The moving from point A to point B is merely a proper fulfillment of our nature. "Being who we are" is moving from point A to point B through the difficult quests of the game—striving, wrestling with God. Understanding that we are beings of action and engagement, rather than inanimate objects like stones that are plagued by unholy animating spirits forcing them to move about, is a key notion to clear up a lot of modern confusion.

We are divine beings, but our divinity is not about an inheritance of infinite

Purpose in Form

rights and pleasures that are being arbitrarily withheld from us by evil systems. Our divinity is about our nature beyond the game. It is what allows us to play this game with joy and compassion. Our characters in this game are here to play. The real key that unlocked this puzzle for me was this poem by Rabindranath Tagore:

> I slept and dreamt that life was joy.
> I awoke and saw that life was service.
> I acted and behold,
> service was joy.

Throughout this book we have analyzed and told stories, and told stories and analyzed. We couldn't leave the end on quite such a poetic note, but here let me try to still leave you with some fantasy, some which does not demand reason to shave down the ideal so much. In David Deutsch's book, which is written perfectly secularly[*] and scientifically, he proclaims two great truths which he says should be carved in stone.

I will take these great modern western scientific truths—which are essential as well to all of Pinker's philosophy—and transfigure them before your eyes into the wisdom of the ages—of Christianity and Jung—of Purpose in Form. The truths Deutsch emphasizes so greatly, inserting a large graphic image of each carven into a stone plaque, are 1) Problems are inevitable, and 2) Problems are soluble. What could be more foundational to the scientific attitude and endeavor? What could be more rational, analytical, and secular?

But the guise is only a matter of diction. These are the same truths we are given divinely, through the intuition of the ages. Take these statements of truth and put the same meanings in a different frame and you will have a formula which is exactly in line with what we have been discussing throughout this book: Problem 1) "Problems are inevitable" becomes "Adventure is out there", for every problem is a purpose or potential purpose. And problem 2) "Problems are soluble" becomes "You are a potential hero", which is exactly the message of Jung, and Neumann traces this idea as the origin of all (self-)consciousness.

---

[*] Though the chapter on a universal beauty and human's part in it sounds like secular support for us being made in the image of God.

Conclusion

This edict of progress and science, like all other humanistic messages which are genuinely positive, is only apparently secular, but hinges on the preliminary and perhaps unconscious acceptance of the divine nature of the individual and the infinite foundational reality of meaning in our lives. It is the call to adventure that has inspired man throughout the ages, merely refined and reworded to suit the idioms and axioms of the age.

As we can see, your purpose and the nature of the game are wound together. It's a difficult game, and you're here to struggle through it. "The best advice is to take it *as if* it had been of your intention."[*] (Campbell, Myth 203) Hopefully now you have been affected in some way; hopefully you are closer to a place of complete acceptance of your life and willingness to work with it, to meet yourself where you are and take up your Personal Legend. Hopefully you have a good start and set of tools to defeat these modern mental demons of purposelessness, meaninglessness, and insignificance, and all the nihilist and antihumanist rhetoric that grows out of it.

Humanity needs to be encouraged, compassionately, to grow and thrive, not told that it is a mistake and is cancerous in its unintended existence. It needs the miraculous and fantastic Truth, rather than malicious and falsely humble lies. I hope that this book is a significant step toward moving past this aversion to self-consciousness in human history. And I hope we begin to grow more clearly and faithfully towards infinity, as we now may know that by it are we nourished.

---

[*] See also Alan Watts "Stop Playing the Victim"

Purpose in Form

Epilogue: Atonement

In this book I have praised and relied heavily on authors such as Deutsch, Tolstoy, Murray, Campbell, Dr. Peterson, and Dogen/Warner. And I have heavily derided others such as Benatar and Harari. I stand by such overall appraisals of their works, but I do not believe in idol worship of particular thinkers, and in line with Deutsch's views on epistemology, I believe that truths can come from any source. As a project of atonement for some intense criticism and rejection, and to bring us toward a more rationalist ideal of impartial assessments I would like to say some things I think those I have heavily criticized got right or did well, and to say where I think those I have supported fall short of perfection (as they must).

Though I strongly disagree with essentially Benatar's entire doctrine, I do think he is being sincere, which is worth a great deal. As I said briefly earlier, when I read his books after listening to his podcast with Dr. Jordan Peterson, my opinion of him changed and my reaction to his words was far less hostile. I think, as far as the podcast discussion goes, Dr. Peterson was in the wrong for his casual dismissal of Benatar's claims and that he did not speak to a clear understanding of what Benatar said in his books. Dr. Peterson was reacting to the sentiment of the perspective Benatar proposes—and he was right in his diagnosis of it as malignant and incoherent; but he did not speak to Benatar in his terms, from a place of understanding.

Further, Benatar stated at least two things within his philosophy which I appreciated and think are very true. For one, he correctly described the relation of purpose/purposelessness to God, and thus I quoted him in a note in the discussion of the Buddhist idea of purposelessness earlier. Secondly, he comes up with this little gem of a quote which I think is both simple and profoundly useful in life, "Not everything that we might wish to be done (or are glad was done) is something that we think should be done (or should have been done)." (BNHB, 155) I think this quote can help us to cultivate an attitude of progress and improvement alongside an attitude of radical acceptance of our pasts—both of which are necessary, but seem paradoxical. This quote, I think, is key in finding the balance between the two and not falling prey to the intellectualism "why not sin so that Grace may abound?" Benatar is right: terrible things happen, and sometimes good comes of them (often the good of our growth, since we are anti-fragile), but that doesn't mean we should seek to create more terrible things.

I take Harari to task throughout the book, perhaps even more vehemently than Benatar. I think his attitude and methodology, along with some of his ideas are atrocious. This might lead one to believe I think of him as a worthless figure and his work as of no more consequence than an illustration of what not to do. This would be wrong.

First of all, Harari's discussion of the current problems of social media and AI and algorithms I think is fantastic and supremely important. This is far from my area of expertise, so there is a possibility that this is merely an example of the Gell-Mann Amnesia effect on my part, but from personal experience observing and being affected by thought bubbles, and light explorations of the topic of algorithms as discussed by others I think he probably does a good job. And even just raising the issue is a great necessity. This constitutes a large section of his book with which I have little or no qualms. I also think it is important that he specifically makes a distinction between consciousness and intelligence when discussing AI—though he does not explain or support this. And his assertion that meditation and the evolution of human consciousness (contradictory to some of his other theses thought it may be) are the keys to our future I think is right on the money.

Harari also makes a wonderful illustration of the processes of knowledge and tradition where he describes the excitement and value of the fringes of knowledge, as well as the advantages of remaining near the central hub of established truths. And he makes a very practical and wise observation that the life of an intellectual requires wasting time. This is an incredibly important truth and perhaps a key insight for intellectuals to combat their prejudices that the salvation of the world rests in everyone becoming an intellectual. Harari has many good ideas; he also is a perfect example of an intellectual who has been unconsciously engulfed by nihilism and preaches it zealously alongside his intended message of hopeful progress, and this is a widespread pattern we must become acutely aware of and begin to uproot.

Though I quote Deutsch liberally and think his book is fantastic, I do think he fails to recognize the significance and reality of consciousness, as a larger claim than reason or intelligence. Deutsch as a brief aside dismisses sweepingly all Psi research as scientists being fooled by "conjurers' tricks" (324). And, though he deeply illustrates the mechanisms and properties of infinite sets, and approaches confronting the reality of the infinity of life more than most secular scientists, he certainly falls short of recognizing the mystical reality it all implies. He also probably veers too close to an intellectual idealist's portrayal of the world, in some ways conflating human potential with broadly actualized reality.

Further, I do not agree with the complete dichotomy he seems to assert between the search for foundational truths and the truth that some realities are emergent at particular levels of analysis (this is a complicated issue and too much to discuss here). Additionally, I think his heavy reliance on Popper may be somewhat of a defect (as my reliance on him may be), especially when he brings politics into discussion and suggests that we may want to move away from compromise in our political systems (again, a complicated issue, and not that there is no truth in it, but I don't take it as Gospel).

He also seems to forward a conception that our ideas should be easily let go of and die quickly on the altar of collective criticism, and that it is lamentable that we hang on so dearly to our ideas. I think that our ideas should die hard. One should not just give up an idea because they hear a compelling argument or two against it; one should grant that the tables seem to have turned, but it is good that our ideas fight tooth and nail for survival—this ensures we don't miss anything by too quickly abandoning everything that seems to be initially refuted by a sophisticated sounding argument. There is much sophistry out there and we need to always be checking our own work and that of others.

Though I think Tolstoy's *A Confession* is perhaps the best answer to the question of suicide that exists in the philosophic literature, and I think his definition of faith and religion are pellucid and inspired, I would be remiss to overlook his affinity for communism scattered liberally through his religious writings. He, like other intellectual idealists, falls prey to this dark underside of finding high standards and ideals and then expecting that all people can and will live up to them, given the necessary support (i.e. control). Similarly, in his essay "The Law of Love and The Law Violence" he adopts the monastic/ascetic ideal and applies its standards to all people, thus negating and neglecting the different but necessary perspective and values of the householder. These issues are terribly interesting and subtle, and deserve far more discussion.

Though in reference to Buddhism I quote nearly exclusively from Dogen/Warner, I do so because that book achieves perhaps the closest pre-prepared parallels to the Christian doctrine that I could hope to find. This also makes the book somewhat peculiar and distant, seemingly, from foundational Buddhist literature. I have personally found that hagiographies are often more illuminating and inspiring than foundational doctrinal texts. But, though the precise connections between the foundational doctrines and Dogen and Warner's words and views may be hard to see, I do think they are there, and I believe the task of relating the East to the West as I have done could be accomplished without looking at Dogen in particular—it just would have taken much more explanatory work on my part. Fortunately, Dogen and Warner had already done this work and are valid representations of their cannon.

That all being said, at the very end of the book, Warner goes off on his own perspectives and ideas and makes some clear errors. Though he scoffs at the ideologies infecting San Francisco and how they are averse to some Buddhist ideas, it is clear in his concluding pages that Warner has not escaped the infection of some relativist memes and ideas which directly contradict much of what he has been saying, and what is true. For one, he makes the nonsensical claim that, "Zen Buddhists have no doctrines and no belief system." (295) Though, he just finished cataloguing just that. He confuses a non-proselytizing approach and a radical "see for yourself" attitude with a lack of doctrines and belief system.

On the side of relativism and the San Francisco-fostered ideologies, Warner echoes, "We regard every person's unique experience of themselves to be fully and equally valid." (296) Another odd incongruity as Dogen frequently calls those he disagrees with in method or message "idiots". And Warner himself recognizes the need for monastic hierarchies and respect for authority. So, if and when a more authoritative monk tells you that you are wrong or missing something or should try something else, you should listen. Buddhists recognize this, and Warner even agrees with Dogen on it. Relativist-identitarians would call that violence and an invalidation of one's unique existence. Sure, people's immediate assessment of their own perceptions and beliefs is "valid" in that it is an acceptable starting point and true "from a certain point of view", but the point of Buddhism is that many (if not nearly all) points of view are flat out wrong, and that you can be instructed on how to see that they are wrong.

Buddhism calls people on their BS and Zen Masters, especially Dogen, are perhaps the most notorious for doing just this. Thus, assuring one that no one's *interpretation* of their own experience "is any less valid" is nothing but a San Francisco-bred platitude to appeal to that mob ideology. (Warner leaves out the "interpretation" part of the personal experience in his sentimental ode to the snowflakes, but this makes the statement essentially meaningless because all we are ever dealing with is the interpretation and if we were all perfectly in the experience there would be no need for Zen.)

I used many quotes from Joseph Campbell throughout the chapters, taking his words as expert testimony on both mythology and essentially mystical truths. Campbell's first and most prolific work, *The Hero with a Thousand Faces*, is hard to find fault with. However, as he continued his career, the way he formulated and reformulated his ideas became less precise and more rounded in favor of popular prejudice—at least in my perception. His lectures often find him speaking more radically on the negative and demagogic nature of the story of Job, above which he elevates Greek humanism. I thoroughly disagree with the juxtaposition he makes on the matter and the diagnosis that our modern confusion is largely due to a Sunday commitment to Job and a Monday through Saturday Greek alignment.

Job is not analogous to Prometheus, as Campbell often claims in his lectures, because God in the Job story is not a deity comparable to Zeus. The point of the leviathan-conquering descriptions of God is not, as Campbell trivializes, "I am a big deity, what can you a small man do about it?" Rather, these allegories and metaphors are to illustrate the beyond beyond comprehensibility of God the infinite—who is beyond any limited archetypal deity. Therefore, the defiance of deity and archetype as exhibited by Prometheus and the humanism that this symbolizes is in no way contradicted by the surrender to the absolute infinite, which is but the necessary truth that we are never separate from the infinite. The failure is not in doctrinal dichotomy of the masses, but in scholarly hubris of reading-in a finite deity where scripture rightly recognizes the infinite and man's relation to it (though again, Campbell seems to avoid this mistake in his earliest work).

Additionally, I think Campbell often speaks so dismissively of the darkness of the world (or romanticizingly of the middle ages) that he comes very close to promoting the Ethical Problem of the East—that once you understand or declare belief in the infinite spirit, all suffering and darkness bows out and life is perfect and simple. Dr. Peterson derides this tendency of Campbell's as epitomized in his maxim, "follow your bliss"—as though the path of a good life were characterized by bliss.

Dr. Jordan B. Peterson's book *12 Rules for Life* is a wonderful book and, though not as foundational as the discussion here, will undoubtedly remain the more accessible and widely effective because of that. However, I think Dr. Peterson is wrong in his assessment that he has made at least a few times that Joseph Campbell got all his ideas from Jung. I also think that when he is involved in political discourse and commentary, he often talks about ideologies possessing people—especially on the political left—and does an incomplete job in dividing this true assessment and condemnation of an active complex in individuals and the behavior it breeds from a condemnation of the individuals themselves.

Especially given the lack of redemption and recourse to repentance that is so endemic in modern secularists, it is extremely important to reemphasize that we do not condemn individuals beyond redemption, nor deny their inherent divinity. Dr. Peterson could be far more clear on the nature of complexes—that they are active in us all—and that while people are and should be responsible for their actions, an individual getting caught up in ego-inflation by a complex and collective unconscious wave is not some aberration which only weak and degenerate people fall prey to; it is an understandable flaw that we all exhibit at some point(s) our lives.

Furthermore, I believe Dr. Peterson has a fundamentally non-Christian reading of Christianity—as many, including Ben Shapiro, have suggested. There may be certain Christian sects, historical or contemporary, which agree with his views, but they are certainly not representative of the mainstream practice and theology of Christianity. This is not so much of a problem when Dr. Peterson is analyzing the Old Testament, but when he talks about the image of Christ he strays from the Christian message drastically.

For example, Dr. Peterson says that the archetypal image of Christ (i.e. the

Atonement

perfection of man) says to humankind "get rid of everything about yourself that isn't perfect" (Akira the Don, "Deadwood"). This is true when looking only at the necessary consequences of the ideal/judge relationship. However, the message of Christ as the Christian messiah is almost precisely the inverse of this; it is not "get rid of that which isn't perfect" but "the perfection which is (and the perfect man which is in accord with this preexisting Glory) loves even this imperfect world to its darkest depths". This is partly because the image of Christ is not, in Christian doctrine, even primarily the image of the perfect man, but rather the image of God himself. Human ideals of perfection do challenge us to rise above ourselves, but Perfect Love—which exists even without man supposing any ideals—loves the imperfect, loves all. The image of Christ is one primarily of Mercy and Grace, far more than it is about overt and exacting human behavioral modification[*].

I think Douglas Murray does a great and brave job at assessing the political absurdities of the age (at least on one end—and the one that primarily objects to free speech and "the idea" of "the truth") and exposes some sinister motives of revenge lurking consciously or unconsciously behind the zealous drives of people commonly assumed to be egalitarians[†]. As I have said earlier, I think he mischaracterizes his assessment as foundational rather than proximal. However, his greatest sin is something only subtly manifest in his book, not

---

[*] I have just recently heard a few podcasts from Dr. Peterson which touch directly on these last two criticisms, where he is explicit about how it is common to be possessed by an ideological complex and that he knows the redemptive side of Christ but is making a point to discuss the inescapable realities of a judge which an ideal must conjure because this is not common enough knowledge in his estimation. And I have not by any means listened to all his material, so I can assume there is more out there. However, I think it can still be said that he could do more to bring up this idea of individual redemption and divinity in direct companionship to ideological possession every time he talks about the latter. And, although it may be true that the understanding of Christ is unbalanced in favor of over-compassion and the unconscious nature of the judge is something to be dealt with, I do not think that the "proper" balance is one that is equal between judgement and mercy—I think it is correct that the Godly side of mercy outweighs the side of judgement and recompense. Thus, though Dr. Peterson's mission to bring to light the unconscious judgement is served by almost exclusively emphasizing the judgement exacted on people by the ideal (compassionate though it be), it does still make him incorrect in his assessment of Christ overall insofar as he makes that side his emphasis.
[†] See 'Tarantulas' by Akira the Don

something he ever claims outright—something he chooses to do as a person, which I strongly disagree with: this man refuses to use the oxford comma!

As you can see, there is no infallible text. There is no catch all formulation. Texts are only good insofar as they can reach us and help us find truth through our fallibility. No single text, lineage, or path appeals to everyone, nor can one be made to. And there is always room for improvement in all.

Equally, though, I would doubt that any text achieved complete untruth (without that being the conscious intent of the author). Thus even in Benatar's bleak work we find a few kernels of truth and insight. Always there remain elements of our consciousness and perceptions that are beyond our conscious control or will. And the unconscious is multifaceted—though it may be plagued by darkness, there will also always be light that creeps in; just as inversely we cannot pretend that suffering does not exist and wish it all away with fantastic idealistic formulations.

In that light, my work here deserves some comment. Now, I dislike when people present their own work along with a self-deprecating remark, as a way of weighting the scales on the negative so that recipients will be more likely to offer praise to balance it out; don't sell yourself short to seek approval. And that is not my intention. I am not going to here list ways I think my work misses points or is unconvincing—if I knew of these it would be my duty to revise and perfect them before moving to publication. However, without this final address I believe my work may come off as somewhat of a counter argument to the majority of Steven Pinker's *Enlightenment Now*, and it should not be seen as such.

Though this book leans religiously apologetic, that does not mean it should encourage blindness to the failings of religion nor to the tremendous successes of science which were truly difficultly won against the bulwark of religion which attempted to hold science back.

I disagree with Pinker that humanism is or can be a foundational morality, as I have extensively argued in connection with secularism. Pinker makes no serious address of nihilistic philosophies or responses to those questioning the value of progress and human life. He relies on the *prima facie* assumption that we are significant, that the ease of our suffering is a good thing, and the unconscious and tacit idea that we are infinitely redeemable, no matter how dark our history or how slow our progress; he assumes the divine nature of the individual and of consciousness, and relies on this intuited faculty in most readers, while dismissing any serious weight of nihilistic counterpoints.

If this works for you, then great; it probably is wholly sufficient for very many people. But the grip of nihilism is very real as well, and a hand waiving account of the appeal to sympathy and progress does nothing to address those who have begun to harbor deeper antihuman sentiments and reject the value or significance of consciousness itself (regardless of its increasingly ameliorated level of suffering). And the fact that secular humanism presents alongside its hopeful, *post hoc*, and only proximally defined morality the very narrative of pointless generation of life (the magical thinking of meaningless "self-replicators") which uproots foundational meaning and breeds nihilism makes it an even worse candidate for a worldwide self-sufficient morality; not only is it incomplete and ineffective in the most extreme cases, it is often the source of generating more of these worst cases.

That issue aside, there is very little else on which I disagree with Pinker. And accepting a properly religious foundation of morality, as I am suggesting, in no way should discourage the vision of progress and science which Pinker heralds. There must be an alloy—a consilience—of these two world visions, each accepting the best the other has to offer, and removing from it what is detrimental. Pinker for the most part supports this idea, though he does occasionally contradict it and himself elsewhere: saying once that modern morality requires a "clean break" from religious conceptions but elsewhere that humanism is not incompatible with religion (394 & 412).

Religion provides the ultimate foundation and attitude toward life. It offers the antidote to nihilism and antihumanism, which secularism has bred (mostly unconsciously) and does not have adequate answers for. And religion should push us to reconsider the foundational story science forwards of the haphazard and meaningless spontaneous genesis of life (just as science should push us to reconsider any literal belief in the spontaneous creation of man *sans*-evolution).

But, no matter how adamantine this basic faith, the successful and effective approach to the world moving forward will have to accept and include complete fallibility, which is something religion has almost entirely failed at throughout the ages. I have made brief cases that scripture is *capable* of supporting the necessary cultural ideas of fallibility and free speech (which are nevertheless undeniably achievements and products of the enlightenment), but there is no shortage of scriptural quotes which undermine these other insights, and more still the organizational practice of religion and its institutions undeniably fostered the exact opposite of these most efficacious virtues, and still do so today.

Science and the enlightenment began as a fight against the religious norms, and they appeared positively demonic; they challenged the view of our significance in the cosmos, and they disregarded the sanctity of the flesh—performing corpse dissections and animal vivisections. Although from the blessed position of health and security hard-won by this process, the grave robbing, vivisections, and more contemporarily the pro-cyborg transhumanists, all violate to some degree my personal sanctity foundation of morality (and I can understand the horror those of the time would have had toward scientists), so does the guinea worm, elephantitis, small pox, the bubonic plague, bloodletting, leprosy, and unorganized and unenlightened disposal of septic waste.

The truth is the natural human condition throughout history is one that violates sanctity (along with so many other moral considerations—at least by the higher standards we hold today, through which we view the past). If it took a deal with the devil to ignore and defy the religious orthodoxy and hack up some dead bodies and torture some animals to get out of constant destitution and dereliction, I'll take it over the guinea worm hands down. I do think that this progress and the underlying philosophy paved the way for the principle of mediocrity and the current swamp of nihilism and loss of meaning—with no shortage of terrible and heartbreaking consequences to date—but every step forward brings new problems, for we are imperfect; we are fallible. And we are in a position to address those now and keep moving forward and hopefully move toward the best of both worlds (after experiencing some of the worst of both).

Reason and science, with their cornerstone of complete fallibility and yet faith in the heroic logos of man, institutions of decentralized power and open cooperation and commerce, have all played key roles in improving the lives of humanity in leaps and bounds so astonishing that, once adapted to, it is no surprise they are uncomprehended and largely forgotten—for they are incomprehensibly significant and miraculous improvements; they are unbelievable.

Just as Hume argued no one could or should believe the testimony of someone else to their witnessing a miracle, so is it nearly pragmatic and reasonable for us to doubt the tales of past human history and our recent salvation from it. Wouldn't any authoritarian despot tell an equally miraculous story of his salvation of his subjects from the horrors of the world? As Hume argued that all reports of miracles are unreliable, doesn't it seem that this fantastic transformation of our world is more likely to be the fabrication and propagandistic sales pitch for the current regime's ideals of reason, science, industry, and capitalism, than the genuine miracle that it is?

I have no idea how to solve this puzzle of human psychological adaptivity, short memory, loss of credulity and perspective, and thus loss of faith in some of our most efficacious virtues. Perhaps by grounding reason, science, and progress in the story of the divine and heroic nature of the human spirit, and keeping alive the romantic and moving affirmation toward our basic nature will motivate more people to take up the mantle of our quest of progress. Perhaps then our multi-century sustained global wildfire of human development and achievement will be seen as the "lightning across the skies"—the second coming of Christ (Luke 17:24)—the divine logos awakening in humankind across the world.

But more than likely, only a few will; we can reasonably hope for gradual and incremental progress. Still, this progress will be enormously significant, and if we can continue to just keep our heads above water[*], and keep enough people properly oriented and striving, we may ease the existential angst of the world, increase the levels of felt meaning and gratitude, spread the mindsets of empowerment and anti-fragility, and further the tremendous progress of modern material achievements and wealth creation. Each degree of improvement in any of these categories will be infinitely significant, and will move us toward more solid ground (technologically, economically, and psychologically/spiritually).

Between the foundational case here for the divinity of the individual, the infinity of life, and the intimate conscious connection between infinite and finite, setting us up to be heroic adventurers in this infinite playground, and the miraculous vision of progress catalogued and championed by Pinker and Deutsch, we have the foundations for a proven positively efficacious set of

---

[*] By our new, higher standards that is; of course compared to 300 years ago we are out of the water, on a safe elevated piece of land, inside a structure with central heating and plentiful food.

values, orienting us in which adventures to pursue and how to keep the ones we select on track. This can be (and I think should be) the modern orthodoxy.

Certainly in modernity we have a plethora of diehard rebels (as we have been actively breeding them), of which I am one, who would revolt at the mere word "orthodoxy", and that will be one of our difficulties in this game going forward. But we should hope that there would be an orthodoxy in our society (and to some extent the world[*])—otherwise there is only anomie, and the depression this breeds (Haidt, 313). Our only hope is to create an orthodoxy which accepts complete fallibility and rejects the justification of knowledge, and so has reform, improvement, and progress built into its worldview, and thus is no stalwart, monolithic antagonist to those of a more rebellious or contrarian nature[†].

Currently, adventurers and heroes are still needed to champion, uphold, and enshrine this orthodoxy, as well as move it forward. The quest, though miraculously successful already, has only just begun. We still sit, as ever, at the beginning of infinity. The choice to accept the quest and engage willingly and positively with life, is yours.

---

[*] Though we must also recognize the need for dissention and differentiation.
[†] "Radicals are only to be feared when you try to suppress them. You must demonstrate that you will use the best of what they offer." (Herbert, 36)

Works Cited

Adyashanti. "The Pouring In of Immensity." *ADYASHANTI*, 3 Feb. 2019, www.adyashanti.org/store/media/audio-downloads/1060.

al-Gharbi, Musa. "Academic Grievance Studies and the Corruption of Scholarship." *Heterodox Academy*, 10 Oct. 2018, heterodoxacademy.org/academic-grievance-studies/.

Alighieri, Dante. *Paradiso*. Book On Demand Ltd, 2013.

Aquinas, Thomas, and Vernon J. Bourke. *Summa Contra Gentiles*. University of Notre Dame Press, 1975.

Aslan, Reza. *God: a Human History*. Random House, 2018.

Aslan, Reza. *Zealot: the Life and Times of Jesus of Nazareth*. Allen & Unwin, 2017.

Benatar, David. *Better Never to Have Been: the Harm of Coming into Existence*. Clarendon Press, 2013.

Benatar, David. *Human Predicament - a Candid Guide to Lifes Biggest Questions*. Oxford University Press, 2017.

Bloom, Paul. *Against Empathy: the Case for Rational Compassion*. Vintage Books, 2018.

Bloom, Paul. "Religion, Morality, Evolution." *Annual Reviews*, Annual Review of Psychology, Jan. 2012, www.annualreviews.org/doi/abs/10.1146/annurev-psych-120710-100334.

Blum, Jeremy. "NBA Commissioner Announces Hope For 'Mutual Respect' With China." *HuffPost*, HuffPost, 1 July 2020, www.huffpost.com/entry/nba-china-adam-silver-mutual-respect_n_5efcbed3c5b6acab284a13a7.

Bodhi, Bhikkhu. *The Discourse on the Fruits of Recluseship: the Sāmaññaphala Sutta and Its Commentaries*. Buddhist Publication Society, 2004.

Boghossian, Peter. *A Manual for Creating Atheists*. Pitchstone, 2013.

Buddha, et al. *The Long Discourses of the Buddha: a Translation of the Dīgha Nikāya*. Wisdom Publications, 1996.

Bugliosi, Vincent. *Divinity of Doubt: God and Atheism on Trial*. Vanguard Press, 2012.

Campbell, Joseph, et al. *The Power of Myth*. Turtleback Books, 2012.

Campbell, Joseph. *The Hero with a Thousand Faces*. New World Library, 2008.

"Carl Gustov Jung & The Red Book (Part 1)." Performance by James Hillman, *YouTube*, Library of Congress, 2013, www.youtube.com/watch?v=Oy-x7BLlBYg.

Davis, Robert B. *Jnana Yoga: a Skeptic's Journey to Knowledge*. Lightning Source, 2016.

Davis, Robert B. "Our Fundamental Access to Truth." *Jnana Yoga Philosophy*, 2016, jnanayogaphilosophy.com/posts/our-fundamental-access-to-truth.

Davis, Robert B. "The Visudhimagga." *Jnana Yoga Philosophy*, 2014, jnanayogaphilosophy.com/posts/the-visudhimagga.

Deutsch, David. *The Beginning of Infinity*. Penguin Books Ltd, 2011.

Dhammaratana, U., and B. Buddhaghosa. *Visuddhimagga*. Buddist Research Society, 1975.

The Don, Akira, director. *Deadwood Ft. Jordan Peterson*. Performance by Jordan Peterson, YouTube, 2018, www.youtube.com/watch?v=DeTmMPtdtX0.

The Don, Akira, director. *Tarantulas*. Performance by Jordan Peterson, YouTube, 2018, www.youtube.com/watch?v=7zIkUkRLJAM.

Doyle, Arthur Conan. *The Sign of the Four: or the Problem of the Sholtos*. Ballantine Books, 1975.

Ekhart, Johannes, and Claud Field. "The Angel's Greeting." *Johannes Eckhart: Meister Eckhart's Sermons - Christian Classics Ethereal Library*, www.ccel.org/ccel/eckhart/sermons.vi.html.

Ellery, John Blaise. *The Collected Speeches of John Stuart Mill with Introduction and Notes*. University of Wisconsin - Madison, 1954.

Emerson, Ralph Waldo, and Stephen E. Whicher. *Selections from Ralph Waldo Emerson: an Organic Anthology*. Houghton-Mifflin, 1976.

Epstein, Alex. *The Moral Case for Fossil Fuels*. Portfolio, 2020.

Follett, Chelsea. "How Anti-Humanism Conquered the Left." *Quillette*, 8 May 2019, quillette.com/2019/05/01/how-anti-humanism-conquered-the-left/.

"God Needs Our Mind to Know the World." Performance by Rupert Spira, YouTube, 17 Feb. 2017, www.youtube.com/watch?v=GyL1uVaXGqU.

Haidt, Jonathan. *The Righteous Mind: Why Good People Are Divided by Politics and Religion*. Vintage Books, 2013.

Harari, Yuval Noah. *21 Lessons for the 21st Century*. Vintage, 2019.

Heraclitus, and Geoffrey S. Kirk. *Heraclitus the Cosmic Fragments*. Cambridge University Press, 1954.

Herbert, Frank, and Brian Herbert. *God Emperor of Dune: Book Four in the Dune Chronicles*. Ace, 2019.

Holy Bible: King James Version. Hendrickson Publishers, 2007.

"How Do You Stop the Mind's Chatter." Performance by Sadhguru, *YouTube*, 2015, www.youtube.com/watch?v=LNyJgNjCDuU.

Howard, Jacqueline. "Suicide Rates Soar among America's Young People,

Study Says." *CNN*, Cable News Network, 18 June 2019, www.cnn.com/2019/06/18/health/suicide-rates-teens-young-adults-us-study/index.html.

Hume, David, and Richard Henry Popkin. *Dialogues Concerning Natural Religion and the Posthumous Essays, Of the Immortality of the Soul, and Of Suicide, and from an Enquiry Concerning Human Understanding Of Miracles*. Hackett Pub., 1998.

"Individuation: A Myth for Modern Man ." Performance by Edward Edinger, *YouTube*, San Diego Friends of Jung, 14 Nov. 2013, www.youtube.com/watch?v=e1OrL4A_b5M.

Jung, C. G. *The Archetypes and the Collective Unconscious*. Translated by Hull, vol. 9, Princeton University Press, 1980.

Jung, C. G. *The Development of Personality*. Vol. 17, Routledge, 1991.

Jung, C. G., and Aniela Jaffé. *Memories, Dreams, Reflections*. Vintage Books, 1989.

Jung, C. G., et al. *The Collected Works of C.G. Jung. Psychology and Religion: West and East*. Princeton University Press, 1991.

Jung, Carl Gustav, et al. *Man and His Symbols*. Dell Publishing, 1969.

Kautz, K. William. *Winter's Grace: How Anguish & Intimacy Transform the Soul*. Outskirts Press, 2012.

Krauss, Lawrence M. *A Universe from Nothing: Why There Is Something Rather than Nothing*. Atria Paperback, 2013.

Laozi, et al. *Laotzu's Tao and Wu-Wei. Second Edition Revised and Enlarged. A New Translation by Bhikshu Wai-Tao and Dwight Goddard. Interpretive Essays by Henry Borel. Outline of Taoist Philosophy and Religion by Dr. Kiang Kang-Hu*. Dwight Goddard, 1935.

Leloup, Jean-Yves, and Joseph Rowe. *The Gospel of Thomas: the Gnostic Wisdom of Jesus*. Inner Traditions, 2005.

"Marxism and Christianity at Odds with Eachother." Performance by Jordan Peterson, *YouTube*, 2019, www.youtube.com/watch?v=Md7X6XS6gMY.

McClure, Barbara J. *Moving Beyond Individualism in Pastoral Care and Counseling Reflections on Theory, Theology, and Practice*. The Lutterworth Press, 2015.

McGonigal, Kelly. *The Upside of Stress: Why Stress Is Good for You, and How to Get Good at It*. Avery, 2016.

McGonigal, Kelly. *The Willpower Instinct: How Self-Control Works, Why It Matters, and What You Can Do to Get More of It*. Avery, 2012.

McTeigue, James, director. *V For Vendetta*. Warner Bros., 2008.

"The Mind." Performance by Alan Watts, *YouTube*, 2014, www.youtube.com/watch?v=emHAoQGoQic.

Mooji. *White Fire: Spiritual Insights and Teachings of Advaita Master Mooji*. Mooji Media Ldt, 2020.

Muller, Charles. "Translation by Charles Muller." *Online Translations of the Tao Te Ching*, labcit.ligo.caltech.edu/~mevans/docs/DDJ-CharlesMuller.

Muller, Richard. *Now: the Physics of Time*. W.W. Norton & Company, 2017.

Murray, Douglas. *The Madness of Crowds: Gender, Race and Identity*. Bloomsbury Continuum, 2019.

"Mysticism, Spirit and the Shadow." Performance by Jordan Peterson, *YouTube*, Rebel Wisdom, 2018, www.youtube.com/watch?v=zAsR6DZTvS8.

Neumann, Erich. *The Origins and History of Consciousness*. Translated by Hull, Princeton University Press, 1954.

Nietzsche, Friedrich Wilhelm, and Walter Kaufmann. *The Portable Nietzsche: Selected and Translated, with an Introduction, Prefaces, and Notes, by Walter Kaufmann*. Penguin, 1976.

"No Goal, No Positive Emotion." Performance by Jordan Peterson, *YouTube*, 2017, www.youtube.com/watch?v=0OscD3RYo6o.

Parmenides, and David Gallop. *Parmenides of Elea: Fragments: a Text and Translation with an Introduction*. University of Toronto Press, 1991.

Pattakos, Alex. "The Crisis of Meaning | Psychology Today." *Psychology Today*, 12 July 2017, www.psychologytoday.com/us/blog/the-meaningful-life/201707/the-crisis-meaning.

"People Say 'The Idea of God as an Old Man in the Sky Is Primitive'." Performance by Jordan Dr. Peterson, *YouTube*, 23 Oct. 2018, www.youtube.com/watch?v=MiVATX0IVYM.

Peterson, Jordan B., et al. *12 Rules for Life: an Antidote to Chaos*. Vintage Canada, 2020.

Peterson, Jordan, director. *2017 Maps of Meaning 12: Final: The Divinity of the Individual*. YouTube, 2017, www.youtube.com/watch?v=6V1eMvGGcXQ.

Peterson, Jordan. "Biblical Series VI: The Psychology of the Flood Transcript." *Jordan Peterson*, 17 Apr. 2018, www.jordanbpeterson.com/transcripts/biblical-series-vi.

Pinker, Steven. *Enlightenment Now: the Case for Reason, Science, Humanism, and Progress*. Penguin Books, 2019.

Pinker, Steven. *The Better Angels of Our Nature: Why Violence Has Declined*. Viking, 2011.

Post, Laurens Van Der. *Jung and the Story of Our Time*. Vintage Publishing, 2002.

Radin, Dean I. *The Conscious Universe: the Scientific Truth of Psychic Phenomena*. HarperOne, 2009.

Reinhold, H. A. *The Soul Afire*. Pantheon, 1944.

"Remain As You Are -- A Guided Meditation with Mooji." Performance by Mooji, *YouTube*, 21 Nov. 2010, www.youtube.com/watch?v=wCkesfE6-gg.

Rubin, Dave. *Muslim Reformers, Islamism, and Combating Extremism*. Performance by Maajid Nawaz, *YouTube*, 2017, www.youtube.com/watch?v=lpit8jc3NeI.

"Sam Harris: Considering a Creator." Performance by Sam Harris, *YouTube*, 2011, www.youtube.com/watch?v=nh7ymp6dVWo.

Sartre, Jean-Paul, et al. *No Exit and Three Other Plays*. Paw Prints, 2008.

Solženicyn Aleksandr, and H. T. Willetts. *The Gulag Archipelago*. Harper & Row, 1978.

Spielberg, Steven, director. *Indiana Jones and the Last Crusade*. Paramount, 1989.

"Stop Playing the Victim." Performance by Alan Watts, *YouTube*, 2017, www.youtube.com/watch?v=Zk5nQrJfcOU.

Tolkien, J. R. R., and Christopher Tolkien. *The Silmarillion*. HarperCollins, 1999.

Tolstoy, Leo. *A Confession and Other Religious Writings*. Translated by Jane Kentish, Penguin Books Limited, 1987.

Warner, Brad. *Don't Be a Jerk and Other Practical Advice from Dōgen, Japan's Greatest Zen Master: a Radical but Reverent Paraphrasing of Dōgen's Treasury of the True Dharma Eye*. New World Library, 2016.

Watts, Alan. *Behold the Spirit: a Study in the Necessity of Mystical Religion*. Vintage Bks., 2011.

Watts, Alan. *The Book on the Taboo against Knowing Who You Are*. Souvenir Press, 2012.

Watts, Alan. *The Supreme Identity; An Essay on Oriental Metaphysics and the Christian Religion, by Alan Watts*. Allegro Editions, 1972.

Welch, Ashley. "Drug Overdoses Killed More Americans Last Year than the Vietnam War." *CBS News*, CBS Interactive, 17 Oct. 2017, www.cbsnews.com/news/opioids-drug-overdose-killed-more-americans-last-year-than-the-vietnam-war/.

Whedon, Josh, director. *Avengers: Age of Ultron*. Walt Disney Studios Home

Entertainment, 2019.

Wilbur, Ken, director. *The Mystic Heart - Part 6*. Performance by Wayne Teasdale, *YouTube*, 2006, www.youtube.com/watch?v=JwpUhCRHjSI.

Yogananda, Paramahansa. *Autobiography of a Yogi: 60th Anniversary Edition*. Self-Realization Fellowship Pub., 1993.

Yogananda, Paramahansa. "Renunciation Is Not an End, It Is the Means to an End." *Aum Amen.com*, aumamen.com/quote/renunciation-is-not-an-end-it-is-the-means-to-an-end.

Yogananda, Paramahansa. "You Are Your Own Enemy and You Don't Know It. You Don't Learn." *Aum Amen.com*, aumamen.com/quote/you-are-your-own-enemy-and-you-don-t-know-it-you-don-t-learn.

www.ingramcontent.com/pod-product-compliance
Lightning Source LLC
Chambersburg PA
CBHW070418010526
44118CB00014B/1800